Faith and Public Life

GLOBAL LIBRARY

Contents

    Series Introduction vii

    Volume Introduction xi

1   A Survey of the Landscape of Christian Public Witness 1

2   Overcoming the Obstacles 37

3   The Biblical Undoing of the Stereotype of "Prostitute" as a Catalyst for Anti-Trafficking Work 61

4   People Living with Disability 79

5   Immigration, Displacements, Hospitality, and the Role of the Church 97

6   Climate Change and Public Witness 113

7   Reconfiguring Christian Public Witness in Africa 131

8   Public Witness in Malaysia 151

9   Live in Christ, Exist for Others 179

10 Contours of Corruption 199

11 Political Ideology and Biblical Interpretation 217

12 Dialogical Model for Engagement in IFES Latin America 241

13 Theological Education as Formation of Prophets for the Church and Society 259

    Contributors 281

Faith and Public Life

Rethinking Church in the 21st Century

General Editors
Riad Kassis and Mark Labberton

Volume Editor
Alfred Sebahene

Series Editor
Joshua Barron

© 2025 Alfred Sebahene

Published 2025 by Langham Global Library
An imprint of Langham Publishing
www.langhampublishing.org

Langham Publishing and its imprints are a ministry of Langham Partnership

Langham Partnership
PO Box 296, Carlisle, Cumbria, CA3 9WZ, UK
www.langham.org

ISBNs:
978-1-78641-100-6 Print
978-1-78641-180-8 ePub
978-1-78641-181-5 PDF
DOI: https://doi.org/10.69811/9781786411006

Alfred Sebahene hereby asserts his moral right to be identified as the Author of the General Editor's part in the Work in accordance with sections 77 and 78 of the Copyright, Designs and Patents Act 1988.

All rights reserved. No part of this publication may be reproduced, stored in a retrieval system or transmitted, in any form or by any means, electronic, mechanical, photocopying, recording or otherwise, without the prior written permission of the publisher or the Copyright Licensing Agency.

Requests to reuse content from Langham Publishing are processed through PLSclear. Please visit www.plsclear.com to complete your request.

Scripture quotations marked (ESV) are taken from The Holy Bible, English Standard Version® (ESV®), copyright © 2001 by Crossway, a publishing ministry of Good News Publishers. Used by permission. All rights reserved.

Scripture quotations marked (NIV) are taken from the Holy Bible, New International Version®, NIV®. Copyright © 1973, 1978, 1984, 2011 by Biblica, Inc.™ Used by permission of Zondervan.

Scripture quotations marked (NET) are taken from the New English Translation (NET). NET Bible® copyright ©1996-2006 by Biblical Studies Press, L.L.C. www.bible.org. Used by permission. All rights reserved worldwide.

Scripture quotations marked (NRSV) are taken from the New Revised Standard Version Bible, copyright © 1989 National Council of the Churches of Christ in the United States of America. Used by permission. All rights reserved.

Scripture quotations marked (NASB) are taken from the New American Standard Bible®, Copyright © 1960, 1962, 1963,1968, 1971, 1972, 1973, 1975, 1977, 1995, 2020 by The Lockman Foundation. Used by permission.

British Library Cataloguing-in-Publication Data
A catalogue record for this book is available from the British Library

ISBN: 978-1-78641-100-6

Cover & Book Design: projectluz.com

Langham Partnership actively supports theological dialogue and an author's right to publish but does not necessarily endorse the views and opinions set forth here or in works referenced within this publication, nor can we guarantee technical and grammatical correctness. Langham Partnership does not accept any responsibility or liability to persons or property as a consequence of the reading, use or interpretation of its published content.

Series Introduction

God's love in Jesus Christ for the salvation and recreation of all things is still the hope of the world. This Christian affirmation is the reality that "holds all things" and "holds all things together." Over the millennia of the biblical narrative, the God revealed in Scripture is present and active to a world in all its glories and agonies, in both personal and collective stories. In seasons when the people of God have flourished in God's faithfulness or doubted, even fought, God's intentions and desires, still God is faithful. The church belongs to its loving, healing, and renewing Saviour and Lord, Jesus Christ. Nothing will separate us from the love of God and even the gates of hell will not prevail against the church.

And yet the church is always a very mixed picture. Great reasons exist for the vitality, truthfulness, and love of Christian communities. Right alongside are all the doubts and insults hurled against God because of the church – from inside and outside – which have been and are profuse. Generation by generation, the church has struggled to discern and practice its spiritual and theological identity in real time and in real places. As we look at the church around the globe today, we give thanks for faithful Christians, often in extreme conditions of poverty, war, violence, and more, who live each day dependent on God, who alone keeps and preserves them. Holding faithful in the midst of authoritarian states, with persecution and suffering constantly at hand, the church faces enormous pressures to surrender its identity, to compromise in the face of such trials, and to neglect or distort its mission. The ever-present danger of the church being hypocritical towards God, towards itself, and towards the world is unavoidable. The church's inclination to teach and preach a gospel it fails to practice, especially in relationship to the poor and the marginalized, adds still more to the list of dangers and challenges faced by the church.

In this global season, it is not difficult to understand why the church is in pain and declining in its Christian and moral influence. No one is surprised in today's world about the fact that many so-called Gen Z's and Millennial's, for example, have no time for the church or Christianity. We can find this pattern around the world, but especially in urban centers. The reasons are many, but "church" and "Christianity" are assumed to be irrelevant, problematic, or probably worse. Furthermore, this is not just a pattern for youth and younger adults, but people in their middle and older years too. For devout people of

Christian faith, such condemning conclusions can seem simplistic and unfair; but for oceans of younger and multi-aged adults, these disaffected opinions are justified and self-evident conclusions. We might even say they are convictions reached by doing what seems to come naturally in this era and in places across the globe.

Every pastor and church leader who may be reading this knows many faces in this sea of disregard and disaffection. Hopefully, we are highly attentive in our roles, listening as carefully and deeply as we can to what this phenomenon is telling us. If we are tending flocks that are dissipating, we need to ask why it is happening, and how we pursue the sheep that are not just lost by circumstances, but by deliberate choice.

ReThinking Church in the 21st Century is an effort begun in 2021 to gather Christian leaders from a diverse range of backgrounds and nationalities online in order to listen to what gratitude and concerns we had about the state of the church as seen from many different angles. We were all Protestants, broadly evangelical, deeply committed to the holistic gospel of Jesus Christ, in varying roles of theological, pastoral, organizational, and congregational responsibility. We came together for an initial six months, and our work has gone on for an additional two and a half years. These three books are the product of the international members (and others) of the group, and the USA leaders have produced a multi-episode podcast. All of us have tried, within the bounds of our many other responsibilities, to contribute to our common cause. The community God has built among us during these years through hours and hours of online video conversations, and through our writing collaboration has been a gift beyond what we could initially have imagined, forming and strengthening enduring friendship in Christ.

The three volumes in this series are responses to the top three priority concerns that we determined are needed: *Suffering and Persecution*, led by Dr. Myrto Theocharous of Greece, *Metaphors the Church Lives By*, led by Dr. Elizabeth Sendek of Colombia, and *Faith and Public Life*, led by Dr. Alfred Sebahene of Tanzania. General Editors are Dr. Riad Kassis and Dr. Mark Labberton. We are very grateful for the contributions of all of our writers in each volume, here briefly summarized by our Volume Editors:

In *Suffering and Persecution* a variety of scholars and church leaders from or in the Majority World interact with writings, mostly from non-Western contexts, on topics such as violence, natural disasters, and ancient and modern persecution, and present their own reflections on these writings. The hope is that this volume will make available a variety of perspectives on suffering and persecution, and invite personal or communal contemplation on these universal themes. —**Myrto Theocharous**

We explore in *Metaphors the Church Lives By* seven biblical metaphors that are foundational for our understanding of the church in the twenty-first century. They transcend historical and sociopolitical categories. Three come from the gospels: yeast, salt, light; another three come from the Pauline epistles: temple, body and ambassadors; and one comes from the Petrine letters: people of God. The aim is to engage readers with the conceptual content of the metaphors and how they intend to shape experience and attitudes, so that we can live them out today. —**Elizabeth Sendek**

Times have changed. The global public space is filled with myriads of challenges. We live in an era which allows new contradictions and opportunities to emerge. But the love of God and the gospel of Christ never changes. How then should the church be engaged in the public space of the twenty-first century? *Faith and Public Life* seeks to answer this pertinent question by inviting Christians to respond with vigor to Christ's call to follow him in whole-life discipleship in this century and beyond. Throughout the pages of this book, Christians from diverse walks of life have given Bible-based testimonies about life in the public square, one of the arenas in which believers' love of God and love of neighbors must be exhibited. The book calls the church and Christian believers to constantly review how to proclaim and serve in the world while appreciating evident signs and wonders witnessing to the nature and character of God, especially his grace. —**Alfred Sebahene**

In these volumes each author speaks for themselves only, and not as a representative of any organization or institution. We offer our great thanks for individuals whose generous financial contributions made this effort possible. They are people with hearts full of the grace of God and love for the church.

Our hope is that these books will prompt pastors and thoughtful Christian leaders to be stimulated by these reflections and admonitions during such a dynamic, vulnerable, and hopeful time as the twenty-first century is presenting. We believe that "God is the same yesterday, today, and forever," and that the church is alive in settings that are constantly changing. This is the intersection we take with great faith and seriousness as we trust the Lord Jesus Christ who reigns in love, justice, and mercy.

To God's glory and honor, and for the welfare of God's church around the globe, we dedicate these books.

Riad Kassis and Mark Labberton

General Editors: Riad Kassis (Lebanon), Mark Labberton (USA)
Series Editor: Joshua Barron (Kenya)
Volume Editors: Alfred Sebahene (Tanzania)
Myrto Theocharous (Greece)
Elizabeth Sendek (Colombia)
Meditations Editor: Milton Acosta (Colombia)
Dialogue Participants: Wojciech Szczerba (Poland), Antonio Carlos Barro (Brazil), David Tarus (Kenya), Jonathan Kavusa (Democratic Republic of Congo), Sergiy Tymchenko (Ukraine), Alejandra Ortiz (Mexico), Antonina Szczerba (illustrator; Poland)
Illustrations: Antonina Szczerba (Poland)
Administration: Stefanii Morton, Mandy Macintosh

Volume Introduction

The twenty-first century has made us more aware of both the opportunities for mission and the fundamental challenges facing the global church. These realities – missional expansion, persistent barriers to human progress, shifts in the composition and centre of gravity of world Christianity, and a growing attention to the need for the church to embrace a radically different way of life – call for a new approach to the role of faith in our public life, to the different ways of witnessing to Christ and stewarding the mysteries of Christian faith.

This book is a response to these concerns. It is an articulation of Christian faith, public witness, and the public relevance of the gospel of Jesus Christ in the twenty-first century. What is, or should be, the role of Christian faith in the public square? At the core of the chapters in this book is the word "witness," which is generally understood by modern Christians to mean "tell someone else about your faith." However, we have chosen to use "witness" as consistently used in the New Testament. As N. T. Wright explains with reference to the Gospel of Luke and Acts, the New Testament uses "witness" to mean "tell someone else that Jesus is the world's true Lord."[1] This book thus speaks of how the gospel of Jesus Christ endlessly relates to the whole world and its reconciliation with God. But we have chosen the title *Faith and Public Life* because from the birth of the church two thousand years ago until today, the public life of Christians has been the most effective witness and most powerful testimony to Christian faith.

The contributors' use of twin foci in this book, *faith and public life* and *faith and public witness*, is thus purposeful and focused. As compassionate Christian witnesses themselves, the authors speak of *public witness* in order to encourage readers to rediscover areas in which they can take part in transforming the church's faith and witness to God's good purposes as revealed in the transforming grace of his Son Jesus Christ. Similarly, the writers refer to *public life* from a desire to encourage readers to reflect on the implications of the gospel for public life – how the gospel vision can be pursued and realized in public life. Our hope is that when our readers have grasped the truth and

---

1. N. T. Wright, *Simply Jesus: A New Vision of Who He Was, What He Did, and Why He Matters* (London: HarperOne, 2011), 214.

recall the values of the kingdom of God herein depicted, they would know their right to participate fully in public life and firmly seek to nourish their churches for Christian witness in all areas of life.

The book is the result of the good work of contributors from across the globe, people who have heard the gospel, believed in it, and in turn have been called to be witnesses. They are from diverse walks of life and expertise: missionaries from Africa and Latin America, biblical scholars, theological educators, senior leaders of a Christian theological educational institution, a Christian ethicist, a lay preacher, a youth ministry expert, a researcher in world Christianity and refugee issues, a senior priest and public theologian, a consultant for churches, NGOs, and governments, and biblical languages specialists. Their vital commitment to this project involved an intensive two years' process of conceptualization, collaboration, and partnership. In their writing they are keenly reconsidering the life of the church in the twenty-first century, a time when Christ's Bride seems exceptionally divided, marred by public desecration of the gospel, a turbulent, guilty, and vulnerable time.

Each chapter of this book is laced with Scripture, a key tool used by writers as they provide a solid grounding and critical reflection for authentic Christian public witness and mission in the twenty-first century. A key assumption of this book is that Christian faith is not merely about *intellectual agreement* with Christian doctrine or *belief* that the narratives of the gospels are true. Instead, Christian faith is a matter of *allegiance to Jesus*,[2] or in the words of contributor Ruth Barron, of *alignment with Jesus*. Such allegiance or alignment necessarily impacts public life. From this perspective, this book offers readers invaluable insight and understanding of public witness in the global church.

The book's weight can best be measured by looking at its articulate and coherent testimonies about the reign of God and believers' participation in God's redemptive mission in the world today. So as one reads through the pages of this book one finds the voices of people who trust that God alone is Lord and that the church is Christ's body and bride, who love and weep for the church, who rejoice in so much of global common life and fellowship, and who are concerned about the prolonged failures among some believers to live into the intended new creation.

Aware of the century's context which is marked by massive changes in the landscape of world Christianity, the writers give witness to the Christian faith

---

2. See Matthew W. Bates, *Salvation by Allegiance Alone: Rethinking Faith, Works, and the Gospel of Jesus the King* (Grand Rapids: Baker Academic, 2017); and Bates, *Gospel Allegiance: What Faith in Jesus Misses for Salvation in Christ* (Grand Rapids: Brazos, 2019).

and remind the reader that, as in all past centuries, in the twenty-first century the church is still called upon to live publicly as a witnessing, healing, and caring community. The church is doing so in a broken world as evidenced in issues addressed in the book, but it cannot do so unless it clearly understands the message it bears witness to and has the right tools to use. The people of God need to understand what they believe in and that it is important to be properly rooted and grounded in God (who is love) before we can witness to the gospel of Christ.

It is therefore my prayer and hope that everyone who reads this book will be reminded of who we are as God's people and how we can best participate in mission, for we not only "live and move and have our being" in God (Acts 17:18) but as humans we are also in our very essence woven into the fabric of our communities and are thus expected to act in the world as people enabled by the Spirit to be light and salt in the world.

May you therefore be inspired and challenged to consider participating in public Christian witness in all areas of life. May you be encouraged by this book to join this movement called to bring the churches into a fellowship in which they see their common role in participating in the wholeness of God's work. It is a noble work of testifying to the goodness and loving kindness of the living Lord who became flesh for us and for our salvation. This is a recommended read for everyone thirsty for faithful public life in the twenty-first century.

May God bless you!

Alfred Uwimana Sebahene, PhD
Head of Department of Theology and Religious Studies
St. John's University of Tanzania
Dodoma, Tanzania
September 2024

1

A Survey of the Landscape of Christian Public Witness

Biblically, Historically, and in Contemporary Africa

Sunday Bobai Agang

Provost, ECWA Theological Seminary, Jos, Nigeria

The much-heralded expansion of Christianity in the southern hemisphere – including Asia, Africa, and Latin America – may have left many who have followed the story of Christianity in Africa bewildered as to why the continent's long-sought-after vision of a "new renaissance" – a rich and welcoming continent – has not materialized.[1] By and large, Christianity has continued to grow in Africa. However, when it comes to their participation in public life, African Christians seem to have a deeply flawed understanding of their faith. Consequently, Africa as God envisions it, where every African can reach his or her full human potential, is a mirage. In no way does Christianity bear responsibility for this. Those who believe in the Christian faith but haven't fully understood its public implications are to blame. Every public place needs to be considered a holy (divine) domain if God's vision for Africa is to come to fruition. In this way, we can come to terms with the reality that Christianity is a faith that has an impact on society at large. The reason for this is that its

---

1. African Union Commission, *Agenda 2063: The Africa We Want; Framework Document* (Addis Ababa: African Union Commission, 2015); see also *Agenda 2063: The Africa We Want; Popular Version* (Addis Ababa: African Union Commission, 2015).

creator, Jesus Christ, was publicly crucified. Because he rules over every aspect of existence, the sacred and the so-called secular realms are inherently related. So our faith in Christ must have an impact on public life. In this chapter, I will provide a historical overview of Christian public witness in the hope that it will encourage Christians today to give serious thought to the tremendous impact they have had and will have in shaping the public sphere for the better.

Introduction

There has been much discussion and controversy in modern society regarding Christian public testimony, which is defined as the tangible display of Christian faith and character traits in public life and the workplace. Some Christians think religion has no place in politics or public life, while others think Christians should be politically involved and utilize their faith to affect public policy. Believers' public deeds and interactions ought to be shaped by their faith, according to those who advocate for Christian public witness. They hold the view that Christians ought to be active in society. Christian public witness has the potential to advance the common good, which is a strong argument in its favour. For the greater good of society, Christians can speak out against injustices such as poverty and inequality, for the preservation of natural resources, and for the advancement of human rights. Organizations such as Catholic Relief Services, which helps with development and humanitarian issues in more than a hundred different countries, are prime examples of this.

But those who think religion has no place in politics and public life oppose Christian public witness. They contend that when people let their religious views shape public policy, it can cause division and even persecution of others who disagree. Some Christian groups have pushed for legislation that other groups view as discriminatory, and this is evident in the conflict over same-sex marriage and reproductive rights. Objectivity and reason in public speech can be undermined by Christian public witness, according to another argument. It becomes more challenging to have arguments based on logic and evidence when people's religious views are given a voice in shaping public policy. Some Christian groups have resisted scientific data because of their beliefs on topics such as evolution and climate change, exemplifying this point.

Ultimately, there are good reasons for and against the need for Christian public witness, and the discussion is far from ended. Christians should live in accordance with the ideas and ideals of their faith, according to proponents, and believers should let their faith guide their public interactions and activities. Whether or not to participate in Christian public testimony is, in the end, a matter of individual conviction. In this chapter, I maintain that the Great Commission encompasses everything, regardless of the reasons presented for or against Christian public witness. Indeed, the idea of Christ's lordship over all of life necessitates Christian discipleship of all spheres of life.

Undoubtedly, incredible changes have taken place on a human and ecological level throughout the course of Christian history, on every continent, in every place where the gospel has been preached and incarnated. The assessment that follows covers only a few historical landscapes of Christian public witness, despite the immense extent of such witness throughout history. In this world of evil and devastation, I primarily concentrate on a handful of examples and frameworks that I think will aid today's church in bearing testimony to God's revealed love. To get there, I'll be looking at the many facets of Christian public witness. This investigation begins with Jesus's ministry and continues through the early church's work and teachings from the apostles. It also includes early modern and postmodern ethicists and theologians from Africa, North America, and Europe, as well as voices from the medieval period of Europe.

My thesis is that the Christian community's outward witness is God's plan to provide humanity with an improved world beyond anything we've ever imagined. Taking on human form and dwelling among us, Jesus Christ ushered us into a future abundant with life. According to the Bible, he came into this world so that everyone who accepts him might have life – abundant life (John 10:10). This completely flips the script of the current global order, which treats human life with desecration and worthlessness. This is particularly evident in the continent of Africa. Because our leaders have finally come to terms with the fact that Africans desire a continent free from corruption, nepotism, social injustices, and violent conflicts which frequently lead to the loss of life and property, it is not surprising that the African *Agenda 2063*, which focuses on "the Africa we want," stresses this desire.

The present situation in Africa has persisted in driving our most brilliant and talented youth to seek refuge on other continents where human life is more highly valued. It is a risk that some of them are willing to take in order to escape the continent via the Mediterranean Sea or the Sahara Desert, with some perishing in the Mediterranean's powerful seas or the desert's sweltering heat. In 2013, African leaders resolved to do all in their power to ensure that the next generation would inherit "an integrated, prosperous and peaceful Africa, driven by its own citizens and representing a dynamic force in the international arena,"[2] in an attempt to stem the tide of youth and intellectual talent leaving the continent. This commitment is to be pursued over the next half century, with the aim of providing young people with more motivation to remain on the continent. Improving all areas of public life and making them alive is a central goal of Christianity, and this is in perfect harmony with *Agenda 2063*. Public witness, then, is rooted in Christianity. It is God's plan to recreate a world that is dying and broken to be a peaceful, prosperous, and fruitful kingdom through the church, which is the body of Christ.

Indeed, the character traits given to all of Jesus's disciples in the Sermon on the Mount (Matt 5–7) are deeply rooted in the public witness of Christians. It is reasonable to say that Christians should live out their new character virtues, which include a moral and ethical existence similar to Christ's, in all areas of society as part of their public witness. To rephrase, being a Christian and living out one's faith in public stewardship allows one to view every area of work as a magnificent chance to be a part of God's grand design of creating a "very good" world (cf. Gen 1:3) by providing salvation via Christ's atoning sacrifice. That is why Ian J. Shaw argues that "Christianity [has] continued to be a profoundly shaping force in matters of national identity."[3] He pointed out how, "in pre-industrial societies, religion had been used by rulers as a way of legitimating their authority, creating close connections between Christianity and national identities. Religion was also associated in stable agrarian societies with the maintenance of traditional values and a sense of common national social and cultural identity."[4] Thus, Christian public witness was relevant to global affairs even before the sacred-secular divide. Putting Christian public witness at the core of global affairs is essential if we are to witness the kind of transformation that can make a better world a reality.

Christians must take seriously the divine proclamation of God-centred Christian public testimony found in Jesus Christ's parting remarks in Matthew 28 and Acts 1, which are meant to inspire us with vision and passion. Mark A. Noll, a church historian, has synthesized the history of Christian public witness from those concluding remarks of Jesus.[5] According to Noll, Christian public

---

2. This is the African Union Commission's vision, as stated in *Agenda 2063* (Framework Document), 5, 11, 12, 23, 29, 47, and 51.

3. Ian J. Shaw, *Churches, Revolutions, and Empires: 1789–1914* (Fearn: Christian Focus, 2012), xi.

4. Shaw, *Churches, Revolutions, and Empires*, 371.

5. Mark A. Noll, *Turning Points: Decisive Moments in the History of Christianity* (Grand Rapids: Baker, 1997), 11.

witness is based on Christ's last words, "You will be my witnesses . . . to the end of the earth" (Acts 1:8),[6] and he contends that

> the Christian faith would take root in particular cultures, and it would profoundly shape individual peoples, regions, and nations. But Christianity itself would belong to none of them. Rather, the church would exist to bear witness to God's love revealed in Christ and to bear that witness throughout the whole world.[7]

When Christ said that we should be his witnesses, he wanted us to be prepared to make a difference in the world by sharing our Christian faith and moral ideals. That meeting Christ will shape us into his likeness is something I think his audience understood quite clearly. Consequently, we won't be noticed until all the systems, institutions, and structures in that realm are fully realized to the point where they bring glory to God. Therefore, the gospel that we are called to testify about has the power to shape the fate of entire nations as well as the lives of the individuals within them.

Insight into God's plan to reveal to humanity, via Jesus Christ, the destiny of those who have placed their trust in Christ can be gained through careful study of the Bible, particularly the New Testament. The Holy Spirit gives such people the calling to be messengers of good news in all aspects of life, encompassing all human vocations, transactions, and efforts. Included within the purview of this directive are the following instructions: "Go therefore and make disciples of all nations, baptizing them in the name of the Father and of the Son and of the Holy Spirit, teaching them to observe all that I have commanded you" (Matt 28:19–20). From these words it is evident that bearing witness in public involves not only reaching out to individuals from various walks of life, but also teaching them about Jesus Christ, the Lord of all, to whom God has entrusted all power on earth and in heaven.

Reading and understanding the Bible is crucial for those who want to be witnesses in the community. If we want to be credible witnesses, we need to know, understand, and trust the defendant. As he said, "Behold, I am with you always, to the end of the age" (Matt 28:20). We ought to have complete faith in this proclamation. In addition, the role and activity of the Holy Spirit are necessary for Christian public witness: "But you will receive power when the Holy Spirit has come upon you, and you will be my witnesses in Jerusalem and in all Judea and Samaria, and to the end of the earth" (Acts 1:8). That Christ

---

6. All quoted Scripture is from the ESV unless otherwise indicated.
7. Noll, 11.

is present and that the Christian testimony will take root and change people, places, cultures, generations, and nations is a great promise. In Noll's words, "the history of Christianity has found its way through vast regions across vast stretches of time and in a vast variety of forms. But it remains the history of those who worship the Lord of Life, who seek to serve him, and whose witnesses they are."[8] So this chapter's goal is to trace the history of Christian public witness and identify its watershed moments. Because Christian public testimony has a long and rich history, this study can cover only a small fraction of that time. I focus on a handful of pivotal events that, in my view, will empower the contemporary church to bear witness to God's revealed love despite the pervasive evil and destruction in our world.

A Historical Landscape of Christian Public Witness

Throughout the two millennia since the arrival of Christ Jesus began the inbreaking of God's kingdom, public witness has been at the heart of the Christian faith. Respect for human dignity, honesty, humility, compassion, and integrity are tenets of Christianity. Christians also bring the values of faith, love, truth, justice, forgiveness, and integrity to public testimony. Christians should demonstrate these qualities in every facet of public life. Consequently, I will analyse these concepts as I traverse the landscape of Christian public testimony, seeking to document their enduring impacts. Christians have been instrumental in influencing many types of cultural, social, and political development over this lengthy period. First I will examine the historical examples of public witness that Jesus provided and how they relate to his disciples today.

Jesus and Public Witness

The incarnation of Christ Jesus and his ministry provide the proper foundation upon which to build our path. It is impossible to ignore the centrality of public witness as we observe his earthly ministry and mission. He healed people, preached sermons, and performed miracles on a regular basis to demonstrate his divine power. Jesus's goal during his public ministry was to destroy the old system which hindered human development. The bold proclamation of the gospel to the impoverished was of great interest to him (Isa 62:1–2a; Luke 4:18–19, NIV). Jesus frequently spoke in public to large crowds. The public events of Jesus's arrest, trial, and crucifixion – described in Luke 22–23 – mark

---

8. Noll, *Turning Points*, 11–12.

the climax of his public ministry. Jesus spent his whole ministry anticipating the hostility of the religious and political elites due to the contentious nature of his teachings. But even though he was in mortal danger, he persisted in his mission and kept on publicly preaching and healing.

The character traits that Christians need to cultivate in order to be effective witnesses are clearly outlined by Jesus in his Sermon on the Mount (Matt 5–7). Jesus's goal in making disciples was to equip people to testify about the good news of God's kingdom in the world. Thus "one day Jesus called together his twelve disciples and gave them *power* and *authority* to cast out all demons and to heal all diseases. Then he sent them out to tell everyone about the Kingdom of God and to heal the sick" (Luke 9:1–2, NLT; emphasis mine). The spiritual, intellectual, cultural, social, physical, moral, economic, political, and environmental aspects are all interconnected in the process of curing the sick. Proclaiming the good news of God's kingdom and showing his supernatural power over all creation via healing and miracles was, in fact, Jesus's main objective. Although he was met with fierce opposition by the Jewish authorities and religious establishment, he stayed committed to this purpose right up to the end.

Public Virtues That Jesus Requires of Christians

Everyone – Christian and non-Christian alike – coexists in the public arena. The life and teachings of Jesus Christ offer us a window into the essential Christian qualities that make for a community that encourages the flourishing of humanity. Repentance, forgiveness, restoration, peace, justice, compassion, faith, perseverance, and a host of other virtues are included. To persevere in a world where morality is a shambles, Christians must prioritize the development of these virtues which are strictly necessary for them to be effective witnesses for God in the world. Jesus spent a great deal of time during his earthly mission teaching about the importance of character virtues. Love, humility, forgiveness, patience, and charity are some of the values he said should characterize a Christian's life. Being the "salt of the earth" and the "light of the world" (Matt 5:13–16), Christians must become light and salt in a world that can be dark and bland.[9] Rather than isolating themselves, Christians should participate in society in a manner that exemplifies their beliefs, values, and ethical perspective.

---

9. Editors' note: These key themes are explored in chapters in the second volume of this series. See Elizabeth Sendek, "The Salt of the Earth," and Sergiy Tymchenko, "Light: The Guiding Force of God's Kingdom," ch. 1 and ch. 6 in Metaphors the Church Lives By, edited by Elizabeth Sendek (Carlisle: Langham Global Library, 2024).

Love, joy, peace, patience, kindness, goodness, faithfulness, gentleness, and self-control are fruits of the Spirit (Gal 5:22–23). Christians must demonstrate these in all their interactions with people, so that they may bring glory to God. This is why Paul stresses the need for Christians to love their neighbours as themselves (Gal 5:14), help each other out (Gal 6:2), and do good to everyone (Gal 6:10), particularly those in the church community. The significance of Christian conduct is also emphasized in the letter of James: "What good is it . . . if someone claims to have faith but has no deeds? Can such faith save them?" (Jas 2:14, NIV). Contrary to some understandings of *sola fide*, Christians must show their faith by doing deeds of justice, kindness, compassion, and love (Jas 2:15–26). My mentor, Glen Stassen, along with his former student David Gushee, elucidate that in our postmodern era, individuals seek to comprehend the practical impact of the gospel on daily existence, questioning assertions of "timeless truths," observing diverse beliefs among cultures and conflicting beliefs within a single culture, and aspiring to authenticate truth not through authoritarian declarations but by observing its manifestation in real-life scenarios.[10] A difficulty we face as a church is the assumption that Christ's teachings in the Sermon on the Mount are abstract principles meant only for individual use. Because of this misunderstanding, many Christians have a much harder time understanding why these principles should be applied to public life. Correcting this confusion, Stassen insists that "the implications of the Sermon on the Mount are not to be limited to just one part of life, or one class of 'super Christians,' or a future eschatological dispensation removed from present history, but for God's rule on earth as in heaven. . . . The Sermon on the Mount is the central Christian text for peacemaking and justicemaking."[11] If Christians fail to exhibit the character virtues, their public witness as Christians will be completely devoid of value.

It is the Christian's duty to act justly, compassionately, and with love towards all people, and to interact with the world in a manner that is consistent with their religion and moral compass. Because Christians are commanded to make a constructive impact on society, this is both a shared and an individual duty. The non-Jews who put themselves in danger to save Jews from the Nazis during the Holocaust were the subject of a meticulous investigation by David P. Gushee. What piqued his interest in particular was the question of why the

---

10. Glen H. Stassen and David P. Gushee, *Kingdom Ethics: Following Jesus in Contemporary Context* (Downers Grove: InterVarsity Press, 2003), 76.

11. Glen H. Stassen, *Just Peacemaking: Transforming Initiatives for Justice and Peace* (Louisville: Westminster John Knox, 1992), 34 and 36.

vast majority of German Christians chose to do nothing or even helped the Nazis destroy their Jewish neighbours. The main cause, as Gushee found out, was not "any kind of self-proclaimed religious or political loyalty, but instead the kinds of moral practices in place among those whose help was sought."[12] For Christians to use character virtues as a road map in their public witness, it is necessary for them to understand what they are all about. As Gushee noted, "Character by itself is an empty vessel. . . . The churches must . . . also work more carefully to define the *kind* of character they want to produce." We must teach

> the fixed perception that every other human being is my equal – in fact, my kin – and thus equally precious and worthy of a decent life. The Christian must be schooled to see that despite important differences among human beings, ultimately our common humanity bears more significance than that which divides us.

We must teach open-heartedness – "an openness to receiving and interacting with the other's joy, pain, sorrow, or whatever else they bring to the encounter . . . a willingness to be vulnerable before and with the other . . . consistent alertness to the needs of the other." We must return central biblical teachings on compassion and love to the forefront of Christian promotion and education.[13]

The church has a responsibility to teach its members love, one of the greatest Christian virtues – indeed, a major tenet of Christianity. In John 15:12, Jesus himself said that his disciples should love one another. Love, which is at the heart of all Christian virtues, is characterized by selflessness and sacrifice. Paul said in his letter to the Corinthians, "And now these three remain: faith, hope, and love. But the greatest of these is love" (1 Cor 13:13, NIV).

Public Witness in Early Christianity

Love and compassion, the apostles said, were to be the hallmarks of public witness. John reminds believers, "Let us not love with words or speech but with actions and in truth" (1 John 3:18, NIV). James likewise emphasized the importance of caring for the poor and marginalized in society (Jas 2:14–17). Last but not least, the apostles knew full well that bearing witness in public could lead to persecution and hardship. Paul tells the Romans, "We . . . glory

---

12. Stassen and Gushee, *Kingdom Ethics*, 77.
13. David P. Gushee, *The Righteous Gentiles of the Holocaust* (Minneapolis: Fortress, 1994), chs. 5–7, quoted in Stassen and Gushee, 78.

in our sufferings, because we know that suffering produces perseverance; perseverance, character; and character, hope" (Rom 5:3–4, NIV). In general, the apostles stressed the significance of bearing witness in public, being holy and upright, loving and compassionate, and ready to endure hardship and persecution for the cause of the gospel.

In the early centuries of Christianity, within the Roman Empire, Christianity was illegal and Christians were at times persecuted. In spite of their marginal and illegal status which prevented them from attaining roles of influence within the empire's power structures, Christians nonetheless made a mark on public affairs. Christian public virtues were consistently "translated into norms of social service and community solidarity" which, like a city on a hill, were impossible to hide.[14] Thus the Christian conviction regarding the worth of every person and the importance of love, fairness, peace, compassion, and mercy influenced the prevailing moral climate of that era. Late in the period, Augustine of Hippo (354–430) urged Christians to be a good example to the pagan society around them. Christians, in his view, should make it their mission to conduct themselves in a way that was consistent with what the Bible says and the example set by Christ. Living a Christlike life in public has always been a powerful way for Christians to change the world. According to Augustine,

> All the devastation, the butchery, the plundering, the conflagrations, and all the anguish which accompanied the recent disaster at Rome [i.e., the unprecedented sack of Rome by the Visigoths under Alaric in August of 410] were in accordance with the general practice of warfare. But there was something which established a new custom, something which changed the whole aspect of the scene; the savagery of the barbarians took on such an aspect of gentleness that the largest basilicas were selected and set aside to be filled with people to be spared by the enemy. No one was to be violently used there, no one snatched away. Many were to be brought there for liberation by merciful foes; none were to be taken from there into captivity even by cruel enemies. This is to be attributed to the name of Christ and the influence of Christianity.[15]

---

14. Rodney Stark, *The Rise of Christianity: How the Obscure, Marginal Jesus Movement Became the Dominant Religious Force in the Western World in a Few Centuries* (San Francisco: HarperSanFrancisco, 1997), 74; see his discussion in ch. 4 of that work, "Epidemics, Networks, and Conversion," 73–94.

15. Augustine of Hippo, *The City of God* 1.7, trans. Henry Bettenson (London: Penguin, 1972), 12–13.

Rome went from being a city that devalued and destroyed human life and property to one that valued and nurtured human dignity, and this quotation explains and highlights the significant role that Christianity and its public representation had in this shift. Rome had a notable transformation as a result of God's use of Christianity to implant a moral consciousness that resulted in a life of selfless devotion and empathy. The significance of love and compassion in public witness was another area in which Augustine made a significant contribution. His concept of virtue was "the condition of right living."[16] The necessity of becoming a good witness to the world was one of Augustine's main contributions.

Public Witness in Modern Christianity

There was a dramatic change to the Christian public sphere in the sixteenth century with the Protestant Reformation. The biblical principle of the universal priesthood was a source of strength for the Reformers as they questioned the Catholic Church's power and placed an emphasis on the significance of personal faith and conscience. The subsequent centuries saw a secularization of society as a result of the Enlightenment's critique of conventional Christian ideas and values. Positively, Enlightenment thinking placed an

> emphasis on the solidarity of the human race, and the natural right of the individual to liberty and happiness . . . [as well as] the growing sense the deep-rooted evils were no longer to be viewed as irremediable. . . . Yet the enlightenment contribution was not entirely positive. With it came the assumptions that Western culture, in which reason was seen to have reached its fullest stage of development, was superior to non-European cultures, which were racially inferior or even savage. . . . The Enlightenment could therefore produce both a "de-Christianised form of scientific racism" and also a clearly articulated ethnology shaped by Scottish Common Sense Philosophy and the Bible, which saw all humans with the same capacity for civilisation and development, and as suitable objects for Christian mission.[17]

---

16. Augustine, 1.16, p. 26.

17. Shaw, *Churches, Revolutions, and Empires*, 139; citing C. Kidd, *The Forging of Races: Race and Scripture in the Protestant Atlantic World, 1600–2000* (Cambridge: Cambridge University Press, 2006), 120.

At its best, post-Enlightenment Western Christian public theology, engagement, and witnessing have been marked by a similar emphasis on human solidarity. The political and social reform movements arising from Enlightenment thinking (whether secular or Christian) saw the ongoing involvement of many Christians.

The pursuit of Christian public testimony has, of course, never been easy. Countries in North America and Europe, where Christianity was widely practised, committed one of the gravest crimes against humanity by instituting slavery. Shaw writes,

> Between the fifteenth century and the late nineteenth century, one of the most appalling and barbaric episodes in world history took place. Some 18 million black Africans were forcibly transported as slaves to the Americas and Asia, where they faced cruel oppression. A further 10 million people had by 1850 been subjected to domestic slavery by their fellow Africans.[18]

Winning the struggle against slavery required Christians to be conscious of the public implications of their faith and to publicly witness to the moral ideals of Christianity. John Wesley (1707–91) was awakened to this when "he witnessed the practice of slavery on his visit to America"; abhorring what he saw, he recognized that public witness *for* Christ necessarily meant public witness *against* slavery. William Wilberforce, who was one of his followers, took the battle to Parliament.[19] His persistent activism was propelled by his strong Christian faith, and he rallied a multitude of people to join his honourable cause.

Wesley is best known, perhaps, for his role in religious renewal. But his work enriched Christian witness in two other key areas:

- Social reform: because of his conviction that the Great Commission entailed discipling entire countries, Wesley placed a premium on public testimony. Christians, in his view, should do more than merely believe in God; they should also work to improve the world around them. Many of England's poor and oppressed people were his concern, and he attempted to alleviate their plight through various

---

18. Shaw, 131, citing H. S. Klein, *The Atlantic Slave Trade* (Cambridge: Cambridge University Press, 1999), 129; P. Manning, *Slavery and African Life: Occidental and African Slave Trades* (Cambridge: Cambridge University Press, 1990), 171; and D. Eltis, S. Behrendt, D. Richardson, and H. Klein, *The Transatlantic Slave Trade 1562–1867: A Database* (Cambridge: Cambridge University Press, 1998).

19. Shaw, *Churches, Revolutions, and Empires*, 141, 143–44.

social reform programmes. In addition to his work to end both the slave trade and slavery itself, the Wesleyan revival led to the creation of schools and health clinics for low-income communities.[20]

- Political reform: despite Wesley's emphasis on social and spiritual improvements, his words and deeds had political ramifications as well. His criticisms of English society ranged far and wide, touching on topics such as the exploitation of the poor and the corruption of public officials. A larger eighteenth-century reform movement in English politics benefited from his stress on individual morality and responsibility. Through Wesley, God raised up men and women who played crucial roles in changing wicked and merciless civilizations.

William Carey (1761–1834) is remembered for his numerous contributions to public testimony in India, where he spent much of his life as a Christian missionary and scholar. Celebrated as one of the pioneers of the modern Protestant missionary movement, "not only did Carey become the founder of the Protestant Church in India, but he also finished six full translations and twenty-four partial translations of the Bible into Indian languages like Sanskrit, as well as grammars, dictionaries, and translations of classical eastern books" (along with William Ward and Joshua Marshman, the so-called Serampore Trio).[21] An integral part of Carey's understanding of public witness was his advocacy of social reform. Akin to Wesley, "Carey's passion was wholeness, extending the lordship of Christ over every department of life and society," as Fountain notes.[22] While fighting for the rights of the downtrodden, he denounced cruel traditions such as sati (widow-burning), infanticide, and caste prejudice. Carey aspired to live out his conviction that Christianity was more than a private religion; it was a power for societal change. The Great Commission, according to Carey, encompassed far more than just translating Scripture, winning souls, and establishing churches. "Discipling the nation" meant instructing a country's citizens in the ways of God's rule.[23] Calling on the church to participate in social justice and transformation was another major contribution Carey made. The gospel, in his view, had far-reaching consequences for society, the economy, and politics. Consequently, he argued that Christians should fight for social fairness, equal schooling opportunities, and more poverty relief. Many

---

20. Jeff Fountain, *Shapers of Our Modern Age: Six Men Who Shaped Nations* (Amsterdam: Schuman Centre Resources, 2018), 15–18.
21. Fountain, *Shapers of Our Modern Age*, 20.
22. Fountain, 21.
23. Fountain, 21.

Christian leaders since Carey's time have echoed this appeal for social justice, and it remains a significant part of the church's witness in the world today.[24]

The influential Dutch politician, journalist, and theologian Abraham Kuyper (1837–1920) made important contributions to Christian public testimony and public theology. At the time of Kuyper's birth, Europe was still in the midst of a political shift from aristocratic and monarchical authority to the more representative democracies of the newly formed states. To address the problems of daily living, Kuyper sought after practical theology. He started to understand how significantly non-biblical beliefs impacted the way churchgoers, including himself, saw life in general. His view was that the church and society at large needed to fight the spirit of the age, modernity, which he defined as the prevailing Enlightenment and rationalist principles. His insistence that God is ultimately sovereign over all spheres of human endeavour – politics, economy, science, and culture – was a major contribution of Kuyper's to public theology, faith, and testimony. Best known as the leader of Dutch neo-Calvinism, Kuyper believed that Christians should work towards subduing all aspects of society to Christ's power, and that God's sovereignty involves redemption not only at the individual level but of the entire created order. Christians, according to Kuyper, should actively participate in society at large. Based on the idea of the sphere of sovereignty, Kuyper argued that Christians should see their jobs as a means to serve God and their neighbours, and that every profession is a divinely inspired calling.

Christians' impact on public life grew massively in the twentieth century. Dietrich Bonhoeffer (1906–45) came to realize that public witness *for* Christ meant public witness *against* the Nazi regime. Eventually martyred for his witness, he argued that "only those who have been placed into the truth can understand themselves in truth. . . . That is to say, they may now recognise themselves as having been created anew from untruth for truth."[25] Christian public figures like Martin Luther King Jr. (1929–68) forcefully thrust such truth into the public square. Playing a pivotal role in the American Civil Rights movement, a watershed event in Christian history, King exemplified not only the necessity of incorporating our Christian ideas and convictions into public

---

24. Fountain, 24.

25. Dietrich Bonhoeffer, *Act and Being: Transcendental Philosophy and Ontology in Systematic Theology*, Dietrich Bonhoeffer Works 2, trans. from the German by Martin Rumscheidt, eds. Wayne W. Floyd Jr. and Hans-Richard Reuter (Minneapolis: Fortress, 1996), 81. For an exploration of Bonhoeffer's legacy of public witness, see Eberhardt Ngugi's chapter in this volume, "Live in Christ, Exist for Others: The Courage and Witness of Dietrich Bonhoeffer in Situations of Rampant Injustice."

discourse, but also the potential for incorporating our theological convictions into matters pertaining to sociopolitical and socio-economic concerns. Within the context of his public testimony, Martin Luther King Jr. highlighted the importance of non-violence as a fundamental Christian principle and a method for bringing about social transformation. Non-violence, in his view, was not merely a practical weapon for achieving justice, but a moral obligation. Incessantly critiquing racism and segregation,[26] King insisted that Christians should struggle for the cause of social justice and speak out against injustice when they encounter it. Building a peaceful and equitable society was the apex of Christian public witness, according to him. King believed that God would finally defeat the evils of the past. He wrote, "God is able to conquer the evils of history. His control is never usurped."[27]

Ron Sider (1939–2022), an American evangelical theologian, social activist, and writer, significantly enriched Christian public testimony. He was an inspiration to many Christian leaders and activists because of his strong faith and dedication to Christ.[28] Best known for his 1977 seminal work, *Rich Christians in an Age of Hunger*, he demonstrated how wicked it is for Christians in the wealthy West, and especially in North America, to turn a blind eye to the plight of their fellow citizens in the Majority World who are struggling financially. A critical consciousness was instilled in the minds of Christians in the West and North America by Sider's understanding of the gospel. This critical consciousness can lead to action to alleviate poverty and economic suffering. Inspired by teachings on holistic human care, Sider combed through the Old and New Testaments to piece together God's story regarding spiritual and physical poverty: "God reveals a special concern for the poor in every part of the Scriptures – both Old Testament and New, prophetic writings and wisdom literature, the Gospels and Epistles."[29] In his view, Christians must maintain a perfect equilibrium between evangelism and social activity if they are to

---

26. Martin Luther King Jr., *Strength to Love* (Minneapolis: Fortress, 2010), 113.

27. King, *Strength to Love*, 114.

28. Mitchell Atencio, "Ron Sider, Who Called Evangelicals to Social Justice, Dies at 82," Sojourners, 29 July 2022, https://sojo.net/articles/ron-sider-who-called-evangelicals-social-justice-dies-82.

29. Ronald J. Sider, with the staff of Evangelicals for Social Action, *Completely Pro-Life: Building a Consistent Stance on Abortion, the Family, Nuclear Weapons, the Poor* (Downers Grove: InterVarsity Press, 1987), 74–75.

be witnesses to the world. Because "God cares so much for the poor," Sider observes, "it is hardly surprising that God wants his people to do the same."[30]

> Nothing excites me more than to hear stories of churches that are leading people to Christ and ministering to the needs of hurting people. I long for the day when every village, town, and city has congregations of Christians so in love with Jesus Christ that they lead scores of people to accept him as personal Savior and Lord every year – and so sensitive to the cry of the poor and oppressed that they work vigorously for justice, peace, and freedom.[31]

Sider combined evangelism with advocacy work for social actions that sought to address the issues of poverty, war, and environmental stewardship, emphasizing the need for Christians to engage in public life and advocate for justice.

Christians nowadays are active in many political and social causes, including those pertaining to economic justice, immigration, and the environment. Although many find fault with the way Christians participate in public life, the influence of Christians on society is undeniable. All things considered, the story of Christians in public life is intricate and varied. Christians have always been, and always will be, a powerful force in moulding the political, cultural, and moral climate of any given era.

The Landscape of Contemporary Christian Public Theology and Witness

Christian public witness and public theology are necessarily related. When I say "theology," what I really mean is that the only way to know God is through his qualities, which we should work hard to develop. Everywhere Christians congregate, they share their faith and the good news of who God is and what he accomplishes. In *African Public Theology*, I define theology as "the study of God [and] how he interacts with his creation."[32] Accordingly, I argue in this section for a public witness and theology that take into account the fact that

---

30. Ronald J. Sider, *Rich Christians in an Age of Hunger: Moving from Affluence to Generosity*, 6th ed. (Nashville: Thomas Nelson, 2015), 61.

31. Ronald J. Sider, *Good News and Good Works: A Theology for the Whole Gospel* (Grand Rapids: Baker, 1999), 18.

32. See Sunday Bobai Agang, "The Need for Public Theology in Africa," ch. 1 in *African Public Theology*, eds. Sunday Bobai Agang, Dion A. Forster, and H. Jurgens Hendriks (Bukuru/Carlisle: HippoBooks, 2020), 7–8.

God is involved in every facet of our public life, and which are consistent with what Jesus said: "All authority in heaven and on earth has been given to me. Therefore go and make disciples of all nations" (Matt 28:18–19, NIV). Christian participation in public life and all issues of life and godliness (including, but not limited to, politics, economics, education, vocation, calling, social justice, and culture) is central to public theology and testimony. It is based on the conviction that Christians should share their faith and use their knowledge of God in public life, and that the gospel affects every aspect of life. Here we will take a quick look at the current state of Christian public theology, focusing on some of the major ideas and figures in this area.

Theology of Public Life

Among those who are dissatisfied with the big picture, you will find Christians in every African country. They often fail to recognize their role as accomplices, though. They too are to blame for the nation's moral, cultural, social, and economic ills, because they fail to understand the public implications of their beliefs. The overall focus of public life theology is the complex relationship between Christianity and modern society. As a place of theological reflection, it seeks to build a consistent theological framework for Christians' engagement with society by exploring the public sphere and the role of the church and individual Christians within it. For Christians, bearing witness in public is not an option, but an essential divine obligation that must be carried out with great care. We are deeply committed to this because we adore and revere the creator of the infinite universe. Furthermore, we are "in truth an emblem of hope, a sign that redemption and healing are possible, even for the living."[33] To rephrase: in a world when everything seems to be falling apart, broken, forlorn, and decaying, we shine like a light. Christians must take part in public witness for this reason. In the face of gloom and doom, we show society that there is hope for a better future through our interactions with one another.

Political theology and ethics, which investigates the connection between religion and politics, is naturally tied to this field of study. Miroslav Volf is a prominent figure in this field; he is a Croatian-American theologian and

---

33. Douglas Burton-Christie, "Athanasius (c.295–373), *The Life of Antony*," in *Christian Spirituality: The Classics*, ed. Arthur Holder (New York: Routledge, 2010), 14. The words describe the early sixteenth-century Isenheim Altarpiece which was created for the Monastery of St. Anthony in Isenheim, Alsace, France. Because it was designed to demonstrate that both Christ and St. Anthony empathize with, and even participate in, our suffering and vulnerability, it also aptly shows how we as Christians should be in our public witness.

has written and contributed greatly to discussions on public theology. In *A Public Faith: How Followers of Christ Should Serve the Common Good*, Volf explains that Christians should participate in public life primarily to advance the general welfare of society. Being the community saved by Christ's death, burial, and resurrection, the church is obligated to participate in society. The Christian faith can impact public life positively in numerous ways, including this one. Christians need to know this if they want to testify in public with any effectiveness: "Faith requires Christians to live lives of integrity, but we find ourselves powerless against the lure of evil. Finite, fragile, and fallible as we are, we easily succumb to the seductions of power, possessions, or glory."[34] Some Christians, oblivious to the peril, avoid involving God in the moral aspects of their professional lives. Volf declared,

> In such situations, faith may not completely fail to shape the lives of people and their social realities [but may be limited] to the life of the soul, to private morality, to family matters, or to church life. As a result, faith becomes idle in important domains in which it, as a prophetic faith, should be active.[35]

That is mostly due to their presumption that God is responsible for rescuing lost souls and guiding individual morality. It slips their minds that

> faith does its most proper work when it (1) sets us on a journey, (2) guides us along the ways, and (3) gives meaning to each step we take. When we embrace faith – when *God* embraces *us* – we become new creatures constituted and called to be part of the people of God. That is the beginning of a journey: our insertion into the story of God's engagement with humanity. As we embark upon it, faith guides us by offering itself as a way of life that indicates paths to be taken and dark alleys or dead-end streets to be avoided, and that tells us what our specific tasks are in the great story of which we are a part.[36]

A prophetic faith fails and does society a disservice whenever Christians keep God in the personal realm instead of allowing God to influence every aspect of their lives. Living out the grace and love that God showed us through

---

34. Miroslav Volf, *A Public Faith: How Followers of Christ Should Serve the Common Good* (Grand Rapids: Brazos, 2011), 13.

35. Volf, *Public Faith*, 14.

36. Volf, 16.

Jesus Christ's incarnation compels Christians to avoid sloth and to instead bear witness to the gospel. According to Volf,

> for Christian faith not to be idle in the world, the work of medical doctors and garbage collectors, business executives and artists, stay-at-home parents and scientists needs to be inserted into God's story of the world. That story needs to provide the most basic rules by which the "game" in all these spheres is played. And that story needs to shape the character of the players.[37]

Thus, for Christians to actively engage in public life, they must acknowledge that the resurrection of Jesus Christ should significantly impact their attitude to every aspect of life, including religious, moral, social, economic, cultural, and political realms. Persistent societal inequities are a constant threat in any field. Thus, the issue of social justice must be central to our public testimony. Hence the church must work tirelessly to foster its members' thorough discipleship and mentorship, equipping them to make a difference in the world through their public witness. Below are the many facets of this public testimony, which spans the fields of politics, social justice, and culture.

Politics

Living out one's faith in all areas of one's life becomes a Christian public testimony. Therefore, Christians, like all people, have a political component, regardless of personal preferences. In classical Greek thought, politics was central to being an engaged citizen of one's city-state, or *polis*. Therefore, Christians are bound up with the social, political, and economic aspects of their God-given communities. Engagement with politics is not without danger. For Christians, the crux of such engagement should be having an allegiance to and alignment with Christ that is greater than all other allegiances and alignments.

Social Justice

Social justice is about Christian values in community. We each have our own set of priorities, interests, and aspirations in life. God created us for a specific reason – to bring him glory by loving him and our neighbours as much as we love ourselves – but our selfish ambitions frequently get in the way of that vision and purpose. A primary focus of Christian public testimony thus becomes social justice, which includes an unwavering commitment to promoting equality and fairness in society, particularly for marginalized and

---

37. Volf, 17.

vulnerable populations. For this reason, Christian social justice activists frequently cite passages in the Bible that speak to the importance of love, fairness, mercy, and compassion. Take Volf's explanation of how "the self-giving love manifested on the cross and demanded by it lies at the core of Christian faith."[38] The complex web of religious, economic, and political considerations that surround the field of public testimony is what Volf draws our attention to here. Paying close attention to these matters, especially questions of social justice, is essential if we desire to be effective witnesses. Volf's work helps Christians to see the enormous difficulty of separating their public witness from their cultural worldview.

Culture

Even if they were saved from within culture, Christians are culturally formed beings. Still, the Scriptures warn us to keep our distance from harmful and sinful cultural factors, and as we go on in this mortal life, we are susceptible to their influence. H. Richard Niebuhr explains that

> the cultural Christian, however, understands that there are great polarities in any civilisation; and that there is a sense in which Jesus Christ affirms movements in philosophy toward the assertion of the world's unity and order . . . and the care for the common good, political concerns for justice, and ecclesiastical interests in honesty in religion.[39]

As a result, public theology also includes the Christian community's involvement with culture. Niebuhr suggests that "culture discerns the rules for culture, because culture is the work of God-given reason in God-given nature."[40] But "human culture is corrupt; and it includes all human work, not simply the achievements of men outside the church but also in it."[41] Therefore, we must keep our focus on Christ's atoning sacrifice on the cross because human culture and deeds are susceptible to corruption. That is why Niebuhr thinks that "Christ defines the issue, and solves the problem of life by his continuous action of revelation, reconciliation, and inspiration."[42] It is impossible to ignore culture because of the crucial function of cultural institutions such

---

38. Miroslav Volf, *Exclusion and Embrace: A Theological Exploration of Identity, Otherness, and Reconciliation* (Nashville: Abingdon, 1996), 25.
39. H. Richard Niebuhr, *Christ and Culture* (New York: Harper Torchlight, 1951), 106.
40. Niebuhr, *Christ and Culture*, 135.
41. Niebuhr, 153.
42. Niebuhr, 160.

as "the family, school, state, and religious community."[43] Christians still live and work within cultural institutions.

> The relation of the authority of Jesus Christ to the authority of culture is such that every Christian must often feel himself claimed by the Lord to reject the world and its kingdoms with their pluralism and temporalism, their makeshift compromises of many interests, their hypnotic obsession by the love of life and the fear of death. The movement of withdrawal and renunciation is a necessary element in every Christian life, even though it be followed by an equally necessary movement of responsible engagement in cultural tasks.[44]

The Transformative Power of Christian Public Witness in Africa

Christian witness has always played a pivotal role in propelling major social shifts in society. A number of countries and areas owe a great deal to the influence of religiously devoted individuals. Across the globe, from the Atlantic coast to the African interior, the stories of these extraordinary individuals bear witness to the ways God has worked through devoted witnesses in all walks of life. This section will examine a few of these cases, focusing on how they have impacted their home nations and the world at large. Ultimately, God's goal in creating human beings is to have them testify about him in whatever they do. For reasons of scope, in this section I will focus on the public witness of world-shaping individuals in Africa.

Africa is hardly a standalone continent, especially in today's interconnected world. The common belief that globalization is something that has happened only recently, in the twentieth or twenty-first century, is incorrect. As long as there have been humans on this planet, there has been globalization. As we travel from the Americas to Africa, it becomes clear that there was not a single element but rather a combination of elements that enabled Christians to have a profound influence on the God-given societal settings in which they lived. Two things stand out: first, the Bible was revered for what it said – that it was God's word – and second, the Great Commission was taken to mean exactly what it said: to make disciples of all countries. Also, there was a pressing need to preach and share the good news because rescuing souls wasn't the only thing

---

43. Niebuhr, 161.
44. Niebuhr, 68.

that mattered; protecting human thought, culture, politics, and economy, and creating prosperity through favourable and fair governmental policies, was also a top priority. We can see this tendency in the lives of the people we talk about below. Their fervour for teaching people God's word and their holistic perspective on the world are inspiring examples of what is possible in public witness.

Byang Kato (1936–75)

A Nigerian theologian and missiologist, Byang Kato was known for his substantial contributions to Christian public witness. Another Nigerian theologian, Tokunboh Adeyemo, has commented on Kato's legacy: "He was a prophet. Like prophets before him, his voice was that of a lonely man in the theological wilderness of his day. His life as a prophet was marked by courage, boldness, moral purity, and discipline. His message was forthright, powerful, uncompromising but always compassionate."[45] Kato was a leading voice in the development of contextual theology, which seeks to integrate the gospel message with local cultural and social contexts. In her book *Byang Kato: Ambassador for Christ*, Sophie de la Haye describes how Kato was able to actively engage in public witness through theological education as a result of his public devotion to Christ and his open following of Christ. While working in the home of a missionary, Kato read a wall plaque which said: "I can do all things through Christ, who strengthens me" (Phil 4:13); that became Kato's life motto.[46]

To prepare him for public witness, de la Haye tells of how

> the ECWA-SIM Scholarship Board decided to give him a scholarship to study at the London Bible College in England, the most expensive one they had ever awarded. . . . [W. Harold] Fuller recalls: "He could have received a similar degree in less time, but the thorough and intensive studies of the London University B.D. provided the disciplined groundwork that would benefit him in future . . . ministry."

Thus Kato was prepared for a life of public witness.[47] He was deeply committed to promoting theological education and scholarship in Africa, and helped to establish several theological institutions and programmes across the continent.

---

45. Tokunboh Adeyemo, "Foreword," in *Byang Kato: Ambassador for Christ; Biography of Dr Byang H. Kato*, by Sophie de La Haye (Achimota: Africa Christian Press, 1986), 11.
46. de la Haye, *Byang Kato*, 24.
47. de la Haye, 35–36.

According to Amanda Pungula, "Byang Kato was passionate about learning, particularly as a Christian. He pursued further studies so that he would be equipped for gospel work in his own context. In this pursuit of education, there was a determination to help shape and fashion theology in the African context."[48] Additionally, Kato had a strong dedication to the propagation of evangelism and discipleship in Africa, and he emphasized the significance of contextualizing these practises in order to make them applicable and efficient. He insisted that "the noble desire to contextualize Christianity in Africa must not be forsaken" and that "an indigenous theology is a necessity,"[49] and sought to elevate the importance of evangelism without neglecting concerns of social justice.[50]

The contributions that Byang Kato made to Christian public witness are evidence of his dedication to the advancement of contextual theology, evangelism and discipleship, African agency and leadership, as well as theological education and research in Africa. Christians who are engaged in the struggle for a more just and genuine manifestation of the gospel in African contexts continue to find inspiration from his work. In addition to being a strong opponent of colonialism and neo-colonialism, Kato was an advocate for the recognition of African agency and leadership in the process of the formation of the African church and society.

David Gitari (1937–2013)

A prominent Christian public witness, David Gitari was a bishop of the Anglican Church in Kenya and an advocate for human rights. He built bridges, preached, prophesied, and led liturgies. When it came to the Kenyan Anglican Communion, he was among the most influential and wise bishops. In his sermons, he would teach the Scriptures and call people to repentance while simultaneously denouncing injustices on a national and local level.

---

48. Amanda Pungula, "Can We Be Christian and African? The Legacy of Byang Kato," The Gospel Coalition, Africa Edition, 1 June 2021. https://africa.thegospelcoalition.org/article/can-we-be-christian-african-the-legacy-of-byang-kato/.

49. Byang H. Kato, "A Critique of Incipient Universalism in Tropical Africa: A Study of the Religious Concepts of the 'Jaba' People of West Africa by the Late Byang H. Kato," *The International Journal of Theology and Philosophy in Africa* 1, no. 1 (1989): 59.

50. Aiah Foday-Khabenje, "From 'Devil's Baby' to Ambassador for Christ: The Evangelical Legacy of Byang H. Kato," *African Christian Theology* 1, no. 1 (2024): 97, citing Wouter Theodoor van Veelan, "'No Other Name!' The Contribution of Byang H. Kato to the Salvation Debate," *Exchange* 50, no. 1 (2021): 69–70.

Advocacy for Human Rights and Democracy, against Corruption and Impunity

Gitari was an outspoken supporter of democracy and human rights. A member of the opposition coalition that fought for multi-party democracy in Kenya in the 1990s, he helped form the National Convention Executive Council (NCEC). Gitari co-founded the Independent Medico-Legal Unit (IMLU), a non-governmental organization (NGO) that offers medical and legal assistance to victims of torture and other human rights abuses. Using his pulpit (literally and figuratively) to insist on biblical justice and integrity, by 1988 his fearless sermons had taken the lead in criticizing political corruption, including the national trend towards voting in front of candidate images rather than a secret ballot. An attempt on his life was foiled in April 1989. He tackled public injustices from every angle. Condemning the slaughter in Rwanda in 1994, Gitari slammed the international world for sitting on its hands and doing nothing to stop the ongoing genocide.[51] As a result, his public witness reached far beyond his own country of Kenya, touching people throughout his area and the African continent. Gitari vehemently opposed corruption and the practice of impunity in Kenya, focusing on both governmental and ecclesial corruption. He was vocal in his disapproval of public officials' inability to be held to account, and the waste of public funds.[52]

Advocacy for Peace, Reconciliation, and the Gospel

During the time of Kenya's political turmoil and bloodshed, Gitari was a vocal supporter of ending the violence and fostering unity. Mediating in disputes and encouraging conversation and reconciliation between opposing factions, he was an influential figure. He was recruited as a mediator by former UN Secretary-General Kofi Annan in the post-election violence that swept Kenya in 2008. Gitari exemplified the kind of public witness that Christians should strive for. Reconciliation with God and with other people were both included in his idea of reconciliation. As a result, he participated in a wide range of social activities alongside his work as an evangelist. Bishop Gitari was the first to serve as leader of the newly established diocese of Mt. Kenya East in 1975. The evangelists he dispatched to each parish had been trained not only in evangelism and church planting but also direct social action. He also assigned

---

51. David Gitari, *Troubled But Not Destroyed: The Autobiography of Archbishop David Gitari* (McLean: Isaac Publishing, 2014), 142.

52. David Gitari, "The Claims of Jesus in African Context," *International Review of Mission* 71, no. 281 (1982): 18.

educators and developmental professionals to every parish in that area.[53] These efforts resulted in an unprecedented rate of growth in both the economy and the number of churches planted during his tenure as bishop of the diocese. As a whole, Gitari's public witness was comprehensive because it was true to Jesus and could reach a lost and wounded world. He had a profound impact on the political, economic, and spiritual climate of his diocese through God's intervention.[54]

John Henry Okullu (1929–95)

Many people remember the late John Henry Okullu, a Kenyan theologian, educated colleague, journalist, and Anglican bishop, who was a notable role model in Christian public witness. A vocal critic of the administration, even when threatened by the state this man's flaming soul would not be quenched. His background in theology, law, and media prepared him to be an effective public witness. As a result, Okullu was a Christian leader who recognized the value of bearing witness in the face of pervasive economic and social inequalities. He was deeply involved in what we may call political theology, which Jemima Atieno Oluoch defines as "a critical corrective of certain tendencies to confine theology to the realm of the private and personal. . . . It aims at 'nationalisation,' taking theological concepts, the language of preaching, out of the private realm."[55] In his public life, he witnessed and contributed to several important causes.

Critique of Corruption and Impunity

Both Archbishop Gitari and Bishop Okullu were outspoken critics of corruption and impunity in Kenyan institutions, especially the church and the government. The independence that Kenya claimed was merely symbolic. Consider the period following independence: "Kenya's colonial heritage – laws, parliament, civil service, police, army, education and provincial administration – remained largely unchanged, unsympathetic and estranged from popu-

---

53. Sider, *Good News*, 23.

54. For further reading on Bishop Gitari, see Stephanie A. Lowery, "A 'Radical,' Prophetic Ecclesiology? Recovering Ecclesiological Insights from Archbishop David Gitari," *African Christian Theology* 1, no. 1 (2022): 121–37.

55. Jemima Atieno Oluoch, *The Christian Political Theology of Dr. John Henry Okullu*, Regnum Studies in Mission (Akropong-Akuapem: Regnum, 2006), xix.

lar vote."[56] Okullu was outspoken in his criticism of government waste and incompetence on many occasions.[57] In a sermon he delivered in 1992, Okullu said, "Corruption is a cancer that is eating away at the fabric of our society. We must root it out if we are to build a just and prosperous nation."[58] In his book *Church and State in Nation Building and Human Development*,[59] Okullu writes about the need for transparency and accountability in governance. He argues that corruption undermines the rule of law, erodes public trust in government, and perpetuates poverty and inequality. To rid society of corruption, church public witness is critical.

Advocacy for Human Rights, Democracy, Peace, and Reconciliation

Okullu was an outspoken supporter of democracy and human rights. In the 1990s, he participated in the fight for multi-party democracy in Kenya as a member of the National Convention Executive Council (NCEC), an alliance of opposition groups. The Christian Council of Kenya, which Okullu helped form, was vital in Kenya's fight for social equality and human rights. At the height of East African political turmoil and bloodshed, Okullu fought tirelessly for a peaceful resolution. Mediating in disputes and encouraging conversation and reconciliation among feuding factions, he was an influential figure. He was assigned to mediate in the Rwandan crisis in 1994 by former UN Secretary-General Boutros Boutros-Ghali.

Okullu's public witness made a tremendous impact in East Africa. When faced with examples of religious, political, economic, and social injustices, he firmly refused to remain silent. He believed that the church was God's special tool for redemption, which would bring about changes in society, politics, economics, and culture.

Mercy Amba Oduyoye (b. 1934)

Renowned for her work in feminist and African theological circles, Mercy Amba Oduyoye is a Ghanaian ecumenist and theologian who has enriched

---

56. Oluoch, *Christian Political Theology*, 2, citing William R. Ochieng', "Structural and Political Changes," in *Decolonization and Independence in Kenya, 1940–93*, eds. B. A. Ogot and W. R. Ochieng', Eastern African Studies (Nairobi: East African Educational, 1995), 104.

57. E.g. J. Henry Okullu, *Church and Politics in East Africa* (Nairobi: Uzima, 1974), 35.

58. John Henry Okullu, "God Sent His Son," sermon preached on Good Friday, 17 April 1992, at St. Stephen's Cathedral, Kisumu, Kenya.

59. John Henry Okullu, *Church and State in Nation Building and Human Development* (Nairobi: Uzima, 1984).

Christian public witness. Her "career has coincided with the tumultuous period of modern African history: the struggle against colonial dominance, political instability following independence, war and violent religious and ethnic strife . . . ecological disasters, famine, the fall of apartheid, and the long road to democracy."[60] In the midst of these monumental social shifts in Africa, Oduyoye has laboriously sought to elevate the voices of women via her work as a feminist theologian and an ecumenical movement leader. If the church gives space for theologizing only to men, it will be a bird with only one wing trying to fly. Oduyoye has been an advocate for a "two-winged" theology,[61] for a church that can soar like an eagle.

As a result, Oduyoye has been an outspoken advocate for the value of women's experiences and viewpoints in theological discussions, and she has been at the forefront of African women's theology. The practice of public witness by Christians is something that Oduyoye has long championed. She argues that "Christians in Africa must deal with the gap between 'Christianity preached' and 'Christianity lived.'"[62] The multi-religious environment in which African Christians live makes this imperative. In her public witness, Oduyoye argues that Christians are called to address the following thought-provoking question: "What does Christianity bring to the table that our people's natural religion does not?"[63]

A leading figure in the international discussion on gender and theology, Oduyoye has long stressed the importance of a theological discourse that is more welcoming of all perspectives. Oduyoye challenges the business-as-usual mentality of African leaders in her chapter "Women and Ritual in Africa," as she pursues the public witness of the church in our societies by declaring that "in the Decade 1988–98 we seek justice for women, to dream 'bold dreams' for new community."[64] Mercy Amba Oduyoye's work in Christian public witness shows how she is dedicated to empowering underrepresented groups, bridging

---

60. Kwok Pui-lan, "Mercy Amba Oduyoye and African Women's Theology," *Journal of Feminist Studies in Religion* 20, no. 1 (2004): 7.

61. E.g. see Mercy Amba Oduyoye, "The Search for a Two-Winged Theology," in *Talitha, qumi! Proceedings of the Convocation of African Women Theologians, Trinity College, Legon-Accra, September 24–October 2, 1989*, eds. Mercy Amba Oduyoye and Musimbi Kanyoro (Accra: SWL, 2001).

62. Mercy Amba Oduyoye, *Hearing and Knowing: Theological Reflections on Christianity in Africa* (Nairobi: Acton, 2000), 9.

63. Oduyoye, *Hearing and Knowing*, 9.

64. Mercy Amba Oduyoye, *Who Will Roll the Stone Away? The Ecumenical Decade of the Churches in Solidarity with Women*, Risk Book Series (Geneva: WCC, 1990), 68.

cultural and religious gaps, and fighting patriarchal and oppressive structures in the church and beyond.

Desmond Mpilo Tutu (1931–2021)

A vocal supporter of Christian public witness, Desmond Mpilo Tutu was a South African Anglican bishop and theologian who played a major role in the anti-apartheid movement and the campaign for social justice and human rights. During the 1980s he performed an unprecedented role in bringing national and international attention to the evils of apartheid. He supported non-violent tactics of protest and encouraged the deployment of economic pressure by countries dealing with South Africa. In 1984 he was awarded the Nobel Peace Prize.

Theological Foundations for Public Witness

Tutu insisted that Christians should base their public witness on the gospel's message of God's love and justice. In his book *Hope and Suffering*, he cautioned his readers to remember that "God cares. God cares about injustice, about oppression, about exploitation. God cares and always takes the side of those who are trodden underfoot. God cares that they want to move you from pillar to post."[65] He held the view that Christians ought to fight for the welfare of all people and denounce injustice when they see it.

Critique of Apartheid

Recognizing that to be a witness for Christ required him to be a witness *against* injustice, Tutu was an outspoken opponent of apartheid in South Africa and a key figure in the fight against it. He writes, "Jesus revolutionised religion by showing that God was really a disreputable God, a God on the side of the social pariahs. He showed God as one who accepted us sinners unconditionally."[66] Tutu rightfully refused to accept that systems of injustice such as the apartheid system could be God's will for humanity. He contended that

> we need to remind ourselves constantly that Jesus was heir to the prophetic tradition. You cannot read any of the major prophets without being struck by at least one thing. They all condemned, as

---

65. Desmond Tutu, *Hope and Suffering: Sermons and Speeches* (Grand Rapids: Eerdmans, 1984), 42.

66. Desmond Tutu, *Crying in the Wilderness: The Struggles for Justice in South Africa* (Grand Rapids: Eerdmans, 1982), 28.

worthless religiosity, a concern with offering God worship when we were unmindful of the socio-political implication of our religion.[67]

He spoke out against apartheid's injustice and persecution from his vantage point as a bishop.

Advocacy for Reconciliation and Forgiveness
In his fight for human rights and social justice, Tutu stressed the significance of forgiveness and reconciliation. Healing and the establishment of a fair and peaceful society depend on reconciliation. In his speech "Between a Nightmare and a Dream," Tutu said,

> I used to tell the Whites "I want liberation for Blacks and Whites – Whites won't be free until we are free." They thought I was spewing irresponsible slogans. We won a victory for everyone, black and white. Now we have all been liberated. Freedom is indivisible. Go and share in the process of healing, the process of reconciliation.[68]

Nelson Mandela, first president of post-apartheid South Africa, nominated Tutu to lead the Truth and Reconciliation Commission in 1995. The commission looked into claims of human rights violations committed during apartheid. Desmond Tutu spearheaded the South African church's effort to stand for truth, justice, forgiveness, and reconciliation via his dedication to church public witness.[69]

Yusufu Turaki (b. 1946)

Nigerian theologian, ethicist, and social critic Yusufu Turaki has done much to advance Christian public witness, especially in contextual theology. Turaki maintains that contextualization is crucial in the fields of theology and mission, and he has written extensively on the connection between Christianity and African culture. Turaki's devotion to public witness is demonstrated in his

---

67. Tutu, *Crying in the Wilderness*, 28.

68. Desmond Tutu, "Between a Nightmare and a Dream: If Reconciliation Can Happen in South Africa, It Can Happen Elsewhere," *Christianity Today* 42, no. 2 (9 Feb. 1998): 25–26; this is a published version of a speech delivered at the South African Press Club in October 1997.

69. Editors' note: Two of the contributors to this volume have recently offered a helpful critique of Tutu's work with the Truth and Reconciliation Commission. See Alfred Sebahene and Ruth Barron, "Without Exceptions: Envisioning Ubuntu Churches Confronting Abuse in Africa, *African Christian Theology* 2, no. 1 (2025): 39–63, https://doi.org/10.69683/n5ebjs21.

published dissertation. He has come to terms with the fact that the colonial past of Nigeria is the source of the present violent conflicts. According to him, "the moral sanction of Islam and the anti-Christian attitude of the Colonial Administration instituted a social and religious conflict between the Muslim and the non-Muslim groups . . . which was never corrected in the post-colonial Nigeria."[70] As such, he argued that to correct this impasse, "the Nigerian society needs to be restructured so as to address the issues of social justice and the existence of structures of inequality, insecurity and incompatibility."[71]

Turaki has also stressed the importance of contextually grounded theological education for African Christians, one that helps them face the opportunities and overcome the obstacles specific to their own social and cultural milieu. In addition, Turaki has been an outspoken supporter of religious tolerance and mutual understanding, especially among Nigeria's Christian and Muslim communities. For Turaki, local leadership, evangelism, and civic engagement are crucial. He contends that "the shaping of African Christian self-expression can be affected either by the conscientious theologian who knows the art of doing theology or by ordinary people whose everyday life and experience provides self-understanding and self-interpretation of their Christian experience."[72]

We must give this Christian experience our full attention if we are to see genuine public witness. Turaki believes that self-criticism and repentance are essential parts of the Christian journey which must be undertaken before any consideration of public engagement can be entertained. He says that missionary Christianity and colonialism tried to change African traditional ideals of kinship and community, but they were unsuccessful. As a result, genocide and civil wars are among the many crises that plague Africa.[73]

Turaki criticized the missionary perspective on missions because he understood the comprehensive nature and scope of the gospel. He observed that the medical policy of the Sudan Interior Mission (SIM) missionaries seemed to imply that true medical mission occurred only when individuals were truly converted to Christ, rather than viewing medical missions as missions in and of themselves. He argued that SIM policy emphasized that the evangelistic activity and winning of souls for Christ that occurred during the medical missions

---

70. Yusufu Turaki, *The British Colonial Legacy in Northern Nigeria: A Social Ethical Analysis of the Colonial and Post-colonial Society and Politics in Nigeria* (Jos: ECWA Challenge Press, 1993), 207–8.

71. Turaki, *British Colonial Legacy*, x.

72. Yusufu Turaki, *Engaging Religions and Worldviews in Africa: A Christian Theological Method* (Bukuru/Carlisle: HippoBooks, 2020), 96.

73. Yusufu Turaki, *The Trinity of Sin* (Bukuru/Carlisle: HippoBooks, 2012), 24.

were more important than the mending and care of the physical body.[74] Finally, Yusufu Turaki's work on Christian public witness shows how much he cared about advancing African leadership in mission and evangelism, contextual theology, theological education, and interfaith cooperation and conversation. For Christians fighting for a more equitable and authentic gospel in Africa, his writings are a source of encouragement and wisdom.

Matthew Hassan Kukah (b. 1952)

Bishop Matthew Hassan Kukah is a native of Northern Nigeria's Kaduna State and is proficient in multiple languages spoken there. His efforts to foster mutual understanding across religious and cultural divides have been truly commendable. He is idealistic in the sense that he thinks the Nigerian people are capable of making their country much better than it currently is. His evaluations of the political and developmental climate of the country are ruthlessly realistic as well. His work as a social critic and human rights champion has propelled him to a prominent position in Nigerian Christian public witness. In 1999, he became a member of the Truth Commission in Nigeria and also served as its secretary. Despite his humility, he saw his role on the commission as that of a divinely appointed commissioner.

In his view, the church is vital to the process of rebuilding a better Nigeria. Consequently, he stated,

> In my analysis, I had come to realise that in many ways, the Churches and their leaders had tended to become redundant after the collapse of dictatorships. The challenges of redefining and repositioning the Churches for a new role were urgent and needed careful thinking. I therefore was determined to ensure that our Churches learnt the lessons and remained relevant in the shaping of a new Nigeria.[75]

Christians in Nigeria now view politics differently because of Kukah.

Advocacy for Social Justice, Human Rights, Peace, and Reconciliation

In Nigeria, Kukah has fought tirelessly for social equality and human rights. He has publicly condemned injustice, corruption, and those in power abusing

---

74. Yusufu Turaki, *Theory and Practice of Christian Missions in Africa: A Century of SIM/ECWA History and Legacy in Nigeria 1983–1993*, vol. 1 (Nairobi: IBS Africa, 1999), 168.

75. Matthew Hassan Kukah, *Witness to Justice: An Insider's Account of Nigeria's Truth Commission* (Ibadan: Bookcraft, 2011), 49–50.

their positions. After violent conflicts broke out in Nigeria between various ethnic and religious groups, Kukah helped to bring about peace. As essential parts of establishing peace, he has stressed the significance of reconciliation and forgiveness.

Critique of Religious Intolerance

When it comes to religious intolerance in Nigeria, Kukah has been outspoken against both Christians and Muslims. In his book *Religion, Politics, and Power in Northern Nigeria*, Kukah writes, "Religious intolerance is one of the most serious problems facing our country today. We need to find ways to promote peaceful coexistence and understanding between people of different faiths."[76] He has stressed the significance of religious communities talking to each other and understanding each other.

Matthew Olusegun Aremu Obasanjo (b. 1937)

Aremu Obasanjo is a retired statesman and former military chief of state from Nigeria. He was the country's leader from 1976 to 1979 and again from 1999 to 2007. He was an active member of the People's Democratic Party (PDP) from 1998 to 2018. His instrumentality in introducing reforms in the country during his tenure as president arose from his Christian public witness and has ameliorated Nigeria's reputation as a politically unstable country plagued by official corruption and vulnerable to military coups. Among Obasanjo's many achievements are the following:

Promotion of Interfaith Dialogue

A firm believer in the need for religious tolerance and mutual understanding, Obasanjo has long championed such causes in Nigeria. He has stressed that Christians and Muslims should work together and appreciate each other. In his book *My Watch*, Obasanjo writes, "We need to promote interfaith dialogue and understanding in Nigeria. This requires a willingness to listen to each other, to learn from each other, and to work together for the common good."[77]

---

76. Matthew Hassan Kukah, *Religion, Politics, and Power in Northern Nigeria* (Ibadan: Spectrum, 1993), 79.

77. Olusegun Obasanjo, *My Watch* (Lagos: Vintage, 2014), 95.

Critique of Corruption

Throughout his presidency and since stepping down, Obasanjo has been an outspoken opponent of corruption in Nigeria. He has demanded an end to the impunity culture that permits corruption to flourish and has stressed the importance of government openness and responsibility.

Advocacy for Peace and Reconciliation

Finally, in Nigeria, Obasanjo has played an active role in restoring harmony following violent clashes between various religious and ethnic factions. As essential parts of establishing peace, he has stressed the significance of reconciliation and forgiveness.

Conclusion

Having an effect on society is an integral part of being a Christian. The only kind of Christian faith that can prevent society from experiencing the good effects of Christianity is a dysfunctional one. As we have seen in this chapter, the Great Commission is so comprehensive that it compels Christians to let their faith, convictions, beliefs, values, and practices permeate every part of society. Therefore, public witnessing is intrinsic to who we are. It is God's plan to undo the world's curse. The central idea of this chapter is that our religion affects society at large. The fact that Jesus emphasized the need to carry the values he taught in the Sermon on the Mount with us wherever we go is one piece of obvious evidence. Allowing other people to perceive God through us is at the heart of what we're doing. Alternatively stated, by emulating Christ's character traits, we are better able to realize the reason why God made us and sustains us here on earth: to bring glory to God by making God visible to those who know him and to those who do not.

Returning to John 20:19–23, we see that once Jesus was resurrected from the dead, he went straight to the house where his followers had taken refuge from the Jewish authorities. "Peace be with you!" Jesus proclaimed as he came to them. After saying this twice he added, "As the Father has sent me, even so I am sending you," followed by, "Receive the Holy Spirit." This means that Jesus Christ, both then and now, sends his followers to various public places all around the globe so that people can have a personal encounter with God. Therefore, Christians are supposed to live in such a way that others can see Jesus in us.

In Antioch, the group of individuals who followed Jesus were known as "Christians" or "Christlike people" because they grasped his teachings so clearly. In every way, the Antioch population viewed them as imitating Jesus Christ. They brought honour to God by demonstrating the Christlike qualities that Christians are called to develop so that we can make a difference in the world. Christians have taken special care since that time to ensure that their faith in Christ has public value, relevance, and meaning, and as a result they have made significant contributions to society. In this chapter, we have summarized the works of prominent Christians from around the world who have continued the work begun by the apostles. They broke ground in spreading the gospel to the masses, ushering in periods of profound personal growth, spiritual revival, national and international progress, and even progress for entire continents.

Bibliography

Adeyemo, Tokunboh. "Foreword." In *Byang Kato: Ambassador for Christ; Biography of Dr Byang H. Kato*, by Sophie de la Haye, 11–13. Achimota: Africa Christian Press, 1986.

African Union Commission. *Agenda 2063: The Africa We Want; Framework Document*. Addis Ababa: African Union Commission, 2015. https://au.int/sites/default/files/documents/33126-doc-framework_document_book.pdf.

———. *Agenda 2063: The Africa We Want; Popular Version*. Addis Ababa: African Union Commission, 2015. https://au.int/sites/default/files/documents/36204-doc-agenda2063_popular_version_en.pdf.

Agang, Sunday Bobai. "The Need for Public Theology in Africa." In *African Public Theology*, edited by Sunday Bobai Agang, Dion A. Forster, and H. Jurgens Hendriks, 3–14. Bukuru/Carlisle: HippoBooks, 2020.

Atencio, Mitchell. "Ron Sider, Who Called Evangelicals to Social Justice, Dies at 82." Sojourners, 29 July 2022, https://sojo.net/articles/ron-sider-who-called-evangelicals-social-justice-dies-82.

Augustine of Hippo. *The City of God*. Translated by Henry Bettenson. London: Penguin, 1972.

Bonhoeffer, Dietrich. *Act and Being: Transcendental Philosophy and Ontology in Systematic Theology*. Dietrich Bonhoeffer Works 2. Translated from the German by Martin Rumscheidt. Edited by Wayne W. Floyd Jr. and Hans-Richard Reuter. Minneapolis: Fortress, 1996.

Burton-Christie, Douglas. "Athanasius (c.295–373), *The Life of Antony*." In *Christian Spirituality: The Classics*, edited by Arthur Holder, 13–24. New York: Routledge, 2010.

Foday-Khabenje, Aiah. "From 'Devil's Baby' to Ambassador for Christ: The Evangelical Legacy of Byang H. Kato." *African Christian Theology* 1, no. 1 (2024): 81–99. https://doi.org/10.69683/mnffcq06.

Fountain, Jeff. *Shapers of Our Modern Age: Six Men Who Shaped Nations*. Amsterdam: Schuman Centre Resources, 2018.

Gitari, David. "The Claims of Jesus in African Context." *International Review of Mission* 71, no. 281 (1982): 12–19.

———. *Troubled But Not Destroyed: The Autobiography of Archbishop David Gitari*. McLean: Isaac Publishing, 2014.

de la Haye, Sophie. *Byang Kato: Ambassador for Christ; Biography of Dr Byang H. Kato*. Achimota: African Christian Press, 1986.

Kato, Byang H. "A Critique of Incipient Universalism in Tropical Africa: A Study of the Religious Concepts of the 'Jaba' People of West Africa by the Late Byang H. Kato." *The International Journal of Theology and Philosophy in Africa* 1, no. 1 (1989): 55–84.

King, Martin Luther, Jr. *Strength to Love*. Minneapolis: Fortress, 2010.

Kukah, Matthew Hassan. *Religion, Politics, and Power in Northern Nigeria*. Ibadan: Spectrum, 1993.

———. *Witness to Justice: An Insider's Account of Nigeria's Truth Commission*. Ibadan: Bookcraft, 2011.

Lowery, Stephanie A. "A 'Radical,' Prophetic Ecclesiology? Recovering Ecclesiological Insights from Archbishop David Gitari." *African Christian Theology* 1, no. 1 (2022): 121–37. https://doi.org/10.69683/0ce6pm16.

Niebuhr, H. Richard. *Christ and Culture*. New York: Harper Torchlight, 1951.

Noll, Mark A. *Turning Points: Decisive Moments in the History of Christianity*. Grand Rapids: Baker, 1997.

Obasanjo, Olusegun. *My Watch*. Lagos: Vintage, 2014.

Oduyoye, Mercy Amba. *Hearing and Knowing: Theological Reflections on Christianity in Africa*. Nairobi: Acton, 2000.

———. "The Search for a Two-Winged Theology." In *Talitha, qumi! Proceedings of the Convocation of African Women Theologians, Trinity College, Legon-Accra, September 24–October 2, 1989*, edited by Mercy Amba Oduyoye and Musimbi Kanyoro, 31–56. Ibadan: Daystar. Reprint ed.: Accra: SWL, 2001.

———. *Who Will Roll the Stone Away? The Ecumenical Decade of the Churches in Solidarity with Women*. Risk Book Series. Geneva: WCC, 1990.

Okullu, John Henry. *Church and Politics in East Africa*. Nairobi: Uzima, 1974.

———. *Church and State in Nation Building and Human Development*. Nairobi: Uzima, 1984.

———. "God Sent His Son." Sermon preached on Good Friday, 17 April 1992, at St. Stephen's Cathedral, Kisumu, Kenya.

Oluoch, Jemima Atieno. *The Christian Political Theology of Dr. John Henry Okullu*. Regnum Studies in Mission. Akropong-Akuapem: Regnum, 2006.

Pui-lan, Kwok. "Mercy Amba Oduyoye and African Women's Theology." *Journal of Feminist Studies in Religion* 20, no. 1 (2004): 7–22.

Pungula, Amanda. "Can We Be Christian and African? The Legacy of Byang Kato." The Gospel Coalition, Africa Edition, 1 June 2021. https://africa.thegospelcoalition.org/article/can-we-be-christian-african-the-legacy-of-byang-kato/.

Shaw, Ian J. *Churches, Revolutions, and Empires: 1789–1914*. Fearn: Christian Focus, 2012.

Sider, Ronald J. *Good News and Good Works: A Theology for the Whole Gospel*. Grand Rapids: Baker, 1999.

———. *Rich Christians in an Age of Hunger: Moving from Affluence to Generosity*. 6th ed. Nashville: Thomas Nelson, 2015. [1st ed.: *Rich Christians in an Age of Hunger: A Biblical Study*. New York: Paulist Press, 1977.]

Sider, Ronald J., with the staff of Evangelicals for Social Action. *Completely Pro-Life: Building a Consistent Stance on Abortion, the Family, Nuclear Weapons, the Poor*. Downers Grove: InterVarsity Press, 1987. Reprint ed.: Eugene: Wipf & Stock, 2010.

Stark, Rodney. *The Rise of Christianity: How the Obscure, Marginal Jesus Movement Became the Dominant Religious Force in the Western World in a Few Centuries*. Princeton: Princeton University Press, 1996. Reprint ed.: San Francisco: HarperSanFrancisco, 1997.

Stassen, Glen H. *Just Peacemaking: Transforming Initiatives for Justice and Peace*. Louisville: Westminster John Knox, 1992.

Stassen, Glen H., and David P. Gushee. *Kingdom Ethics: Following Jesus in Contemporary Context*. Downers Grove: InterVarsity Press, 2003.

Turaki, Yusufu. *The British Colonial Legacy in Northern Nigeria: A Social Ethical Analysis of the Colonial and Post-colonial Society and Politics in Nigeria*. Jos: ECWA Challenge Press, 1993.

———. *Engaging Religions and Worldviews in Africa: A Christian Theological Method*. Bukuru/Carlisle: HippoBooks, 2020.

———. *Theory and Practice of Christian Missions in Africa: A Century of SIM/ECWA History and Legacy in Nigeria, 1983–1993*. Volume 1. Nairobi: IBS Africa, 1999.

———. *The Trinity of Sin*. Bukuru/Carlisle: HippoBooks, 2011.

Tutu, Desmond. "Between a Nightmare and a Dream: If Reconciliation Can Happen in South Africa, It Can Happen Elsewhere." *Christianity Today* 42, no. 2 (9 Feb. 1998): 25–26.

———. *Crying in the Wilderness: The Struggles for Justice in South Africa*. Grand Rapids: Eerdmans, 1982.

———. *Hope and Suffering: Sermons and Speeches*. Grand Rapids: Eerdmans, 1984.

Volf, Miroslav. *Exclusion and Embrace: A Theological Exploration of Identity, Otherness, and Reconciliation*. Nashville: Abingdon, 1996.

———. *A Public Faith: How Followers of Christ Should Serve the Common Good*. Grand Rapids: Brazos, 2011.

2

Overcoming the Obstacles

Challenging the Church's Public Witness in Response to Abuse

Ruth Barron

Curriculum Developer, MissionStream, Kenya

We cannot speak out against bigotry while abusing people within our churches or neighborhoods. We cannot decry injustices while hoarding resources for ourselves. Witness must take seriously what it means to embody the kingdom of God within the confessing community, and then what it means to live out that reality openly within and for the public realm.[1]

There is abundant evidence that one of the key areas where God is now at work lies in exposing and calling out abuse and abuse cover-ups in the church. In our day, this work of God began nearly forty years ago with the public exposure of the Roman Catholic Church's cover-ups of rampant sexual abuse by priests, and this work has expanded to expose multiple churches and ministries of every size, on every continent, and includes multiple forms of abuse. Yet even as we hear of abuse being exposed and called out, too often the church has resisted joining this work of God and instead stands in the way of it. This chapter explores five obstacles to the church addressing abuse well. These obstacles are (1) incorrectly identifying abuse, (2) prioritizing institutions over vulnerable members, (3) misusing Scripture to justify policies that enable abuse, (4) sacrificing victims to protect charismatic leaders with prominent

---

1. Gregg Okesson, *A Public Missiology: How Local Churches Witness to a Complex World* (Grand Rapids: Baker Academic, 2020), 255.

platforms, and (5) condemning the victims to excuse our refusal to help. In my examination, I will also offer parables to help us understand these obstacles more deeply. I write this chapter to encourage Christians to overcome these obstacles and engage in this work of God to protect the vulnerable within the church rather than their abusers.[2]

The Pandemic of Abuse

Abuse is a pandemic. More than 400 million children worldwide experience sexual exploitation and abuse every year.[3] If we broaden the scope to include physical and emotional abuse as well as neglect, an estimated one billion children experience violence every year.[4] Among women aged fifteen and over, approximately 736 million have experienced physical or sexual violence one or more times in their lives.[5] In a 2021 survey of workplace harassment and violence spanning 121 countries, 22 percent of participants said that they had experienced one or more types of workplace abuse.[6] None of these statistics include spiritual abuse or abuse of authority by Christian leaders. What has been the public witness of the church in the face of this pandemic?

---

2. There are other obstacles as well. E.g. Tarana Burke, the African American who founded the #MeToo movement, notes that "in the Black community, the culture of secrecy and silence" about sexual violence "is more complex than just wanting to protect the perpetrator" but is tangled with "the long history of false accusations of sexual violence against Black men along with our tumultuous relationship with law enforcement"; in addition, "the general ranking of sexual violence as minor in the face of things like structural racism and crippling poverty also play[s] a role in how hard it is for us to stare down the monster that is sexual violence and call it out by name." *Unbound: My Story of Liberation and the Birth of the Me Too Movement* (New York: Flatiron Books, 2021), 211–12. In the same paragraph, Burke mentions two of the obstacles which I examine: excusing the abuser, and blaming victims for the abuse they have suffered.

3. Economist Impact, *Out of the Shadows: Index 2022*, 2, https://cdn.outoftheshadows.global/uploads/documents/Out-of-the-Shadows-Index-2022-Global-Report.pdf.

4. World Health Organization, *Global Status Report on Preventing Violence against Children 2020*, v, x, 8, 12, 61, https://www.who.int/teams/social-determinants-of-health/violence-prevention/global-status-report-on-violence-against-children-2020.

5. UN Women, "Facts and Figures: Ending Violence against Women," February 2022, https://www.unwomen.org/en/what-we-do/ending-violence-against-women/facts-and-figures.

6. Edith M. Lederer, "Global Survey: Workplace Violence, Harassment Is Widespread," AP News, 5 December 2022, https://apnews.com/article/business-violence-united-nations-workplace-04e3626ffb0ceb8478ccfa12d6f4457f.

The Roman Catholic sexual abuse scandal[7] began to awaken the church, but we remain very naïve, assuming that abuse is not a serious issue in our own churches or denominations and that the vulnerable are safer in our churches than in "the world." Unfortunately not. Boz Tchividjian, grandson of Billy Graham and founder of GRACE (Godly Response to Abuse in the Christian Environment), reviewed multiple studies and found that abuse is actually more likely in religious spaces than in secular spaces. One study, Tchividjian notes, found that 93 percent of sex offenders consider themselves religious and that religious sex offenders are often the most dangerous, with younger and larger numbers of victims.[8]

One survey found that 75 percent of pastors "underestimate the level of violence experienced within their congregations."[9] As one pastor told me, he preaches to abuse victims to forgive their abusers because he has abuse victims in his church, but he doesn't preach to abusers to stop abusing because he doesn't *have* any abusers in his church. This is a very dangerous assumption for pastors to make. The majority of pastors speak about abuse at most once a year, and when pastors *do* speak about abuse, most speak in ways that perpetuate rather than address the harm.[10]

Many church teachings enable abuse. For instance, the emphasis on offering grace to sinners becomes dangerous when combined with doctrines that equalize sins, such that abuse is seen as no worse than having an irritable moment. Yet Jesus taught that it was better to drown oneself than to cause a little one to stumble (Matt 18:6; Luke 17:2), suggesting that harming the vulnerable is a great sin. When churches enable abuse, predators find churches a highly appealing target. As a convicted sex offender told interviewer Dr. Ann Salter, "I considered church people easy to fool . . . They have a trust that comes

---

7. In just one state of the USA, "more than 450 credibly accused child sex abusers" continued to minister in the Roman Catholic Church "over almost seven decades," with "at least 1,997 children" having been abused during that time." Ruth Graham, "Sex Abuse in Catholic Church: Over 1,900 Minors Abused in Illinois, State Says," *New York Times* online, 23 May 2023, https://www.nytimes.com/2023/05/23/us/illinois-catholic-church-sex-abuse.html.

8. Boz Tchividjian, "Startling Statistics: Child Sexual Abuse and What the Church Can Begin Doing about It," RNS (Religion News Service), 9 January 2014, https://religionnews.com/2014/01/09/startling-statistics/; citing "the Abel and Harlow Study", see Gene G. Abel and Nora Harlow, "The Abel and Harlow Child Molestation Study," Child Molestation Research & Prevention Institute," April 2002, https://www.childmolestationprevention.org/_files/ugd/4b2901_d91e1a1c004d4e68b7d2b45157971961.pdf. This study is an updated excerpt from Abel and Harlow, *The Stop Child Molestation Book* (Bloomington, Indiana: Xlibris, 2001).

9. "Adult Clergy Sexual Abuse Survey," Not in Our Church, n.d., http://www.notinourchurch.com/statistics.html.

10. "Adult Clergy Sexual Abuse Survey."

from being Christians. They tend to be better folks all around and seem to want to believe in the good that exists in people."[11]

Churches also groom children and women and other vulnerable people to accept abuse. After her children were abused at a missionary boarding school, one mother stated, "In some ways, missionary parents unwittingly set their children up for abuse. We taught them to be very compliant, very obedient. We talked about how important our work was for God. We even used words like, 'You need to be a good little soldier for Jesus.'"[12] Yet teachings that emphasize compliance ignore the many stories of vulnerable people standing up to the more powerful in the Scriptures, such as the woman who answered back to Jesus: "Even the dogs eat the crumbs that fall from their master's table" (Matt 15:27, NIV).[13]

Other teachings encourage onlookers to ignore and enable abuse. I will focus on this aspect in this chapter. There are a growing number of reports on the failures of prominent Christian organizations to address abuse allegations properly: the Catholic Church, Hillsong, RZIM (the ministry of Ravi Zacharias), the Southern Baptist Convention, New Tribes Mission, and many, many more. Many Christians acknowledge that abuse is a serious issue but teach that we must focus on our mission: "to seek and to save the lost" (Jesus's words in Luke 19:10). This understanding of the mission of the church is deeply flawed. The protection and safety of the vulnerable *is not separate from, but is a central part of, the mission of the church*, as Agbonkhianmeghe E. Orobator argues.[14] In fact, to continue the sheep parable Jesus used, if there is a predator in the sheepfold it is *safer for the sheep to be outside the sheepfold*. As we have seen, the predators in religious spaces tend to have *more and younger victims*. If there are predators in the sheepfold, we must first make the sheepfold safe for the sheep before bringing in more sheep. Jesus's strong words of warning for any

---

11. Quoted by Tchividjian, "Startling Statistics"; see also Anna C. Salter, *Predators: Pedophiles, Rapists, and Other Sex Offenders: Why They Are, How They Operate, and How We Can Protect Ourselves and Our Children* (New York: Basic Books, 2003, 2004).

12. Sarah Eekhoff Zylstra, "When Abuse Comes to Light," *Christianity Today* 58, no. 2 (March 2014): 46.

13. Except where otherwise noted, all biblical quotations are taken from the NIV.

14. Agbonkhianmeghe E. Orobator, "Between Ecclesiology and Ethics: Promoting a Culture of Protection and Care in Church and Society," *Theological Studies* 80, no. 4 (December 2019): 897–915. Specifically, he notes that "the manner in which the church ought to regard and treat children rests on the foundation of a moral duty incumbent on the church and mandated by Christ. . . . The theological self-understanding of the church is held to account by a set of ethical imperatives that warrant an unwavering commitment to the care and protection of children inside and outside the church. . . . This commitment is constitutive of the mission and identity of the church" (898).

who would harm the vulnerable alert us to the extreme seriousness with which God approaches the sin of abuse. Taken together with the above statistics, and the painful reality that religious spaces are often havens for predators, I would argue that it is immoral to bring new sheep into a sheepfold without doing everything possible to first ensure it is safe.

In light of these statistics, what is the church to do? As we rethink church in the twenty-first century, we do not need to rethink whether the church *should address abuse*. It is abundantly evident that we must. Instead, we need to rethink the obstacles to our *doing what we know to be right and just*. In the following sections, I will identify five obstacles to addressing abuse, and explore how they have contributed to the church's perpetuation of abuse.

Incorrectly Identifying Abuse

The first and most difficult obstacle to addressing abuse is incorrectly identifying what abuse is. What distinguishes abuse from non-abuse? Surely "all parts of a community must share a clearly defined theory of violence to coordinate effective intervention strategies."[15] Yet many parts of the church hold vastly different definitions of abuse from abuse researchers and human rights groups. For example, the UN defines abuse as "physical, sexual, emotional, economic or psychological actions or threats of actions that influence another person. This includes any behaviors that frighten, intimidate, terrorize, manipulate, hurt, humiliate, blame, injure, or wound someone."[16] The Domestic Abuse Intervention Project (DAIP) formulated a useful tool, the Power and Control Wheel, to chart the methods that abusers use to control their spouses.[17] In identifying abuse, both the UN and DAIP focus on the impact actions have on vulnerable people.

Yet the church often bypasses the perspective of the vulnerable. Many Christians look to "what God says in the Bible" to define abuse because we look to the most powerful to define right and wrong. They think that only the actions and behaviours which God specifically and explicitly designates as abuse are abusive. But God turns us back to the vulnerable to determine what

---

15. The Advocates for Human Rights, "Evolution of Theories of Violence," Stop Violence Against Women, April 2015, https://www.stopvaw.org/Evolution_of_Theories_of_Violence.

16. United Nations, "What Is Domestic Abuse?," n.d., https://www.un.org/en/coronavirus/what-is-domestic-abuse.

17. Advocates for Human Rights, "Evolution of Theories of Violence."

is sinful and abusive. Greg Gifford of the Biblical Counseling Coalition offers what he calls a "biblical definition of abuse":

> Abuse entails physical violence (Acts 16:19), threats of physical violence (Eph. 6:9), persecution (Matt. 5:44), sexual mistreatment (Judg. 19:25), reviling (Luke 6:28; 1 Pet. 2:23), speaking evil (James 4:11), or being under the misused power of another person or group of people (Gen. 16:6; 1 Sam. 2:16; Ezra 5:12).[18]

He developed his definition of abuse by looking for specific actions which God condemns in Scripture. The powerful, not the vulnerable, defines abuse. Why is this problematic?

Gifford's definition does not adequately address issues of power and vulnerability. Let's consider this through a parable: A young man is severely burned. His father visits him in the hospital and gives him a tight hug. The young man cries out in pain. His father insists that hugs are loving actions and repeatedly hugs his son, ignoring his son's cries. The hug does not hurt the father, and so he insists that the problem is his son's perception, not his own actions. When the father continues to disregard the cries of his son, the son begins to describe his father's behaviour as abusive, but the father insists that his son is delusional. He only gave his son hugs. He didn't do anything abusive. Instead, he says that his son is abusing him by telling others that his behaviour was abusive.

As DAIP tells us, we must consider power and vulnerability as we identify abuse:

> [Abuse is the] logical outcome of relationships of dominance and inequality – relationships shaped not simply by the personal choices or desires of some men to [dominate] their wives but by how we, as a society, construct social and economic relationships between men and women and within marriage (or intimate domestic relationships) and families. Our task is to understand how our response to violence creates a climate of intolerance or acceptance to the force used in intimate relationships.[19]

God does not define abuse by what offends God but by what harms the vulnerable. The "royal law" to love (Jas 2:8) means that "love does no harm" to the vulnerable person whom we are able to protect or help (Rom 13:10;

---

18. Greg Gifford, "A Biblical Definition of Abuse," Biblical Counseling Coalition, 14 January 2019, https://www.biblicalcounselingcoalition.org/2019/01/14/a-biblical-definition-of-abuse/.

19. Advocates for Human Rights, "Evolution of Theories of Violence."

Mark 12:28–31; Luke 10:25–37). Failure to offer protection and help to the vulnerable is harmful.

Too often, churches ignore issues of power and vulnerability. For example, many pastors present the story of David and Bathsheba as a story of a consensual affair rather than as a story of rape,[20] but viewing this story as an affair disregards the power of David and the vulnerability of both Bathsheba and her husband, Uriah.[21] It also disregards God's own views as stated in Nathan's parable to David (2 Sam 12:1–4). In the parable, God focuses specifically on the aspect of power and vulnerability. Bathsheba becomes a lamb, a symbol of innocence and vulnerability. Uriah becomes a poor man who loves and nurtures his single lamb well. David becomes a rich man with many sheep who steals the single lamb of the poor man, wreaking destruction on the poor man. God's judgement of David centres on the issue of power and vulnerability.

In a more current example, we see the church's disregard for the vulnerable in the Catholic Church's response to the sexual abuse crisis. During the Mass of Reparations for that crisis, one of the abuse survivors, Chris O'Leary, stood on a sidewalk outside the cathedral holding a picture of himself with other survivors. He reports that the priests and archbishop refused to acknowledge him in any way throughout the event, and he adds:

> The reason the priests and my archbishop ignored me at the Mass of Reparation – why they made it clear they weren't INTERESTED in me – was, at best, because they weren't THERE for me.

---

20. Such preachers follow misguided scholars who often have blamed Bathsheba; e.g. Randall C. Bailey, *David in Love and War: The Pursuit of Power in 2 Samuel 10–12*, Journal for the Study of the Old Testament Supplement Series 75 (Sheffield: JSOT Press, 1990), 86–88; Hans Wilhelm Hertzberg, *I and II Samuel: A Commentary*, Old Testament Library (London: SCM, 1964), 309; Cheryl A. Kirk-Dunggan, "Slingshots, Ships, and Personal Psychosis: Murder, Sexual Intrigue," in *Pregnant Passion: Gender, Sex, and Violence in the Bible*, ed. Cheryl A. Kirk-Dunggan, 37–70, Semeia Studies 44 (Leiden: Brill, 2003), 59. For the harm that these types of interpretations cause, see Rachael Denhollander, *What Is a Girl Worth? My Story of Breaking the Silence and Exposing the Truth about Larry Nassar and USA Gymnastics* (Carol Stream: Tyndale Momentum, 2019), 89–90; and also ERLC, "What Is a Girl Worth? A Conversation with Rachael Denhollander and Russell Moore on the Church's Abuse Crisis," 8 October 2019, Vimeo, https://vimeo.com/showcase/6383529/video/365072432.

21. There are a growing number of examples of responsible scholarship which does not blame the victim; e.g. Richard M. Davidson, *Flame of Yahweh: Sexuality in the Old Testament* (Peabody: Hendrickson, 2007), 523–32. For a popular treatment, see David E. Garland and Diana R. Garland, "Bathsheba's Story: Surviving Abuse and Devastating Loss," ch. 6 in *Flawed Families of the Bible: How God's Grace Works through Imperfect Relationships* (Grand Rapids: Brazos, 2007), 153–77. For a scholarly yet accessible review of the historical reception of Bathsheba and the different interpretations of her, see Sara M. Koenig, *Bathsheba Survives*, Studies on Personalities of the Old Testament (Columbia: University of South Carolina Press, 2018).

> Or any survivor.
> I was irrelevant.
> As their callous indifference made all too clear.
> Rather, they were there for God.
> Because God matters.
> And priests matter.
> And survivors don't.[22]

The Catholic leaders' response to the scandal reflects David's own perspective of his sin, which erased the vulnerable Bathsheba and Uriah. He told God, "Against you, you only, have I sinned and done what is evil in your sight" (Ps 51:4). These responses do not reflect the perspective of God in Nathan's parable to David, which spotlights the harm the king caused the vulnerable. To summarize, we can apply the words of Jesus here: the church searches the Scriptures to identify abuse (see John 5:39), but in that search we miss seeing the vulnerable among us whom God is calling us to help. We cannot faithfully address the issue of abuse without recognizing and reckoning with issues of power and vulnerability. We must value the voice of the vulnerable as we seek to identify abuse.

Prioritizing Institutions over Vulnerable Members

The second obstacle to confronting abuse is our prioritizing of the interests of the church as an institution over the needs of the church as a body made up of many parts, each of which is valuable. During an Alaska state House Judiciary Committee discussion on the societal costs of abuse, David Eastman, a Christian-affiliating Representative, suggested that fatal child abuse was "actually a benefit to society."[23] This attitude is extreme, but it epitomizes a common sentiment that dealing with the aftermath of abuse is too costly to our institutions. One pastor shared a similar sentiment with me: I should focus on calling the church to prevent abuse rather than on calling the church

---

22. Chris O'Leary, "This Nightmare," *Sacrificed*, 8 February 2021, https://www.chrisoleary.com/sacrificed/episode/002-This-Nightmare.html; emphasis original.

23. Jonathan Edwards and Azi Paybarah, "Lawmaker Censured for Asking if Fatal Child Abuse Saves Taxpayers Money," *The Washington Post* online, 23 February 2023, https://www.washingtonpost.com/nation/2023/02/23/david-eastman-alaska-child-abuse/.

to address abuse well when it happens, because focusing on addressing abuse that has happened will damage the church.[24]

Again, a parable can help us understand this issue more deeply. Schools do everything they can to ensure that their students are safe, but despite those efforts, schools cannot guarantee that their students will never experience serious injuries such as broken arms. One day, a child does break an arm at school. That injury can be healed with proper care, but the school fears its reputation will be damaged by acknowledging that the child was injured at school, and refuses to take the child to the hospital. Likewise, the parents just wrap the arm instead of asking a doctor to set it. The arm heals crookedly. The child received a serious but treatable wound, but because of the failure of the school and the parents to ensure that the arm received proper treatment, the child now has a lasting disability. The failure to treat the break caused greater harm than the break itself. The school, which exists to serve the needs of its students, has instead become self-serving.

It seems counter-intuitive to realize that the church's response to abuse allegations may actually cause more harm to the victim than the abuse itself, yet the wounds of abuse can be healed if treated promptly and properly. When churches fail to do so, they cause the victims much more harm than the abuse itself did. Psychologist Jennifer J. Freyd calls this "institutional betrayal."[25] Abuse survivor O'Leary aptly names it "the abuse of the abused."[26] Multiple studies document the harm such actions cause to victims. As Danya Ruttenberg writes, how institutions respond to abuse "has a lasting impact on how easily or quickly victims heal from that harm and whether it causes them additional pain or even lasting trauma."[27]

Medical research substantiates Ruttenberg's claim, as paediatrician Nadine Burke Harris dramatically highlights in the opening of her TED Talk:

> In the mid-90's, the CDC and Kaiser Permanente discovered an exposure that dramatically increased the risk for seven out of 10 of the leading causes of death in the United States. In high doses, it affects brain development, the immune system, hormonal sys-

---

24. Similarly, see Diane Langberg's discussion on covering up abuse in order to "protect the name of Jesus" and "the work of the Lord": *Redeeming Power: Understanding Authority and Abuse in the Church* (Grand Rapids: Brazos, 2020), 81.
25. In Danya Ruttenberg, *On Repentance and Repair: Making Amends in an Unapologetic World* (Boston: Beacon, 2022), 105.
26. O'Leary, "This Nightmare."
27. Ruttenberg, *Repentance and Repair*, 105.

tems, and even the way our DNA is read and described. Folks who are exposed in very high doses have triple the lifetime risk of heart disease and lung cancer and a 20-year difference in life expectancy.[28]

What is this exposure that causes such drastic effects? Childhood trauma. This and other research demonstrates the serious damage abuse does to the physical bodies of the victims, far beyond the actual physical injuries inflicted by the abuser.

The injuries inflicted by abuse go far beyond the physical. Psychologist and global trauma researcher Dr. Diane Langberg says, "Abuse of any kind is always damaging to the image of God in humans. The self is shattered, fractured, and silenced and cannot speak who it is into the world."[29] Through her interviews with victims of violence, she found that abuse causes three core wounds to victims, wounding (1) the victims' voices, (2) their relationships, and (3) their agency, or their ability to influence the world around them.[30] Jesus affirms this in the parable of the sheep and the goats, insisting that what we do to "the least of these" is done to Jesus himself (Matt 25:31–46).

Jesus identified himself with the vulnerable people, not the religious institution. He called out the failures of the religious institution to meet the needs of the vulnerable. Yet, as Dr Langberg argues, we often deceive ourselves in our interpretations of what it means to be Christlike, asserting that when we prioritize the well-being of a ministry, "we then make decisions that silence unwelcome truths about fraud or abuse and tell ourselves the cover-up 'preserves God's honor.'"[31] We claim we are protecting Christ from being dishonoured, yet when Jesus was faced with the dishonour of a conviction and a humiliating crucifixion, he did not protect himself. Indeed, when Peter tried to defend Jesus from that shame, Jesus reprimanded him. Are we to protect Jesus from a shame from which he does not protect himself? As a church, we

---

28. Nadine Burke Harris, "How Childhood Trauma Affects Health across a Lifetime – Nadine Burke Harris," TEDEd, TED Talk video, September 2014, https://ed.ted.com/lessons/eczPoVp6; for a transcript, see https://www.ted.com/talks/nadine_burke_harris_how_childhood_trauma_affects_health_across_a_lifetime/transcript?subtitle=en; see also Guy Raz and Nadine Burke Harris, "Nadine Burke Harris: How Does Trauma Affect a Child's DNA?," TED Radio Hour, NPR Interview transcript, 25 August 2017, https://www.npr.org/transcripts/545092982.

29. Langberg, *Redeeming Power*, 7.

30. Langberg, 7.

31. Langberg, 62.

must show the same value for the vulnerable over the institutions that Jesus himself demonstrated.

Misusing Scripture to Justify Policies That Enable Abuse

A third obstacle to addressing abuse is the misuse of Scripture to justify policies that enable abuse, even when those policies clearly harm victims. One such example is the demand for victims to "follow Matthew 18," which outlines how to proceed if "your brother or sister sins against you." This is a misapplication of the passage which ignores power differentials. A brother or sister is an equal. An abuser has immense power over the victim. It would be extremely dangerous for a victim to confront his or her abuser privately. However, church leaders often insist that the Bible, or rather, their interpretations of the Bible, trump the needs of victims.

Let us consider a parable. Some parents attend a meeting. They leave a list of tasks for their children to accomplish before they arrive home, and they leave the oldest child in authority. The role of the oldest is to ensure that everyone, including himself, works together to complete the tasks, but instead he interprets the list in a way that exempts himself: he only has to tell his siblings what to do, and they have to do all the work. He keeps the list to himself, not allowing the younger children to read and interpret it for themselves. Then he tells his younger siblings that their parents will be displeased with *them* if the tasks are not done completely *and* if they complain about his authority. After all, their parents entrusted him with this role. He has now developed a system that benefits himself and unjustly burdens his siblings, and has claimed parental endorsement of that system.

An examination of how Jesus interpreted Scripture demonstrates the priorities the church should hold as we interpret Scripture. The religious leaders in the gospels valued their interpretations of Scripture above the needs of the people. They repeatedly condemned Jesus for violating what they claimed to be clear scriptural Sabbath standards. Jesus responded that the Sabbath was made for people and not people for the Sabbath (Mark 2:27). He told the leaders to consider the impact of their interpretation on the vulnerable: "should not this woman, a daughter of Abraham, whom Satan has kept bound for eighteen long years, be set free on the Sabbath day from what bound her?" (Luke 13:16). Jesus considered the lives and well-being of the sick and vulnerable to be more important than their "clear reading" of Scripture. He reprimanded the religious leaders, asking whether the Sabbath law allowed them to do evil or good, to save life or to destroy it (Matt 12:1–13; Mark 2:23 – 3:5; Luke 6:1–9;

13:10–17; 14:1–6). In critiquing the "Corban" teaching, Jesus again focused on the impact of the interpretation on the well-being of elderly parents (Mark 7:9–13). Jesus did not define sin by what a "clear reading" of Scripture says offends God, but rather by what harms the vulnerable.

Wade Mullen, whose PhD research focused on the language organizations use to cover up abuse, writes, "Sometimes abusive organizations use their own policies and procedures to eliminate the threat the legal system poses."[32] One example he gives is the use of church membership or employment contracts which specifically prohibit lawsuits. Institutions which utilize such contracts can easily point to 1 Corinthians 6:1–8 as a biblical basis for them. Yet lawyer and abuse survivor Rachel Denhollander states that civil suits serve an essential role in holding institutions and their leaders "accountable for enabling abuse. . . . Far too often, the people who run institutions are motivated by money and reputation. In such cases, the only way to make them change is to force consequences that are significant enough that they want to do better the next time."[33] We need to develop policies and procedures that demonstrate Jesus's values. Scriptural teachings are to serve people, not people to serve the Scriptures. Our policies should serve the vulnerable, not bind them.

Sacrificing Victims to Protect Charismatic Leaders with Prominent Platforms

Another obstacle is that many abusers are charismatic leaders with prominent platforms. These gifts and platforms obscure abuse by building loyal followers who are not willing to investigate abuse. Jesus tells us, "Watch out for false prophets. They come to you in sheep's clothing, but inwardly they are ferocious wolves" (Matt 7:15). Paul adds, "And no wonder, for Satan himself masquerades as an angel of light. It is not surprising, then, if his servants also masquerade as servants of righteousness" (2 Cor 11:14–15).

Jesus teaches us to examine the fruits of a leader: "By their fruit you will recognise them. . . . A good tree cannot bear bad fruit, and a bad tree cannot bear good fruit. Every tree that does not bear good fruit is cut down and thrown into the fire. Thus, by their fruit you will recognise them" (Matt 7:16–20), but we often focus on the appearance of the fruit. Although we tend to think of abusers as *others* or *strangers*, abusers are often well respected and trusted by

---

32. Wade Mullen, *Something's Not Right: Decoding the Hidden Tactics of Abuse – and Freeing Yourself from Its Power* (Carol Stream: Tyndale Momentum, 2020), 72.
33. Denhollander, *What Is a Girl Worth?*, 233.

the family, church, or community. It is this very trust that enables abuse. Rachel Denhollander described her abuser: "He's extremely personable. Extremely gregarious. Very warm. Very caring. . . . He's the type of person that knows how to make you want to trust him. There's a reason he's risen to his place of prominence."[34] Wade Mullen writes, "Tactics of charm lead to devastating abuse, but the aftereffects are also long lasting for survivors. It's part of what's so disorienting and disillusioning about abuse: the realization that the kindness you once enjoyed and appreciated was actually a deception intended to harm you."[35] As Eve saw, the fruit looks "good for food and pleasing to the eye" (Gen 3:6).

Jesus describes it this way:

> Not everyone who says to me, "Lord, Lord," will enter the kingdom of heaven, but only the one who does the will of my Father who is in heaven. Many will say to me on that day, "Lord, Lord, did we not prophesy in your name and in your name drive out demons and in your name perform many miracles?" Then I will tell them plainly, "I never knew you. Away from me, you evildoers!" (Matt 7:21–23)

The public performance and leadership position of the abuser obscures his or her actions, so we *must investigate suspicious behaviour and/or allegations carefully and not judge by appearances.* John MacArthur, whom we will discuss further at the end of this chapter, says that when an accusation against a leader is brought to him, "My first reaction is always to deny that. . . . Until it would be confirmed significantly by two or three, whose confidence I would trust, and then properly investigated, a deaf ear is the best thing you can turn to someone who falsely accuses."[36] He assumes the accusation is false, before investigation, unless the victim provides two or three witnesses he deems trustworthy, and he requires no witnesses from the accused. MacArthur centres the accused and his own judgement rather than the needs of the victims.

I offer a parable. A woman is waiting at an intersection for the traffic light to turn green. When it does, she accelerates to cross the road, but suddenly another car, driven by an influential pastor, slams into the driver's side of her

---

34. Denhollander, 162.
35. Mullen, *Something's Not Right*, 48.
36. John MacArthur, "Restoring Biblical Eldership, Part 2," sermon delivered at Grace Community Church, Sun Valley, California, 18 January 1987. The transcript is available on MacArthur's Grace to You website, https://www.gty.org/library/sermons-library/54-41/restoring-biblical-eldership-part-2.

car. She is badly injured. Someone calls for emergency assistance, but when the first responders come, they stop to exchange warm greetings with the pastor, ignoring the woman screaming and crying for help. Eventually, they turn to her, but they insist she first tell them calmly and correctly every detail of the accident. When she cannot meet their demand, they refuse to help her and leave her bleeding to death in her vehicle. They ignore the physical evidence and, when the pastor calmly assures them that he had nothing to do with her injuries, they allow him to leave without any accountability for the harm he caused.

Such demands place a heavy burden on victims. Because abuse is a deed of darkness, it often happens without corroborating eyewitnesses. There are two voices: the voice of the powerful, highly trusted leader, and the voice of the vulnerable victim. The victim displays symptoms of trauma, making him or her seem irrational and untrustworthy. And so we listen only to the voice we deem trustworthy. Yet in the parable of the sheep and the goats, Jesus says to powerful leaders: "Truly I tell you, whatever you did not do for one of the least of these, you did not do for me" (Matt 25:45). Jesus demands an account from powerful leaders regarding their behaviour towards the vulnerable.

The Jewish leaders also demanded that Jesus produce witnesses. He replied, "I have testimony weightier than that of John. For the works that the Father has given me to finish – the very works that I am doing – testify that the Father has sent me" (John 5:36). There are two key points to note here: (1) a witness does not have to be a person, and (2) Jesus asserts that the non-verbal testimony is greater than the verbal testimony. *The evidence of the victim's trauma should be counted as a corroborating witness!* Too often, we interpret the victim's symptoms of abuse as proof that the victim is deluded or conniving, rather than seeing the symptoms themselves as one of the witnesses to the abuse. For example, like the woman in our parable, victims often struggle to tell the abuse story clearly. The details they offer can seem contradictory. Victims are often distraught while the abuser is calm, and we interpret the pain of betrayal in the victim's voice as sinful bitterness and the abuser's calm as innocence.

Even when abuse is fully confirmed by an investigation, the church often responds inappropriately. Jesus says, "Away from me, you evildoers!" Yet the church continues to honour the abuser. One poignant example of this was captured in a viral video[37] of a pastor "apologizing" for, or rather minimizing, his repeated rape of a girl. He told the congregation:

> That's why I'm here today, to follow the Biblical process of confession, repentance, and forgiveness. If God wants anything out of us . . . it's to bring healing to all who are involved. The church is engaged in a healthy Biblical process to restore your trust to the ministry here. . . . I hope you believe that God called you here perhaps for such a time as this, to believe, to forgive, to heal, so that God can reveal his goodness to you.

The abuser's focus in his apology is forgiveness, rather than accountability, for himself. He completely ignores the needs of his victim. In the biblical story of Esther, to which the pastor alludes, the king orders the abusive Haman to be killed on the gallows he had built for his primary victim and writes an edict which protects all the victims. Yet this pastor misuses the Esther story, encouraging the church to focus on extending him forgiveness, rather than on holding him accountable and helping his victim. The church gave the pastor a standing ovation.

In the video, the victim, now a grown woman, stood up to confront the pastor regarding his continued lies and deflections. She described the destructiveness of the abuse in her life. She described how she had needed help but no one gave it. She described how a former associate pastor of the same church had molested his daughters, and the church had helped that pastor move to a new congregation, leaving the daughters with their abuser and increasing the vulnerability of the other church. As she left, a few people hugged her, but then *many* members of the congregation gathered around the predator to pray for him.

Let us examine two elements of this church's response to known incidents of sexual abuse. One is the leadership's moving of a known predator to a new sheepfold, protecting the predator rather than the sheep. The other is the congregation's actions demonstrating love, concern, and praise for the predator rather than for the wounded sheep. The wounded sheep must be offered love, concern, and praise for her or his courage in speaking up. The predator

---

37. This took place at New Life Christian Church & World Outreach in Warsaw, Indiana, on 22 May 2022; the video is available on YouTube: The DCShorts, "#METOO: Woman Confronts Her Pastor about Alleged Past Abuse," n.d., https://youtu.be/hsSdj4Wp97k. See also Peter Smith and Holly Meyer, "#ChurchToo Revelations Growing, Years after Movement Began," *Cochrane Eagle*, 12 June 2022, https://www.cochraneeagle.ca/amp/world-news/churchtoo-revelations-growing-years-after-movement-began-5469940.

must be permanently removed from any position of authority over vulnerable sheep. This includes his or her own home. Jesus's words to evildoers, "Away from me!," are a stark reminder of the firm boundary which Jesus drew *to protect* the vulnerable from leaders who use their gifts and platforms *to harm* the vulnerable. I assert that this principle also extends to leaders who protect abusers. Just as recovered alcoholics cannot return to the bars that tempt them to drink, so leaders who do not protect the sheep must never again be given authority over vulnerable sheep. We have a promise that the lion will lie down with the lamb, but we are not yet living in the time of fulfilled hope. We must not practise idolatry by sacrificing the vulnerable to gain the gifts and platforms offered by abusive leaders.

Condemning Victims to Justify Our Refusal to Help

A final obstacle to addressing abuse is a belief that the victim somehow deserved the abuse, even if not its full measure. The book of Job is a powerful story about the ways we justify suffering and abuse rather than alleviate it. It offers two perspectives of the victim: God's and Satan's. Yahweh states: "There is no one on earth like him; he is blameless and upright, a man who fears God and shuns evil" (Job 1:8; see also 2:3). Satan replies, "Does Job fear God for nothing? . . . Have you not put a hedge around him and his household and everything he has? . . . But now stretch out your hand and strike everything he has, and he will surely curse you to your face" (Job 1:9–11; see also 2:4–5). As we listen to stories of abuse, we *must* hold onto Yahweh's perspective: *The victim is blameless. Nothing the victim has done justifies abuse.* When we hold Satan's perspective, we subvert justice: "the spotlight is wrongly put on the victim, and the scales are tipped toward the abuser."[38]

In John 9:1–2, the disciples meet a man who was born blind and ask Jesus, "Who sinned, this man or his parents . . . ?" Though startling, I suggest that they were essentially asking, "How does his suffering display the goodness of God?" If the man had sinned, the suffering could be seen as the discipline of a good Father, and who are they to interfere with God's discipline? Jesus disrupts their expectations. He tells them that the goodness of God is displayed not in the blind man's suffering, but in the alleviation of his suffering. Like the disciples, church leaders often see themselves as powerless to address abuse, and so they employ a framework for the goodness of God that focuses on the victim's culpability for his or her own abuse, rather than on what the church

---

38. Mullen, *Something's Not Right*, 113.

should do to address the abuse. In this way, the church displays a form of godliness, but denies its power (2 Tim 3:5).

Let us examine a final parable. Suppose that, as the congregation is talking together after the church service, one member draws a knife and stabs another. The church members gather around the victim and condemn him for bleeding. If the victim were truly holy, the knife wound would not bleed. They ignore the aggressor's actions, but demand that the victim instantly forgive him. When the victim cannot, they excommunicate him and tell him that God will condemn him to hell.

Even when we can find no sin in the victim's life before the abuse, Satan offers us a framework for arguing that the victim still deserved the abuse. As quoted above, Satan points to Job's potential future response to abuse as a justification for abuse. This perspective utilizes circular reasoning, and Job's anguished cries show us how this increases the suffering of the victims. God's declaration in Job 42:7 that Job had spoken well of him clearly demonstrates that God does not see an anguished response to injustice as sin deserving of abuse. In fact, God alleviates Job's unjust suffering by restoring double what he had lost. Job himself directly demolishes Satan's argument: "To the one in despair, kindness should come from his friend / even if he forsakes the fear of the Almighty" (Job 6:14, NET). Even if victims are in despair, and even if they abandon God because of the abuse the church has enabled, their blamelessness for their own abuse remains, and the victims still deserve justice and kindness. We must still display the goodness of God by alleviating their unjust suffering.

Why does the church so often believe the voice of Satan rather than the voice of Yahweh? Bryan Maier writes that victims come to believe the accusation that they deserved the abuse because this allows them to hold onto the belief in a world that is just in the face of injustice. He argues:

> As discouraging as this interpretation ("the offense was justified") might be, it is often the interpretation of choice compared with an even more horrifying explanation – that perhaps there is no such thing as justice after all or a judge who can enforce the law, and the strong can indeed exploit the weak with impunity. In this scenario, no matter what the victim does, she cannot prevent re-abuse.[39]

We in the church are called to meet the victim's need for justice and safety from abuse. Instead, we have too often adopted the role of Job's friends, insist-

---

39. Bryan Maier, *Forgiveness and Justice: A Christian Approach* (Grand Rapids: Kregel, 2017), 49.

ing God must have had a reason for allowing the abuse. Their response is markedly different from God's own response: restitutionary justice for all Job's losses. Job calls the church to account for its failure to represent God well:

> Will you speak wickedly on God's behalf?
> > Will you speak deceitfully for him?
> Will you show him partiality?
> > Will you argue the case for God?
> Would it turn out well if he examined you?
> > Could you deceive him as you might deceive a mortal?
> He would surely call you to account
> > if you secretly showed partiality. (Job 13:7–10)

To summarize, the church must display a powerful godliness and display the goodness of God in alleviating the suffering of abuse victims rather than seeking justification for our inaction. We must make a full account of the losses and harm caused to the victim so we can emulate God by making full restitution.

A Case Study of These Obstacles

We can see each of these obstacles at work in the response of Grace Community Church (GCC) in California when a woman named Eileen Gray reported to the church that her husband David, then a children's Bible and music teacher at the church, was severely abusing her and her children. There was sufficient evidence that when she later turned to the legal system, he was convicted and is currently serving twenty-one years in prison. California law required the church to report child abuse allegations, yet the church did not report the abuse. Instead, they pressured Eileen Gray to restore her abusive husband to the home. Associate pastor Carey Hardy even told Eileen Gray that "she needed to model for her children how to 'suffer for Jesus' by enduring David's abuse."[40] Finally, senior pastor John MacArthur publicly shamed and excommunicated Eileen Gray for refusing to obey the elders' demand that she forgive her husband, urging the church to "treat her as an unbeliever."[41] At the same

---

40. Julie Roys, "John MacArthur Shamed, Excommunicated Mother for Refusing to Take Back Child Abuser," The Roys Report, 8 March 2022, https://julieroys.com/macarthur-shamed-excommunicated-mother-take-back-child-abuser/. Hardy was charged with two misdemeanors for failure to report and for pressuring a witness, though his case was dismissed (Roys, "John MacArthur").

41. Roys.

time, he told the church, "Pray for David, for the sympathy and compassion and the lovingkindness of God to be his portion."[42] After David Gray confessed to child abuse, GCC did not renew his teaching contract, yet MacArthur and GCC continued to defend his leadership role in his home and insisted that his wife remain with her abusive husband.

Eileen Gray maintained her silence until her children were grown, fearing retribution from MacArthur's many devoted followers. After she spoke publicly in 2022, GCC's board asked lawyer and then elder Hohn Cho to investigate the church's actions regarding the Gray case. Cho found that even after the courts found David Gray guilty of child molestation, the church had continued to censure Eileen Gray. Cho submitted a letter to the GCC board, telling them, "Now that the facts are indeed known, it is not too late to 'do justice' even at this late stage, almost 20 years later. One's own integrity, and upholding justice and righteousness, and being faithful even in the small things, even for something 20 years ago, all matter immensely."[43]

He also reported that he had found other cases where the church had supported abusers and opposed victims who sought safety, continuing up to the time of his report. In response, leaders ordered Cho to rescind his report.[44] When he refused, they removed him from eldership and even went so far as to remove every sermon he had preached from their website.[45]

In response to public pressure, GCC posted on its website that they do "not discuss details publicly arising from counseling and discipline cases on social media, nor do we litigate disputes about such matters in online forums. Grace Church deals with accusations personally and privately in accordance with biblical principles."[46] Yet, in a sermon in 1987, MacArthur told his congregation, "If I ever sin a sin – and the category of sins is very large – if I ever continue in some sin . . . I'm asking you to do to me exactly what this text says

---

42. Roys.

43. Julie Roys, "Former Elder at John MacArthur's Church Confronts 'Awful Patterns' of Endangering Abuse Victims," The Roys Report, 9 February 2023, https://julieroys.com/former-elder-at-john-macarthurs-church-confronts-awful-patterns-of-endangering-abuse-victims/.

44. Kate Shellnut, "Grace Community Church Rejected Elder's Calls to 'Do Justice' in Abuse Case," Christianity Today, 9 February 2023, https://www.christianitytoday.com/news/2023/february/grace-community-church-elder-biblical-counseling-abuse.html.

45. Christine Pack (@SolaSisters), "Zero search results now for 'Hohn Cho sermons' on GCC now [link to GCC] vs. Pages of his sermons here [link to Internet Archive] All these sermons have been scrubbed from the GCC website," Twitter, 13 February 2023, https://twitter.com/SolaSisters/status/1624881853462114304. For proof of Cho's sermons previously being on the church's website, see the Internet Archive, https://web.archive.org/web/20210126080511/https://www.gracechurch.org/teachings/leader/cho/hohn.

46. Roys, "Former Elder."

to be done, and that is public exposure."[47] GCC's response is in direct contradiction to MacArthur's own teaching.

GCC did not overcome these five obstacles as they responded to abuse.

1. They did not correctly identify abuse, instead labelling it as "suffering for Jesus," and they themselves further abused Eileen Gray.
2. They prioritized the reputation of GCC over the needs of Eileen Gray by refusing to acknowledge the harm they had caused.
3. They claimed to follow biblical principles to excuse their failures.
4. John MacArthur's charismatic gifts created a prominent platform of devoted followers. Eileen Gray feared retribution if she spoke up, and GCC used their platform to silence both her and Hohn Cho. They failed to hold abusive leaders accountable for the harm they had caused.
5. They accused Eileen Gray of sin for her responses to the abuse and failed to make restitution for the harm Eileen Gray experienced.

Conclusion

In response to the public exposure of the Southern Baptist Convention (SBC), August Boto, a member of the SBC's Executive Committee from 1995 to 2019 and former vice president of that body, claimed: "The whole thing should be seen for what it is. It is a satanic scheme to completely distract us from evangelism. It is not the gospel. It is not even a part of the gospel. It is a misdirection play."[48] In Matthew 12, the religious leaders accused Jesus of casting out demons by Beelzebul. Jesus told them it was by the Spirit that he cast out demons. It is not by Satan that we call out abuse and abuse cover-ups in the church. It is by the Spirit and is the very fulfilment of the gospel. Jesus promised that the Spirit of truth would lead us into all truth, and thus in the widespread reports

---

47. MacArthur, "Restoring Biblical Eldership." This is an older sermon (January 1987), but according to a Christianity Today interview, MacArthur has not changed his stance on any of his major doctrinal positions. See Morgan Lee, "John MacArthur is No Stranger to Controversy," Christianity Today, 23 October 2019, https://www.christianitytoday.com/ct/podcasts/quick-to-listen/john-macarthur-beth-moore-controversy.html.

48. This was widely reported; e.g. Sarah Einselen, "Former SBC Leader Says Abuse Survivor Advocates Are Part of 'Satanic Scheme' to Derail Evangelism," The Roys Report, 8 July 2021, https://julieroys.com/august-boto-satanic-scheme/; Kate Shellnut, "Southern Baptists Refused to Act on Abuse, Despite Secret List of Pastors," Christianity Today, 22 May 2022, https://www.christianitytoday.com/news/2022/may/southern-baptist-abuse-investigation-sbc-ec-legal-survivors.html.

exposing the truth of the church's failure to address abuse well we must recognize the voice of the Spirit of truth, calling the church to account for our failure to do justly on behalf of victims.

As a church, we must decide whether we will quench the Spirit or join with the Spirit in displaying the goodness of God. As Christians, in our public life, will our alignment be with Jesus, or be with abusers? As we rethink the church's response to abuse, may we echo Joshua and say, "As for me and my church, we will heed the call of the Spirit and the cries of the victims, and we will do justly regarding abuse" (adapted from Josh 24:15). The voice of Mordecai prophesies the consequences of abstaining to act: "If you remain silent at this time, relief and deliverance for the victims of abuse will arise from another place, but you and your church will perish. And who knows but that you have come to your place in the church for such a time as this?" (adapted from Esth 4:14).

Bibliography

Abel, Gene G., and Nora Harlow. "The Abel and Harlow Child Molestation Study." Child Molestation Research & Prevention Institute. April 2002. https://www.childmolestationprevention.org/research.

"Adult Clergy Sexual Abuse Survey." Not in Our Church. N.d. http://www.notinourchurch.com/statistics.html.

The Advocates for Human Rights. "Evolution of Theories of Violence." Stop Violence Against Women. April 2015. https://www.stopvaw.org/Evolution_of_Theories_of_Violence.

Bailey, Randall C. *David in Love and War: The Pursuit of Power in 2 Samuel 10–12*. Journal for the Study of the Old Testament Supplement Series 75. Sheffield: JSOT Press, 1990.

Burke, Tarana. *Unbound: My Story of Liberation and the Birth of the Me Too Movement*. New York: Flatiron Books, 2021.

Davidson, Richard M. *Flame of Yahweh: Sexuality in the Old Testament*. Peabody: Hendrickson, 2007.

The DCShorts. "#METOO: Woman Confronts Her Pastor about Alleged Past Abuse." N.d. https://youtu.be/hsSdj4Wp97k.

Denhollander, Rachael. *What Is a Girl Worth? My Story of Breaking the Silence and Exposing the Truth about Larry Nassar and USA Gymnastics*. Carol Stream: Tyndale Momentum, 2019.

Economist Impact. *Out of the Shadows: Index 2022*. https://cdn.outoftheshadows.global/uploads/documents/Out-of-the-Shadows-Index-2022-Global-Report.pdf.

Edwards, Jonathan, and Azi Paybarah. "Lawmaker Censured for Asking if Fatal Child Abuse Saves Taxpayers Money." *The Washington Post* online. 23 February 2023. https://www.washingtonpost.com/nation/2023/02/23/david-eastman-alaska-child-abuse/.

Einselen, Sarah. "Former SBC Leader Says Abuse Survivor Advocates Are Part of 'Satanic Scheme' to Derail Evangelism." The Roys Report. 8 July 2021. https://julieroys.com/august-boto-satanic-scheme/.

ERLC. "What Is a Girl Worth? A Conversation with Rachael Denhollander and Russell Moore on the Church's Abuse Crisis." 8 October 2019. Vimeo. https://vimeo.com/showcase/6383529/video/365072432.

Garland, David E., and Diana R. Garland. "Bathsheba's Story: Surviving Abuse and Devastating Loss." Chapter 6 in *Flawed Families of the Bible: How God's Grace Works through Imperfect Relationships*, 153–77. Grand Rapids: Brazos, 2007.

Gifford, Greg. "A Biblical Definition of Abuse." Biblical Counseling Coalition. 14 January 2019. https://www.biblicalcounselingcoalition.org/2019/01/14/a-biblical-definition-of-abuse/.

Graham, Ruth. "Sex Abuse in Catholic Church: Over 1,900 Minors Abused in Illinois, State Says." *New York Times* online. 23 May 2023. https://www.nytimes.com/2023/05/23/us/illinois-catholic-church-sex-abuse.html.

Harris, Nadine Burke. "How Childhood Trauma Affects Health across a Lifetime – Nadine Burke Harris." TEDEd. TED Talk video. September 2014. https://ed.ted.com/lessons/eczPoVp6.

Hertzberg, Hans Wilhelm. *I and II Samuel: A Commentary*. Old Testament Library. London: SCM, 1964.

Kirk-Dunggan, Cheryl A. "Slingshots, Ships, and Personal Psychosis: Murder, Sexual Intrigue." In *Pregnant Passion: Gender, Sex, and Violence in the Bible*, edited by Cheryl A. Kirk-Dunggan, 37–70. Semeia Studies 44. Leiden: Brill, 2003.

Koenig, Sara M. *Bathsheba Survives*. Studies on Personalities of the Old Testament. Columbia: University of South Carolina Press, 2018.

Langberg, Diane. *Redeeming Power: Understanding Authority and Abuse in the Church*. Grand Rapids: Brazos, 2020.

Lederer, Edith M. "Global Survey: Workplace Violence, Harassment Is Widespread." AP News. 5 December 2022. https://apnews.com/article/business-violence-united-nations-workplace-04e3626ffb0ceb8478ccfa12d6f4457f.

Lee, Morgan. "John MacArthur Is No Stranger to Controversy." Christianity Today. 23 October 2019. https://www.christianitytoday.com/ct/podcasts/quick-to-listen/john-macarthur-beth-moore-controversy.html.

MacArthur, John. "Restoring Biblical Eldership, Part 2." Sermon delivered at Grace Community Church, Sun Valley, California, 18 January 1987. Grace to You. https://www.gty.org/library/sermons-library/54-41/restoring-biblical-eldership-part-2.

Maier, Bryan. *Forgiveness and Justice: A Christian Approach*. Grand Rapids: Kregel, 2017.

Mullen, Wade. *Something's Not Right: Decoding the Hidden Tactics of Abuse – and Freeing Yourself from Its Power*. Carol Stream: Tyndale Momentum, 2020.

Okesson, Gregg. *A Public Missiology: How Local Churches Witness to a Complex World.* Grand Rapids: Baker Academic, 2020.

O'Leary, Chris. "This Nightmare." Sacrificed. 8 February 2021. https://www.chrisoleary.com/sacrificed/episode/002-This-Nightmare.html.

Orobator, Agbonkhianmeghe E. "Between Ecclesiology and Ethics: Promoting a Culture of Protection and Care in Church and Society." *Theological Studies* 80, no. 4 (December 2019): 897–915.

Raz, Guy, and Nadine Burke Harris. "Nadine Burke Harris: How Does Trauma Affect a Child's DNA?" TED Radio Hour. NPR. Interview transcript. 25 August 2017. https://www.npr.org/transcripts/545092982.

Roys, Julie. "Former Elder at John MacArthur's Church Confronts 'Awful Patterns' of Endangering Abuse Victims." The Roys Report. 9 February 2023. https://julieroys.com/former-elder-at-john-macarthurs-church-confronts-awful-patterns-of-endangering-abuse-victims/.

———. "John MacArthur Shamed, Excommunicated Mother for Refusing to Take Back Child Abuser." The Roys Report. 8 March 2022. https://julieroys.com/macarthur-shamed-excommunicated-mother-take-back-child-abuser/.

Ruttenberg, Danya. *On Repentance and Repair: Making Amends in an Unapologetic World.* Boston: Beacon, 2022.

Salter, Anna C. *Predators: Pedophiles, Rapists, and Other Sex Offenders: Why They Are, How They Operate, and How We Can Protect Ourselves and Our Children.* New York: Basic Books, 2003, 2004.

Shellnutt, Kate. "Grace Community Church Rejected Elder's Calls to 'Do Justice' in Abuse Case." Christianity Today. 9 February 2023. https://www.christianitytoday.com/news/2023/february/grace-community-church-elder-biblical-counseling-abuse.html.

———. "Southern Baptists Refused to Act on Abuse, Despite Secret List of Pastors." Christianity Today. 22 May 2022. https://www.christianitytoday.com/news/2022/may/southern-baptist-abuse-investigation-sbc-ec-legal-survivors.html.

Smith, Peter, and Holly Meyer. "#ChurchToo Revelations Growing, Years after Movement Began." *Cochrane Eagle.* 12 June 2022. https://www.cochraneeagle.ca/amp/world-news/churchtoo-revelations-growing-years-after-movement-began-5469940.

Tchividjian, Boz. "Startling Statistics: Child Sexual Abuse and What the Church Can Begin Doing about It." RNS (Religion News Service). 9 January 2014. https://religionnews.com/2014/01/09/startling-statistics/.

United Nations. "What Is Domestic Abuse?" N.d. https://www.un.org/en/coronavirus/what-is-domestic-abuse.

UN Women. "Facts and Figures: Ending Violence against Women." February 2022. https://www.unwomen.org/en/what-we-do/ending-violence-against-women/facts-and-figures.

World Health Organization. *Global Status Report on Preventing Violence against Children 2020*. https://www.who.int/teams/social-determinants-of-health/violence-prevention/global-status-report-on-violence-against-children-2020.

Zylstra, Sarah Eekhoff. "When Abuse Comes to Light." *Christianity Today* 58, no. 2 (March 2014): 44–47.

3

The Biblical Undoing of the Stereotype of "Prostitute" as a Catalyst for Anti-Trafficking Work

Myrto Theocharous

Professor of Hebrew and Old Testament, Greek Bible College, Athens, Greece

Introduction

The issue of trafficking, particularly the trafficking of humans into the sex industry known as "sex trafficking," combines two phenomena: the phenomenon of slavery and the phenomenon of prostitution. Both slavery and prostitution have always been present throughout the history of our world, with the only difference that, in the case of slavery, as Miltiades Vantsos notes,

> There is no longer any ethical dilemma on whether it is right, since it is rejected by everyone and utterly condemned in a formal way. The acknowledgment and securing of basic human rights in the universal declaration of the United Nations and in many other analogous declarations discourages any sort of consideration of the human being as a slave, i.e. as an object that may be sold or bought.[1]

However, when it comes to prostitution, there is no consensus regarding its ethical evaluation and how the legislation of each country should respond

---

1. Miltiades Vantsos, *Η Εμπορευματοποίηση του Ανθρώπινου Σώματος: Ηθική Θεώρηση της Δουλείας και της Πορνείας* [The Commercialization of the Human Body: The Ethical Understanding of Slavery and Prostitution] (Thessaloniki: Ostracon, 2019), 3; my translation.

to it.² The truth is, however, that while slavery has been formally rejected in our modern world, it has not been eliminated, but has hidden itself within the practice of prostitution. To give an example of the problem, while a given country may legalize prostitution and offer licences to brothels, it is difficult to know whether the women working in a certain brothel are there by their own free choice or whether they are victims of trafficking.³ Consequently, the manner with which each country responds to prostitution directly affects sex trafficking which in turn responds to the demand for the sex industry and feeds the market with women "products," often at the lowest possible price. It is, therefore, imperative that sex trafficking be examined in conjunction with the phenomenon of prostitution.

How, then, do we detect a sex trafficking victim? This question is particularly pressing for the church. A dominant constituent of the church's public life is the care of the poor and marginalized, not only within the church family but beyond, since we serve a God who "makes his sun rise on the evil and on the good, and sends rain on the righteous and on the unrighteous" (Matt 5:45, NRSV). On the basis of many years of experience with anti-trafficking work, my answer is that initially we meet the victim of human trafficking unknowingly as a "prostitute"⁴ and it may take months or even years for us to discover whether this "prostitute" belongs to the category of a sex trafficking victim. Women in prostitution will not reveal their trafficked state right away. They are held in this position via threats of violence or death for them and/or their family members, fictitious debts they must work to repay, false promises of marriage, and other forms of coercion. Rather, they will insist that they willingly chose this profession, that they feel fine with it, that they are making lots of money and are in no need of any kind of help. Gradual revelations of the true state of affairs will come only once the victim feels secure enough and a relationship of trust has had time to develop. In other words, one must become

---

2. For the current state of legislation on prostitution around the world, see World Population Review, "Countries Where Prostitution Is Legal 2023," n.d., https://worldpopulationreview.com/country-rankings/countries-where-prostitution-is-legal.

3. Often traffickers are discovered when raids are carried out in brothels, which is proof enough that traffickers often hide behind licensed brothels. See for example the police raids in Athens: "Αττική: Σπείρα Σωματεμπορίας Εξαρθρώθηκε από την ΕΛΑΣ [Attica: A Spiral of Human Trafficking Was Dismantled by ELAS]," Η Καθημερινή [Kathimerini], 2 May 2017, https://www.kathimerini.gr/society/907638/attiki-speira-somatemporias-exarthrothike-apo-tin-elas/.

4. I am using this term in quotation marks because this has been (and remains) an inappropriate yet stereotypical way of referring to women in prostitution in many cultures throughout the ages. The rest of the chapter will show how problematic this stereotype is. Nowadays people refer to women engaged in prostitution as sex workers.

a friend of "prostitutes," for liberation happens in a context of friendship. However, the main obstacle to forming a friendship with a "prostitute" is the stereotype that keeps us from attempting such connections.

The "Prostitute" Stereotype

One of the major obstacles in locating victims of sex trafficking is the ancient stereotype of the "prostitute." This stereotype is difficult to overcome as the negative connotations of this stereotype (i.e. unethical, unreliable, dangerous) make us (including governmental bodies) uninterested and distant and therefore participants in the marginalization and dehumanization of these individuals. This stereotype has been solidified in many cultures through time and was the main factor that caused and continues to cause the alienation and marginalization of these individuals, making it extremely difficult for the evil of sex trafficking to be revealed. Those raised with the Scriptures are well acquainted with texts that refer to prostitution with contempt and disgust. However, if we look more closely, we will see that what is actually condemned is not women who use sex as a means for economic survival but mainly covenant infidelity.

The biblical metaphor of "the prostitute" is primarily used for the Israelite idolater (e.g. Hos 2:12–13; Mic 1:7; Ezek 16:31), and this identification may possibly derive from Canaanite practices of sacred prostitution.[5] The prophet Ezekiel in chapter 16, for example, is not referring to the typical understanding of prostitution where a woman receives money for her sexual services, but rather describes a type of prostitute who behaves in this manner in order to satisfy her *own* insatiable sexual desire. In fact, the prophet keeps repeating that this prostitute is *not* charging money for her services but, instead, is the one who is paying the bypassers in order to attract them (Ezek 16:31, 34, 41; see also Exod 34:15–16; Num 15:39; 25:1; Deut 31:16; Judg 2:17; 8:27, 33; 1 Chr 5:25). Phyllis Bird states that the disgust the audience feels towards the sexual image of this kind of prostitution is used in order to raise an accusation (and disgust) against something else and not the prostitute herself.[6] Along with idolatry, Israel's prostitution often refers to her alliances with other political forces (e.g. Hos 9:1–3).

---

5. Exod 34:15–16; Lev 17:7; 20:5–6; Deut 23:17. There is a prohibition for priests to marry a woman defiled by prostitution (Lev 21:7, 14), a prohibition for the daughters of priests to become prostitutes (21:9), and a prohibition for offerings that come from the earnings of prostitution (Deut 23:18).

6. Phyllis Bird, "Of Whores and Hounds: A New Interpretation of Deut 23:19," *Vetus Testamentum* 65 (2015): 360–61.

To formulate our attitude towards the "prostitute" from the use of this metaphor against Israel is to misunderstand and even ignore what Old Testament texts have to say about women who engage in prostitution. While the biblical word is often the same (זוֹנָה / *zōnah*), it is used to describe completely different things and we must be careful to discern what is condemned each time this word is used.

A General Survey of Prostitution in the Old Testament

As a corrective to the stereotyping of the prostitute it will be useful to begin with a short survey of the attitude of various Old Testament texts towards prostitution. When we examine the Bible with the purpose of seeing the biblical approach or approaches on a topic, we must keep a basic methodological principle in mind: the Bible must be distinguished from ancient Israel. What is meant by this is that the practices of ancient Israel that are observed in the biblical texts or extra-biblical texts, or come to the surface through archaeological discoveries, and the biblical view on a certain issue are two different things. In the majority of the Bible, the writers of the canonical books, despite the fact that they are people of their own time, place, and patriarchal culture, are opposed to the mentality and practices of their co-Israelites and they usually write with a critical eye with the purpose of reforming their own context. It would, therefore, be naïve to say that "in the Bible we observe the phenomenon of prostitution; therefore, the Bible promotes, or accepts, or supports prostitution." Without a careful narrative analysis of the texts it would be presumptuous for one to identify the Israelite phenomenon that is reflected in the texts with the author's stance on it. Unfortunately, this important distinction is not always made.

We may begin with the story of the rape of Dinah in Genesis 34. In this narrative we see her brothers justify their revenge with the following question: "Should our sister be treated like a whore [or prostitute]?" (34:31).[7] Their indignation betrays that the prostitution of a woman brings shame on the men who are responsible for the protection of her sexuality. In other words, Shechem, Dinah's rapist, did not acknowledge that this woman was a member of a much larger network of relationships and the damage inflicted was equal to offending the entire patriarchal household to which she belonged. This story is situated in a patriarchal ancient Near Eastern society where human sexuality was not a private individual matter but a precious good under the responsibility and

---

7. All biblical quotations in this chapter are from the NRSV.

protection of the patriarchal house. Therefore, the expression that Shechem treated Dinah as a prostitute does not mean that he paid for her sexual services. It means that he treated her as if her household lacked any responsible protectors; as if she was an abandoned and neglected woman. Regardless of whether the reaction of Dinah's brothers was justified, their expression does shed light on the other narratives we will explore, precisely because it was the neglected and unprotected women who faced the highest risk of finding themselves in prostitution.[8]

In the case of Tamar, in Genesis 38, we are given some indication of how a woman could end up in prostitution. Tamar is both a widow and childless, and, according to the law of levirate marriage (Deut 25:5–10), it was the duty of a close relative, usually the brother of the deceased, to marry her and provide for her needs.[9] Now, Judah neglected Tamar, failing to give his son Shelah to her, even though he was now of a marriageable age (38:14). Judah's neglect towards the widow is in fact a legal injustice against her. Bill T. Arnold notes that not only has she been abandoned, but she is perhaps also branded a dangerous woman on account of Judah's reluctance to keep her in his household. "An unmarriageable, childless widow" is perhaps "the most vulnerable state of ancient Semitic society,"[10] a state that drives her to her risky plan: to disguise herself as a prostitute, entice Judah, acquire descendants, and, in this way, secure her future well-being. The only social power this woman had left was her sexual power to entice.

The narrative presents the widow as having the law on her side while at the same time it demonstrates the dangers into which the neglect of the law could push a woman who would resort to such measures for survival. The story, therefore, draws attention to the problem of potential neglect towards vulnerable groups by the patriarchs of Israel and, in some way, it offers an explanation for this social problem. Moreover, the narrative invites the audience to a deeper and fairer assessment of the women one might encounter on the side of the street. On the lips of Judah the author places the following declaration: "She is more in the right than I, since I did not give her to my son Shelah" (38:26). The moral agent behind a transgression may not always be who we think it is.

---

8. Someone's wife becoming a prostitute was considered as equally horrific as the death of one's descendants and the elimination of their line from the land (Amos 7:17).

9. Claus Westermann, *Genesis*, trans. David E. Green (London: T&T Clark, 2004), 269.

10. Bill T. Arnold, *Genesis*, New Cambridge Bible Commentary (Cambridge: Cambridge University Press, 2009), 327.

The narrative raises another issue as well: the superficial implementation of the law. A superficial and/or hasty application of the law often ends up condemning the just (the prostitute) while protecting the reputation of the unjust (the client; "otherwise we will be laughed at" [38:23]). The law-abiding Israelites, rather than searching to discover the deeper causes of her act, were quick to demand the punishment of Tamar, thus condemning in their zeal the victim of this injustice herself.

A similar risk is faced by the widow Ruth who is also a foreigner in the land of Israel. The danger of a potential physical or sexual assault against the foreign widow is evident in the words of Boaz himself who thought it necessary to give instructions to his workers not to touch her (Ruth 2:9).[11] This is confirmed by Naomi, her mother-in-law, who warns her that in other fields it is very likely that she would be raped or assaulted (2:22),[12] a danger that must have been exacerbated by the fact that she was a foreigner without a male protector in the land.

The survival of these two women is again dependent on whether the law will be kept, in particular the law of the redemption of their property by their closest relative (Lev 25:25), but also through the observance of levirate marriage. Boaz is not readily motivated towards the application of this law, something that forces the women to take risky measures.[13] Ruth's risk is to lie down next to Boaz one night with the single hope that his desire will lead him to marry her, as the law prescribes, rather than treating her as a prostitute.

These examples do not show the phenomenon of prostitution per se but they present the conditions and circumstances that would often lead women, especially widows, to resort to unwanted, dangerous, sexual ways of survival. The primary reason apparent for all these is the neglect of justice, or stalling of justice, towards the widow from the patriarchal house together with the challenging circumstances for survival. The case of Rahab, a woman actually engaged in prostitution, will be examined in more detail later on.

---

11. Also Marion Ann Taylor, *Ruth, Esther*, The Story of God Bible Commentary (Grand Rapids: Zondervan Academic, 2020), 44.

12. Also Taylor: "the verb [וּפְגָעוּ] also suggests sexual pressure such as she might have received from the men whom Boaz had earlier instructed not to touch Ruth (2:9, 22)." *Ruth, Esther*, 48.

13. Boaz appears to know about the state of Ruth and Naomi (1:19; 2:11) and he also knew that they were relatives (3:12), but he seems to have left the responsibility to the other relative without enquiring as to whether procedures for the levirate marriage have been initiated. His "activation" is a result of Ruth's risky acts.

The Causes of Prostitution in the Old Testament

There are indications that, in poor families, girls were most likely pushed into prostitution in order to supply the whole family with the necessary income for survival.[14] This phenomenon continues to this day and, although it may be rare in some parts of the world, it is not completely absent. Recently, all of Greece was shocked to discover that a twelve-year-old girl was prostituted in Athens with the knowledge, or perhaps the pimping, of her own mother.[15] Leviticus 19:29 presupposes the existence of a similar practice in Israel, since the biblical writers oppose it by a legal prohibition ("Do not profane your daughter by making her a prostitute, so that the land may not become prostituted and full of depravity"; see also Deut 23:18).[16]

Poverty and hunger are the basic causes of the existence of prostitution. According to Proverbs 6:26 it is known that a prostitute will sell herself for only a loaf of bread, a verse indicating how near starvation did not leave these individuals with much choice. Deuteronomy, also, keeps repeating the command to care for the widow and the orphan (e.g. 14:29; 25:20), because, as we already saw, the loss of patriarchal or spousal care would often drive these individuals to prostitution. These commandments, however, are taken as mere exhortations and would be impossible to enforce in a context of power inequality. It would be unlikely for a widow or an orphan to take an Israelite patriarch to court with the accusation of neglect. The economic power of the patriarch in court would automatically determine the outcome of any trial against a poor, defenceless, and unprotected individual. This is the reason why God takes the side of the widow and the orphan, presenting himself as their defender and judge who is incapable of being bribed: "For the LORD your God is God of gods and Lord of lords, the great God, mighty and awesome, who is not partial and takes no bribe, who executes justice for the orphan and the widow, and who loves the strangers, providing them with food and clothing" (Deut 10:17–18).

If one were to systematize the legal stipulations of Israel, we would see that the legislators leave no room for the practice of prostitution. Since it is

---

14. Rahab seems to have been prostituting herself with the knowledge of her family (Josh 6:23).

15. See reports in Kathimerini and Euronews: https://www.kathimerini.gr/society/562185556/ypothesi-12chronis-apo-ton-kolono-neo-entalma-syllipsis-gia-ton-michali/; and https://gr.euronews.com/2022/10/13/pyothesh-12xronhw-kolonos-prothesmia-gia-na-apologhthei-elabe-h-mhtera.

16. Margaret Davies, "On Prostitution," in *The Bible in Human Society: Essays in Honour of John Rogerson*, eds. M. Daniel Carroll R., David J. A. Clines, and Philip R. Davies, JSOTSup 200 (Sheffield: Sheffield Academic, 1995), 228–29.

prohibited for Israelites to prostitute their own daughters (Lev 19:29) and since, at the same time, there is a prohibition on sexual activity with an unmarried woman without that being followed by an agreement with her father for restoring her honour through marriage (Deut 22:28–29), then how could prostitution find room to exist in Israel? One would need to move outside the law, or outside Israelite territory, to find foreign women or Israelite women lacking male protection. Israelite women who would be forced into prostitution would probably have to move beyond Israelite borders since that is where they would most likely find their clients (as Tamar did).

What is interesting is that Judas, in Genesis 38, is looking for a prostitute outside the boundaries of Israel, in the territory of Timnah, where he goes for the shearing of his sheep. Timnah is a Philistine town and is known from the visit of Samson in Judges 14 where he is seeking a wife. Later on, Samson is looking for a prostitute in Gaza, another Philistine town, which possibly indicates that the individual looking for the services of a prostitute would not be able to find one easily within Israelite towns. Perhaps there was no tolerance for such a market in Israelite territory, but it might also be that he would prefer anonymity for this shameful act. However, Margaret Davies identifies clues in the Bible that suggest that perhaps one could see prostitutes in the streets and squares of Israel (Jer 3:2; Ezek 16:24–25; Prov 7:12; 9:14), playing music and singing (Isa 23:16), and even having distinct clothing (Prov 7:10).[17]

In the light of biblical law, then, prostitution could arise only under circumstances of an absent father, spouse, or relative – that is, where defence, protection, and the basic means of survival were lacking. And, even though God presents himself as stepping in as the defender of the defenceless and the father of the fatherless, most Israelites would hardly let this theological point deter them from exploiting these individuals, much less allow it to inspire *imitatio Dei*. Prostitution, then, is a symptom of the failure of the Israelites to "love your neighbour as yourself" and apply the justice that they were called to live.

To sum up, on the basis of what we have seen in this short survey, we may conclude that prostitution results mainly from economic deprivation and the neglect of Israelite patriarchs to do justice towards widows, orphans, and abandoned women in general. God identifies with these women and there is no law condemning them. In fact, the writers seem to be taking their side in the narratives that we have covered.

---

17. Davies, "On Prostitution," 229.

Conscious Undoing of the Stereotype: the Example of Rahab

Nevertheless, the stereotype of the "prostitute" continues to contribute to the marginalization of these individuals. With respect to prostitution and trafficking in the present, the immovable social stereotype of the "prostitute" obstructs the immediate response of responsible bodies and institutions to listen, help, and protect these women.

Naturally, the following question then arises: how may a transformation in my perspective take place? How do I move from seeing before me a "prostitute" to seeing before me a valuable human being, an abused victim, a person in need of liberation, an equal? This question may also be applied more broadly to the wider area of sexual violence, where the stereotype of the "prostitute-like" woman, the woman who tempts, the unreliable one who has only herself to blame for provoking any sexual move against her, also prevents incidents of sexual violence from coming to light and interferes with the justice process. These are the kinds of stereotypes that discourage every woman from speaking up, even more so the women trapped in prostitution. Intentional work at deconstructing this stereotype is urgently needed.

We shall now examine such an intentional deconstruction of the "prostitute" stereotype by a biblical author. In the second chapter of the book of Joshua we have one of the most ancient examples of a conscious attempt to eliminate this stereotype. Right from the beginning of the story we are introduced to this woman as "a prostitute" (זוֹנָה / *zōnah*). According to a tradition we encounter in the writings of the historian Josephus (*Antiquities* 5.1–2), Rahab was not really a prostitute but an innkeeper. However, this version is most likely an attempt to present the woman who played a fundamental role in Israel's history in a more positive light. Also, even if Rahab was an innkeeper, that does not rule out that she could also have worked as a prostitute.[18]

The Greek translation of the Old Testament, the Septuagint, on the other hand, does not shy away from rendering the Hebrew term זוֹנָה (*zōnah*) as πόρνη (*pórnē*, "prostitute"), and this version is carried into the New Testament where Rahab's profession does not seem to subtract from the honour given to her by the church. However, before we get to the New Testament, we will see that already the narrative of the Old Testament is written in such a way as to give honour to this woman.

---

18. For the ancient Near Eastern innkeeper as the background for Rahab's occupation, see Donald J. Wiseman, "Rahab of Jericho," *Tyndale Bulletin* 14 (1964): 8–11.

Rahab versus Lot

There is a long tradition in the Old Testament about offering hospitality to strangers. Abraham and Sarah come readily to mind, when they hosted three unknown men in their tent (Gen 18). The visit to Sarah and Abraham is a peaceful one where the visitors bring good news to the couple: the promise of the birth of Isaac (Gen 18:10). We also have the story of the Shunammite woman who hosts the prophet Elisha in her home and, like Abraham and Sarah, receives a promise of the birth of her son (2 Kgs 4:15–16). The story, however, that seems to have the most similarities (as well as contrasts) with the story of Rahab who hosted the Israelite spies in her home is the story of Lot's hospitality in the land of Sodom.

In Genesis 19 two men visit Sodom, and Lot invites them to his home, prepares food for them, and offers to put them up for the night (Gen 19:1–3). Similarly, in the story of Rahab, two men come into Jericho and visit her house so that they can stay for the night, or rather, hide (Josh 2:1).

In both narratives, the hosted men are threatened by the hostile environment and their hosts are asked to hand them over immediately. In the case of Lot, the city of Sodom is a city of immorality which is under God's predetermined judgement (Gen 13:10, 13; see also Ezek 16:49–50). In the story of Rahab, the same holds true for Jericho, as God has already decided to judge the city and deliver it to the Israelites.

The men of Sodom demand that Lot gives up his guests for the sexual gratification of the locals, while in Rahab's account, the king of Jericho, having been informed that the men had arrived to spy out the land, orders Rahab to deliver them into his hands (Josh 2:2–3). The command of the Sodomites to Lot and the command of the king of Jericho to Rahab are expressed in the same words ("bring out the men who came to you"), further linking the two narratives intertextually, and thus activating in the mind of the reader a comparison between the two incidents (see the similar wording in the boxes in the table).

Joshua 2:3	Genesis 19:5
יאִיצֹה רמֹאל בחֶר־לֹא וחִירִי דְּלֶמ חלשִיוּ יכ דְּתֵיבֵל וַאבְ־רִשַׁא דְּיִלַא סיאִבה סיִשְׁנַאֶה וַאבְ יִרְאַהַ־לִבְ־תָא רִפּחַל:	סִישְׁנַאָה הָיֵא וֹל וּרמאיוַ טוֹל־לֶא וּארְקיַוַ הָעדנֵוּ וּניִלֵא םאיִצוֹה הָלְיַלה דְּיִלֵא וּאבְ־רִשַׁא םתא:

What are Lot's and Rahab's responses to this command? They both refuse to hand over their visitors. Lot, however, risks the lives of his daughters in order to protect the two men. He offers his daughters as an alternative to appease the sexual appetites of the mob of Sodom.

In contrast, Rahab risks only her own life in her attempt to mislead the king's emissaries, and the danger appears to be much greater. Not only does she refuse to place her family's life at risk, but, as we will see later, saving her family was her primary concern in dealing with the spies (Josh 2:13). Note that the gap in social status between Rahab, a harlot, and the king is vast, so defying the king's orders required much more bravery from Rahab than from Lot who was presumably a respectable resident in the town of Sodom.

Lot obviously fails to protect his guests and ends up in need of protection himself. The two men join forces and act themselves as saviours for Lot and his family. Taking care of Lot's family is their initiative, not his. They are the ones who seek out his relatives (Gen 19:12).

The author of the book of Joshua, however, places Rahab in the position of the saviour. A harlot, a foreigner, a heathen Canaanite, becomes the saviour of Israel – not only of the two strangers who visited her, but of the entire people of Israel, as she contributes decisively to their mission. Such a narrative turns a foreign prostitute into a founding member, so to speak, of the Israelite nation. The patriarchal role that Lot failed to live up to, our author, through these echoes and intertextual connections, manages to attribute to Rahab. Rahab becomes, therefore, right from the very first chapters of the book of Joshua, the door, the instrument, the servant of God, for the fulfilment of his vows: to deliver the land to his people as he promised to their ancestors.

Rahab's Ethics

Rahab's superiority is evident not only in her actions but also in the presentation of her moral character. We will see that through his descriptions, the author presents Rahab as a type of the ideal Israelite who fulfils the Ten Commandments of Moses.

Upon their entry into Jericho, one would expect that the two Israelites would act based on the well-known stereotype of the evil Canaanites who sought to lure them into idolatry. Much more a Canaanite harlot who specialized in professional seduction would be expected to behave that way. Already the Israelites' history is marred by their failure to resist the Moabite and Midianite women who, by means of sexual luring, led them to worship their gods, as the book of Numbers records in chapter 25. With this experience in mind, one would expect that the author would present the two spies as model Israelites who were not foolish enough to repeat the mistakes of their countrymen. They would prove themselves to be men able to resist, careful to avoid any contact, let alone agreement, with a Canaanite prostitute. Surprisingly, we see the opposite.

This stereotype of the dangerous seductress is completely absent. Ethnicity and gender, as well as social status, are put to the side and the lens focuses on Rahab's inner qualities. The Old Testament scholar Joshua Berman, in his book *Ani Maamin*, demonstrates that in the dialogue between the Israelite spies and Rahab, there are references to the first five commandments of the Decalogue. Berman says that these references are emphasized in order to secure Rahab's place in Israel's future. We see Rahab's social acceptance and social integration textually prepared, thus cultivating the imagination of the reader.[19]

Some of these references are the following:

First, the Israelites know their God as he was introduced to them in the first commandment in Exodus 20:2 ("I am the LORD your God, who brought you out of the land of Egypt, out of the house of slavery"). The Canaanite Rahab perceives the identity and role of Israel's God in similar terms as she approaches and converses with the spies: "We have heard how the LORD dried up the water of the Red Sea before you when you came out of Egypt" (Josh 2:10). She knows, that is, the God of Israel in the way that an Israelite who stood at the foot of Sinai would know him.

Second, no other person in the Old Testament acts for the good of his or her father and mother and explicitly mentions his or her "father" and "mother." Only in the case of Rahab does this happen: "Give me a sign of good faith that you will spare my father and mother . . ." (Josh 2:12–13). This passage is directly related to Exodus 20:12 and the reward, too, that comes with honouring father and mother appears to be relevant for Rahab's story: "Honour your father and your mother, so that your days may be long in the land that the LORD your God is giving you." The writer in Joshua 6:25 shows the reader that Rahab finally receives this divine gift: "But Rahab the prostitute, with her family and all who belonged to her, Joshua spared. Her family has lived in Israel ever since."

Third, Rahab recognizes God as ruler of heaven and earth. She says in 2:11: "The LORD your God is indeed God in heaven above and on earth below." For Berman, this acknowledgement is linked to the Sabbath commandment that presents God as the creator of heaven and earth: "For in six days the LORD made heaven and earth, the sea, and all that is in them, but rested the seventh day; therefore the LORD blessed the sabbath day and consecrated it" (Exod 20:11).[20]

---

19. Joshua Berman, *Ani Maamin: Biblical Criticism, Historical Truth, and the Thirteen Principles of Faith* (Jerusalem: Maggid Books, 2020), Kindle, ch. 2.

20. Berman, *Ani Maamin*, ch. 2.

Rahab has before her the representatives of the slaves of Egypt, the fugitives of Pharaoh, the wandering refugees of the desert, and she is a first-hand witness and, at the same time, believer that this God who took their side, who gave them rest from their oppression, is able to see her own suffering as well. Only the God who gives rest to the poor and resists the empires of this world could be the God of heaven and earth. Only he could rightfully claim that title – the God who is not ruled by any other power in heaven or on earth.

We may conclude, then, that the biblical writer, by portraying the prostitute in this manner, by allowing the reader to hear the echoes of the Decalogue in Rahab's words, by showing her brave salvific actions towards the two spies in stark contrast to the actions of the weaker Lot, succeeds in deconstructing the stereotype of the prostitute. Marion L. S. Carson says that in the story of Rahab "the idea of the prostitute as sinner par excellence [is] overturned" and warns Christians, especially, to "be very careful about branding people who are caught up in prostitution as sinners – for, like Tamar and Rahab, they may well turn out to be more righteous than those who seem to adhere to cultural and religious norms."[21] The author offers us an alternative way of encountering and perceiving these people; he supplies us with a different set of criteria for their morality, unlike the superficial criteria imposed by stereotypes. The author frees the Israelites so that they may be able to see a true Israelite behind the veil of the foreign prostitute, a woman they needed much more than they had thought, a woman with whom an encounter was first and foremost lifesaving for them and secondarily lifesaving for her.[22]

Rahab in the New Testament

In the New Testament, Rahab is known as "Rahab the prostitute," with this identification appearing twice, in Hebrews 11:31 and James 2:25. In both letters she is praised for her hospitality: in the first account the emphasis is on her faith that prompted her to act, but in the second account the emphasis is on the fact that it was her actions that justified her. And here it is worth reflecting on these actions, not only of Rahab, but of all women who are, in one way or another, caught in prostitution. How do we perceive their actions? Do we see women who sacrifice for their families, who risk their lives, who are forgotten

---

21. Marion L. S. Carson, *Human Trafficking, the Bible, and the Church: An Interdisciplinary Study* (Eugene: Cascade, 2016), 90, 107.

22. For a negative perspective on the ethical characterization of Rahab, see Ronald Charles, "Rahab: A Righteous Whore in James," *Neotestamentica* 45, no. 2 (2011): 206–20.

by the kings of their people and remembered only when they are to blame for the ills of their society? Do we justify them or condemn them, remaining attached to our stereotype?

The third mention of Rahab's name in the New Testament, this time without the accompanying epithet "the prostitute," is found in Matthew 1:5, where she is now fully incorporated into the people of Israel, not simply as Israel's benefactor, but as a carrier of Israel's messiah. Again, just as in Jericho, she appears as the instrument of the coming salvation, only this time it is the salvation of the whole world.

Going back now to Joshua 6:25 and rereading "Rahab the prostitute, with her family and all who belonged to her . . . has lived in Israel ever since" we may perceive another dimension, prophetic so to speak, in this passage. Her descendants who live to this day include her great descendant, Messiah Jesus himself, who lives and will live to the ages, but also her descendants begotten by her great son Messiah Jesus – you and I, the children of Rahab the prostitute.

Approaching Sex Trafficking Today

We have seen a wonderful example of how the author of the book of Joshua successfully undertakes the undoing of the dominant stereotype of the prostitute that holds these individuals in perpetual marginalization. As Margaret Eletta Guider notes,

> Rahab was a harlot when she made her declaration of faith, and she was a harlot when she took action on behalf of the Israelites. Her harlotry does not seem to be an issue for the God who includes her as a partner in bringing about the divine plan. No amount of nuancing or glossing can change that fact.[23]

Moreover, the New Testament continues to reflect on Rahab's example as a model of active faith. The hope is that the readers of these texts, having experienced this unexpected unveiling of Rahab's qualities, would question their stereotype of the prostitute, would open up to other possible unveilings of individuals in prostitution, and would begin to move into closer proximity to them with new-found respect and anticipation of discovering people of immeasurable value in their encounters with them. Only then do women in

---

23. Margaret Eletta Guider, *Daughters of Rahab: Prostitution and the Church of Liberation in Brazil* (Minneapolis: Fortress, 1995), 35.

prostitution have a chance for their voices to be truly heeded and only then do we have a chance to discover if they are victims of sex trafficking.

Unfortunately, the track record for combating sex trafficking around the world has not been great. For the majority of countries there have been no specific laws dealing with trafficking as a distinct crime. They could not categorize it as slavery since it did not resemble the institution of slavery everyone was familiar with, and it could not be categorized as prostitution either. Therefore, cases that had to do with the trafficking of women for the purposes of prostitution were approached as instances of illegal immigration or illegal prostitution, rather than of illegal coercion.[24]

From our experience with our anti-trafficking organization Nea Zoi, this is a fact that we witness constantly in the streets of Athens. We regularly see that women engaged in prostitution, as soon as they see the police patrolling their area, will under no circumstances run to them to be rescued. In fact, they will run in the opposite direction since they know that falling into the hands of the police will mean that they will be immediately arrested for illegal prostitution and/or illegal immigration. On the basis of the latter, the authorities must immediately deport them back to their country, which basically throws them back into the hands of their traffickers. The only criminal this scenario knows is the victim herself.

Antonia Pothoulaki confirms that immigration laws do not provide for exceptions in illegal immigrants who are victims of trafficking. Only in such cases where the victim would press charges would she be considered a trafficking victim and only then is she given asylum, protection, care, and an opportunity to return to her country only if she chooses to. However, most victims do not seek the help of the police out of fear that they will be arrested, detained, or deported, and being terrified of their traffickers deters them from pressing charges. It is, therefore, a rare phenomenon for accusations to reach the courts and for trafficking rings to be prosecuted.[25]

Despite the legal adjustments and gradual improvements in outlining the laws for sex trafficking,[26] what the state is able to do is extremely limited.

---

24. Edward Newman and Sally Cameron, "Introduction: Understanding Human Trafficking," ch. 1 in *Trafficking in Humans: Social, Cultural and Political Dimensions*, eds. Sally Cameron and Edward Newman (Tokyo: United Nations University Press, 2008), 6. See also Kimberly A. McCabe and Sabita Manian, eds., *Sex Trafficking: A Global Perspective* (Plymouth: Lexington Books, 2010), 152.

25. Antonia Pothoulaki, *Trafficking: Εσωτερικές «Πορείες» σε Εκτός Νόμου «Διαδρομές»* [Trafficking: Internal "Directions" in "Roads" outside the Law] (Athens: Pedio, 2019), 122.

26. For the legal developments to the Greek law see Pothoulaki, *Trafficking*, 65–75.

State representatives often lack the sensitivity and the discernment required to understand when a woman is a victim and in need of special care and protection. State bureaucracy combined with the strong social stereotypes about the foreign woman engaged in prostitution have already predetermined what sort of treatment they will receive.

Most importantly, the state cannot inspire a woman who is a victim of trafficking with the necessary strength and decisiveness required to stand up against her traffickers and take them to court. Such a decision presupposes a constancy of care and loving support by people who are committed to stand in solidarity with her. It goes without saying that the church has a debt to Christ and a debt to those with whom Christ identifies. By consciously putting to death the inherited stereotype of the prostitute and approaching these individuals as if approaching Rahab herself, the church can accompany them in their journey of liberation and restoration. While the Pharisees often wondered why Jesus befriended the marginalized and "ethically suspect" individuals of this world, Christ's public witness was precisely this: not to be close to the healthy but to the sick (Matt 9:12; Mark 2:17; Luke 5:31).[27]

Conclusion

It should be apparent by now how the stereotype of the "prostitute" is a major factor in the marginalization and continuous oppression of individuals involved in prostitution, in every society and throughout the ages. Moreover, it is a hindrance to relating to, befriending, and identifying victims of sex trafficking in desperate need of help. Without a conscious mortification of this inherited stereotype, by taking our cue from the work of the biblical authors and especially from the portrayal of Rahab in the book of Joshua, we will always approach these individuals from a position of superiority, relating to them paternalistically and one-sidedly, as if we were their saviours. The biblical record, however, demonstrates that these individuals may often be ethically superior to us, may be in touch with their creator in ways that we are not aware of, and may even be able to save us just as much as we may be able to save them.

> Truly I tell you, the tax-collectors and the prostitutes are going into the kingdom of God ahead of you. (Matt 21:31)

---

27. I believe Jesus's statements are ironic. The sick and the sinners were actually the Pharisees who were opposing Jesus's ministry. This irony is most evident in the parable of the Pharisee and the tax collector (Luke 18:9–14).

Bibliography

Arnold, Bill T. *Genesis*. New Cambridge Bible Commentary. Cambridge: Cambridge University Press, 2009.

"Αττική: Σπείρα Σωματεμπορίας Εξαρθρώθηκε από την ΕΛΑΣ [Attica: A Spiral of Human Trafficking Was Dismantled by ELAS]." Η Καθημερινή [Kathimerini]. 2 May 2017. https://www.kathimerini.gr/society/907638/attiki-speira-somatemporias-exarthrothike-apo-tin-elas/.

Berman, Joshua. *Ani Maamin: Biblical Criticism, Historical Truth, and the Thirteen Principles of Faith*. Jerusalem: Maggid Books, 2020. Kindle.

Bird, Phyllis. "Of Whores and Hounds: A New Interpretation of Deut 23:19." *Vetus Testamentum* 65 (2015): 352–64.

Cameron, Sally, and Edward Newman. "Trafficking in Humans: Structural Factors." Chapter 2 in *Trafficking in Humans: Social, Cultural and Political Dimensions*, edited by Sally Cameron and Edward Newman, 21–57. New York: United Nations University Press, 2008.

Carson, Marion L. S. *Human Trafficking, the Bible, and the Church: An Interdisciplinary Study*. Eugene: Cascade, 2016.

Charles, Ronald. "Rahab: A Righteous Whore in James." *Neotestamentica* 45, no. 2 (2011): 206–20.

Davies, Margaret. "On Prostitution." In *The Bible in Human Society: Essays in Honour of John Rogerson*, edited by M. Daniel Carroll R., David J. A. Clines, and Philip R. Davies, 225–48. JSOTSup 200. Sheffield: Sheffield Academic, 1995.

Guider, Margaret Eletta. *Daughters of Rahab: Prostitution and the Church of Liberation in Brazil*. Minneapolis: Fortress, 1995.

McCabe, Kimberly A., and Sabita Manian, eds. *Sex Trafficking: A Global Perspective*. Plymouth: Lexington Books, 2010.

Newman, Edward, and Sally Cameron. "Introduction: Understanding Human Trafficking." Chapter 1 in *Trafficking in Humans: Social, Cultural and Political Dimensions*, edited by Sally Cameron and Edward Newman, 1–17. Tokyo: United Nations University Press, 2008.

Pothoulaki, Antonia [Ποθουλάκη, Αντωνία]. *Trafficking*: Εσωτερικές «Πορείες» σε Εκτός Νόμου «Διαδρομές» [Trafficking: Internal "Directions" in "Roads" outside the Law]. Athens: Pedio, 2019.

Taylor, Marion Ann. *Ruth, Esther*. The Story of God Bible Commentary. Grand Rapids: Zondervan Academic, 2020.

"Υπόθεση 12χρονης από τον Κολωνό: Προθεσμία για να απολογηθεί έλαβε η μητέρα [Case of a 12-Year-Old Girl from Kolonos: Deadline for the Mother to Apologize]." Euronews. 13 October 2022. https://gr.euronews.com/2022/10/13/pyothesh-12xronhw-kolonos-prothesmia-gia-na-apologhthei-elabe-h-mhtera.

"Υπόθεση 12χρονης στον Κολωνό: Νέο ένταλμα σύλληψης για τον «Μιχάλη» [Case of a 12-Year-Old Girl in Kolonos: New Arrest Warrant for "Michael"]." Η

Καθημερινή [Kathimerini]. 14 December 2022. https://www.kathimerini.gr/society/562185556/ypothesi-12chronis-apo-ton-kolono-neo-entalma-syllipsis-gia-ton-michali/.

Vantsos, Miltiades [Βάντσος, Μιλτιάδης]. Η Εμπορευματοποίηση του Ανθρώπινου Σώματος: Ηθική Θεώρηση της Δουλείας και της Πορνείας [The Commercialization of the Human Body: The Ethical Understanding of Slavery and Prostitution]. Thessaloniki: Ostracon, 2019.

Westermann, Claus. *Genesis*. Translated by David E. Green. London: T&T Clark, 2004.

Wiseman, Donald J. "Rahab of Jericho." *Tyndale Bulletin* 14 (1964): 8–11.

World Population Review. "Countries Where Prostitution Is Legal 2023." N.d. https://worldpopulationreview.com/country-rankings/countries-where-prostitution-is-legal.

4

People Living with Disability

Present, Participating, and Pertinent

Brenda Darke

Latin Link, Costa Rica

People living with some kind of disability should have access to church, be facilitated to participate fully, and be enabled to find pertinence and meaning in their faith. Yet historically this group of people, though extremely diverse and numerous, has been largely excluded from church and marginalized in society. Sometimes their exclusion or other mistreatment is justified by theological perspectives which in turn arise from myth-perpetuating and distorted readings of Scripture. Recent attempts to include those with different experiences of disability have concentrated on giving aid and compassionate pastoral care. Although this is undoubtably important, if it were the only response it could lead to a degree of paternalism. Careful study of Scripture provides a recognition and new understanding of the role of people with disabilities within the church and its mission as a largely untapped resource of people who have spiritual gifts and acquired wisdom. As churches seek to become more accessible, frequently in line with changes in society and new anti-discrimination legislation, it is important to examine questions of human dignity and worth. The church must amplify its central message of acceptance and welcoming into fellowship of all those who, whether disabled or non-disabled, profess faith in Jesus Christ.

State of Play

The lives and experiences of people with disabilities have until recently been a subject upon which little has been known or written from within the context of church communities. However, people with disabilities have always been present, sometimes hidden from view, and frequently excluded from mainstream society. The families of people with disabilities and perhaps some friends have had insight into their lives but in our fellowships there have often been too few opportunities to engage. In part this has been due to long-held ideas leading to discrimination, prejudice, and fear. Too frequently, people living with some form of disability have faced isolation and social distance. Even in churches, many families have experienced this same discrimination, based on false, and theologically dubious, ideas. This chapter will seek to replace some of the myths that have been believed with more relevant biblical truths. The public witness of the church will be true to God's word only as it takes note of this aspect of human experience.

It is important to listen to what people living with disability tell us. Roy McCloughry shares his experience: "I was advised, as a young man, not to apply for training as a priest for the Church of England as it would not ordain an 'epileptic,' but I have since spoken from hundreds of Church of England pulpits."[1] Paul Lindoewood, who is a wheelchair user with limited dexterity and communication impairments, says, "By far the biggest issues I have faced as a person with a disability relate to how people react to my existence, rather than a feeling of bereavement over what I can or cannot do."[2] But not only does a person with a disability face stigma and fear, there are also real physical barriers to accessing church. The barriers are part of the disability as many advocates for social change would assert. As disability is such a multifaceted concept, the kinds of adaptations necessary to open up our churches are also very varied. For someone who is a wheelchair user, it could mean accessible transport to get to church, good pavements, a wide entrance without steps or with a ramp or lift, spaces for a wheelchair in the different areas of the building, especially in the main body of the church and any raised area for leading the service, and accessible toilet facilities as well as any other help needed. For someone with a visual disability, it might mean something quite different, such as Bibles

---

1. Roy McCloughry, *The Enabled Life: Christianity in a Disabling World* (London: SPCK, 2013), 14.

2. Paul writes about his time as a mission partner working with the Methodist Church in Kenya in "Being a Mission Partner with Disability in Kenya," ch. 7 in *Disability in Mission: The Church's Hidden Treasure*, eds. David C. Deuel and Nathan G. John, Lausanne Library (Peabody: Hendrickson, 2019), 83.

in accessible formats, good lighting, and wide, uncluttered passageways. But in every case, the most important way of welcoming people with disabilities into church is by our attitudes. No longer should outdated language such as "handicapped" be used, nor equally patronizing and ambiguous words such as "special." New, respectful, and more biblical attitudes should be emerging so that the church in its public witness can truly welcome those with disabilities as well as all those who, to this point, do not live with a disability.

Within our lifetimes this area has been opened up to scrutiny. There have been new approaches in education, much more social interaction, and the paralympic movement, all underpinned at international as well as national level by new laws and regulations seeking to improve the lives of people with disabilities. While previously people with disabilities were largely hidden away, now they are a part of our communities, and, in many countries they have the same legal rights as other citizens.

Why Should This Be of Interest in the Twenty-First-Century Church?

Although this group of people is extremely diverse, it represents not only the largest minority group in the world but quite possibly the least evangelized. Joni Eareckson Tada, founder and CEO of Joni and Friends International Disability Center, reports that only 5–10 percent of all people with disabilities have been "effectively reached with the Gospel."[3] Clearly there is work to do. The concept of disability is wider than many might think. As disability is defined as some kind of bodily limitation affecting daily living in social contexts, usually over a long period of time, there is huge diversity, ranging from the most visible to almost completely invisible disabilities. The United Nations Convention on the Rights of Persons with Disabilities describes persons with disabilities as "those who have long-term physical, mental, intellectual or sensory impairments which in interaction with various barriers may hinder their full and effective participation in society on an equal basis with others."[4] The World Health Organization's studies have found that a minimum of 15 percent of the world's population has some form of disability, often categorized as physical,

---

3. Quoted at CURE, "CURE Provides a Practical Theology of Disability to Communities Across Its Network of Hospitals," 18 March 22, https://cure.org/2022/03/cure-provides-a-practical-theology-of-disability-to-communities-across-its-network-of-hospitals/.

4. UN General Assembly, Resolution 61/106, Convention on the Rights of Persons with Disabilities, A/RES/61/106 (13 December 2006), Article 1, https://www.un.org/en/development/desa/population/migration/generalassembly/docs/globalcompact/A_RES_61_106.pdf.

sensory, cognitive, or psycho-behavioural.[5] There are many who obviously live with multiple disabilities while others have hidden disabilities.

On a personal level it is increasingly clear that each member of a congregation could become a person with a disability at some point in their life. While the number of babies born with a disability is high, perhaps 6 percent (and some of these may not survive long),[6] we live in a world of ever more ageing populations. Many members of congregations are already partially disabled although they may not recognize this as true. The social context is an important factor; a person who uses a wheelchair may be able to function very well in some situations, perhaps holding down a demanding job, and not be at any disadvantage. However, in a different social context the barriers to access might prevent that person from carrying out the same role. Physical barriers are an enormous obstacle for many, but as Paul Lindoewood says, the greatest barrier is a negative attitude.

In the past, many people would hide their disabilities because of stigma or discrimination. Parents frequently hid a child born with a disability, mainly as a response to the false guilt and shame they felt for having given birth to such a child. Today, with much greater knowledge of the possible reasons for having a disability, many parents are accepting and supportive of their children, although there are still some cultures in which babies born with a disability are hidden. There has been an increased interest in advocacy and human rights for people with disabilities, leading to improved quality of life and much more independent living. Many people with disabilities are their own very capable advocates, but others are not able to communicate verbally and can be left behind, especially those with cognitive or mental health disabilities.

The response of the church has been equally varied. In some congregations people with disabilities are truly welcomed, perhaps because someone in their family is already a member or because they are able to integrate easily. Sadly, in many churches where there is little or no experience of disability and frequently where the pastor has had no exposure to a biblical theology of disability, the idea of people with disabilities being part of the church has not been seen positively. Some negative myths still circulate, essentially blaming

---

5. World Health Organization and The World Bank, *World Report on Disability* (Geneva: WHO, 2011), 29.

6. World Health Organization, "Congenital Disorders," n.d., https://www.who.int/health-topics/congenital-anomalies#tab=tab_1. UNICEF gives data showing an overall 10 percent of children living with a disability: nearly 240 million children in the world today have some form of disability. UNICEF, *Seen, Counted, Included: Using Data to Shed Light on the Well-Being of Children with Disabilities* (New York: UNICEF, 2021), 6, 18, 152.

the person or his or her parents for the condition. This old idea that disability is a punishment from God for sinful behaviour is still prevalent in cultures all over the world but is being challenged by many. Bridget Hathaway and Flavian Kishekwa say, "The Bible makes it clear that we are sinners and that our parents were sinners. If this is so, why were we not all born with disabilities? Theologically it makes no sense to say that God sends a disability as a punishment in an arbitrary fashion."[7]

Pastors, church leaders, and congregations can find the need to make adjustments too costly, economically or socially. In the past, fear of difference, and of the unknown, played a significant part in discouraging inclusion. Sunday school teachers would question how they could welcome a disabled child, perhaps with cerebral palsy or visual impairment, into their classroom. Pastors might not find the presence of a noisy member of the congregation easy to support. As people with disabilities become more visible in our schools, social groups, parks, and shopping centres, we need to find new ways of including them in our churches. Some might be seen as valued and useful members, gifted people who only require some reasonable adjustments in order to be able to participate and work alongside the rest of the church team. But how does a church welcome someone with a severe cognitive disability or with non-verbal autism? These are practical questions that can mask a lack of biblical thought.

Theology of Disability

The Bible has much to say about disability, contrary to what most Christians would assume. When working professionally with children with severe cognitive disabilities, I still failed to understand what the Scriptures taught about people living with disability and their place in the kingdom. As a closer look is taken at key passages, it becomes clear that the church is obligated to respond. This might at first seem to bring additional responsibility and tasks to the church, but only until it is understood that the kingdom of God includes people with disabilities who put their faith in Jesus Christ. As members of the body of Christ they too have gifts and abilities that should be used to build up the church. Not only are people with disabilities present in churches, they are called to participate. They should be present as part of the public witness of the church.

The answer to the question "Who are people with disabilities?" is really no different from the answer to "Who am I?" Genesis speaks of man and woman

---

7. Bridget Hathaway and Flavian Kishekwa, *Included and Valued: A Practical Theology of Disability* (Carlisle: Langham Global Library, 2019), 66.

made in the image of God. There can be no reason for negating this concept for someone who has a disability. Where would such a line be drawn? Someone who is non-verbal? Someone who has very little mental capacity? Someone who is deaf and blind? Someone born with no arms or legs? Many have grappled with whether people with severe disability can be seen as persons who can experience spiritual life. The theologian Frances Young found this hard to accept for her own son who was born with profound disabilities. In an early account of his life she says, "There are people, like Arthur and more limited than Arthur, of whom it is very difficult to speak of 'person,' distinct from the brain-damaged body, which might or might not survive death."[8] Years later she writes of being with a group of very disabled adults: "Here were some of the most vulnerable persons in our society, yet each was a self, each had value, and before God we were all equally vulnerable human beings in need of God's grace."[9] Frances Young had been able to move from confusion to certainty, and so must we.

Parents of children with multiple disabilities often tell the same story: that they have found that words are not essential to personhood. Their children are persons created in God's image, dearly loved and precious. There are many ways of communicating, and the ability to do so verbally is not a prerequisite for personhood. We are all equally loved and valued by our creator God, in all of our individual diversities:

> For you created my inmost being;
>   you knit me together in my mother's womb.
> I praise you because I am fearfully and wonderfully made;
>   your works are wonderful,
>   I know that full well.
> My frame was not hidden from you
>   when I was made in the secret place,
>   when I was woven together in the depths of the earth.
> Your eyes saw my unformed body;
>   all the days ordained for me were written in your book
>   before one of them came to be. (Ps 139:13–16)[10]

---

8. Frances Young, *Face to Face: A Narrative Essay in the Theology of Suffering* (Edinburgh: T&T Clark, 1990), 61.

9. Frances Young, *Arthur's Call: A Journey of Faith in the Face of Severe Learning Disability* (London: SPCK, 2014), 49.

10. All biblical quotations in this chapter are from the NIV.

This positive and lovely song of praise to the God who created us, as it were "by hand," each of us different and unique, informs us of the beauty of each person, made in God's image and due respect and dignity solely because of our place in the created world. There are no degrees of humanity; we are all raised to the same level by our creator, who loves each of us equally, disregarding our different abilities or disabilities. In fact, God takes personal responsibility when, in response to Moses using his difficulty in speech as an excuse not to confront Pharaoh, he poses the question, "Who gave human beings their mouths?" (Exod 4:11a). There is diversity built into the human race: some with disabilities and others not. The Bible teaches that we live in a fallen world. Roy McCloughry and Wayne Morris comment that "we are all made by God and yet we are all born into a compromised world,"[11] and they observe, "The fact is that all of our lives are touched by living in a world that no longer reflects God's intentions."[12]

Against this, several very positive truths can be acknowledged. God's dealing with Moses actually affirmed that people with disabilities are among those called to undertake tasks far beyond their natural abilities. What becomes clear is that disability does not preclude faith nor indeed exercise of gifts. In the passage mentioned above, God instructed Moses to start working and promised to support him in the task: "Now go; I will help you speak and will teach you what to say" (Exod 4:12). Moses argued that he was totally unfit to speak with Pharaoh, but God made a "reasonable adjustment" (something required in most legislation in line with the International Convention on Human Rights for People with Disabilities). God sent Aaron with Moses to speak his words while Moses performed miracles. The Bible affirms that a person with disabilities can carry out God's will and, with God's help, be the means to further the kingdom.

Turning to Leviticus, there has been a concern that God discriminated against people with disabilities in the laws about priests and their entry into the holy of holies. While this may not be a complete answer, it is worth noting that only men from the tribe of Levi could be priests, and only once a year was one of the priests allowed to enter this most dangerous of places. All the other privileges of the priesthood were open to the males of the tribe of Levi, whether they had a disability or not. They could eat the bread that was "most holy" and were thus given status and dignity. Most of the other Israelites, those not of the tribe of Levi as well as all women, were forbidden this. There seems

---

11. Roy McCloughry and Wayne Morris, *Making a World of Difference: Christian Reflections on Disability* (London: SPCK, 2002), 31.

12. McCloughry and Morris, *World of Difference*, 33.

to be symbolism around the idea of perfection, as the disabilities mentioned are all visible and obvious. There may have been an element of protection involved, for the holy of holies was a dangerous place. McCloughry and Morris quote a Jewish academic, Rabbi Judith Abrams, who "compares the priests who officiated in the temple with extremely fit and highly trained marines who survive the rigours of battle where the rest of us would not."[13] Thus anyone with physical limitations would have been vulnerable. As Christ has paid the ultimate price for sin by dying on the cross, we can be assured that God now allows all of us who profess faith to draw near to him, without any fear of death or discrimination.

More importantly for the church today is Leviticus 19:14, where we read: "Do not curse the deaf or put a stumbling-block in front of the blind, but fear your God. I am the LORD." This is part of the listing of God's laws that his people had to obey in order to be holy as required. So there is clear evidence of God's specific protection of people with disabilities. In two "test" cases, a blind person and a deaf person, the people of Israel were warned against abuse. The reasoning is that God calls his people to be holy ("Be holy because I, the LORD your God, am holy," Lev 19:2). Any abuse by attacking the weakest point of a deaf or blind person would be contrary to God's holiness. This text is a reminder to the church to maintain God's holiness by refusing to abuse anyone with a disability, especially in ways in which they would be unable to defend themselves. This seems to be God defending the "human rights" of people with disabilities thousands of years before humankind ever used that term. But the context and motivation is one of honouring God in his holiness.

Turning to the New Testament, Jesus's own ministry is often seen as centred on people in need. The crowds followed him as he healed and restored people with illness and disability to dignified lives. The healings were a sign of his divinity and point forward to the full realization of the kingdom of God. There was no distinction between illness and disability, although today they are rightly seen as two different situations. A person with a disability may affirm that he or she is not ill, although illness may sometimes cause disability. Jesus healed many people living with disabilities, recognizing their suffering in a socio-historic context of stigma and poverty associated with any disability. There would have been very little medical knowledge or treatment available and those without families to care for them became beggars and outcasts. It is in this particular context that we read of Jesus's deep concern for people living

---

13. McCloughry and Morris, 38.

with disabilities. Time and time again the evangelists record how Jesus called people with disabilities to himself, healed body, mind, and spirit, and restored them to both a right relationship with God and a place in society.

His emphasis on the spiritual health of the person is instructive. There are those who assert that some people with disabilities, especially those with cognitive disabilities such as Down's syndrome, are like "angels" and are already counted within the kingdom of God. This is a powerful myth as it releases us from the responsibility to teach biblical truth to those who seem to have very little understanding of abstract concepts. But all are in need of salvation, and even those with limited intellectual ability can be taught about Jesus and his saving sacrifice. This does require us to spend time alongside these people, and to live out our own faith in tangible ways, but ultimately it is the Holy Spirit who imparts faith. It is not for us to make assumptions about a person's ability to understand and respond in faith. Biblical teaching should be accessible for all. Jesus actually taught that we need to become like children to enter the kingdom of heaven: "Truly I tell you, unless you change and become like little children, you will never enter the kingdom of heaven" (Matt 18:3).

But Jesus did more than heal: he also taught some very important lessons. Jesus was careful to teach that disability is not necessarily linked to sin, whether that of parents or oneself (John 9:1–3). This must have been a pivotal moment for the blind man – to have his blindness declared to be for other reasons and not due to his sin or his parents' sin. Human sin can sometimes be implicated in disability – for instance, in disabilities resulting from the violence of war or drug abuse. However, this text is a reminder that no such connection should be assumed. If sin were the cause of disability, no one would escape, as all people are in need of forgiveness of sins. The disciples were confused, as were the religious leaders of the day, and Jesus's words would have been a source of comfort to this man. No small wonder, then, that he was willing to obey Jesus's commands and, once healed, went on to defend Jesus against the powerful Pharisees.

In the Gospel of Luke, and especially in chapter 14, more can be read about Jesus's attitude to people with disabilities. Jesus was invited to a Pharisee's home for a meal. There seems to have been some attempt to trick him as it was the Sabbath, but Jesus, with great compassion, healed a man, thus breaking the religious law. Later, at the same meal, it is recorded that Jesus started to teach, telling his listeners that they should not try to be at the top of the table (Luke 14:8–11). In verses 12–14 he begins to talk about the importance of inviting people to a meal:

> Then Jesus said to his host, "When you give a luncheon or dinner, do not invite your friends, your brothers or sisters, your relatives, or your rich neighbours; if you do, they may invite you back and so you will be repaid. But when you give a banquet, invite the poor, the crippled, the lame, the blind, and you will be blessed. Although they cannot repay you, you will be repaid at the resurrection of the righteous."

This teaching seems to have been very countercultural. It is, of course, common practice to extend invitations first to family and friends. Jesus may have wanted to draw attention in a dramatic way to a social situation and probably was not saying that family and friends were not to be included for a meal. The central idea is that those who are disadvantaged by poverty or disability should be included in the invitation. Again in the historic context (and sadly also today), these two factors of poverty and disability were closely linked, those with disabilities almost always being among the poorest. Poverty is also recognized as being one of the root causes of disability. This teaching should provoke some reflection as to how welcoming our churches are of those with disabilities and the most impoverished. How uncomfortable would it feel to intentionally invite these groups of people into our congregations?

Although Jesus had just healed a man, he drew attention to those who were not healed. Not being healed from a disability was not a reason to exclude people; rather they should be given special assistance. The parable Jesus then told reinforced these new ideas (Luke 14:15–24). Again, two groups, people with disabilities and poor people, are linked together. This parable about a rich man who invited his friends to a banquet, each of whom gave an excuse as to why they could not attend, is often seen as a metaphor about the Jews and Gentiles. But many theologians writing about disability have a more direct reading of the text. Brett Webb-Mitchell writes, "If the Church is to be like the Kingdom of God, then it too must invite, welcome and accept the presence of those who are considered poor, 'the crippled, the blind and the lame' in our world today."[14] After the refusal of his friends, the rich man of the parable then sent his servant to invite the poor and those with disabilities. The servant returned to report that there was still room. It seems in this parable that those people, disabled and poor, accepted the invitation but there was still space and food for others. Making room for those with disabilities does not

---

14. Brett Webb-Mitchell, *Unexpected Guests at God's Banquet: Welcoming People with Disabilities into the Church* (New York: Crossroad, 1994), 20.

exclude others. There were no conditions for entry to the feast: no one had to be healed or educated in order to take part. They did not have to pay an entry fee or change into better clothes. This is a marvellously liberating parable for those who doubt that they might be eligible to enter the kingdom of God. The entry is free and all who trust in Jesus may enter. Disability in this light is not a reason for exclusion from the kingdom of God.

Disability is often closely linked to suffering. Jesus himself suffered in multiple ways, especially on the cross, and then at his resurrection he showed his disciples his wounded hands and feet. This has been read by some as Jesus (and thereby God) himself experiencing disability. Nancy L. Eiesland writing in her ground-breaking book *The Disabled God* says, "In presenting his impaired hands and feet to his startled friends, the resurrected Jesus is revealed as the disabled God."[15] She goes on to affirm, "The disabled God repudiates the conception of disability as a consequence of individual sin."[16] Eiesland herself was a wheelchair user and had struggled to find her place in church. This rereading of the significance of the resurrection body of Jesus was powerfully cathartic for her and many others. For someone who has no ability to move arms or legs, this understanding of the disabled God might be of special significance. Most importantly we know that Jesus suffered in mind, body, and spirit, surely something which can bring comfort to those who live with pain of body or mind. Jesus was not immune to pain and trouble; he endured and did not sin.

Moving on from the gospels, Paul's letters are full of references to those who are humanly weak. While it would not be right to conflate the ideas of disability and weakness, nevertheless these texts can be liberating. They reveal God's heart for people with disabilities, perhaps especially those with profound and complex disabilities. Paul wrote about the church as the body of Christ (1 Cor 12:12–27). This text is important in any disability reading as it is clearly calling for true inclusion or pertinence within the church. Every part of the body has a role and a function, Paul says, especially that which seems "unimportant." The less-honoured and insignificant part of the body, which might be covered up, might actually be indispensable: "The eye cannot say to the hand, 'I don't need you!' And the head cannot say to the feet, 'I don't need you!' On the contrary, those parts of the body that seem to be weaker are indispensable" (1 Cor 12:21–22). So a person living with a disability, reading this, could understand that he or she too has a part to play. It also alerts us

---

15. Nancy L. Eiesland, *The Disabled God: Toward a Liberatory Theology of Disability* (Nashville: Abingdon, 1994), 100.

16. Eiesland, *Disabled God*, 101.

to the reality of our overlooking someone in our community of faith who is gifted but unrecognized for his or her contribution. On a practical level, while there is often emphasis within disability circles on independent living, this text reminds us that as Christians we are not called to live independently but interdependently. We are dependent on God's saving grace, and as part of the body of Christ we should be living as a functioning interdependent church. Thus someone with an obvious need of physical support might also be the person who prays most consistently for another member of the congregation.

Paul also speaks about his own experience of "unanswered" prayer in 2 Corinthians 12:7–10. He asked God to take away the thorn in his flesh (it is a matter of speculation what this might have been; Pablo Martinez thinks that it might have been some kind of physical disability),[17] but he did not receive his request. The text points to a deeper experience of faithfulness in the face of suffering which in turn leads to a greater reliance on God himself and his grace. Many of those who live with disability and have experienced the distress of unanswered prayer for healing, whether initiated by themselves or by their congregation, have found comfort in Paul's testimony. Clearly Paul was a man of faith, yet he was not released from his pain and weakness. This simple truth speaks into the difficulty that some find when they are told they lack enough faith to be healed. God does answer our prayers; however, it is not always in the way we most desire, but rather to bring glory to his name.

Finally the New Testament ends by revealing something of the new heaven and new earth:

> And I heard a loud voice from the throne saying, "Look! God's dwelling-place is now among the people, and he will dwell with them. They will be his people, and God himself will be with them and be their God. 'He will wipe every tear from their eyes. There will be no more death' or mourning or crying or pain, for the old order of things has passed away." (Rev 21:3–4)

One day there will be no suffering and no exclusion from God's presence for all those who put their trust in Jesus Christ. This message of hope is true for all, whether we have a disability or not. We are called to live together now in fellowship as we look for the renewal of all things and the kingdom of God in all its glory.

---

17. Pablo Martinez, *A Thorn in the Flesh: Finding Strength and Hope amid Suffering* (Nottingham: Inter-Varsity Press, 2007), 22.

How Should We Welcome People with Disabilities into Our Churches?

As we have seen, people with disabilities have always been present but not always welcomed. How then should they find their place in church? How does this change the witness of the church? God calls them too to participate actively in churches, in mission, and in using their gifts. The social model of disability, which is widely espoused around the world, would seem to explain that people are disabled as far as their environment and context include barriers to their full participation. From a Christian worldview we might make the case for a more biblical understanding of disability, but it cannot be denied that the witness of our churches is impacted negatively by the lack of proper attention given to the needs of people living with disabilities, whatever their context or disability. The list of possible adjustments may seem overwhelming and leave any pastor or church feeling that it is just too much to ask. The truth is that there is always need in the church, and other priorities might seem more important than that of the old person who can no longer read his Bible or the girl on the autistic spectrum who needs a quiet space with one-to-one help. Nevertheless, every church can make small changes, starting with the language used around disability and personal interactions with people coming into church. People with disabilities report that they are more concerned with a welcoming and friendly environment than with having every adjustment made, although it must be emphasized that where there are loving relationships the adjustments will gradually come about too.

Inclusion, even though a challenge for most churches, is clearly not enough. For people who live with the experience of disability, the need for friendship and belonging is paramount. In a world where they are often ignored or discriminated against, the church can be a place of welcome and pertinence. Sadly this has not often been the case. John Swinton writes in his book *Becoming Friends of Time: Disability, Timefullness and Gentle Discipleship*:

> The idea of inclusion . . . works well at the level of politics and social justice. . . . It is, however, much less successful in opening up spaces wherein "mere encounters" can lead to meaningful friendship, belonging and love. *It is the ability to love, not the ability to include or tolerate, that is a primary mark of discipleship.*[18]

Thus, Swinton notes, someone can be included within the fellowship of the church but might not truly belong.

---

18. John Swinton, *Becoming Friends of Time: Disability, Timefullness and Gentle Discipleship* (London: SCM, 2017), 93; emphasis original.

It is important to remain connected to the real world with lived experiences guiding us. Complexity inevitably means that not all expectations can be met immediately. This is not necessarily a problem if those in leadership take time to consult with the person with disability to understand his or her most pressing needs. Then even one small improvement can make that person feel welcomed. If it is understood that efforts are being made and that they are being welcomed in spite of the lack of equipment or resources, then disabled people are more likely to find their place in the church. If they are consulted about their needs and what would be best for them to be able to fully participate in church, there are grounds for hope as the process continues to improve their access.

What are the barriers to this process being put in place? One of the most obvious stumbling blocks is unfortunately the pastor and leadership team. This is not usually because of any real prejudice against people with disabilities, but rather because of a lack of information and theological education. They may not have a good grasp of biblical thought around the idea of disability. It is unlikely they will have knowledge of good contemporary practice. It is possible they may still hold stereotypes and even myths around the concept of disability. It seems that this element in theological preparation for pastoral ministry is lacking in most seminaries or included only as an option. A way forward would be to require all pastors to study something of the theology of disability with a view to incorporating good practice in church as a necessary and normal part of congregational life. Implicit in this would be some pastoral training regarding both people with disabilities themselves and also their families.

Nearly twenty years ago I challenged some of my students to undertake some practical work in our church. This developed into a support group for families with children with severe and complex disabilities. These families came from several churches but all were keen to have a space in which they could be heard and supported, something they did not always feel was adequate in their own congregations. Over the years they have gained confidence and a reliance on God. Many are lone parents and have found strength by feeding on God's word and by sharing their joys as well as their distress in prayer together. The children, now young people, have had their own Bible club, learning something of God, having fun, and sharing their own lived experience together while releasing their caregivers for a short time. The team of helpers has learned how to support the two sides of this small ministry, even though they are not professionals in the field but simply church members who recognize God's love for each person and have been willing to give their time and energy as part of the church's public witness. This model is just one of many ideas; some churches have developed more ambitious ministries. Parachurch ministries also exist and secular associations are also very helpful. Lamar Hardwick, a pastor diagnosed with autism, writes, "Disability ministry will cost you something but not doing it may well cost you everything."[19]

Sharing the Path with People with Disabilities

In order for the church's witness to be true to God's word, the church has to better understand that people with disabilities are part of this witness. The task is to acknowledge their presence, facilitate their participation, and enable them to find their pertinence and place in the fellowship of the saints. Our fellowship with people with disabilities should be genuine; they should not be seen as a project. As Thomas E. Reynolds notes, "Disability is not a way for non-disabled Christians to grow in charity."[20] The Scriptures teach us that people with disabilities should not be seen as "other" or "less." They are like all of us, created and loved by God. Their presence should never be put in doubt. People with disabilities are called to respond to God's grace as the Holy Spirit speaks to their hearts and then gifts them as they become children of God. As part of the body of Christ they are a vital part of church life – its witness and work. This is not to make them somehow more special or sanctified. Noel Fernandez, a Baptist pastor and disability advocacy leader from Cuba who has lived with visual disability most of his life, attests that people with disabilities are neither more nor less sinful than anyone else.[21]

We are all richer if we enable people with disabilities to be truly part of the community, using their gifts. This may first require facilitating their education and training. They may need help and some adjustments in order to participate fully. Do we ever think about our Bible colleges and whether they are accessible? Perhaps we have a too restricted idea of who might be leading our churches. Roy McCloughry reminds us that "we often see involvement in the church as restricted to the competent. Churches are frequently run by a small group of committed people while others sit on the sidelines and cannot find their place despite the fact that they have gifts to offer."[22] In whatever

---

19. Lamar Hardwick, *Disability and the Church: A Vision for Diversity and Inclusion* (Downers Grove: InterVarsity Press, 2021), 48.

20. Thomas E. Reynolds, *Vulnerable Communion: A Theology of Disability and Hospitality* (Grand Rapids: Brazos, 2008), 39.

21. Personal conversations in meetings of the Latin American group of the Ecumenical Disability Advocacy Network (EDAN); Noel Fernandez was its coordinator for many years.

22. McCloughry, *Enabled Life*, 105.

way people living with the experience of disability are gifted, they all need to feel at home. They belong with us in our churches, our Sunday schools, our Bible studies, our worship times, and our fellowship groups. They are part of the body of Christ, part of the public witness of the church. Are we willing to walk alongside them? This may mean, as John Swinton comments, that we walk more slowly: "In God's time there is always time to sit together and learn the meaning of love. . . . In God's time the difference that disability brings is perceived quite differently."[23] Are we willing to learn from them and value them? For people with disabilities to find pertinence in the church, they need to feel wanted and valued, they need to be at home – not just allowed entry but welcomed in.

The public witness of the church should be held to account by the way it treats, welcomes, and enables people with disabilities to find their home within it. It can be said that a church shows itself to be biblical and healthy in part by the way in which it includes people with disabilities. Can this be a way of testing the spiritual temperature of the church? Should we not question why churches do not have many people living with disabilities as members? We may be surprised by what we find when we start to build friendships with such people. A lady with visual impairment I met when visiting her church told me that she loves cooking and frequently invites friends into her home. So for her, Jesus's words about inviting those with disabilities for meals (Luke 14:12–14) cause her to reflect on how she is able to do more than be a passive recipient. She is present, participating, and finding her place in the body of Christ. We, the twenty-first-century church, need to reread the biblical texts and assess our public witness in their light. Does our witness accord with God's word? If it does, we should look forward to welcoming in many more people with disabilities as active, indispensable members of the body of Christ. As the 2010 Lausanne statement on disability in the *Cape Town Commitment* affirms: "We encourage church and mission leaders to think not only of mission *among* those with a disability, but to recognize, affirm and facilitate the missional calling of believers with disabilities themselves as part of the Body of Christ."[24] Scripture shows that people living with the experience of disability should be present, participating, and finding their place in today's church.

---

23. Swinton, *Becoming Friends of Time*, 15–16.

24. Lausanne Movement, *The Cape Town Commitment: A Confession of Faith and a Call to Action; The Third Lausanne Congress* (Peabody: Hendrickson, 2011), II.B.4.(B), 71.

Bibliography

Brock, Brian, and John Swinton, eds. *Disability in the Christian Tradition: A Reader*. Grand Rapids: Eerdmans, 2012.

CURE. "CURE Provides a Practical Theology of Disability to Communities Across Its Network of Hospitals." 18 March 2022. https://cure.org/2022/03/cure-provides-a-practical-theology-of-disability-to-communities-across-its-network-of-hospitals/.

Darke, Brenda. *Un Camino compartido: hacia la plena inclusión de la persona con discapacidad en las iglesias*. 2nd ed. Lima: Ediciones Puma, 2020.

Deuel, David C., and Nathan G. John, eds. *Disability in Mission: The Church's Hidden Treasure*. Lausanne Library. Peabody: Hendrickson, 2019.

Eiesland, Nancy L. *The Disabled God: Toward a Liberatory Theology of Disability*. Nashville: Abingdon, 1994.

Hardwick, Lamar. *Disability and the Church: A Vision for Diversity and Inclusion*. Downers Grove: InterVarsity Press, 2021.

Hathaway, Bridget, and Flavian Kishekwa. *Included and Valued: A Practical Theology of Disability*. Carlisle: Langham Global Library, 2019.

Lausanne Movement. *The Cape Town Commitment: A Confession of Faith and a Call to Action; The Third Lausanne Congress*. Peabody: Hendrickson, 2011. https://www.lausanne.org/content/ctcommitment.

Lindoewood, Paul. "Being a Mission Partner with Disability in Kenya." Chapter 7 in *Disability in Mission: The Church's Hidden Treasure*, edited by David C. Deuel and Nathan G. John. Lausanne Library. Peabody: Hendrickson, 2019.

Mackenney Jeffs, Frances. *Reconceptualising Disability for the Contemporary Church*. London: SCM, 2021.

Martinez, Pablo. *A Thorn in the Flesh: Finding Strength and Hope amid Suffering*. Nottingham: Inter-Varsity Press, 2007.

McCloughry, Roy. *The Enabled Life: Christianity in a Disabling World*. London: SPCK, 2013.

McCloughry, Roy, and Wayne Morris. *Making a World of Difference: Christian Reflections on Disability*. London: SPCK, 2002.

McKinney Fox, Bethany. *Disability and the Way of Jesus: Holistic Healing in the Gospels and the Church*. Downers Grove: IVP Academic, 2019.

Reiners, Hans S. *Receiving the Gift of Friendship: Profound Disability, Theological Anthropology and Ethics*. Grand Rapids: Eerdmans, 2008.

Reynolds, Thomas E. *Vulnerable Communion: A Theology of Disability and Hospitality*. Grand Rapids: Brazos, 2008.

Swinton, John. *Becoming Friends of Time: Disability, Timefullness and Gentle Discipleship*. London: SCM, 2017.

———. *Finding Jesus in the Storm: The Spiritual Lives of Christians with Mental Health Challenges*. Grand Rapids: Eerdmans, 2020.

Swinton, John, ed. *Critical Reflections on Stanley Hauerwas' Theology of Disability: Disabling Society, Enabling Theology*. Binghamton: Haworth Pastoral, 2004.

UN General Assembly. Resolution 61/106. Convention on the Rights of Persons with Disabilities. A/RES/61/106. 13 December 2006. https://www.un.org/en/development/desa/population/migration/generalassembly/docs/globalcompact/A_RES_61_106.pdf.

UNICEF. *Seen, Counted, Included: Using Data to Shed Light on the Well-Being of Children with Disabilities*. New York: UNICEF, 2021.

Webb-Mitchell, Brett. *Beyond Accessibility: Toward Full Inclusion of People with Disabilities in Faith Communities*. New York: Church Publishing, 2010.

———. *Dancing with Disabilities: Opening the Church to All God's Children*. Cleveland: Pilgrim, 1996.

———. *Unexpected Guests at God's Banquet: Welcoming People with Disabilities into the Church*. New York: Crossroad, 1994.

Wen Pin, Leow, and Anne Wong-Png, eds. *Call Me by Name: Stories of Faith, Identity and Special Needs*. Singapore: Family Inclusion Network, 2018.

World Health Organization. "Congenital Disorders." N.d. https://www.who.int/health-topics/congenital-anomalies#tab=tab_1.

World Health Organization and The World Bank. *World Report on Disability*. Geneva: WHO, 2011.

Yong, Amos. *The Bible, Disability and the Church: A New Vision of the People of God*. Grand Rapids: Eerdmans, 2011.

———. *Theology and Down Syndrome: Reimagining Disability in Late Modernity*. Waco: Baylor University Press, 2007.

Young, Frances. *Arthur's Call: A Journey of Faith in the Face of Severe Learning Disability*. London: SPCK, 2014.

———. *Face to Face: A Narrative Essay in the Theology of Suffering*. Edinburgh: T&T Clark, 1990.

5

Immigration, Displacements, Hospitality, and the Role of the Church

A Focus on the Middle East Region

Lucy Schouten

Centre for the Study of World Christianity, University of Edinburgh

Introduction

"You'll need to use a different word when you talk to the congregation," he told me. "If you say 'hospitality,' they will think you mean putting out cakes for guests."[1] George Al-Kopti, an Anglican minister in Amman, Jordan, paired his trademark sense of humour with wry advice on the research pursuit that had brought me to the Middle East. This Arab pastor was sympathetic to my quest to learn about practical hospitality from his congregation, which had transformed from an impoverished monument to a Christian past into a busy headquarters for Christian fellowship that cut across national boundaries and boasted a majority-refugee membership. But he also warned me – prophetically, it turned out – that language would slow me down. It was not only that the Egyptian migrants and Iraqi refugees spoke noticeably different dialects of Arabic from their Jordanian hosts ("Don't worry about the Iraqi dialect," the pastor's wife, Mary Al-Kopti, once reassured me. "When they talk among

---

1. George Al-Kopti, interview by author, St. Paul's Anglican Church, Amman, Jordan, 5 March 2019.

themselves, even we can't understand them"), but also the concept of hospitality I sought proved elusive. Communicating "hospitality," I learned during six months of fieldwork in Amman, is much more than a linguistic puzzle. Rather, it requires a deeper exploration into the needs of the guest, the resources of the host, and the mission Christ has given to the church in a given context.

The twenty-first century has frequently been called an "age of migration," for it has already presented the church and related institutions with almost unprecedented challenges associated with forced displacement and hypermobility. The question emerges: how can Christians demonstrate hospitality to a growing number of strangers in their churches and their communities? Scholarship has engaged fruitfully with this question, especially the concept of hospitality. Notably, theologians have identified a need to consider the refugee as representing the person of Christ before the church. I also discovered this approach among churches on the ground in the Middle East during research in a context undergoing a dramatic experience with refugees and displacement: Amman, Jordan, in 2018 and 2019. In this chapter, I draw on fieldwork observations from several Arab churches in Jordan that hosted Syrian and Iraqi refugees from 2012 to 2019. These observations offer a window into the transformative, everyday hospitality of the church on the borders of violent conflict. The church can consider the refugee as the figure of Christ on the cross, forsaken by all, and thereby find a model for responding to refugees with hospitality. To meet the needs of the displaced around the world, the church must observe the model of the world's earliest Christians in caring for the forsaken Christ on the cross: first a claiming of the body of Christ, then a removal from the cross, and finally a selfless bringing into one's own place. Such hospitality on the part of the church can, in turn, create a space for the grace of God to craft a new life in place of what was destroyed.

Hospitality in Scholarly Literature

Responding to displacement and migration is one of the more persistent issues facing churches in the twenty-first century. The evidence of a contemporary "age of migration"[2] is increasingly apparent in some form in nearly every clime,

---

2. Limitations of space do not permit this chapter to consider fully the fruitful engagement between migration in the modern world and the theological and demographic development of both Middle Eastern and world Christianity; however, useful analysis of the still-limited numerical data on the idea of an "age of migration" in various regions of the world, as well as its ongoing effects on world Christianity, may be found in Jehu J. Hanciles, "Beyond Christendom: African Migration and Transformations in Global Christianity," *Studies in World Christianity* 10, no. 1

and its effect on the growing dynamics of world Christianity led Jehu Hanciles to remark, "Every Christian migrant is a potential missionary."[3] Specifically, the immediate aftermath of involuntary migration, sometimes called displacement, has become such a sticky problem in international politics that churches increasingly search for a distinct response that might "leaven" the often harsh policies or even mass imprisonment of involuntary migrants, often called refugees.[4] In 2015, refugees from Syria and elsewhere made headlines for unprecedented numbers of sea voyages to Europe. By 2018, however, an estimated 86 percent of the world's refugees still resided outside Europe and North America.[5] This fact creates a particularly pressing need for responses to displacement appropriate to the Global South and not necessarily requiring stable governments or economies. Many Christian theologians have suggested hospitality as a possible approach for churches responding to refugees. Indeed, Ross Langmead identifies hospitality directly with Christian witness, wherein "our guest becomes our host or . . . more profoundly, the Jesus we serve through the poor and hungry becomes our host."[6] He describes hospitality as follows:

> Hospitality is a strong concept which includes justice-seeking, political action, inclusion around our tables, intercultural friendship, pursuing a hospitable multicultural approach to church life, practical assistance, long-term commitment, learning from those who are different, sensitivity to the power dynamics of "welcome," a willingness to "let go" as well as "embrace," interfaith dialogue and discovering the intertwining of the guest and host roles which is embedded in Biblical and theological understandings of God's activity amongst us.[7]

(2004): 93–113. Further historical and theological reflection on the topic may also be found in Andrew F. Walls, *The Cross-Cultural Process in Christian History* (Maryknoll: Orbis, 2002).

3. Jehu J. Hanciles, *Migration and the Making of Global Christianity* (Grand Rapids: Eerdmans, 2021), 1; emphasis original..

4. Kristin E. Heyer, "Reframing Displacement and Membership: Ethics of Migration," *Theological Studies* 73, no. 1 (2012): 201.

5. United Nations reports in 2015 suggested the number of refugees displaced at that time exceeded any since the Second World War. See UNHCR, *Global Trends: Forced Displacement in 2015* (Geneva: United Nations High Commissioner for Refugees, 2016), 2, https://www.unhcr.org/media/unhcr-global-trends-2015.

6. Ross Langmead, "Refugees as Guests and Hosts: Towards a Theology of Mission among Refugees and Asylum Seekers," in *Religion, Migration and Identity: Methodological and Theological Explorations*, eds. Martha Frederiks and Dorottya Nagy, Theology and Mission in World Christianity 2 (Boston: Brill, 2016), 184.

7. Langmead, "Refugees as Guests and Hosts," 171.

On a more practical level, Christine Pohl identifies a need for the churches to "recover" hospitality as a deeply scriptural practice. "The practice of Christian hospitality," Pohl writes, "is always located within the larger picture of Jesus's sacrificial welcome to all who come to him," and the earliest Christians differentiated themselves from other Jews and Romans by welcoming the poor and outcasts to their homes and tables.[8] Notably, both these scholars begin to approach hospitality by identifying the refugee directly with the person of Jesus Christ.

Hospitality in Jordan

Intriguingly, the notion that hospitality requires the host to see Christ in the refugee's place emerged repeatedly in my research into hospitality in Jordan. The most forceful articulation of this concept came from Reverend Archpriest Father Bassam Shahatit.[9] Speaking on behalf of the Melkite Catholic Church in Jordan, he described his colossal task of the preceding five years: to craft and coordinate the response of Jordan's second-largest church family, the Eastern or *Rum* Catholics, to the sudden arrival of thousands of Iraqi refugees after their expulsion from ISIS-controlled Mosul.[10] Many – though not all – of these refugees were Christian, but they were far more distressed by the betrayal of their own Iraqi neighbours than even the atrocities of Islamic militants. A leader for many years in this unique Middle Eastern church family, Shahatit described his church's role in the financial and logistical struggle to respond to refugees in Jordan, a story that receives further attention later in this chapter. But the biggest challenge that faced the Christian hosts, he believed, was to assist in a way that strengthened rather than weakened the dignity of the refugees. The attention that his region was receiving, the international aid money, and the intense vulnerability of the refugees themselves, he insisted, all combined to create a spiritually dangerous situation, a situation in which

---

8. Christine Pohl, *Making Room: Recovering Hospitality as a Christian Tradition* (Grand Rapids: Eerdmans, 1999), 17.

9. Bassam Shahatit, interview by author, St. George Rum Melkite Cathedral, Amman, Jordan, 14 October 2019, English/Arabic translation by author. *Melkite* refers to a Syriac/Arabic Christian tradition; the first Melkites remained with the denomination of the Byzantine emperor (*melek*) in the great schisms resulting from christological controversies in the fifth century. *Melkite* derives from a Greek transliteration of the Syriac term. These Christians are also called *Rum*, from the Arabic transliteration of the Greek word for "Romans," because their ancestors followed the official doctrine of the Roman Empire (then based in Constantinople, also known as Byzantium).

10. Shahatit, interview.

competition, money, and personal prestige became more potent motivators than Christlike love. The proper alternative to such competition, he said, came from the refugees themselves: an Iraqi woman had shared with him a painting that expressed the collective sorrow of herself and her fellow refugees. She had painted the *Maseehi il-matrook*,[11] the figure of Christ on the cross, forsaken by all. Like Pohl, Langmead, and others, Shahatit identified the refugees in need with Christ himself. Importantly, however, he specified that the focus was not the Lord glorified, or even as the host of a sacramental meal, but Christ betrayed, abandoned, and then crucified on behalf of another's sins. Shahatit insisted that this recognition should colour the church's response to refugees as well. "This is the situation that the refugee is passing through," he told me. "So it's very important to be sensitive."[12]

This chapter seeks to explore the need for Christian hospitality to the refugee, not through the metaphor of a meal or a home – as important as those elements are to the practice of hospitality – but by considering the figure of Christ on the cross. Building on pre-existing explorations into Christian hospitality, this chapter aims to articulate a pragmatic response to migration and displacement for churches on the ground. In doing so, I draw from a total of six months of interviews and participant observation research with several Arabic-speaking congregations in Amman, Jordan,[13] in 2018 and 2019.[14] I argue that the church's response to migration and displacement should be one of Christ-centred hospitality. In the sections that follow, I introduce a three-part model for hospitality with a view towards the forsaken Christ on the cross. Because the practice of hospitality requires pragmatic attention to

---

11. المسيحي المتروك, or "the forsaken Christ."

12. Shahatit, interview.

13. Christians account for just over 1 percent of Jordan's population, which is mostly Sunni Muslim, but they identify strongly with the two-thousand-year-old history of Christianity in the area. Most Christians living in Amman would describe themselves as Palestinians, having fled homes around Jerusalem or the Galilee after the wars of 1948 and 1967. Many of these deployed their educational and other resources to help drive Jordan's economic growth over the past century, and – largely barred from government service on the basis of their Palestinian heritage – they have thrived as professionals or in private enterprise. On the other hand, most Christians in rural Jordan have long roots in the area's Bedouin, tribal past, and many maintain strong ties to the lands where they live. For more information, see Paulo Maggiolini and Iyad Twal, "Jordan," in *Christianity in North Africa and West Asia*, eds. Kenneth R. Ross, Mariz Tadros, and Todd M. Johnson, Edinburgh Companions to Global Christianity (Edinburgh: Edinburgh University Press, 2018), 152–63.

14. I completed this research as part of the requirements for a doctoral research degree at the Centre for the Study of World Christianity at the University of Edinburgh.

context, I illustrate each stage of this model with stories from the welcoming congregations of Jordan.

The Forsaken Christ: A Model for Hospitality

In considering the refugee as one who has been betrayed and forsaken, we see at once that certain kinds of responses are inappropriate. Cathy Ross, for instance, notes that hospitality loses force when – as the Jordanian pastor warned me – it is reduced to cake and beverages. Instead, Ross writes, "The practice of hospitality allows for creating space – space that allows room for both host and guest or stranger."[15] Instead of merely prolonging the refugee's difficult situation by offering the bare necessities of life, hospitality calls for Christians to proactively provide the refugee with a new place to belong. Indeed, while the proliferation of private, governmental, and even Christian aid has increasingly emphasized the provision of goods in response to displacement and related struggles, Luke Bretherton urges caution. A single-minded focus on meeting the refugee's material needs is not merely short-sighted; it risks displacing the refugee permanently. Bretherton writes, "The problem with only responding in a humanitarian as opposed to a conscious way that addresses structural issues is that questions of justice are unaddressed, so that while the symptoms may be ameliorated, the causes of the problem are at best ignored and at worst legitimated or colluded with."[16] The refugee becomes displaced by losing social and political ties, thus becoming "placeless." Ultimately, what the refugee needs the most is a new place to belong. And hospitality is the act of creating it.

Likewise, in responding to displacement, churches must be cautious about alliances that inadvertently reinforce the refugee's plight. Joshua Ralston has cautioned against the tendency of many churches and Christian organizations to become partners with their respective states, inasmuch as they permit national governments to dictate the terms of engagement with those in need. Ralston writes:

> By dislocating refugee engagement from its ecclesial context and placing it primarily with state-funded NGOs contracted with USORR [US Office of Refugee Resettlement], the church has allowed the state to set the terms of Christian engagement. These

---

15. Cathy Ross, "Creating Space: Hospitality as a Metaphor for Mission," *Anvil* 25, no. 3 (2008): 167.

16. Luke Bretherton, *Christianity and Contemporary Politics: The Conditions and Possibilities of Faithful Witness* (Chichester: Wiley-Blackwell, 2010), 141.

NGOs end up mimicking the state in prioritizing service provision over solidarity, mutual exchange, and growth in personhood.[17]

Thus, any hospitality that relies solely on the provision of goods is inadequate, or even damaging. Like Christ on the cross, the refugee is suffering from physical pain and privation. Food, shelter, the dressing of wounds: all of these are needed in due course. Ultimately, however, such goods will not resolve the refugee's situation any more than they would, on their own, restore the slain Saviour to life.

The plight of the refugee is complex, but creating a space to encounter such difficulty can help to bring the church forward to the feet of the forsaken Christ. As Ross notes, "Strangers save us from cosy, domesticated hospitality and force us out of our comfort zones. Strangers may transform us and challenge us."[18] The human being became a refugee through the same means that brought Jesus to Calvary: the betrayal and abandonment of friends, neighbours, and local leadership. Thus, the Christian who wishes to help refugees may follow in the footsteps of those first Christians who saw their Master on the cross. The New Testament disciples acted in three important ways, and these three steps become a model for twenty-first-century Christians to follow as we respond to displacement: first, the body of Christ must be boldly claimed before the leaders of this world; second, his body must be brought down from the cross; and third, he, like the refugee, must be brought inside and laid to rest in the place that we prepared for ourselves. This three-stage model, illustrated in detail throughout the remainder of this chapter, enables the church to respond to refugees with a robust hospitality that remains loyal to Christ, avoiding the pitfalls of collusion or "cosiness."

Claiming the Refugee

In claiming the refugee, the church must not expect the applause of the world's leaders, whether social, economic, or political. The nations made the refugee; we should not be surprised when they object to his or her rehabilitation. In many countries, of course, Christians can work within their societies or governments to craft kinder policies to rescue the refugee from the excesses of a neighbouring government. But how might churches respond amid the indifference or even hostility of their respective governments? How can Christians

---

17. Joshua Ralston, "Toward a Political Theology of Refugee Resettlement," *Theological Studies* 73, no. 2 (2012): 388.

18. Ross, "Creating Space," 170.

use the resources they do possess to claim the refugee when they lack political power? The answer comes from the Scripture text: "Joseph of Arimathaea, an honourable counsellor, which also waited for the kingdom of God, came, and went in boldly unto Pilate, and craved the body of Jesus" (Mark 15:43).[19] Joseph of Arimathaea approached his political leader with boldness to state his claim. He used his position to obtain an audience with Pilate, not for his own advantage, but on behalf of Christ. In this way, he made a conscious decision to request rather than abandon the body of Jesus, even if it required him to risk his own reputation and resources. Likewise, the church responds to displacement with hospitality when it reclaims the refugee from the potential indifference or violence of the world's leaders.

Such claiming may be illustrated by a group of church leaders in Jordan in 2014. That summer, the Islamic State militant group successfully conquered large areas of Iraq. But although Iraqi refugees had often fled to Jordan during previous conflicts, the Jordanian government, citing concerns about the large numbers of Syrian refugees already in the country, closed the border. In response, a group of Jordan's Catholic bishops, along with in-country representatives from Caritas,[20] contacted the Vatican ambassador to Iraq and Jordan. They were joined by the Italian Council of Bishops, and, together, this alliance of church leaders approached the Jordanian government to negotiate on behalf of the refugees. The border was opened, and the Catholic leaders promised that their churches and charitable associations would provide for the refugees, who would not be permitted to work legally in Jordan. In the years that followed, thousands of Iraqi refugees would not only receive direct assistance from Caritas, but would actually reside inside the church facilities of congregations across Jordan. Father Bassam Shahatit of the Eastern Catholic Church described the administrative struggle of opening new church services for the sudden rush of new members, as well as the deeply personal sacrifice of Jordanian Catholics whose church classrooms, offices, and community halls became the residence of refugees for months on end.[21] Shahatit noted the struggle of not only the leaders involved in complex diplomacy, but also the local priests and laity who created space for the refugees: "Maybe the bathroom is not clean because twenty Iraqi girls were using two bathrooms," he noted

---

19. All Scripture quotations in this chapter are from the KJV.

20. Caritas is known in certain countries as Catholic Charities, the global humanitarian organization of the Roman Catholic Church.

21. Maggiolini and Twal, "Jordan," 160.

among a myriad of other difficulties. "But the churches help."[22] In this way, the Catholic churches of Jordan claimed the Iraqi refugees who needed a voice before the governments of the world.

In summary, the church can respond to refugees with hospitality by claiming the refugee before the political leaders of the day. This act of claiming the refugee mirrors the actions of Joseph of Arimathaea when he claimed Christ's body from the Roman authorities. This act requires the church to draw on its own resources and reputation on behalf of those suffering from displacement. In this illustration, the Catholic churches of Jordan marshalled their own transnational resources to negotiate entry for the Iraqi refugees into Jordan. This act of claiming enabled further engagement with refugees, as this chapter will explore in the next two sections, for the Catholic churches not only invited these refugees into their country, but they also brought them out of harm's way and into their own local churches.

Taking the Refugee from the Cross

The second aspect of hospitality to the refugees may be seen in the removal of Christ's body from the cross. The Scriptures describe these events as follows:

> Joseph of Arimathaea . . . besought Pilate that he might take away the body of Jesus: and Pilate gave him leave. He came therefore, and took the body of Jesus.
> And there came also Nicodemus. . . . Then took they the body of Jesus, and wound it in linen clothes with the spices. (John 19:38–40)

As the text notes, Joseph of Arimathaea and Nicodemus personally confronted those who had killed Jesus in an effort to restore his body to friendly hands. These New Testament disciples employed their own political power in service to this act. Their bold action confronted, challenged, and ultimately halted further Roman abuse and enabled them and others to instead care for the body of Jesus. Such messy engagement with the forces of this world is likewise needed when the church responds to twenty-first-century refugees. In many cases, a person or group becomes a refugee by fleeing the attacks of their own government. Again, I note the comments of Ross, Bretherton, and Ralston above, that while the refugees may experience hunger, homelessness, or poverty as a result of this displacement, such privations do not themselves

---

22. Shahatit, interview.

constitute the plight of the refugee. As such, offering food, shelter, or even education and healthcare services does not constitute a taking down from the cross. Rather, taking Christ from the cross requires engagement with the forces that have displaced the refugee.

An illustration of such engagement may be found in the story of several Jesuit priests living in Amman in 2015. For several years prior, a number of Sudanese had resided in Jordan, having fled conflict in Sudan. Many were officially awaiting decisions from the refugee assistance branch of the United Nations, or even from individual embassies, in hopes of eventually receiving permission to leave the region and resettle permanently elsewhere. In December 2015, Father Michael Linden of the Amman Jesuit Center told me that many Sudanese received text messages telling them that a plane was waiting at the airport to take them to new homes.[23] When they arrived, however, the Jordanian police were waiting to place them on planes – not to new homes in the United States or Canada, but back to Sudan, where the government was offering a bounty for refugees.[24] The Jesuit Center had been offering pastoral and other support to the Sudanese in Jordan, and Linden discovered the plot from a Sudanese friend working in the Jesuit Center. Linden believed that the Jordanian police had intentionally acted during the Christmas holidays, when many professional foreign aid workers or United Nations staff would be busy or absent. With the assistance of his Sudanese friend, Linden began to drive through the streets where many Sudanese lived, warning them away from the airport and ultimately hiding many inside the Jesuit Center until the episode ended.[25]

I note that, unlike the Jordanian *Rum* Catholics, these Jesuits were Americans, foreigners living in Jordan for the express purpose of providing a Christian witness to another land. What is notable about their service, however, and in direct contrast to much of the relief work done by many churches in Jordan at this time, is that these Jesuits were not terribly different from their Jordanian counterparts in the *Rum* Catholic churches. In seeking to serve a foreign land, they had chosen to live in the foreign land. They built an institution to do so.

---

23. Michael Linden, interview by author, Jesuit Center, Amman, Jordan, 4 March 2019, English.

24. This incident is not widely known – or at least, widely discussed – in Jordan, but the Human Rights Watch has corroborated the episode, claiming that eight hundred Sudanese men, women, and children were deported to Sudan in December 2015. Human Rights Watch, "Jordan: Deporting Sudanese Asylum Seekers," 16 December 2015, https://www.hrw.org/news/2015/12/16/jordan-deporting-sudanese-asylum-seekers.

25. Linden, interview.

They had built up the Jesuit Center over years, even planting and cultivating extensive gardens over decades, for they had settled in Jordan long before the 2015 "refugee crisis" brought floods of foreign humanitarian aid to the Middle East. They built partnerships not with other global organizations but with locals in the area they intended to serve. They obeyed the local government, but they did not serve it. Rather, when government officials plotted to sell the vulnerable Sudanese back to their captors, even calculating a time when other aid organizations would not be present to stop them, the Jesuits acted quickly and decisively in opposition. They were able to do so, not only because they remained in Jordan over the Christmas holidays, but also because they had offered employment and friendship to these refugees for years earlier. Not all the Sudanese were rescued, but many were taken from the hands of their persecutors and brought into the place that these Jesuits had built as a refuge.

In summary, the second stage of this model of hospitality is to remove the body of Christ from the cross, as did Joseph of Arimathaea and Nicodemus. This requires the church to engage with political or other leaders who would harm refugees, using its own resources to halt further violence. This becomes important in situations where the refugees cannot obtain government assistance because the government itself has initiated violence against them. Such difficulties can remind the church to focus its own identity in the witness of Christ, as Ross notes: "We need the stranger – partly because we never know whom we may be welcoming and partly because they may show us new dimensions and new aspects of God that we have never seen before."[26] I have illustrated this stage with an anecdote from a group of Jesuits in Jordan. These Jesuits offered hospitality by rescuing the Sudanese refugees from exploitation by the Jordanian police and offering instead a needed refuge in their own home, the Jesuit Center.

Welcoming the Refugee into One's Space

The third stage of hospitality to refugees involves welcoming the refugee into one's own space. After Jesus was slain on the cross, Joseph of Arimathaea placed the body of Jesus into a new tomb. This space was owned personally by this disciple, prepared for the purpose, and offered at his own expense, as the scripture reads: "And when Joseph had taken the body, he wrapped it in a clean linen cloth, and laid it in his own tomb, which he had hewn out in the rock: and he rolled a great stone to the door of the sepulchre" (Matt 27:59–60).

---

26. Ross, "Creating Space," 170.

Because Joseph welcomed the body of Christ into his own space, his tomb became the site of an unprecedented miracle. Joseph's sacrifice was met by the grace of God to create – or rather, to recreate – new life through resurrection. This process of creating space for the refugee – and for God's life-restoring work – is also part of the church's hospitality to refugees. Just as the slain Christ needed a place to rest, so the refugee needs welcome in the homes, hearts, or institutions of today's Christians. Space fails me to elaborate on the wonder of the new growth that can follow life-shattering migration, but I point to the recent and able documentation of other scholars among British[27] and Congolese[28] churches, and indeed, the expansion of Christianity across the globe in its "first three-quarters"[29] of history.[30] This is, perhaps, the most obvious element of hospitality, but I hope to highlight the importance not only of offering a new home, but of allowing the newcomer to feel at home by appreciating the refugee's unique contributions.

St. Paul's Anglican parish in Amman – where George and Mary Al-Kopti served as leaders – illustrated the importance of creating a place for refugees. The Al-Koptis had been sent to a poor inner-city parish in 2013 with instructions to try to revitalize the now-dwindling church. They soon realized that hundreds of Syrian refugees were also living in the neighbourhood, however, and in desperate circumstances. Acting with only the limited resources of an already impoverished church, the Al-Koptis and other members of this church began offering the refugees the only thing they had: fellowship. They opened their church physically, allowing many refugees to reside in the church facility until better homes could be found. They also opened the church spiritually, by visiting and praying with the discouraged refugees and ultimately creating new ministries at the church to encourage them. Regular prayer and Bible study sessions, a youth group, children's camps, and special women's meetings were launched. When Iraqi refugees began joining the Syrians, the church became ever more diverse and regularly exceeded its seating capacity. These new activities, Al-Kopti explained, were open to refugees and locals alike, in an effort to promote unity and fellowship. "We try our best to make [refugees in the parish] feel that they are part of the community," Al-Kopti told me in an interview. "Our philosophy is, 'I was a stranger, and you took me in.' Not

---

27. Susanna Snyder, *Asylum-Seeking, Migration and Church* (Farnham: Ashgate, 2012).

28. Emma Wild-Wood, *Migration and Christian Identity in Congo (DRC)*, (Leiden: Brill, 2008).

29. Philip Jenkins, "Foreword," in Hanciles, *Migration*, xi–xii.

30. Hanciles, *Migration*.

in the backyard, not in the basement, not in a tent – we welcome them in."[31] By mentioning a tent, he questioned the common notion of a refugee camp, where many refugees in Jordan were forcibly kept.[32] By contrast, St. Paul's Anglican Church encouraged the refugees to eat, pray, ask questions, and otherwise participate in full fellowship alongside its members. The refugees in this now-robust congregation joined the Jordanians in prayer and worship, helped to select the topics for meetings and discussion groups, and even sponsored Sunday lunch gatherings on occasion. Al-Kopti even described with emotion how one Iraqi woman had donated a small sum to a fundraiser to buy chairs for the church. When he urged her to keep the money, she replied that she wished to contribute to the light of Christ. He celebrated her willingness to contribute to the church, in which she had become, through hospitality, a tangible participant.

To summarize, hospitality includes a need to welcome the refugee into one's own space, to resolve the refugee's "placelessness" by providing new relationships. The Anglican congregation in Amman had very little to offer to refugees financially, but in offering fellowship and a chance to belong somewhere new in Jordan, they provided hospitality to Syrian and Iraqi refugees. Likewise, the disciples did not permit the body of Christ to be thrown aside by the leaders of their day, but rather they carried him into a clean space carefully prepared by and for the disciple Joseph of Arimathaea. Importantly, this new home for Christ's body in turn became the site of a miracle of God's grace. Joseph of Arimathaea provided a space not only for the body of Christ, but for the resurrection and recreation of new life, as the life that was lost returns with new splendour. His act of hospitality, his sacrificial offering of space, was met in turn by God's grace to yield a salvific miracle of new life. Likewise, as the church works to offer a space to those who are betrayed and displaced by violence, twenty-first-century disciples who practise hospitality may look forward to the miracle of new life after displacement.

---

31. Al-Kopti, interview.

32. A frequent topic in these conversations was the infamous Camp Zaatari, a tent settlement in Jordan's northern desert that was built in 2012 for Syrian refugees. Refugees arriving at the Jordanian border were escorted to the camp by Jordanian soldiers, and a fence with armed guards kept them inside.

Conclusion

To conclude, the notion that churches must see Christ in the figure of the refugee is well established in scholarship and also emerged organically from my observations and interviews with welcoming churches in Jordan. Specifically, church leaders suggested that certain errors in the responses they saw in 2018 and 2019 could be countered by considering the refugee as the *Maseehi il-matrook*, the figure of Christ forsaken on the cross. Thus, this chapter has explored the actions of Joseph of Arimathaea and Nicodemus after Jesus was slain on the cross. From their actions, we see a model for how the churches can respond to refugees with hospitality. This model of those first Christians at the cross offers a response for today's churches: first, we must claim the refugees; second, we must bring them down from the cross and remove them from the hands of their persecutors; and third, we must bring them into our own place. This chapter has illustrated each of these steps with episodes from the congregations of Amman, who sought to welcome the refugees fleeing conflict in and around the Middle East. Their activities were conducted with deep attention to their own context of Jordan, as well as to the needs of the refugees to contribute meaningfully to a new society. Their engagement provides a useful study of hospitality to the displaced in action, and it was generally conducted by non-professionals.

My desire to translate "hospitality" into the lived experience of these welcoming Jordanians and the displaced Iraqis drew me much deeper into the Middle East's rich Christian tradition than I had anticipated. Even when the evidence of deeper fellowship and friendly welcome stood before my eyes, I struggled to translate my search for Christian hospitality into a word – in any language – that could communicate something more than "cake." While my experience included a real translation process between English and Arabic, it persuaded me that hospitality itself requires the same attention to nuance usually associated with foreign language translation. To understand, and indeed to practise, Christian hospitality requires an intimate working knowledge of the history, customs, and scriptures of the host context, as well as of the problems and politics that have diminished a unique human soul into one of many "refugees." With this working knowledge, a deep attention to context and to the model of Joseph of Arimathaea enables the church to respond to refugees with life-renewing hospitality, a hospitality that truly provides the space for a glorious recreation of new life.

Bibliography
Scholarly Sources

Bretherton, Luke. *Christianity and Contemporary Politics: The Conditions and Possibilities of Faithful Witness*. Chichester: Wiley-Blackwell, 2010.

Hanciles, Jehu J. "Beyond Christendom: African Migration and Transformations in Global Christianity." *Studies in World Christianity* 10, no. 1 (2004): 93–113.

———. *Migration and the Making of Global Christianity*. Grand Rapids: Eerdmans, 2021.

Heyer, Kristin E. "Reframing Displacement and Membership: Ethics of Migration." *Theological Studies* 73, no. 1 (2012): 188–206.

Jenkins, Philip. "Foreword." In *Migration and the Making of Global Christianity*, by Jehu J. Hanciles, xi–xiii. Chicago: Eerdmans, 2021.

Langmead, Ross. "Refugees as Guests and Hosts: Towards a Theology of Mission among Refugees and Asylum Seekers." In *Religion, Migration and Identity: Methodological and Theological Explorations*, edited by Martha Frederiks and Dorottya Nagy, 171–88. Theology and Mission in World Christianity 2. Boston: Brill, 2016.

Maggiolini, Paulo, and Iyad Twal. "Jordan." In *Christianity in North Africa and West Asia*, edited by Kenneth R. Ross, Mariz Tadros, and Todd M. Johnson, 152–63. Edinburgh Companions to Global Christianity. Edinburgh: Edinburgh University Press, 2018.

Pohl, Christine. *Making Room: Recovering Hospitality as a Christian Tradition*. Grand Rapids: Eerdmans, 1999.

Ralston, Joshua. "Toward a Political Theology of Refugee Resettlement." *Theological Studies* 73, no. 2 (2012): 363–90.

Ross, Cathy. "Creating Space: Hospitality as a Metaphor for Mission." *Anvil* 25, no. 3 (2008): 167–76.

Snyder, Susanna. *Asylum-Seeking, Migration and Church*. Farnham: Ashgate, 2012.

Walls, Andrew F. *The Cross-Cultural Process in Christian History*. Maryknoll: Orbis, 2002.

Wild-Wood, Emma. *Migration and Christian Identity in Congo (DRC)*. Leiden: Brill, 2008.

Interviews and Related Sources

Al-Kopti, George. Interview by author. St. Paul's Anglican Church, Amman, Jordan. 5 March 2019.

Human Rights Watch. "Jordan: Deporting Sudanese Asylum Seekers." 16 December 2015. https://www.hrw.org/news/2015/12/16/jordan-deporting-sudanese-asylum-seekers.

Linden, Michael. Interview by author. Jesuit Center, Amman, Jordan. 4 March 2019.

Shahatit, Bassam. Interview by author. St. George Rum Melchite Cathedral, Amman, Jordan. 14 October 2019. English/Arabic translation by author.

UNHCR. *Global Trends: Forced Displacement in 2015.* Geneva: United Nations High Commissioner for Refugees, 2016. http://www.unhcr.org/576408cd7.

6

Climate Change and Public Witness

An Eschatological-Geological Approach to Mission

Víctor Manuel Morales V.
Am Waldhof Gymnasium, Bielefeld, Germany

When I was invited to write a chapter on this hot topic early in 2023, I was not aware how the following summer would turn out to be for the northern hemisphere. July 2023 was the hottest July to date in modern history. Climate-related disasters have normally happened outside the West; however, in recent years these events have become more frequent in Europe and North America, wreaking havoc in places once thought to be safe, for instance, for holidaymakers. In the midst of the pain of loss, mounting insecurity, and paralysing fear, what about our faith and mission call as the body of Christ and New Humanity? How are we to come to grips with this new state of affairs? In this chapter I will offer some food for thought and pointers on these critical questions and burning issues from the vantage point of a global player with an academic biography of having lived and studied in Africa, North America, and Europe, where I currently reside.

An Eschatological-Geological Approach to the Church's Mission and Public Witness

Continuous learning is key to success in life. The natural world is in permanent motion. Our personal and social lives are subject to constant change. Adapting to new situations is a strategic skill not only in the labour market but for the whole of our daily lives. When it comes to coming to terms with the obliteration of the life conditions we used to know and the rise of new scenarios it is imperative to be aware of how necessary a lifelong learning approach is for us, both as individuals and also in terms of our ultimate commitments, namely, our allegiance to God's kingly purposes of reconciling the world to himself in Christ Jesus.

Granted, it is difficult to think in cosmic terms. We are not used, in our daily lives, to making an effort to see beyond ourselves and our immediate surroundings. In fact, that is normally the case since there is a difference between our world and the earth. Our worries, primary needs, and our loved ones are our greatest concerns, and they should be. However, the current climate crises are forcing us to lift our eyes and see further afield. It is no longer an option to think globally and act locally. We have to do both: think and act both locally and globally. My world has to encompass the earth, thought of as a system of which I am part. It is compulsory to learn to see myself anew by looking beyond my personal desires and aspirations and picturing myself from a worldwide scale.

But does it matter, really? Is the earth not doomed to be destroyed anyway? This wrong-headed point of view has been dominant in the way we understand mission. Reading 2 Peter 3 at first gives us the impression that it is about the final cataclysm. However, on closer inspection we notice that the passage has a rather moral focus, stressing that the new creation will be characterized by the presence of justice. So what is implied in this passage is the need of stripping God's world of injustice which is basically located in human nature. It is *us in relation to the world and to others* where the problem lies. Injustice must be removed radically, this time with fire instead of water – water being the means used the first time God purified his creation. Christians should learn to see anew and gain new perspectives on what God is currently doing in his world. That means looking at creation as it unfolds. I suggest that we should learn to integrate salvation history and geological history as one event rather than conceiving them separately or estranged from each other. That means that we must acquire a *deep-time* approach to life and to mission, particularly in the public square.¹ God is working wonders all around us in the midst of the injustices we suffer and also cause, willingly or unwillingly.

I will speak of a mission *didactics* centred in the eschatological-geological thinking whereby we learn to see anew our historical place in God's dynamic world and his action within it, in us, and through us on a wider scale. Such a skill will shape our actions, which will in turn become ultimately good habits in line with the new humanity anticipated in Christ. The connection between knowing, acting, and being lies at the core of this learning process we must come to realize when understanding the deep implications of our mission in today's world: it is about proclaiming existentially that God is reconciling the world in Christ; it is about participating in bringing about a new world characterized by justice. The church plays no small role here but is the main character in God's salvation history, God having appointed human beings right at the beginning as his representatives and deputies in keeping and tilling his garden in his name. Human beings are becoming aware of the scope of the effects of their actions in the real world and in themselves. This ability to transform our environment and ourselves is what technology is all about. Our technical power is God-given; however, it has to undergo the same process of transformation by the power of reconciliation God is operating in Christ. It has to contribute to greater justice. Such transformation is part and parcel of the ways in which we understand the church's mission and public witness in the twenty-first century. The fact that we live technically, in a world being radically transformed by technical means, offers us a challenge and an opportunity for us as Christians to understand the times and not only the changes in the weather patterns, as Jesus rightly criticized the Jewish authorities for regarding their hypocrisy and short-sightedness in relation to his presence among them:

> He said to the crowd: "When you see a cloud rising in the west, immediately you say, 'It's going to rain,' and it does. And when the south wind blows, you say, 'It's going to be hot,' and it is. Hypocrites! You know how to interpret the appearance of the earth and

---

1. What is "deep time"? It is a broad geological perspective which stretches back into the past and also forward beyond the ordinary individual human perspectives of *chronos* and *kairos*. Ted Toadvine explains that "our everyday experience of time has been transformed by the scientific discovery of the geological past and predictions of anthropogenic environmental impacts extending into the far future.... The deep past and deep future ... are ... radically heterogeneous ruptures within our everyday temporal experience." Quoted in David Wood, *Deep Time, Dark Times: On Being Geologically Human*, Thinking Out Loud: The Sydney Lectures in Philosophy and Society (New York: Fordham University Press, 2019), 7; citing Ted Toadvine, "Deep Past, Deep Future: Anachronicity in the Anthropocene," unpublished research proposal (2014). Chapter 1 of Wood's book is evocatively titled "Herding the Cats of Deep Time."

the sky. How is it that you don't know how to interpret this present time? (Luke 12:54–56, NIV)

What Is Climate Change?

Let us turn to the concrete issue of climate change. It is not an aspect of our daily lives that we care about unless some kind of disaster knocks on our door. On the whole, Christians have paid very little attention to earthly things due to a wrongheaded worldview which practically despises the order of creation by stressing its perishable state or by misunderstanding how we fit into God's care for creation. Another reason is the ill conception of what science is all about. For many Christians, the gospel has nothing to do with science and the earthly matters which are the object of its endeavours. Hence it can be awkward for many to read a chapter on the topic of climate change in a book about the church's mission and public witness. Yet as I have already suggested in the previous section, it is important to cultivate an integrated and integral understanding of God's business, as it were, in his world. And one way of doing so is to think in eschatological and geological terms, where historical processes reveal God's actions in the radical transformation of his world.

As a boy I always marvelled at the beauty of rocks and minerals to such an extent that collecting them became an important hobby at the time and a cherished childhood memory now. Today, as an environmental theologian and philosopher, I have rediscovered the beauty of geology particularly as a historical document to be interpreted. Geological history speaks volumes about God's action in the world. One particular aspect of the earth is its unique atmosphere. The fact that there is a thin layer surrounding the globe is a miracle. The blue skies communicate God's glory. Beauty and meaning are everywhere around us, including in the lithosphere, that is, the crust or outer layer of the earth formed by rocks. The interrelationships between the atmosphere, the lithosphere, the biosphere, the hydrosphere, and the cryosphere are not only a fascinating topic but a necessary subject, especially now that our livelihoods will undergo radical changes worldwide due to climate change. It is crucial to gain a proper understanding and knowledge of the earth as a system resting on a mesh of interconnections whose dynamics form the basis of our existence.

It is against this backdrop that we should understand climate change as an ongoing natural process characteristic of our Planet Earth due to the laws of thermodynamics, particularly the second law about heat flow and instability, also known as entropy. In other words, as energy is always being transferred and relocated, a given order will fall into disarray.[2] Changes arise out of the tension between chaos and stability. This applies to weather patterns as well. When looking at the earth's history it becomes clear that there have been novel climate arrangements across unfathomable slots of time. The interactions between the various layers or spheres bring about temporary stability to our planet. In particular, it is astonishing how the interdependency of the atmosphere and the biosphere allows for the production of the so-called greenhouse gases such as carbon dioxide, ozone, and methane. These gases regulate how much heat in the form of radiation should be absorbed from the sun, our main energy provider. Most of the radiation coming from the sun is reflected back into space. The energy intake filtered out by these gases enables the ideal conditions for life to flourish; for instance, the right temperature: without them the earth's temperature would drop to −18°C (−0.4°F) on average, thus they prevent an ice age. However, too much of them causes an unnecessary increase in temperature, the effects of which are equally threatening to life on Earth. The debate centres around the question whether or not recent changes in weather patterns are due to anthropogenic causes, that is, to human activity.

Geologically, the interaction between the biosphere and the atmosphere has produced changes that have been conducive to the development of all organisms. At an early stage of the earth's history, the presence of cyanobacteria or blue bacteria was responsible for the release of oxygen in our atmosphere due to their way of processing sunlight, or photosynthesis. In the same way, today in industrial and post-industrial times human beings have released more carbon dioxide into the atmosphere by the use of fossil sources of energy. The rapid increase in the amounts of these kinds of greenhouse gases has mainly caused a temperature rise around the globe whereby more heat is kept than released. Accordingly, since the Industrial Revolution back in the nineteenth century, weather patterns worldwide have gradually altered, increasingly becoming more extreme. So the entropy kept in check during past geological ages is running out of control, to the degree that the familiar conditions under which human life flourishes are being transformed radically and rapidly. The question is how to understand these processes. The earth's system is equipped with sinks such as forests, moors, and oceans, where the excesses of any kind are processed and made ready for reuse. However, the amounts of greenhouse

---

2. This can be easily observed in our households and offices as we constantly try to keep them in order. However, as time passes, chaos sets in.

gases circulating in the atmosphere have exceeded the capacities of the *remaining sinks* to cope with the recycling, and therefore the effects are being felt.[3]

Let us now broach the issue by looking first at the power of narratives as laying the context for understanding climate change broadly.

Narratives and Stories as Epistemic Devices

An epistemic device is an instrument for knowing or understanding an issue or set of issues. This means that our access to figuring out what the meaning of something is requires a context which becomes the basis by which something can be grasped. It means that nothing is fathomed in isolation but always in relation to something else. In this particular case, stories or narratives represent coherent and comprehensive views of reality with the ability to bring them home since they address us personally. The formidable power of a good story lies in the fact that it appeals to our imagination and our emotions, and not only to our reason. Therefore, I shall address the great stories or metanarratives currently on the market, as it were, regarding the issue of climate change. It is indeed the case that climate change is not only a natural phenomenon but a cultural issue with political, economic, aesthetic, social, and ethical meanings. I shall address these narratives in terms of the worldview they portray. They represent a particular way of understanding ourselves and our place in the world. Narratives entail the rise of a problem and the possibility of finding out what the solution is. In so doing there is a change in the situation of the agents or actors of the story, who can be better or worse off afterwards.

Emplotting Climate Change

In most cases, modern human beings picture the environment, including climate, as an element that is foreign to their daily lives. For the majority of the

---

3. It is obvious that the destruction of natural sinks can only amount to self-destruction in the name of irrational economic growth. But I have dealt with this topic in various conference papers and in my own postdoctoral research (Habilitation) on the topic of sustainable development: a theological and philosophical discourse analysis. E.g., see Víctor Manuel Morales, "Jésus bouleverse le marché: Une critique éco-théologique de l'aspect utilitariste de la définition «faible» de développement durable ['Jesus upsets the market: An eco-theological critique of the utilitarian aspect of the "weak" definition of sustainable development']," in Penser les relations écologiques en théologie à l'ère de l'anthropocène: Contributions œcumeniques en théologie de l'écologie ['Thinking about Ecological Relations in Theology in the Age of the Anthropocene: Ecumenical contributions to ecological theology'], ed. Fabien Revol, Louk Andrianos, and Guillermo Kerber, 253–268, Cerf Patrimoines (Paris: Éditions du Cerf, 2023).

world's population, modern life happens in an increasingly artificial world. As such, nature has become a concept that is difficult to fathom. However, its otherness is real. One should bear in mind the dynamic interrelationship between nature and human action. The issue of climate change is a case in point. In relation to scientific models of climate change, Mario Molina, José Sarukhán, and Julia Carabias argue, "*La idea central de estas metodologías es que la sociedad modifica el clima y la naturaleza, y es a la vez afectada por los desequilibrios que se derivan de esto* [The central idea of these methodologies is that society modifies climate and nature, and is at the same time affected by the imbalances that result]."[4]

Indeed, any organism will modify its environment and will be modified by it as well. Cultural life is nothing other than the human capacity to modify the environment according to our needs and imagination. The formative power to transform a given situation is a reality. The question is, how are we supposed to do it? This is a moral issue.[5] Molina, Sarukhán, and Carabias contend that the issue of climate change is not only the concern of the scientific community, but is a social, political, and economic problem. It is urgent to act responsibly and promptly on behalf of all creatures, since creaturely life is under threat.[6] They believe that alternative models of development based on the transformation of our economic system together with technological innovations can reduce the risks implied by climate change.[7] However, they also point out that energy consumption is a key piece of the puzzle, as it were. Our lifestyles, that is, the

---

4. Mario Molina, José Sarukhán, and Julia Carabias, *El cambio climático: Causas, efectos y soluciones* [Climate change: Causes, effects, and solutions], La Ciencia para Todos 241 (Mexico City: Fondo de Cultura Económica, 2017), 158; my translations throughout.

5. As Molina, Sarukhán, and Carabias explain, "Tres grandes E definirán el futuro de la actividad económica e industrial del planeta y, en consecuencia, el futuro de la humanidad : ética, economía y ecología [Three major Es will define the future of the planet's economic and industrial activity and, consequently, the future of humanity: ethics, economics, and ecology]." *El cambio climático*, 197.

6. As Molina et al. explain, "Estamos viviendo tiempos marcados por profundos cambios sociales, políticos, económicos y de retos éticos, cuyos motores principales son, por un lado, la naturaleza y , por otro lado, la creciente insatisfacción social de muchos millones de habitantes del planeta que están sufriendo los primeros embates impuestos por el cambio climático, y quienes además no pueden satisfacer sus necesidades básicas de mejoría y bienestar personal y familiar [We are living in times marked by profound social, political, economic, and ethical challenges, the main drivers of which are, on the one hand, nature and, on the other hand, the growing social dissatisfaction of many millions of inhabitants of the planet who are suffering the first impacts imposed by climate change, and who are also unable to meet their basic needs for personal and family improvement and well-being]" (197).

7. Molina et al. assert that "los cambios estructurales de la economía mundial y las nuevas tecnologías pueden ayudarnos a transitar a un mejor modelo de desarrollo en todos los países, a la vez que disminuimos el riesgo del cambio climático [Structural changes in the global economy

way we live, certainly determine whether we will ever reduce the amount of anthropogenic greenhouse gases to safe levels.[8]

The description of this state of affairs and the courses of action we will take must be contextualized. An analysis of the modern metanarratives can contribute to clarifying conflicts of interest and to sponsoring an honest dialogue between conflicting parties. In discussing the metanarratives of climate change, I shall start with the overall modern scientific metanarrative, which branches off into the narrative of scepticism, the narrative of technofixes, and the Gaia narrative.

The Modern Metanarrative: Francis Bacon's Project

As to the metanarrative of modernity, it reflects on the whole the polarization between nature, on the one hand, and human beings, on the other. In environmental ethics this tension is captured by two ideologies, namely, biocentrism and anthropocentrism. The neo-Calvinist position proposes that this state of affairs is the result of an inner tension between an absolute view of nature and an absolute view of human freedom as autonomy. Such a tension characterizes the modern worldview which the so-called Baconian project expresses well: "Man by the fall fell at the same time from his state of innocency and from his dominion over nature. Both of these losses, however, can even in this life be in some part repaired; the former by religion and faith, the latter by the arts and sciences."[9]

In this regard, the intrinsic value of creation turns out to be such a conundrum to the modern mind because its existence is explained away as stuff to be exploited and replaced. Consequently, human beings can eventually be replaced as well. On the whole, the task of forging a proper understanding of what it means to have a common future in a world with extreme and unprecedented climate patterns depends on recognizing and assessing the current narratives which set at play the totality of human life along a particular plot line.

---

and new technologies can help us move towards a better development model in all countries, while reducing the risk of climate change]" (176).

8. Molina et al. conclude that "en consecuencia, el estilo de vida que seleccionamos, nuestro grado de consumo de bienes y recursos, los niveles de comodidad que elegimos, etc., tienen un impacto sobre las demandas de energía y consecuentemente sobre las emisiones de gases de efecto invernadero [Consequently, the lifestyles we choose, our degree of consumption of goods and resources, the levels of comfort we choose, etc., have an impact on energy demands and consequently on greenhouse gas emissions]" (61).

9. Francis Bacon, *Novum Organum* (1620), 295; quoted in Francis A. Schaeffer, *Pollution and the Death of Man: The Christian View of Ecology* (London: Hodder & Stoughton, 1970), 50.

From the European Enlightenment stemmed the idea of progress, the great myth by which western modernity has lived. The idea of progress was a myth of universal history. It claimed that humanity is on a path of progress towards a better, ultimately Utopian future. . . . The means of progress were education, technology and imperialism.[10]

The Narrative of Scepticism

The scepticism and even resistance and refusal to accept anything like the idea of global warming in large sectors of, for example, US society is the first modern scientific narrative to be dealt with. Professor of Sustainable Enterprise at the University of Michigan Andrew Hoffman attributes this resistance to the power worldviews and cultural lenses exercise on people's attitudes and actions. He explains,

> While physical scientists explore the mechanics and implications of a changing climate, the social scientist explores the cultural and cognitive reasons why people support or reject their conclusions. What social scientists find is that physical scientists do not have the final word in public debate. Instead, we interpret and validate conclusions from the scientific community by filtering their statements through our own world-views. Through what is called motivated reasoning, we relate to climate change through our prior ideological preferences, personal experiences, and knowledge. We search for information and reach conclusions about highly complex and politically contested issues in a way that will lead us to find supportive evidence of our pre-existing beliefs.[11]

I shall argue that the growing distrust of science and scientists when it comes to climate change is rooted in the generalized cultural perception that their work is an attack not only on the American dream but on the economic welfare of the West. No amount of information will ever change the attitude and way-of-being-in-the world of those citizens in their adamant denial. Their reluctance to act has been reinforced by failed attempts to convince them with

---

10. Richard Bauckham, *Bible and Mission: Christian Witness in a Postmodern World* (Grand Rapids: Baker Academic, 2003), 5.
11. Andrew J. Hoffman, *How Culture Shapes the Climate Change Debate* (Stanford: Stanford University Press, 2015), 3–4.

arguments based on scientific research. Andrew Hoffman even reports personal threats and attacks made on him and other colleagues.[12] I contend that this cultural perception is grounded in the core belief that the USA is the land of opportunities and that their history has been a success story right from the outset. It is almost impossible to convince people of the need for austerity once their lifestyles are hooked to economic prosperity. It is a hard habit to break, and a painful one too. The current ruling political party in Germany is steering the political agenda of austerity and driving it forward at the cost of losing their gains to the extreme right-wing party, which supports the sceptical narrative.

The Narrative of Technofixes

The scientific project as ideologically articulated in the seventeenth century by Francis Bacon (1561–1626) has been the dominant narrative characterizing human enterprise and endeavours in modern times. The language of domination and mastery is typical of modern discourse. Early and late modernity also display both the idea of progress, which manifests a deep-seated desire to break free from any external bondage such as God, and also of nature. The modern ideal of freedom necessarily requires the subjection of nature to the exclusion of God. Knowledge is power. Practical scientific knowledge and technical power are basically the modus operandi leading to greater transformations in reality. The shape of things escapes us, though.

On the issue of the "technofix of geoengineering," Clive Hamilton says that "the appeal of climate engineering runs deeper, for as an answer to global warming it dovetails perfectly with the modernist urge to exert control over nature by technological means, a predisposition."[13] An important feature of the narrative of technofixes is what has been dubbed "the technological hubris."[14] Blind faith in our technical capacity not only to solve problems, but to exert control over our whole planet, particularly in relation to the issue of climate change, fosters arrogance and haughtiness.

At this juncture, it becomes clear that an analysis of the attitudes characteristic of a particular account is all-important. This attitude goes hand in hand with the conviction that the earth has been and can be technically transformed

---

12. Andrew Hoffman says, "Some of my collection of hate mail includes: 'you are doing the work of Satan.'" Hoffman, *Climate Change Debate*, 31.

13. Clive Hamilton, *Earth Masters: The Dawn of the Age of Climate Engineering* (New Haven: Yale University Press, 2013), 107.

14. Hamilton, *Earth Masters*, 109.

in our image just as the biblical narrative tells us that we have been made in God's image. Being made in God's image rests on the fact that human beings were to foster God's character in their lives.

> [Bran Allenby] begins with the observation that humans have not merely transformed the landscape but have imprinted themselves on every cubic metre of air and water, to the point where the Earth has become a human artefact. There is no more "natural" so we must cast off all romantic notions and take responsibility for conscious planetary management.[15]

Planetary management is in need of realizing that we are held accountable to the triune Creator and Redeemer. The solution to the human predicament cannot be exclusively immanent. The kind of planetary management implied by geoengineers is fuelled by efficiency rather than justice.[16] The denial of transcendence and the sense of community will not produce sustainable ways of living proper to human flourishing and world flourishing.

The Gaia Narrative

Lastly, as awareness of the dimensions of the ecological crisis was taking hold globally in the twentieth century, environmental theology and philosophy began to draw heavily on the idea that the earth is a living organism. Their conviction challenged the belief that human beings were accorded a special place in the ecological network. James Lovelock popularized the picture of Gaia, or Mother Earth, which is commonly taken to designate what has been otherwise dubbed the "Earth system." The latter designation suppresses any religious overtones. However, Bruno Latour offers us an alternative interpretation of James Lovelock's Gaia.[17] His interpretation defies the concepts of

---

15. Hamilton, 110–11.

16. Clive Hamilton discusses Brad Allenby's definition of geoengineering: "Earth systems engineering and management may be defined as the capability to rationally engineer and manage human technology systems and related elements of natural systems in such a way as to provide the requisite functionality while facilitating the active management of strongly coupled natural systems" (111).

17. This lengthy comment is worth repeating (English translation follows): "S'il n'y a aucun cadre, aucun but, aucune direction, nous devons considérer Gaïa comme le nom du processus par lequel des occasions variables et contingentes ont obtenu l'opportunité de rendre les événements ultérieurs plus probables. En ce sens, Gaïa n'est plus une créature du hasard que de la nécessité. Ce qui veut dire qu'elle ressemble beaucoup à ce que nous avons fini par considérer comme l'histoire elle-même [If there is no framework, no goal, no direction, we must consider Gaia as the name of the process by which variable and contingent occasions have obtained the

totality and teleology. In other words, Gaia is nothing other than the process of *becoming* based merely on the random character of events caused by the simultaneous actions of actors in the geological drama without any purpose or meaning. According to this view, the earth is not the creation which points to its designer. Hence nothing is directly responsible for sustaining it, but it is the result of a combination of vast elements. To his mind, this is the reason why it is not appropriate to apply technical metaphors when describing our planet, such as that of the spaceship.[18]

Since the earth is not a mechanism which can be repaired, Bruno Latour questions any attempt to re-engineer it and to manage it as any other system. This is a direct challenge to technological hubris. It forces us to acknowledge the boundaries of our technical capacity as well as the limits of our managerial approach to complex issues which we are only starting to comprehend.[19] Certainly, the Gaia narrative draws our attention to the complexities involved in gaining insight into the problem of climate change. However, it leaves out entirely any notion of unity, purpose, meaning, and transcendence. The fact that human beings are moral agents implies the obligation to act responsibly according to a given set of norms derived from a specific story. It is difficult to grasp how we are supposed to act responsibly in the face of pure contingency.

The Christian Narrative

Inspired by the work of biblical scholars and systematic theologians such as N. T. Wright, Craig Bartholomew, Brian Walsh, and Richard Middleton, I have drawn on the concept of biblical story as the theological basis for the kinds of

---

opportunity to make subsequent events more probable. In this sense, Gaia is no longer a creature of chance but of necessity. Which is to say, she's a lot like what we've come to think of as history itself]." Bruno Latour, *Face à Gaïa: Huit conférences sur le nouveau régime climatique* [Facing Gaia: Eight lectures on the new climatic regime] (Paris: Éditions La Découverte, 2015), 142.

18. Latour explains: "Or il est évident qu'on ne peut durablement appliquer de métaphore technique à la Terre : elle n'a pas été fabriquée ; personne ne l'entretient : même si c'était un « vaisseau spatiale » - comparaison que Lovelock combat sans relâche -, il n'aurait pas de pilote [Now it's obvious that we cannot sustainably apply a technical metaphor to the earth; it hasn't been manufactured; nobody maintains it: even if it were a 'spaceship' - a comparison which Lovelock battles relentlessly - it wouldn't have a pilot]." *Face à Gaïa*, 129.

19. Latour explains: "C'est parce qu'il n'y a pas d'ingénieur à l'œuvre, pas d'horloger divin, qu'une conception holistique de Gaïa ne peut être soutenue. Et comme Gaïa ne peut être comparée à une machine, elle ne peut être soumise à un quelconque re-engineering [sic] [It is because there is no engineer at work, no divine watchmaker, that a holistic conception of Gaia cannot be supported. And as Gaia cannot be compared to a machine, she cannot be subjected to any re-engineering]" (129).

suggestions I am making. As such the concept of a biblical story constitutes the horizon within which the church should understand its call and kingly duty. In other words, it is its hermeneutical key, which understands reality as creation in need of redemption and new creation as the result of the redemptive work of the Lord Jesus Christ freeing it from the brokenness of sin and death. In this respect, the church's public life must be suffused by the dynamic of the biblical story in order to attest to its pervasive transforming effects in all areas of the created order, which includes the sciences and complex issues such as climate change.

Appropriating the message of the Scriptures means seeing reality and myself as part of salvation history as my metanarrative. Serious readers should expect their expectations and current understanding to be radically unsettled by the biblical story which offers them a new mode of being. For instance, I can understand myself as a steward entrusted with the duty to care for the property of someone else, and not as its master. And this is what, according to Ricoeur, appropriating the message of a text is all about.[20]

The biblical belief that God relates to his creatures and his creatures relate to one another enables us to account for the unity and diversity of our planet. However, the Bible also tells us that this interplay of relationships is broken because of the fall of humankind into sin. God made covenants whereby his faithfulness to his creation and his people was safeguarded. For that reason, Jesus Christ came to heal these broken relationships which will be completely restored at the end of time. On these grounds, healing courses of action can be taken in a really sustainable and hopeful way. When it comes to climate change, this means ensuring that our courses of action reflect humility[21] and justice in relation to our *Mitwelt*, that is, to all creatures.[22]

---

20. See Paul Ricoeur's essay "Appropriation," chapter 7 in *Paul Ricoeur: Hermeneutics and the human sciences: Essays on language, action and interpretation*, trans., ed., and introduced by John B. Thompson, 182–93 (Cambridge: Cambridge University Press, 1981). Ricoeur notes that the act of reading well "is always a question of entering into an alien work, of divesting oneself of the earlier 'me' in order to receive, as in play, the self conferred by the work itself . . . It is the text, with its universal power of unveiling, which gives a *self* to the *ego*"; 190, 193; emphasis original.

21. "While advances in climate science ought to be teaching us to be more humble," Hamilton remonstrates, "advocates of schemes aimed at regulating sunlight or interfering in Earth-system processes seem to draw the very opposite conclusion." Hamilton, *Earth Masters*, 116.

22. The German term *Mitwelt* is often glossed in English as "environment" but is a richer term, more properly defined as *Gesamtheit der Mitmenschen* (entirety of our fellow human beings) and in German existential thought refers to the entirety of one's social or cultural environment.

The biblical metanarrative constitutes the framework within which believers interpret themselves and look for wisdom. Celia Deane-Drummond proposes,

> Not only is wisdom fruitful in delineating the relationship between God and creation in the context of contemporary science, but also wisdom becomes most fruitful in the context of the Christian community when it is understood as a Trinitarian theological term. Such Wisdom holds together the ideas of creation with redemption: Christ as Logos is also Sophia incarnate.[23]

Likewise, Horst W. Beck contends that salvation history is the ultimate context within which we can fully understand ourselves.[24] It is the story of God's acting in favour of his people. This metanarrative integrates the historical events of creation and redemption in Jesus Christ, providing the framework for wisdom required by the moral agency of believers. Celia Deane-Drummond argues that the absence of such a framework will hamper any attempt to establish a true ethic of nature[25] and, I would add, a new understanding and morality in relation to climate change.

Practicalities

Having discussed background analysis to the issue of climate change, we can now reflect on the courses of action to be taken according to an eschatological-geological approach. I would like to delineate three concrete aspects, namely, the ethical, the semiotic, and the political. The kernel of the first is love and justice, that of the second is information and critical thinking, and that of the third is power and willingness to act.

---

23. Celia E. Deane-Drummond, *The Ethics of Nature*, New Dimensions to Religious Ethics 4 (Malden: Blackwell, 2004), 19.

24. He writes: "Das Heilshandeln Gottes – entfaltet im angezeigten weitesten und tiefsten biblischen Grundbild – ist der letzte kategoriale Grundhorizont, auf den hin Mensch sich auslegen kann [God's salvific action – unfolded in the broadest and deepest basic biblical picture indicated – is the last categorical basic horizon towards which man can interpret himself]." Horst W. Beck, *Schritte über Grenzen zwischen Technik und Theologie, Teil 2: Schöpfung und Vollendung – Perspektiven einer Theologie der Natur* [Steps across borders between technology and theology, Part 2: Creation and completion – Perspectives of a theology of nature] (Neuhausen-Stuttgart: Hänssler-Verlag, 1979), 202.

25. "However," she writes, "I suggest that unless we look to ourselves and are critical of what we might become or have become, then ethics simply directed towards nature becomes a false dawn. It emerges, further, from a disjointed sense of who we are as persons, a projection of self into the cosmos as in deep ecology, without any sense of what that self might be like." Deane-Drummond, *Ethics of Nature*, 19.

Bringing together conceptually and theologically *salvation history* and *geological history* is to underline purpose and meaning in the mesh of events where God, human beings, and creatures-other-than-humans participate in transforming events. I will refer to this practical aspect as the Jonah paradigm. The Jonah story brings together all these elements into the salvific purposes of God in relation to the city of Nineveh. God calls Jonah to fulfil his mission of bringing the message of judgement and repentance to the Assyrians who are enemies of Israel. Jonah decides to do otherwise and takes the wrong course of action. However, God will bring him back onto the right track. For that purpose, God brings into play elements of the atmosphere, the hydrosphere, and the biosphere so that Jonah can carry out his duty as God's appointed messenger. Thus the storm, the sea, the big fish, the ship, and the sailors become characters in God's story. Jonah's attitude has to be transformed too and aligned with God's purposes. God deals with Jonah's reluctance using for a second time elements of the biosphere and the atmosphere, namely, the plant, the worm, and the hot wind. It is fascinating to see all these working together to accomplish God's purpose to change Jonah too, so that he sees what God sees. This paradigm also appears dramatically in Jesus's mission when he meets the crowd whom he describes as sheep without a shepherd.

When thinking of the current state of altered weather patterns and the ensuing geological change we can either adopt a deistic position where God is distant and the earthly processes are happening as the logical result of a chain reaction caused by human intervention; or we can learn to see God's hand at work, leading humankind to repentance. The origin of the current climate change is human hubris, that is, human beings taking pride in their technical prowess, managing their own lives *irresponsibly* in the sense that they believe they are accountable to no one but themselves. However, this technical prowess is not without a cost. Progress has led to planetary injustice, which translates into climate injustice. The idol will not deliver the goods. It cannot. Instead, there will continue to be many more victims as a wrong-headed progress makes its way as "inevitable." What shall we do?

First, it becomes apparent that Christians have to integrate this eschatological-geological dimension into their mission and public witness by thinking in *deep-time* terms. We must consider not only the recent past but the overall picture of the earth's history in order to realize the power of God's creative work and our place in the dynamic of the planetary network. Human beings are called to represent God in keeping and caring for his creation and its future development too. As such we are the ones who can open up the moral aspect built into the created order. We are called to live eschatologically and geologically since our ways of life will impact deep time. We simply cannot allow God's beautiful planet to go to waste. We need to learn to love what God loves and realize its cosmic dimension.

Second, we must also not only be better and more critically informed about what is happening, but we must be eager to cultivate an interest in God's wonderful creation, in what it is all about. Only then can we really learn how to keep it and till it. We must be aware of the consequences of so-called information overload. We have to be able to navigate this ocean of information, most of which is sheer rubbish. Thinking critically implies keeping your feet on the ground, that is, cultivating real and earthly relationships with your community and your surroundings: thinking as an *earthling*; taking time and slowing down; cultivating *phronesis*, that is, the virtue of prudence by asking God to open our eyes to his present working and by keeping an eye on his overall salvific purpose of cosmic reconciliation in Jesus Christ, who is the source of wisdom, love, and justice. It is important to cultivate a life anchored in this world which does not belong to us but is God's. We must resist being taken up with alternative and virtual worlds with the ensuing severing of real ties. Cultivate a garden, cultivate friendships, and cultivate yourself!

The third and last aspect has to do with taking up our civil responsibility of being global players and becoming political actors. Constructive political action is crucial for bringing forth changes in society. We need to be imaginative and creative when it comes to altering the structures and processes that have led to climate injustice. We need to be actively transforming economic models, the school system, the way science operates, and the *moral* development and *rightful* application of technology. Climate change is offering us the opportunity to do mission in an integral way by attending to people individually and collectively as we also take care of the rest of God's world. We have reached a point of no return. We will not be doing business as usual. But instead of lamenting our losses, let us repent and ask God to teach us to distinguish the right from the left.

Conclusion

Addressing this important issue has to prompt us to think of the church's mission in much broader terms and its public witness in particular. We cannot simply keep thinking in gnostic terms, namely, practically abhorring the material world and praising the spiritual dimension. Climate change defies us to reshape our understanding of God's mission in eschatological-geological ways, where human beings and all other creatures matter. As we celebrate the reality of the new creation where justice reigns, let us shape our lives accordingly today in concrete ways. Let us actively cultivate lifestyles that reflect God's character, and so let us model them for others too. In doing so we witness to the power of our resurrected Lord, not only in the private but also in the public sphere. Ignoring contemporary pressing issues such as climate change will only hamper the effectiveness of our mission in the public square as our message will then become increasingly alienated and irrelevant, leaving it up to others to shape our world according to their competing metanarratives and underlying worldviews. Integrating critically and creatively into our mission an understanding of the now daily issue of the reality of climate change is a golden opportunity for the church to publicly witness to the good news of God's reconciling the world in Christ!

Bibliography
Works Cited
Bauckham, Richard. *Bible and Mission: Christian Witness in a Postmodern World*. Grand Rapids: Baker Academic, 2003.

Beck, Horst W. *Schritte über Grenzen zwischen Technik und Theologie, Teil 2: Schöpfung und Vollendung – Perspektiven einer Theologie der Natur* [Steps across borders between technology and theology, Part 2: Creation and completion – Perspectives of a theology of nature]. Neuhausen-Stuttgart: Hänssler-Verlag, 1979.

Deane-Drummond, Celia E. *The Ethics of Nature*. New Dimensions to Religious Ethics 4. Malden: Blackwell, 2004.

Hamilton, Clive. *Earth Masters: The Dawn of the Age of Climate Engineering*. New Haven: Yale University Press, 2013.

Hoffman, Andrew J. *How Culture Shapes the Climate Change Debate*. Stanford: Stanford University Press, 2015.

Latour, Bruno. *Face à Gaïa: Huit conférences sur le nouveau régime climatique* [Facing Gaia: Eight lectures on the new climatic regime]. Paris: Éditions La Découverte, 2015.

Molina, Mario, José Sarukhán, and Julia Carabias, with Georgina García Méndez and Wendy García Calderón. *El cambio climático: Causas, efectos y soluciones* [Climate change: Causes, effects, and solutions]. La Ciencia para Todos 241. Mexico City: Fondo de Cultura Económica, 2017.

Ricoeur, Paul. *Paul Ricoeur: Hermeneutics and the human sciences: Essays on language, action and interpretation*. Translated and edited with an Introduction by John B. Thompson. Cambridge: Cambridge University Press, 1981.

Schaeffer, Francis A. *Pollution and the Death of Man: The Christian View of Ecology*. London: Hodder & Stoughton, 1970.

Wood, David. *Deep Time, Dark Times: On Being Geologically Human.* Thinking Out Loud: The Sydney Lectures in Philosophy and Society. New York: Fordham University Press, 2019.

Works Consulted / For Further Reading

Bourg, Dominique, and Alain Papaux. *Dictionnaire de la pensée écologique* [Dictionary of Ecological Thought]. Paris: Presses Universitaires de France, 2015.

Hulme, Mike. *Why We Disagree about Climate Change: Understanding Controversy, Inaction and Opportunity.* Cambridge: Cambridge University Press, 2009.

Lienkamp, Andreas. *Klimawandel und Gerechtigkeit: Eine Ethik der Nachhaltigkeit in christlicher Perspektive* [Climate change and justice: An ethics of sustainability from a Christian perspective]. Paderborn: Ferdinand Schöningh, 2009.

Maslin, Mark. *Climate Change: A Very Short Introduction.* 3rd ed. Oxford: Oxford University Press, 2014.

Morales, Víctor Manuel. "Jésus bouleverse le marché: Une critique éco-théologique de l'aspect utilitariste de la définition «faible» de développement durable ['Jesus upsets the market: An eco-theological critique of the utilitarian aspect of the "weak" definition of sustainable development']." In *Penser les relations écologiques en théologie à l'ère de l'anthropocène: Contributions œcumeniques en théologie de l'écologie* ['Thinking about Ecological Relations in Theology in the Age of the Anthropocene: Ecumenical contributions to ecological theology'], edited by Fabien Revol, Louk Andrianos, and Guillermo Kerber, 253–268. Cerf Patrimoine. Paris: Éditions du Cerf, 2023.

Schäfer, Lothar. *Das Bacon-Projekt: Von der Erkenntnis, Nutzung und Schonung der Natur* [The Bacon Project: Understanding, using, and protecting nature]. Frankfurt am Main: Suhrkamp, 1993.

van Ypersele, Jean-Pascal, ed. *El Clima: Cambios, peligros y perspectivas* [Climate: Changes, dangers, and prospects]. Madrid: Editorial Popular, 2007.

7

Reconfiguring Christian Public Witness in Africa

Challenges and Lessons Learned Integrating Spiritual Care in Hospital Settings in Western Kenya

Eunice Kamaara

Professor, Department of Philosophy, Religion and Theology, Moi University, Eldoret, Kenya

James A. Lemons, MD

Professor of Pediatrics Practice, Indiana University School of Medicine, Indianapolis, Indiana, USA

Introduction

The human race is facing multiple and complex crises which often seem unprecedented. Old threats to human life and well-being are increasing instead of being eliminated. Family breakdown, climate change, and poverty, among others, seem to be worsening in extent and intensity. In spite of enormous scientific and technological advancements, old and new communicable and non-communicable diseases threaten to overwhelm public health services. Though evidence clearly points to the need for interdisciplinary and intersectoral approaches to addressing health, the biomedical and biopsychosocial models of health continue to be privileged in hospital settings. Clinical pastoral care (spiritual care) is rarely mentioned and rarely offered in hospitals across Africa in spite of the highly spiritual and religious nature of Africans. One would expect that Christianity, the numerically dominant religion in Africa, would prioritize spiritual care in hospitals as part of its public life. Not so. In this chapter, we postulate that spirituality is at the core of human health. Using illustrations from an ongoing clinical pastoral education (CPE) project that aims to integrate professional spiritual care in hospitals in western Kenya, we highlight the critical role of the church in health and healing. At the same time, we share some of the challenges faced in the CPE project to argue that the church needs to reconfigure its public witness in health provision for effective public ministry in the twenty-first century. Towards this we offer some suggestions based on our conclusions.

Among the challenges one would expect the enormous scientific and technological developments of the modern world to have solved is disease. The reality is otherwise. Old and new non-communicable diseases (NCDs) such as cancer, diabetes, cardiovascular disorders, and mental illnesses have become so common that the situation is dire. Add to this new and old communicable diseases (CDs) and conditions, such as malaria, AIDS, ebola, and more lately COVID-19, and the global health crisis threatens to be overwhelming. Doomsday seems imminent. One does not need to mention the interactions of the various crises to appreciate the precarious situation within which humans are living. This is in spite (or because) of enormous scientific and technological advancements.

Evidence clearly points to the need for interdisciplinary perspectives and intersectoral approaches to addressing health. Yet in practice many researchers and development practitioners continue to operate in silos even when they are part of multidisciplinary teams. Certain perspectives, areas of knowledge, and experiences continue to be privileged and to be dominant in real life while others are suppressed.[1] In the field of healthcare, interprofessional teams contribute significantly to patient care and safety. However, barriers to effective interdisciplinary collaboration which negatively impact patient care remain; these include power dynamics and mistrust among team members,

---

1. E.g. see Eric R. Masese, "Moral Values and Personhood: The Missing Link in International Development Interventions in Africa," ch. 8 in *Values, Identity, and Sustainable Development in Africa*, eds. Ezra Chitando and Eunice Kamaara, Sustainable Development Goals Series (New York: Palgrave Macmillan, 2022), 159–74; and Emily K. Jenkins, "The Politics of Knowledge: Implications for Understanding and Addressing Mental Health and Illness," *Nursing Inquiry* 21, no. 1 (2014): 3–10.

contrasting ideologies, interests, and levels of engagement among clinicians, and disciplinary territoriality.[2]

In this chapter, we highlight the relationship between religion/spirituality and health and argue that spirituality is at the core of human health. More specifically, we focus on the church to present its twofold mission – that is, liberation on the sociopolitical and economic planes, in the here and now, and salvation in the world to come. In so doing we bring out the critical public role of the church in preventing ill health and in healing (restoring health) and promoting health. However, this role is faced with major challenges with counterproductive results.

The first part of the chapter offers operational definitions of various terms. Against the current global crises, many people are becoming disillusioned with the church, with some moving around from one church to another while others are becoming atheists. In the second section, we interrogate the public witness of the church in the area of health to indicate what the church needs to rethink and what it needs to do differently for impactful public ministry in the health sector. In this section we bring out some of the barriers to impactful public ministry using illustrations from an ongoing work at Moi University, Eldoret, Kenya. In the last section we summarize key observations and conclusions and suggest actions for the church for impactful public ministry in the twenty-first century.

Operational Definitions of Terms

Words, in whatever human language, are used in context. Therefore, they often have multiple meanings. A necessary practice in any piece of academic writing, therefore, is to provide operational definitions of key terms. In this chapter, we begin by explaining the different meanings of the terms we will use.

Religion/Spirituality

Often, the word "spirituality" conjures up sacred images of religious worship so that spirituality and healing are equated with faith healing, prayers, miracles, and demon exorcism. In other contexts, especially in Western societies, spirituality is not necessarily sacred: religion is only a small component of

---

2. Paulchris Okpala, "Addressing Power Dynamics in Interprofessional Health Care Teams," *International Journal of Healthcare Management* 14, no. 4 (2021): 1–7.

spirituality. The conception of spirituality as being synonymous with religion is not far-fetched, especially in Africa.

Across indigenous communities in Africa (and perhaps across the world), there is no distinction between what is sacred and what is profane. To live is to be religious and to be spiritual because everything that one does is related to the Holy Other. As John S. Mbiti observed, indigenous Africans carry with them their religious beliefs wherever they go and whatever they do; even the act of greeting a fellow tribesman is a religious activity.[3] Please note that there are no words for "culture," "religion," and "spirituality" in many local African languages. There is only one holistic reference to all of these: "way of life." Within this worldview, all relationships occur within the "ethical community" which comprises everything in the world – living and non-living things found in water (such as reptiles, sea plants, and rocks), the air (such as birds, insects), and on land (such as reptiles, insects, animals, plants, and humans), but also the metaphysical world beyond, comprising ancestors, spirits, and God. Humans and all in the ethical community flourish when they all uphold healthy relationships governed by such values as trust, honesty, forgiveness, and love.

In this context, as much as we would wish to think of religion as synonymous with spirituality, we find it practical to suggest that the two are distinct but closely related. In the context of contemporary Africa where life is compartmentalized into social, economic, political, cultural, and so on, it is prudent to separate religion and spirituality, if only for clarity and inclusivity. In so doing, hopefully we make room for provision of spiritual care to all humans regardless of their religious belonging.

Much broader than religion is "spirituality." "Spirituality" is conceptualized as all relationships regardless of whether they are with the supernatural or not. In this sense, therefore, religion may be considered a subset of spirituality.

(Holistic) Health/Well-Being

The World Health Organization defines health as "a state of complete physical, mental and social well-being and not merely the absence of disease or infirmity."[4] The definition has been hailed as holistic and criticized as inadequate in equal measure. Without getting into the arguments for or against the

---

3. John S. Mbiti, *African Religions and Philosophy* (Nairobi: Heinemann, 1969), 1.
4. Oche Joseph Otorkpa, "World Health Organization (WHO) Definition of Health," Public Health Nigeria, https://www.publichealth.com.ng/world-health-organizationwho-definition-of-health/.

definition, we observe that in practice, the biomedical and the biopsychosocial models of healthcare provision remain dominant especially in hospital settings across the globe. Both models privilege biomedicine, with the biopsychosocial model allowing for some psychological services, with only a little in the way of social services.[5] Besides, in that definition, what we conceive as the fourth and central dimension of health,[6] namely, spiritual health, is assumed to be subsumed in social health and is barely offered. This dimension is most critical, especially in Africa. In resource-poor contexts where people are "notoriously religious,"[7] spiritual care would be most impactful.[8]

In ordinary English, the term "well-being" needs no definition. But for discussions about public health, definitions are necessary. According to the World Health Organization, "well-being is a positive state experienced by individuals and societies. . . . A society's well-being can be observed by the extent to which they are resilient, build capacity for action, and are prepared to transcend challenges."[9] The Centers for Disease Control and Prevention (CDC) define well-being "as judging life positively and feeling good."[10] But what does "judging life positively" mean? And what does "feeling good" mean? It gets murky when CDC attempts to distinguish between physical, mental, economic, environmental, spiritual, and other forms of well-being. Then it becomes one and the same thing with holistic health. The term "holistic health" presupposes that there is health which is not holistic. Yet there is no controversy whatsoever that lack of health in any one dimension causes ill health in other spheres.

---

5. George L. Engel, "The Need for a New Medical Model: A Challenge for Biomedicine," *Science* 196, no. 4286 (April 1977): 129–36.

6. Paul Nyongesa et al., "Integrating Spiritual Care into Maternity Care at a University Teaching and Referral Hospital in Eldoret, Kenya: Challenges, Lessons and Way Forward," *Health and Social Care Chaplaincy* 7, no. 2 (2019): 168–215.

7. John S. Mbiti famously began his influential text with the assertion that "Africans are notoriously religious"; *African Religions*, 1. This assertion has been both widely cited and, at times, contested; see, e.g., Jan Platvoet and Henk van Rinsum, "Is Africa Incurably Religious? Confessing and Contesting an Invention," *Exchange* 32, no. 2 (2003): 123–53; and Mercy Amba Oduyoye, "The Value of African Religious Beliefs and Practices for Christian Theology," ch. 10 in *African Theology en Route: Papers from the Pan-African Conference of Third World Theologians, December 17–23, 1977, Accra, Ghana*, eds. Kofi Appiah-Kubi and Sergio Torres (Maryknoll: Orbis, 1979), 109–10.

8. Mavis Asare and Samuel A. Danquah, "The African Belief System and the Patient's Choice of Treatment from Existing Health Models: The Case of Ghana," *ACTA Psychopathologica* 3, no. 4:49 (2017): 1–4.

9. World Health Organization, *Health Promotion Glossary of Terms 2021* (Geneva: World Health Organization, 2021), 10.

10. Centers for Disease Control and Prevention, "Well-Being Concepts," CDC Archive, archived 9 September 2023, https://archive.cdc.gov/www_cdc_gov/hrqol/wellbeing.htm.

In this chapter, therefore, we consider the three terms – well-being, health, and holistic health – to mean the same and we therefore use them interchangeably. In any case, all the terms used by any researcher or institution to describe the structure and/or functioning of humans – for example, physical, mental, emotional, and spiritual functioning – would be preceded by the word "healthy" or "unhealthy," "ill" or "well," "positive" or "negative," "good" or "bad," and so on, to refer to (dis)ease of whatever kind.

Sustainable Development

"Sustainable development" is a tricky concept because it is not only fluid and dynamic but is in as many interrelated domains as health. Without getting into the contradiction within the term "sustainable development,"[11] we note that the term presupposes the need to integrate all domains of health. Therefore, disciplines, all professions, and all sectors need to work together if a continuous process of improvement to human life, that is, sustainable development, is to be realized.

Church

One of the major development agents in the world, especially in Africa, is religion. In Kenya, for example, church and church-based institutions account for a significant proportion of healthcare provision. But what exactly is "church"?

First, "church" may be defined as a building set apart for Christian worship. Certain designs are associated with churches across the world. For example, churches may have a cross, the symbol of Christianity in later times (initially the symbol of Christianity was a fish). Second, the term "church" may be used to mean a congregation, that is, a group of Christians meeting for worship purposes, whether they are meeting in a church building or not. Third, "church" may refer to a specific denomination of the global group of Christians distinguished by their historical, ecclesiological (organizational and governance structure), and doctrinal positions. For example, in Africa we have what are referred to as mainline churches, such as the Roman Catholic Church, the Anglican Church of Kenya, and the Presbyterian Church of East Africa. But "church" may also refer to a host of indigenous churches (commonly known

---

11. Christiano Nogueira, "Contradictions in the Concept of Sustainable Development: An Analysis in Social, Economic, and Political Contexts," *Environmental Development* 30 (2019): 129–35.

as African Independent Churches or AICs), such as the Legio Maria in Kenya and the Church of the Lord Aladura (COLA) in Nigeria, or to new religious movements such as Christ Is The Answer Ministry (CITAM) and Deliverance Church. Fourth, sometimes spelled with a capital letter, "church" may refer to the entire global body of people who claim to believe and follow Jesus Christ (Christians), and to consequently profess the one holy, apostolic, catholic (universal) church. Fifth, and finally, the term "church" may refer to the leadership within the organizational institutional management structure of individual church denominations. Often Christian leaders are ordained ministers (clergy) whose vocation is to serve Christians. The public witness of the church lies heavily on this leadership. Context will indicate when each of these definitions applies in this chapter. However, the subject matter is Christian clergy and the message is directed to the universal church.

Public Witness in Health and the Church in Africa

Against the global health crises in the modern world, many people seem disillusioned by the church, claiming that the church is no longer fulfilling its role. But what exactly is the role of the church? Regardless of time and place, the church has a two-in-one role of evangelization: to liberate persons on the sociopolitical and economic planes and to lead humanity to salvation in the world to come. In this, liberation necessarily comes first because it doesn't make sense to try to convince someone that there is life in the world to come without addressing that person's immediate needs in the here and now (liberation). Application of "the doctrine of *kenōsis*," a key aspect of the "Christological theological framework,"[12] underscores servanthood and unpacks the term "public witness" as a key description of the role of the church in public life. Jere argues for the public involvement of the church in anti-corruption activities in Africa. In the context of this chapter, we limit our discussion of public witness to the role of the ordained leadership of churches in the area of public health.

In public witness, one would expect church and church-based organizations and local faith communities to complement government activities. Historically, the church in Africa has not disappointed. Religious institutions are major development agents in all spheres of life. In some regions in the continent, the church is the only "government" that people know. In terms of

---

12. Qeko Jere, "Public Role of the Church in Anti-Corruption: An Assessment of the CCAP1 Livingstonia Synod in Malawi from a *Kenōsis* Perspective," *Verbum et Ecclesia* 39, no. 1 (2018): Article 1776, 3.

public healthcare provision, church-based organizations, with their expansive and long history of development programming, are second only to national governments. Moreover, religion plays a big role in (re)construction of relationships, a major component of which is health, especially in communal societies.[13] Fifty-five years after Mbiti made the observation that "Africans are notoriously religious,"[14] the situation remains: the overwhelming majority of Africans confess and practise a specific faith. In Kenya, for example, the 2019 Kenya Population and Housing Census estimated that 97 percent of the population ascribed to a specific religion, 75 percent of those being Christian and 11 percent Muslim.[15]

Yet there is more potential in the church than has been realized. Faith leaders have great potential to inculcate desired beliefs and practices. Given the rich history of health programming and the existing health infrastructure, their numerical strength, constant and regular forums, expansive international networks, grassroots structures with a good understanding of contextual patterns, and continued command in terms of respect and authority, church leaders are often unrivalled in influence.[16] Writing on the influence of the church with specific reference to HIV prevention and intervention, Christian Aid observed:

> Faith values are not invoked once a week at a religious service; they permeate people's lives, decision making and processes of understanding. For this reason, working with communities where faith is a significant aspect within the culture, a response to HIV which does not communicate with relevance to faith has a potentially much more difficult route to achieving its aims.[17]

---

13. See Yuval Levin, "The Case of Wooden Pews: Why Hard Religion Is More Important Than Ever," *Deseret News*, 27 January 2021, https://www.deseret.com/indepth/2021/1/18/21564215/why-hard-religion-is-important-american-faith-yuval-levin-gallup-declining-trust-in-institutions/.

14. Mbiti, *African Religions*, 1.

15. Kenya National Bureau of Statistics, *2019 Kenya Population and Housing Census, vol IV: Distribution of Population by Socio-economic Characteristics* (Nairobi: Kenya National Bureau of Statistics, 2019), 12.

16. E.g. see Edward C. Green, *Faith-Based Organizations: Contributions to HIV Prevention* (Washington, DC: US Agency for International Development, 2003); Christian Aid, "Evaluation of the Impact of Christian Aid's Support of Faith-Based Responses to HIV," Internal and External Evaluation report, 2012; and Zita Lazzarini, *Human Rights and HIV/AIDS*, Discussion Papers on HIV/AIDS Care and Support, Paper no. 2 (Washington, DC: United States Agency for International Development, 1998).

17. Christian Aid, "Evaluation of the Impact," 11.

The same may be said of ill health in general. In terms of sphere and level of influence of faith leaders in shaping knowledge, attitudes, values, beliefs, and behaviour related to health, the potential of the church leaders can never be overestimated. But that now seems to be history. In this twenty-first century, a time characterized by expansive and fast changes, it would appear that the church has not kept pace with these developments and is therefore losing its grip in authority and influence; in the words of Ivan Mesa, "traditional Christian faith is increasingly implausible."[18] Consequently, it is increasingly missing opportunities for public witness, especially in the area of health provision.

Here we must be quick to emphasize that it is not for lack of engagement of the church in healthcare today that we write this chapter. Far from it; the public witness of the church in the area of health remains substantial. We have witnessed individual clergy and individual churches mobilize the faithful to selflessly and tirelessly share food and water and other kinds of material support to the needy for their well-being. I, Eunice, most recently witnessed individual priests from different Christian denominations put their lives on the frontline to offer spiritual care in hospital settings in Kenya at the height of COVID-19. Talk of faith with actions! Our concern is that the church is not making adequate effort to keep pace with scientific and technological advancements in order to fully exploit its potential to fill the gaps and opportunities presented by current health crises. As we all know, adapting to and adopting change is one of the twenty-first-century's survival skills. As we pointed out in the introduction, this chapter is meant to identify the challenges that make Christian public witness a profession rather than a lived witness. It is also meant to provide lessons to church leaders for the future. In so doing, we echo what others have said but also identify new challenges and new lessons in the context of health. We use the case of the CPE project at Moi University/Moi Teaching and Referral Hospital to illustrate the challenges, gaps, and opportunities.

The CPE Project

The biomedical model dominated healthcare provision in hospital settings especially after the Industrial Revolution. In this model, the human person is treated like a machine and health is defined as absence of illness.[19] But by the

---

18. Ivan Mesa, "Introduction," in *Before You Lose Your Faith: Deconstructing Doubt in the Church*, ed. Ivan Mesa (Austin: The Gospel Coalition, 2021), 1–2.

19. Karen Willis and Shandell Elmer, *Society, Culture and Health: An Introduction to Sociology for Nurses* (Sydney: Oxford University Press, 2007), 22–34.

beginning of the twentieth century, questions were raised as studies in sociology of health and psychology intensified. Consequently, the biomedical model began to mutate into the biopsychosocial model.[20] However, the emphasis of hospital-based healthcare has remained largely biomedical.

While there seems to be consensus that the human person is made up of the body, the mind, and the spirit, little attention has been given to the psychosocial and spiritual human person. Much less attention has been paid to the symbiotic relationship between spirituality and all other aspects of health. Convinced of the need for spiritual care in hospital settings especially in Africa, an interdisciplinary team comprising lecturers from the schools of arts and social sciences, medicine, public health, and nursing partnered with a team from Indiana University School of Medicine, Indiana University Health and Values, and the Christian Theological Seminary in Indianapolis, IN, USA, to initiate the Clinical Pastoral Education Project at Moi University and Clinical Pastoral Care Moi Teaching and Referral Hospital, beginning with the Riley Mother and Baby Hospital (RMBH). The project was designed as an academic model and is therefore three-pronged: (1) teaching/training (clinical pastoral education); (2) clinical pastoral service (spiritual care); and (3) a policy-engaging research component. This model ensures that training and service are evidence based and generate new knowledge to guide teaching and learning, training, and service delivery.

The very first activity that we carried out was to collect baseline data through a mixed-method situational analysis of the Quality of Care (QoC) at the Riley Mother and Baby Hospital of the Moi Teaching and Referral Hospital (MTRH), Eldoret. The results suggested that physical care at the hospital is of a high quality and is in high demand, and the supply is adequate. Psychological care was of a low quality, was moderately in demand, and was moderately supplied, with two serving psychological care providers serving a population of at least 100 mothers every day. Social care was barely available and focused on assessment of clients' (in)ability to pay for services rendered. Yet demand for psychological counselling and social support is high: mothers reported that they felt isolated from their families and they also felt lonely.[21] Spiritual care was completely lacking, even though demand was extremely high.[22] Further, we

---

20. Engel, "New Medical Model," 129–36.

21. Eunice Kamaara et al., "Hospital-Based Spiritual Care for Mothers of Neonates at RMBH in Eldoret, Kenya: A Situational Analysis," *Health and Social Care Chaplaincy* 7, no. 2 (2019): 159.

22. Kamaara et al., "Hospital-Based Spiritual Care," 146–47, 160, 162.

observed that there were mixed feelings on the quality of communication, with some saying that communication was of a high quality while others said it was not. But psychological care providers are few. From observation we noted that a patient would be referred from a physician to a psychologist, and, if need be, to a social worker and ultimately to a "hospital chaplain" independently. We put the term "hospital chaplain" in quotation marks because these chaplains had no training whatsoever in healthcare or even hospital settings. They preached and prayed for patients en masse and would often be called on when someone died to give the news to the relatives of the deceased.

The focus at RMBH was largely biomedical. So as maternity services become increasingly technocratic, structured, and standardized, spirituality has not been given emphasis in the care of mothers and their newborns.[23] This approach was not holistic. The collaborative effort to integrate spiritual care at the RMBH, therefore, aimed at a holistic approach to health, to improve the quality of care, and to reduce maternal and neonatal deaths in Western Kenya.

The Intervention

In view of the above-presented results, the CPE committee resolved to implement an intervention that was three-pronged:

Teaching/Training and Service

This involved developing and implementing a curriculum for a postgraduate diploma in clinical pastoral education. Following nearly ten years of engagement with stakeholders, the curriculum was approved by Moi University and by the Commission for University Education in Kenya in September 2015. The Department of Philosophy, Religion, and Theology in collaboration with the Moi University College of Health Sciences started piloting the curriculum at the Riley Mother and Baby Hospital (RMBH) of the Moi Teaching and Referral Hospital (MTRH). Five cohorts of postgraduate students have been trained since and a sixth cohort was in session as of February 2023.

Clinical Pastoral Care Services

Training in CPE is largely through practicums where students learn at the bedside from "the human document" as they offer spiritual care services at the hospital under the supervision by mentors. After qualification, CPE students

---

23. Susan Crowther and Jennifer Hall, "Spirituality and Spiritual Care in and around Childbirth," *Women and Birth: Journal of the Australian College of Midwives* 28, no. 2 (2015): 173–78.

are engaged in a three-month residency programme at the RMBH in order to offer service at the teaching hospital and at community level.

Research in Spirituality
To improve teaching/training and service, we conduct research on spirituality/religion and health for contextual evidence.

CPE Awareness Campaigns
After intervention over three years, we engaged in CPE awareness campaigns and policy advocacy.

Achievements of the CPE Project

Barely five years after the implementation of CPE, we recorded major achievements, thanks to the high demand for spiritual care. First and foremost, as noted above, the Moi University Senate and the Commission for University Education approved the curriculum for a postgraduate diploma in CPE. This was the first in Eastern and Central Africa. Second, we received recognition from the top management of the Moi Teaching and Referral Hospital (MTRH); the management board established a full-fledged department of Clinical Pastoral Services reporting directly to the chief executive officer (previously, the chaplaincy was a small section reporting to the public relations officer) and resolved to increase the number of chaplains at the hospital from four to ten and that no untrained chaplain would be employed at the MTRH. Volunteer chaplains who would come in on an ad hoc basis were discontinued. Further, we have received chaplains from various healthcare institutions at our Chaplaincy Training Centre (CTC) to benchmark and receive training from us; this includes the Kenyatta National Hospital in Nairobi, the first and oldest national and referral hospital in Kenya. Third, as we write this, five cohorts have completed training and all of them have been absorbed in various institutions as chaplains or, because of their postgraduate qualification, in CPE and training. Four, as far as we know, ours is the first research into clinical pastoral care (hospital-based spiritual care) in Eastern and Central Africa. While our initial efforts at research were full of challenges related to the lack of contextual literature on the subject, we now boast some significant publications. Five, we have created awareness of spiritual care and its central place in health and healing across the entire community of the Moi Teaching and Referral Hospital and Moi University.

At the time of writing in March 2023, we can confidently assert that we have achieved our goal of integrating spiritual care at the Moi Teaching and Referral Hospital. However, much more is needed to fully integrate the care into all service areas and to see all healthcare providers work in an interdisciplinary way so that a biomedical care provider can identify the need for and/or offer (rudimentary) first aid spiritual care before referring patients to chaplains or other relevant caregivers for specialized care. Nevertheless, we faced major challenges in our efforts to integrate spiritual care in hospital settings. These included lack of resource materials since we were starting a new kind of service; lack of research funds because many funding agencies are not interested in "invisible realities"; lack of structures for accreditation of CPE; and inability to meet the demand for professional chaplaincy. We now turn to one of the major challenges we faced that is of central concern in this chapter.

The Complex Challenge of Christian Public Life

We anticipated many challenges in seeking to integrate spiritual care at the MTRH. We expected that the major areas of these challenges would be resistance from top-level management/policy makers of the teaching hospital and also from biomedical healthcare providers. To our pleasant surprise, this turned out to be the least of our challenges. In fact, the support and encouragement that we have received from these groups of people has been enormous, making the influence and success of the CPE project come sooner than we expected. We remain forever grateful to these people.

Our major challenge was not anticipated and therefore caught us by surprise. It is the bittersweet challenge of success. The successful implementation of the CPE project has created a huge demand for professional chaplains and therefore for CPE, a demand that we are unable to meet. This translates into a severe and most urgent challenge for the public witness of the church in Africa.

Perceptions matter. The common perception in Africa is that chaplains – whether for school, prison, or hospital settings – must be ordained ministers, that is, church leaders. And this is not without reason. As has already been mentioned in the section on definitions of terms, religion and spirituality are not separable in many contexts in Africa. Moreover, persons in spiritual distress will often require religious services and rituals such as sacraments which are ordinarily performed by clergy. Indeed, chaplaincy provides the church in Africa with a huge opportunity for public witness in the different settings that require it. Unfortunately, low-quality academic and professional training among the clergy is a major barrier to effective service, especially as general populations become highly educated and therefore more critical of what they see and hear – even regarding the church. The challenge is made worse by the current global appreciation of the importance of interdisciplinary and intersectoral approaches to training and consequently to service delivery.

Take the case of the CPE project. One of our considerations in deciding to develop and implement a curriculum at postgraduate level is that chaplains' work involves interacting intensively with professional healthcare providers such as medical doctors, psychiatrists, psychologists, pharmacists, and nurses. In our specific context of MTRH, a level 6 (national and referral) facility, human resources would be highly trained in different specialities and therefore the level of training was not debatable. And since ours is an academic model, an undergraduate level of education would be the minimum requirement as training has to be done while serving in hospitals.

Although whenever we advertise for enrolment of new cohorts we clarify that any person with an undergraduate degree in health, religion, or theology and related subjects will qualify, we receive huge numbers of applicants, almost all of whom are church (mostly ordained) leaders. They are highly interested in the programme, with a significant number of them already working as hospital chaplains. Sadly, more than three-quarters of these applicants do not qualify for the postgraduate diploma in CPE because they lack degree certificates. Of those with degree certificates, a significant number will have certificates from institutions that are not recognized by the Kenya National Qualifications Board and therefore not approved by the Commission for University Education. Furthermore, many of those with degree certificates will not have achieved the minimum entry requirements for universities and not undergone a "bridging course" and so there will be gaps in transition from secondary school to university. Many other clergy applicants, especially in Pentecostal and indigenous churches, will be without any theological training whatsoever. Others will have honorary doctoral degrees.

It turns out that many church-based tertiary-level institutions in Kenya have accreditation challenges.[24] This is not to say that church leaders do not have quality education. Yet accreditation is important because it indicates that an institution has met the standards and requirements set by national governments or other regulatory bodies. Without accreditation, one becomes unemployable. This has not been an issue for graduates of theological institutions because many of them are employed by the church and by church-

---

24. Paul Bowers, "Theological Education in Africa: Why Does It Matter?," *Africa Journal of Evangelical Theology* 26, no. 2 (2007): 135–49.

related institutions, institutions that will recognize their qualifications. When employed outside church and church-related institutions, the employees work on a voluntary basis or on low salaries, which has implications for quality service provision.

Traditionally, the church has always served people of different educational backgrounds, professions, social standing, and persuasions in spite of the level of education and training of the church leaders. This was viable a few years back, especially because the church leadership was still ahead of the general congregation in education. Many in church leadership would be teachers and healthcare workers. But it is no longer viable. What has changed? Congregations now have more and more education and seem to be overtaking the church leaders. With higher education, congregations are more critical of what church leaders tell them. Moreover, with an increasing emphasis on interdisciplinary approaches and intersectoral approaches in the era of Sustainable Development Goals, this way of church operation will become obsolete. The era when religious leaders will have to come out of their silos to work in and with other professions/professionals is nigh. It is critical that all educational institutions including church-based institutions meet the required standards and be accredited if their education is to be recognized as quality and relevant across different contexts. This calls for self-assessment and continuous quality improvements which seem to be lacking in many church-based education invitations.

Laba writes:

> Most of the leaders in African churches do not see the need for higher education. A common misunderstanding circulates among church members that to carry on pastoral duties, there is no need for further studies. There is even a saying in my country that "Higher theological learning does not produce a good pastor; it is rather the Holy Spirit on the field." This view not only reveals an inappropriate reading of the Bible, but also the limited understanding of pastoral ministry/church ministry. Churches and Christian Higher Education in Africa denominational budgets reflect this anti-intellectualism.[25]

Closely related to the challenge of low academic and professional qualifications, another challenge we have experienced in the CPE project is that some students are so dogmatically attached to their religious identities that

---

25. John Balema Laba, "Christian Higher Education in Africa: Past, Present and Future," *Africa Journal of Evangelical Theology* 24, no. 2 (2005): 159.

they are unable to tolerate views from lecturers or students from other faiths or denominations. Efforts to have them offer service to clients at the hospital without judgement become difficult. Doctrinal and historical differences across faiths become a barrier with the inability of Christian student chaplains to rise above their faiths and denominations. Among the key values for twenty-first-century teaching and learning are critical thinking, creativity, collaboration, communication, and continuous learning. None of these values will be applicable without understanding the other. This has meant that our classes have been small (three to six) and largely Christian rather than ecumenical and academic. We are therefore unable to promote critical thinking.

We appreciate that financial challenges dog many theological institutions which operate in a context of poverty, and running a credible academic institution is quite expensive.[26] As Laba notes, this is manifested in that existing Christian theological institutions in Africa have persistently cried out for financial help from associated denominations.[27] Laba adds that "it is very common in Africa to graduate students who still owe money to the school. They are given a chance to work and pay back. This, unfortunately, does not happen. Institutions run with unpaid debts threatening to exterminate them."[28] Sadly, this becomes a cycle of poverty where theological institutions offer education almost for free, which then is not quality, and graduates, in turn, have to seek voluntary or low-paying jobs in churches and church-related institutions with a heavy reliance on congregations. This cannot go on. As congregations become more critical and demand transparency, they give less and the situation will prove unsustainable.

Crises always offer opportunities. Paradoxically, as church leaders run out of funding, opportunities for them to do better are on the increase. Who would have thought that hospital chaplaincy would become so professional that public universities would train chaplains? The opportunity offered by the current context of requirement for values beyond knowledge and skills favours Christian and other religions. However, opportunities are always for those who are ready. The question remains: Will Christian leaders seize the moment to reconfigure their public life for the twenty-first century?

---

26. Laba, "Christian Higher Education," 159.
27. Laba, 159.
28. Laba, 160.

Summary, Conclusions, and Suggestions for the Future of Christian Public Witness

In spite (or because) of enormous scientific and technological advancements, human health crises are devastating in nearly all spheres of life. Yet, like all crises, they provide exceptional opportunities for individuals and organizations to reconfigure their roles in order to remain relevant and to offer new and better services in line with the times. This chapter suggests that the church (referring in this context specifically to the clergy, its officially recognized leadership) is a uniform force which therefore has a major role to play within its sole twofold mission of liberating people in the sociopolitical and economic sphere in the here and now, and leading them to salvation in the world to come. Playing this role is the very mandate of the church because it is following the example of Christ, the one who came to serve and not to be served. While the church has historically made great public witness in the area of health in a most commendable way, the church has not adequately reconstructed its role to negotiate its place in the current context. Yet there are lessons for the church for the future, as sure as the sun rises.

Towards effective reconfiguring of the public life of the church in the area of health, we make the following suggestions to church leaders in Africa:

1. Prepare for the role. Nobody goes to war unprepared. Learn, learn, learn. Your audience is now literate and critical.

2. Unity is strength. The church might want to go back to the root of ecumenism and pool spatial, time, and organizational structures, and human resources, and use them effectively in identifying and meeting the real needs of vulnerable populations in hospital settings regardless of their religious belonging.

3. Finally, get ready for more and more engagement in health crises. Both science and history, as well as our own experience (most recently of COVID-19), tell us that human crises will be experienced in the future. And science and technology are completely inadequate to address many of these crises. Science and technology will require people with values to be of sustainable use to humanity. Chaplains must be prepared for this.

The church's public witness regarding salvation in the world to come will not be effective if we ignore the needs of people for liberation in the sociopolitical and economic sphere in this world.

Bibliography

Asare, Mavis, and Samuel A. Danquah. "The African Belief System and the Patient's Choice of Treatment from Existing Health Models: The Case of Ghana." *ACTA Psychopathologica* 3, no. 4:49 (2017): 1–4.

Bowers, Paul. "Theological Education in Africa: Why Does It Matter?" *Africa Journal of Evangelical Theology* 26, no. 2 (2007): 135–49.

Centers for Disease Control and Prevention. "Well-Being Concepts." CDC Archive. Archived 9 September 2023. https://archive.cdc.gov/www_cdc_gov/hrqol/wellbeing.htm.

Christian Aid. "Evaluation of the Impact of Christian Aid's Support of Faith-Based Responses to HIV." Internal and External Evaluation Report, 2012. http://www.christianaid.org.uk/images/evaluation-of-the-impact-of-Christian-Aids-support-of-faith-based-responses-to-HIV.pdf (defunct link). Accessed 9 December 2013. Archived at https://jliflc.com/wp-content/uploads/2014/06/evaluation-of-the-impact-of-christian-aids-support-of-faith-based-responses-to-hiv-2.pdf.

Crowther, Susan, and Jennifer Hall. "Spirituality and Spiritual Care in and around Childbirth." *Women and Birth: Journal of the Australian College of Midwives* 28, no. 2 (2015): 173–78. https://doi.org/10.1016/j.wombi.2015.01.001.

Engel, George L. "The Need for a New Medical Model: A Challenge for Biomedicine." *Science* 196, no. 4286 (April 1977): 129–36. https://doi.org/10.1126/science.847460.

Green, Edward C. *Faith-Based Organizations: Contributions to HIV Prevention*. Washington, DC: US Agency for International Development, 2003.

Jenkins, Emily K. "The Politics of Knowledge: Implications for Understanding and Addressing Mental Health and Illness." *Nursing Inquiry* 21, no. 1 (2014): 3–10. https://doi.org/10.1111/nin.12026.

Jere, Qeko. "Public Role of the Church in Anti-Corruption: An Assessment of the CCAP1 Livingstonia Synod in Malawi from a *Kenōsis* Perspective." *Verbum et Ecclesia* 39, no. 1 (2018): Article 1776. 10 pages. https://doi.org/10.4102/ve.v39i1.1776.

Kamaara, Eunice, Paul Nyongesa, Hazel O. Ayanga, Emily J. Choge-Kerama, Dinah Chelagat, Joseph K. Koech, Mohamed Mraja, Edith K. Chemorion, Joseph Mothaly, Lucy Kiyiapi, Joseph Katwa, Jack Odunga, and James Lemons. "Hospital-Based Spiritual Care for Mothers of Neonates at RMBH in Eldoret, Kenya: A Situational Analysis." *Health and Social Care Chaplaincy* 7, no. 2 (2019): 145–67. https://doi.org/10.1558/hscc.37265.

Kenya National Bureau of Statistics. *2019 Kenya Population and Housing Census, Vol IV: Distribution of Population by Socio-economic Characteristics*. Nairobi: Kenya National Bureau of Statistics, 2019. https://www.knbs.or.ke/wp-content/uploads/2023/09/2019-Kenya-population-and-Housing-Census-Volume-4-Distribution-of-Population-by-Socio-Economic-Characteristics.pdf.

Laba, John Balema. "Christian Higher Education in Africa: Past, Present and Future." *Africa Journal of Evangelical Theology* 24, no. 2 (2005): 153–64.

Lazzarini, Zita. *Human Rights and HIV/AIDS*. Discussion Papers on HIV/AIDS Care and Support. Paper no. 2. Washington, DC: United States Agency for International Development, 1998.

Levin, Yuval. "The Case of Wooden Pews: Why Hard Religion Is More Important Than Ever." *Deseret News*, 27 January 2021. https://www.deseret.com/indepth/2021/1/18/21564215/why-hard-religion-is-important-american-faith-yuval-levin-gallup-declining-trust-in-institutions/.

Masese, Eric R. "Moral Values and Personhood: The Missing Link in International Development Interventions in Africa." Chapter 8 in *Values, Identity, and Sustainable Development in Africa*, edited by Ezra Chitando and Eunice Kamaara, 159–74. Sustainable Development Goals Series. New York: Palgrave Macmillan, 2022.

Mbiti, John S. *African Religions and Philosophy*. Nairobi: Heinemann, 1969.

Mesa, Ivan. "Introduction." In *Before You Lose Your Faith: Deconstructing Doubt in the Church*, edited by Ivan Mesa, 1–4. Austin: The Gospel Coalition, 2021. Open access pdf: https://media.thegospelcoalition.org/private/before-you-lose-your-faith.pdf.

Nogueira, Christiano. "Contradictions in the Concept of Sustainable Development: An Analysis in Social, Economic, and Political Contexts." *Environmental Development* 30 (2019): 129–35. https://doi.org/10.1016/j.envdev.2019.04.004.

Nyongesa, Paul, Eunice Kamaara, Hazel O. Ayanga, Joseph Mothaly, Simon Peter Akim, Steven Ivy, and James Lemons. "Integrating Spiritual Care into Maternity Care at a University Teaching and Referral Hospital in Eldoret, Kenya: Challenges, Lessons and Way Forward." *Health and Social Care Chaplaincy* 7, no. 2 (2019): 168–215. https://doi.org/10.1558/hscc.37583.

Oduyoye, Mercy Amba. "The Value of African Religious Beliefs and Practices for Christian Theology." Chapter 10 in *African Theology en Route: Papers from the Pan-African Conference of Third World Theologians, December 17–23, 1977, Accra, Ghana*, edited by Kofi Appiah-Kubi and Sergio Torres, 109–16. Maryknoll: Orbis, 1979.

Okpala, Paulchris. "Addressing Power Dynamics in Interprofessional Health Care Teams." *International Journal of Healthcare Management* 14, no. 4 (2021): 1–7. https://doi.org/10.1080/20479700.2020.1758894.

Otorkpa, Oche Joseph. "World Health Organization (WHO) Definition of Health." Public Health Nigeria. https://www.publichealth.com.ng/world-health-organizationwho-definition-of-health/.

Platvoet, Jan, and Henk van Rinsum. "Is Africa Incurably Religious? Confessing and Contesting an Invention." *Exchange* 32, no. 2 (2003): 123–53. https://doi.org/10.1163/157254303X00190.

Willis, Karen, and Shandell Elmer. *Society, Culture and Health: An Introduction to Sociology for Nurses*. Sydney: Oxford University Press, 2007.

World Health Organization. *Health Promotion Glossary of Terms 2021.* Geneva: World Health Organization, 2021. https://iris.who.int/bitstream/handle/10665/350161/9789240038349-eng.pdf.

Acknowledgement

The authors acknowledge the cooperation of Clinical Pastoral Education committees in both Moi University, Eldoret, Kenya, and Indiana University, Indianapolis, Indiana, USA.

8

Public Witness in Malaysia

A Case Study on Contextual Pentecostalism and the Reshaping of Missional Approaches in the Twenty-First Century[1]

Eva Wong Suk Kyun

Director of Malaysia Pentecostal Research Centre, Bible College of Malaysia

This chapter is part of a case study on the Assemblies of God regarding contextual Pentecostalism in Malaysia from a missiological perspective. This research seeks to understand how classical Pentecostalism was contextualized during the revival period with early missional strategies in the diverse ethnic and cultural context of the mid twentieth century. There have been changes over time as the movement has transitioned from homogeneity in the pioneering years to diversity in the movement's growth years with church-growth strategies. Missiological factors, mainly the shift in theological motivation, the new hermeneutical development in eschatology, and the shift in mission ownership, have gradually led to the reshaping of the missional approach over the decades. The development of modern missiology involves the broadening and diversification of the mission field towards holistic missions and social concern ministry, and a reconceptualization of Christian service and mis-

---

1. This chapter is an extract on missions and adaptation of my 2022 PhD dissertation entitled "Contextualised Pentecostalism from a Classical Pentecostal Movement to a Contemporary Pentecostal Church Movement: A Study of the Assemblies of God of Malaysia with Special Reference to Joel 2:28–32" (Oxford Centre for Mission Studies).

sional approach. Malaysian Christians have been responding and adapting with innovative missional developments. Ultimately, Malaysian social influences are crucial in shaping the Malaysian church and its engagement in integral mission through public witness and nation-building in the twenty-first century.

Contextual Pentecostalism from a Missiological Perspective

Regarding contextual Pentecostalism, Wonsuk Ma describes common traits in the Asian Pentecostal movement whereby there is an "interaction between the Pentecostal movement and its new-found environment, that is the Asian cultural religious 'soil' on the one hand, and the contemporary 'weather' (including the politico-economic) on the other."[2] He notes that "Asian classical Pentecostalism is not so 'classical,' that is, it does not always reflect the early Pentecostal beliefs and practices faithfully. This discrepancy is often found among the non-English speaking Asian nations."[3] He discusses the context of Malaysian Pentecostalism in which evangelism to majority Muslims is prohibited by law and complicated by racial tensions, and notes that Pentecostal churches in Malaysia are more actively involved in social concern ministries and programmes, such as drug rehabilitation centres, orphanages, homes for the elderly, kidney dialysis centres, and so on, which are successful and creative ways of demonstrating God's love in action.[4] As a contextualized Pentecostal movement, the Assemblies of God Malaysia (AGM) has undergone the processes which Wonsuk Ma explains. Mission methods and approaches have evolved over time from more open evangelism to public witness, particularly in social concern ministries, holistic and integral missions, marketplace ministries, and nation-building in this twenty-first century.

Revival and Early Missional Strategies

Classical Pentecostalism began to be contextualized in Malaysia during the revival period with early missional strategies in the diverse ethnic and cultural contexts of the mid twentieth century. Malaysian Pentecostal leaders appropriated and adapted strategies inherited from Assemblies of God USA

---

2. Wonsuk Ma, "Asian (Classical) Pentecostal Theology in Context," in *Asian and Pentecostal: The Charismatic Face of Christianity in Asia*, eds. Allan Anderson and Edmond Tang, Regnum Studies in Mission / Asian Journal of Pentecostal Studies Series 3 (Baguio: APTS, 2005), 60.

3. Ma, "Asian (Classical) Pentecostal Theology," 78.

4. Ma, 60–61, 77–78, 81.

(AGUSA) missionaries and applied them in their local contexts. The historical background of the Assemblies of God Malaysia's Pentecostalism can be traced to the roots of American Pentecostalism. Pentecostal historians and scholars affirm the centrality of Joel 2 and Acts 2 in the birth of classical Pentecostalism and early Pentecostal missionary strategies. These foundational scriptures have been at the very core of the Pentecostal movement since the Azusa Street Revival of 1906–08,[5] with Spirit-baptism being the empowerment for missions. Within a century, Pentecostalism had become a major part of the multidimensional global missionary movement.[6] AGUSA became one of the largest Pentecostal movements, urgently sending out missionaries to every part of the world, including Malaya and Singapore, as AGUSA Foreign Missions reported in the first half of the twentieth century.[7]

Pentecostal scholars – such as Allan Anderson, Stephen Jack Land, David W. Faupel, Frank Macchia, Julie Ma, and Veli-Matti Kärkkäinen – unanimously agree that the understanding of the early Pentecostals at the time of the outpouring of the Spirit in the Azusa Street Revival was that they were living in "the last days." This gave them an eschatological fervour to preach the "full gospel" to the world in order to hasten the imminent return of Christ. The apocalyptic vision or "crisis eschatology" understanding of "the last days" ignited the early Pentecostals' missionary zeal for evangelism and universal missions empowered by the Spirit (Acts 2:17) and spurred the worldwide revival which grew into global Pentecostalism.[8] Robert P. Menzies states that

---

5. Harold Hunter and Cecil M. Robeck Jr., "Introduction," in *The Azusa Street Revival and Its Legacy*, eds. Harold Hunter and Cecil M. Robeck, 13–26 (Eugene: Wipf & Stock, 2009), 22.

6. Allan Heaton Anderson, "The Emergence of a Multidimensional Global Missionary Movement: A Historical Review," in *Pentecostal Mission and Global Christianity*, eds. Wonsuk Ma, Veli-Matti Kärkkäinen, and J. Kwabena Asamoah-Gyadu, Regnum Edinburgh Centenary Series 20 (Oxford: Regnum, 2014), 12, 23.

7. L. O. McKinney, "A Glimpse of Malaya" (1943), 13–19 (archive material); "Singapore, Malaya," *Global Conquest* (March 1961; archive material). *Global Conquest* is published bimonthly by the Assemblies of God Foreign Missions Department, Springfield, MO.

8. Allan Anderson, *An Introduction to Pentecostalism: Global Charismatic Christianity*, 2nd ed. (Cambridge: Cambridge University Press, 2014), 198–202; Steven Jack Land, *Pentecostal Spirituality: A Passion for the Kingdom*, Journal of Pentecostal Theology Supplement Series 1 (Cleveland: CPT, 2010), 59–63; David W. Faupel, *The Everlasting Gospel: The Significance of Eschatology in the Development of Pentecostal Thought*, Journal of Pentecostal Theology Supplement Series 10 (Sheffield: Sheffield Academic, 1996), 21–22; Frank D. Macchia, "The Struggle for Global Witness: Shifting Paradigms in Pentecostal Theology," in *The Globalization of Pentecostalism: A Religion Made to Travel*, eds. Murray W. Dempster, Byron D. Klaus, and Douglas Petersen (Oxford: Regnum, 1999), 17; Anderson, "Emergence," 25; Veli-Matti Kärkkäinen, "The Pentecostal Understanding of Mission," in Ma, Kärkkäinen, and Asamoah-Gyadu, *Pentecostal Mission*, 27; Julie C. Ma, "Pentecostal Evangelism, Church Planting, and Church Growth," in Ma, Kärkkäinen, and Asamoah-Gyadu, 87, 90.

all Pentecostals believe in living out the book of Acts today and understand Spirit-baptism to be essential to empower missions, with the initial physical evidence being speaking in tongues, and they believe that all spiritual gifts, miracles, signs, and wonders are for the church today.[9]

Assemblies of God (AG) missionaries and the early AG congregations in this region had similar traits and practices to those of early American Pentecostalism. They established a general council with organizational and administrative structures after starting some missionary work. With typical eschatological and missionary fervour, AG missionaries and local ministers engaged in evangelism, healing rallies, evangelistic crusades, church planting, and the establishment of Bible schools, with the goal of raising up both local ministers and missionaries. Julie Ma identifies the main modus operandi of Pentecostal mission from its beginning as being evangelism and church planting, with divine healing being a demonstration of supernatural power making inroads for the gospel.[10] Indeed, these main mission approaches – namely, evangelism and church planting, open-air or healing crusades, and publications – had been used by early AGUSA missionaries in Malaya and AGM since the pioneering period. The main missional strategy of AGUSA missionaries in many nations around the world is the establishment of the AG general council and Pentecostal Bible schools to train and raise up national leadership for the local field to plant and pastor churches.[11]

Historically, colonization affected many countries in parts of Asia and South-East Asia. When national independence was gained, the foreign powers departed and time was up for most foreign missionaries. As national patriotism intensified in some countries, foreigners were politically evicted by newly instituted immigration laws. Many missionaries returned to their home countries and AG general councils transitioned to indigenous leadership. Malaya gained independence in 1957, followed by the formation of Malaysia in 1963. In 1967, Malaysian immigration regulations imposed new guidelines on foreign missionaries, limiting the time they could work in the country to ten years. From

---

9. Robert P. Menzies, *Pentecost: This Story Is Our Story* (Springfield: ACTP, 2013), 160–73.

10. Julie Ma, "Pentecostal Evangelism," 87.

11. Collective interview data from two sets of in-depth interviews. The first set took place from 21 March to 26 May 2017 with forty-five pioneers, senior ministers, and young pastors and leaders from the Assemblies of God Malaysia; the interviewee pool reflected balanced representation from the executive committee, district committee members, senior pastors, and associate/assistant pastors nationwide. The second interview took place from 21 July to 28 August 2019, with nine executive committee and senior ministers for the leadership's views, visions, and strategies for the contemporary Pentecostal church movement.

the 1970s, most foreign missionaries across all Christian denominations had to leave Malaysia due to this immigration restriction, as recorded in the Bible Institute of Malaya Report,[12] and the Azusa Street Revival – the Pentecostal heritage which provided the theological foundation of the movement – passed on to Malaysian leadership in 1974.

The AGM and the early missional strategies had taken root during the times of revival when the outpouring of the Spirit in the baptism in the Holy Spirit (BHS) became widespread in Malaysia.[13] The uniformity of the strong emphasis on BHS and the purpose of empowerment of the Spirit for life and service, especially zeal in missions and evangelism, ignited exponential growth with intensive church-planting endeavours and church-growth initiatives in the formative pioneering periods as a classical Pentecostal movement.

Diverse Ethnicity and Culture

Although the early AGUSA's missional strategies and endeavours were similar to those of many countries that inherited the espoused classical Pentecostalism, AGM is a Malaysian Pentecostal movement in its diverse ethnicity and culture, as emphasized by its leadership and pioneers.[14] For example, certain Western church methods and formal Western attire taught by the early missionaries at the Bible schools in the formative years were not so applicable at the grassroots level. Missionaries and church planters in small towns and villages had

---

12. Bible Institute of Malaya Report, "Malaysia, Missionary Force Depleting Due to the Strict Regulations Imposed by the Malaysian Government upon Missionary Visas, and Local Leadership Is Much Needed in This Country" (May 1981; archive material); "Worldwide," *Pentecostal Evangel* 2786 (1 Oct. 1967), 7 (archive material).

13. Collective interview data. There were revivals and spiritual renewals in mainline denominational churches from the 1970s to 1980s. There were also pockets of revivals in indigenous villages such as Ba'kelalan of Bario Highlands, Ranau, and Taginambur in East Malaysia. See Jin Huat Tan, *Planting an Indigenous Church: The Case of the Borneo Evangelical Mission*, Regnum Studies in Mission (Oxford: Regnum, 2011), 214–15 and 225–43. See also Solomon Bulan and Lillian Bulan-Dorai, *The Bario Revival* (Kuala Lumpur: HomeMatters Network, 2012); Christopher Choo, *The Ba Kelalan Revival of East Malaysia* (Petaling Jaya: El Shaddai, 1994); Jason Law, "The Bario Revival: Its Background Context and Beginnings," Christianity Malaysia, 17 July 2015, http://christianitymalaysia.com/wp/the-bario-revival-its-background-context-and-beginnings/; and Kok Eng Chan, "A Brief Note on Church Growth in Malaysia, 1960–1985," in *Christianity in Malaysia: A Denominational History*, eds. Robert A. Hunt, Lee Kam Hing, and John Roxborough (Petaling Jaya: Pelanduk, 1992), 354–78.

14. Collective interview data; interview with Rev. Ong Sek Leang, AGM General Superintendent, on 7 April 2017 and 26 July 2019 at the pastor's office, Metro Tabernacle AG, Batu Caves; interview with Rev. Dr. Chan Nam Chen, AGM pioneer and Executive Director of Asia Collaborative Mission Services (AsiaCMS), on 28 March 2017 and 21 July 2019 at Bible College of Malaysia, Petaling Jaya.

to learn to adapt to the culture and indigenous perspectives when engaging with the local people, meeting their needs in practical ways, and preaching the gospel in grassroots realities.[15] Missions and the methods and approaches of evangelism need adaptation to the local environment, culture, and context.

In understanding AGM's historical context of Pentecostalism, contextualized studies on Asian, Asia Pacific, and South-East Asian Pentecostalism, particularly regarding AGUSA missionaries sent to these parts of the world, present some similarities in their indigenizing and contextualizing in the different nations.[16] The AGM's contextualized Pentecostalism is also quite similar to that of nations which have multiracial or multi-ethnic, multicultural, and multireligious populations. Similar to Pentecostalism in the larger context, the contextualization of AGM has been fast and adaptable.

Missional Diversity in the Movement's Growth Years

There have been changes over time as the movement transitioned from homogeneity in the pioneering years to diversity in the movement's growth years with church-growth strategies. In the pioneering days, there was homogeneity in the focus on classical Pentecostal theology and practice inherited from the early missionaries in the classical formation from its inception in 1957 to the mid 1980s. Interviews demonstrate that the theological emphases of church sermons were on BHS, the Holy Spirit, the Spirit-filled life, Spirit empowering, the working of the Holy Spirit, the book of Acts, missions, church planting, the end times (eschatology), soul winning, faith, giving, evangelism, financial giving, missions, faith promises, discipleship, holiness, going to the nations, and so on. Sermons given by the influential and popular church leader Yonggi

---

15. Interview with Chan.

16. For Asian Pentecostalism, Asia Pacific Pentecostalism, and contextual studies in South-East Asia and the South Pacific, see, among others, Allan Anderson and Edmond Tang, eds., *Asian and Pentecostal: The Charismatic Face of Christianity in Asia*, 2nd ed., Regnum Studies in Mission (Oxford: Regnum, 2011); Denise A. Austin, Jacqueline Grey, and Paul W. Lewis, eds., *Asia Pacific Pentecostalism*, Global Pentecostal and Charismatic Studies 31 (Leiden: Brill, 2019); Chin Kua Khai, *The Cross among Pagodas: A History of the Assemblies of God in Myanmar* (Baguio: APTS, 2003); Tavita Pagaialii, *Pentecost to the Uttermost: A History of the Assemblies of God in Samoa* (Baguio: APTS, 2006); Dave Johnson, *Theology in Context: A Case Study in the Philippines* (Baguio: APTS, 2012); Dynnice Rosanny D. Engcoy, *Pentecostal Pioneer: The Life and Legacy of Rudy Esperanza in the Early Years of the Assemblies of God in the Philippines*, Pentecostalism around the World 4 (Baguio: APTS, 2014); Joshua J. Lovelace, *From Seedtime to Harvest: The History of the Assemblies of God in Cambodia*, Pentecost around the World 5 (Baguio: APTS, 2019); Fred G. Abeysekera, *The History of the Assemblies of God in Singapore, 1928–1992* (Singapore: Abundant Press, 1992).

Cho (1936–2021) emphasized the second coming of Christ, the "full gospel," and "Christ as Healer." In media the popular movie *Thief in the Night* carried an urgent message, and there was a deep sense of urgency to win souls for Christ.[17]

The movement's growth days were a period of church growth and diversification of ministries, emphases, and focus. Churches adopted programmes and popular strategies in church growth which had worked well in other parts of the world or other churches. Cho's preaching, teaching, and books became very popular.[18] Cho had been a strong influence on AGM and charismatic churches in Malaysia, especially from the late 1970s to the 2000s. AGM churches have been greatly impacted by his strategies in church growth, administration, leadership, prayer, giving, faith, enhancing church programmes with cell groups, lay leadership, Christian education, and so on. In Korea, church planting and church growth are seen as alternative strategies. Later, in the 2000s, Rick Warren's "Purpose Driven" curricula also became a popular programme in AGM churches,[19] focusing on how a member can contribute to church growth. This period of consolidation and building up of ministries shifted the emphases and focus from outward evangelism to addressing the needs of the culture in church and for the people.[20]

Missiological Factors Reshaping the Missional Approach

As the Pentecostal movement has changed from its classical homogeneity in emphases to diversification in focus and practices, inevitably the missional aspect has also gradually evolved. Many factors have contributed to the change. The main missiological factors, namely, the shift in theological motivation, the new hermeneutical development in eschatology, and the shift in mission

---

17. Collective interview data.

18. Dr. David Yonggi Cho was a South Korean Christian minister and founder of Yoido Full Gospel Church, the largest church in the world. His book titles include *Successful Living* (1977); *Solving Life's Problems* (1980); *Successful Home Cell Groups* (1981); *The Leap of Faith* (1984); *Prayer: Key to Revival* (1984); *The Fourth Dimension* (1979, 1983); *Salvation, Health and Prosperity* (1987); *The Holy Spirit My Senior Partner: Understanding the Holy Spirit and His Gifts* (1989); *The Body of Christ's Present-Day Provision for Divine Healing* (co-authored 1989); *Born to Be Blessed* (1993); *How to Pray: Patterns of Prayer* (1997); *Spirit Led Reader: The Holy Spirit My Senior Partner / The Next Move of God / There's a Miracle in Your House* (co-authored 1999); *Prayer That Brings Revival* (1998); *How Can I Be Healed?* (1999); *Spiritual Leadership for the New Millennium* (2003); *Unleashing the Power of Faith* (2006); *4th Dimensional Living in a 3 Dimensional World* (2006); *Ministering Hope for 50 Years* (2008).

19. Rick Warren, *The Purpose Driven Life* (Grand Rapids: Zondervan, 2002) and *The Purpose Driven Church* (Grand Rapids: Zondervan, 1995).

20. Collective interview data.

ownership, have gradually led to the reshaping of the missional approach over the decades.

Shifts in Theological Motivation in Missions

The paradigm shifts in theological and missional motivation or driving forces have impacted the methods and approaches in doing missions over the decades. These shifts and motivations range from eschatological fervour and BHS empowerment for life and service, or missions and witnessing, to different understandings of "the last days" and, because of charismatic influences, the purpose of BHS not necessarily being empowerment for witness and missions.

New Hermeneutical Development in Eschatology

The main theological factors affecting the waning of the eschatological fervour and missional motivation of the classical formation period have to do with new hermeneutical developments. The shift in eschatological motivation for evangelism and mission from the 1980s is evident in the waning "crisis eschatology" of "the last days" and "second coming of Christ" and missionary fervour driven by this underlying motivation. These shifts are evident in the discontinuity of preaching and teaching topics on "the last days" and "return of Christ" over the period, as well as of certain early classical Pentecostal practices such as "tarrying meetings" and evangelism approaches such as "door-to-door evangelism," which were driven by "crisis eschatology."[21]

The early Pentecostals interpreted the "last days" chronologically and this "crisis" eschatology was the dispensational premillennial view where the world was near its impending doom at the end of tribulation, hence the early Pentecostals were urged to launch universal missions lest it be too late before the return of Christ. Anderson, Kärkkäinen, and Julie Ma affirm that the early Pentecostals' eschatological fervour in their mission emphasis on the "last days" was received through BHS with the Spirit's empowerment (Acts 1:8; 2:17; 5:12–16).[22] However, over time there have been doctrinal issues in Pentecostal eschatology, in that modern Pentecostal scholars do not agree with some eschatological perspectives taught by the early Pentecostal writers. The *Dictionary of Pentecostal and Charismatic Movements* records that in this new

---

21. Collective interview data.
22. Kärkkäinen, "Pentecostal Understanding," 27; Julie Ma, "Pentecostal Evangelism," 87–93.

century, modern Pentecostals understand the "last days" very differently; they do not believe the phrase should be taken in a chronological sense but should be understood from the perspective of salvation history, pointing to the last age of salvation history which began with the incarnation and will end with the parousia. Modern Pentecostals believe that Peter's phrase "the last days" (Acts 2:17) means "the entire period between the first and second advents of Christ."[23]

The shift in the underlying theology of the "crisis" eschatology fervour of early Pentecostalism to the modern theological interpretation of "the last days" and "the latter rain" has resulted in changes in missionary fervour and missional approach. This is a good drift towards the Bible, coming from evangelical traditions outside the dispensational tradition, and embraced by contemporary Pentecostal theologians and scholars when AGM joined the evangelical family in the 1980s. Although it is a corrective adjustment, what is worrying is the disappearance of the eschatological message altogether from Pentecostal pulpits. Missionary fervour is still a strong distinctive feature of Pentecostals but it has a more biblical-theological perspective on "the last days." Wonsuk Ma highlights, "As the movement enters the third generation, eschatological messages from Pentecostal pulpits have gradually disappeared to be replaced by this-worldly concerns, such as church growth, the message of blessings and health."[24]

Besides the missional development within Pentecostalism, some missional theories by Doug Matacio and Ralph D. Winter about the global trends of modern churches also explain the changing landscape and focus of churches in contemporary times. According to one theory, the decrease in missions and evangelistic fervour can be explained by centripetal versus centrifugal mission, in that churches are being inward-looking rather than outward-looking.[25] A similar kind of theory is about church organizations being focused on modality versus sodality, meaning churches focused on local church structure versus

---

23. John Rea, "Book of Joel," in *Dictionary of Pentecostal and Charismatic Movements*, eds. Stanley M. Burgess, Gary B. McGee, and Patrick H. Alexander (Grand Rapids: Regency Reference Library, 1988), 495.

24. Wonsuk Ma, "The Theological Motivations for Pentecostal Mission," in *Pentecostal Mission and Global Christianity: An Edinburgh Centenary Reader*, eds. Younghoon Lee and Wonsuk Ma, with Kuewon Lee, Regnum Studies in Mission (Oxford: Regnum, 2018), 36–37. The correlation between Pentecostal eschatology and mission is found in Wonsuk Ma, "Pentecostal Eschatology: What Happened When the Wave Hit the West End of the Ocean," in *The Azusa Street Revival and Its Legacy*, eds. Harold Hunter and Cecil M. Robeck (Cleveland: Pathway, 2006), 227–42; and Wonsuk Ma, "The Holy Spirit in Pentecostal Mission: The Shaping of Mission Awareness and Practice," *International Bulletin of Mission Research* 41, no. 3 (2017): 227–38.

25. Doug Matacio, "Centripetal and 'Centrifugal' Mission: Solomon and Jesus," *Journal of Adventist Mission Studies* 4, no. 1 (2008): 31–42.

churches focused on missions.[26] In the postmodern period, churches are generally becoming centripetal and modality-focused. These are the global changes of declining missional emphasis which are prevalent in the world of Christianity today. In these modern times, churches need a balance of good structure and to be intentionally missional focused in the midst of diversified emphases, and to mobilize a more holistic approach in missions and evangelism, particularly in reaching out and impacting the community. Despite a different understanding of the "last days" and a different eschatological fervour from the formative period, the Pentecostal missionary emphasis is not diminished. There are new missional methods, approaches, perspectives, ideas, strategies, and specific roles that better suit the changing times and generations, as well as the Malaysian sociopolitical context.

Shifts in Mission Ownership

The paradigm shift in missions is mainly the shift in responsibility from Spirit-baptized believers to mission organizations and mission departments of churches, as well as the diversification of the mission field. As a result, the modus operandi of missions has changed drastically and many classical ways of doing missions have been discontinued. There has been less emphasis on the missional purpose of BHS but more emphasis on spiritual gifts and the edification of believers, which has impacted individual zeal and passion for missions as compared with the earlier decades, when the teachings on BHS were consistent and there was strong emphasis on empowerment for life and service, especially for witness and missions.

As global missiology advances and evolves, the "specialized" role of missions and evangelism has been taken over by mission organizations and agencies, such as Operation Mobilisation, Youth With A Mission, Interserve, OMF International, and many others. Church souvenir books over the decades show there are designated missions departments and missionaries in local churches, hence the responsibility for missions, evangelism, and witness has shifted in Malaysian churches. Local-church-initiated mission operations have been noticed in the West for some time, especially by megachurches. Churches are also networking and partnering with mission organizations, and more

---

26. Ralph D. Winter, "The Two Structures of God's Redemptive Mission," ch. 35 in *Perspectives on the World Christian Movement: A Reader*, eds. Ralph D. Winter and Steven C. Hawthorne, 3rd ed. (Pasadena: William Carey Library, 1999), 220–30; first given as an address to the All-Asia Mission Consultation in Seoul, Korea, in August 1973 (at the Asia Mission Association's founding).

church members' participation in missions is through prayer support and mission giving.

Contemporary Missional Approach

The development of the contemporary missional approach involves a broadening mission perspective and diversification of the mission field towards holistic missions and more social concern ministries and the reconceptualization of Christian service. Malaysian Christians have been responding and adapting with innovative missional developments. This is very significant in the context of the changes in AGM's missiological stance over the historical period.

Holistic Missions and Social Concern Ministry

There has been a shift in missionary fervour from the classical Pentecostal approaches of "door-to-door evangelism," "tracting," and "open-air meetings," to contemporary mission approaches of churches organizing short-term mission trips for members' participation and evangelism programmes such as the Alpha Course for pre-believers, as well as encouraging more friendship evangelism. Besides this, a more interesting shift in missional approach is from the previous model of only church planting and evangelism, to now also engaging with the socio-economic context and integral mission.[27]

AGM's missions have been moving beyond evangelism and church expansion into social concern ministry, which Wonsuk Ma calls "mercy ministry,"[28] such as caring for the poor and needy, the marginalized, and the suffering, and touching the real world outside the four walls of the church. Since the 1990s, there has been a shift in understanding the need to diversify missions and social concern ministry as the times change. The AGM National Department now has a Social Concern Department with a broadening and diversification of missions and social concern ministries, many of which are new frontiers. In general, people are becoming more aware of social concern ministries and the needs of the community today.

Churches are also shifting their approaches and methodologies of missions and evangelism by organizing more mission trips and encouraging members to engage in personal evangelism.[29] There have been more local outreaches to

---

27. Collective interview data.
28. Wonsuk Ma, "Theological Motivations," 26.
29. Collective interview data.

Orang Asli (native) settlements, social concern ministries, community services, and partnerships with mission organizations in financial support for missionaries and mission work. At the time of writing there are at least thirty-seven organized and registered social concern works in AGM, mainly homes for orphans and underprivileged children, youth, and elderly men and women, day care for the elderly, homes for homeless and destitute women, homes for unwed mothers with unplanned pregnancies, homes for delinquent children, dialysis centres, rehabilitation centres for drug addicts, gamblers, and alcoholics, community centres, food banks, e-learning tuition, tuition centres for marginalized communities, learning centres for refugee children, training of persons with learning disabilities, and home-schooling for children with learning disabilities.[30] These social concern works are greatly impacting the community with God's love, the gospel, and a message of hope in the contemporary world. There are many more missions, outreaches, and community services done by churches on a smaller scale within the governance of the churches.[31]

Since the slowdown in AGM's local church planting endeavours in the 1990s, there has been an expansion in overseas missions including church planting and outreaches. For example, Calvary Church started Westside Pentecostal Church, a daughter church in Canada, in 1991, as well as Calvary Family AG in Medan and Parapat, Indonesia, in 1994 and 1995 respectively; in Nairobi, Kenya, in 2000; and Yei, Sudan, in 2006.[32] Bigger churches have continued to plant and support other churches and outreaches locally and abroad from the 1990s to the present. Metro Tabernacle established mission partnerships with and support for churches and ministries in Thailand, Indonesia, Vietnam, Romania, the Philippines, Bangladesh, Sudan, China, and so on.[33] Since the 1990s there has been a shift in focus to foreign mission trips, such as Glad Tiding's mission teams to nine nations including the Philippines, Thailand, Cambodia, China, and India.[34] There are churches that have been going strong in missions during the movement's growth period amid expansion and diversification. Ongoing missions, church planting, outreaches, and com-

---

30. Social Concern Works, Assemblies of God Malaysia Directory 2018–2020, 151–59 (archive material).

31. Glad Tidings Assembly of God, *Celebrating 50 Years of God's Empowering 1963–2013: A Jubilee and Dedication Celebration*, souvenir magazine (2013), 66 (archive material).

32. Calvary Church (Assembly of God Kuala Lumpur), "Calvary Church 40th Anniversary," souvenir book (2008), 50, 56 (archive material).

33. Metro Tabernacle, "30th Anniversary 1982–2012: Rejoice and Celebrate God's Favour in These Remarkable 30 Years," *Connect*, Special Edition (August 2012), 4 (archive material).

34. Glad Tidings Assembly of God, *Celebrating 50 Years*, 58, 72 (archive material).

munity service remain the main focus of some big churches, such as Calvary, Glad Tidings, Metro Tabernacle, and Agape Community Church.

The exploration of missions into new frontiers in social concern ministries and reaching out to the communities goes in tandem with the changes in global Pentecostal missions expanding in "social engagement," following the evangelicals' response to the Lausanne Conference in 1974. Julie Ma remarks, "The most visible turning point is the adoption of the Lausanne Covenant, which declares proclamation and social service as 'partners' of mission." The waning eschatological urgency in missions with a new hermeneutical understanding of "the last days" has prompted Pentecostals to follow the evangelicals in their missional change to include the "social dimension," such as "poverty, social injustice, children at risk, disaster relief and others."[35] A few AGM churches started social concern work in the pioneering years, mainly drug rehabilitation centres and homes for orphans and underprivileged children. Awareness of holistic missions, social issues, and engagement in new frontiers has been a gradual process over the decades as Malaysian churches have become more active in reaching out to society and taking part in nation-building in contemporary times. One possible and strong evidence may be the attitude of pastors towards Pentecostal mission.

Reconceptualization of Christian Service and Missional Approach

In the growing business and corporate world, there is also a new area of "marketplace ministry" led by Christians who have professional careers, businesses, or corporate vocations, and witness to Christ in their workplaces.[36] This is a current trend in Malaysia. Church members are exposed to the more popular response to God's call by professionals and laity serving God in "marketplace

---

35. Julie C. Ma, "A Pentecostal Perspective: Challenges, Contributions and Commitment of Pentecostals in Missionary Work among Other Faiths," in *Witnessing to Christ in a Pluralistic World: Christian Mission among Other Faiths*, eds. Lalsangkima Pachuau and Knud Jørgensen, Regnum Edinburgh 2010 Series (Oxford: Regnum, 2011), 81.

36. Rev. Dr. Amos Yong, Mr. Sreedhar Subramaniam, and Rev. Sophia Tan, "Pentecostal in the Market Place," BCM Public Seminar, 15–17 July 2013 (archive material); Rev. Paulus Wong Too Tiang, "Anointed Marketplace Leadership," Chinese Language Division Supervisor Report, 2nd Chinese Language Division, Young Adult Starlife Camp, 16–19 July 2015; Rev. Joeann Chong and Zac Gou Hao Zheng, "Together Encounter God, Empower the Church, Enforce the Kingdom, Encourage One Another," AG Biennial Report 2014–2016, 30 May – 2 June 2016 (archive material).

ministry"[37] without the sacred-secular divide. There are many opportunities to serve God without having to be attached to a church as a "full-time" clergy member or worker.

The reconceptualization of Christian service and missional approach in contemporary times has directly impacted theological education. This is evident in the demographics of the student body and the adaptations of the Bible College of Malaysia (BCM) in the twenty-first century. Registration records show that there is an increasing number in the enrolment of non-full-time students alongside a drastic reduction in the number of full-time students who have a calling as full-time pastors. The average number of full-time students in the past eight years has decreased from more than forty to around twelve in 2023, whereas the number of non-full-time students, many of whom are lay leaders, has tripled to more than 700 currently.[38] Although AGM places top priority on providing credentials to ministers with a conventional full-time calling, BCM has been designing and offering new programmes and courses that are well suited for equipping lay leaders, particularly counselling and leadership which are needed in churches and the marketplace.

Other Bible colleges have also been upgrading and improving their theological training programmes to meet the needs of the altered spiritual dynamics. Davina Soh recently undertook a case study on "Fostering Vocation" at ACTS College, AG Bible College in Singapore, which shows a similar trend in the change in the conventional understanding of full-time calling to the wide spectrum of vocation as Christian service in the world. The meaning of "vocation" has been redefined, and nowadays Christians believe that they are called to serve anywhere in the marketplace, industries, and other arenas in society, with service no longer confined to full-time pastors and church workers. As such, the role of Bible schools or theological education has advanced from training pastors and missionaries to "equipping the saints" or lay leaders for any kind of service unto the Lord.[39]

In the twenty-first century, more focus is given to "equipping the saints" with knowledge and diversified ministry skillsets and vocations in the marketplace.

---

37. Rev. Stephen Ong, "Pentecostal Movement," Bible College of Malaysia chapel service sermon on the Chinese Pentecostal movement in Malaysia and marketplace missions, 14 February 2019. Ong is a pastor of First Assembly of God Church, Kuala Lumpur, Malaysia (archive material).

38. Bible College of Malaysia, student information report, 2015–23.

39. Soh Hui Leng Davina, "Fostering Vocation in the Here and Now: A Case Study," *Pentecostal Education: A Journal of the World Alliance for Pentecostal Theological Education* 5, nos. 1–2 (2020): 33–43.

Malaysian Social Influences

Malaysian social influences, especially the majority Muslim setting and the multi-ethnic, multireligious environment, are crucial in shaping the religious landscape of the country. Along with other faiths in the minority group, Christianity by and large exists with many restrictions governed by federal and state laws, policies, and regulations. The Malays' strong nationalistic fervour in Malaysianization, Islamic revivalism, and Islamization create political, religious, and racial sensitivity in the nation, and limit the way Malaysian churches function in worship, practice, evangelism, and missions.[40] Muzaffar defines Islamic resurgence as "the endeavour to re-establish Islamic values, Islamic practices, Islamic institutions, Islamic laws, indeed Islam in its entirety, in the lives of Muslims everywhere."[41] Islam is the national religion, as stated in the Independence Constitution of 1957, and the "religion of the federation," according to the Federal Constitution of 1963. The constitution allows freedom of religion with specified limitations (Articles 3 and 11). All Malays are Muslim (Article 160 [2]), and propagation of any religion among Muslims may be controlled and restricted by state law (Article 11, clause 4).

The global Islamic resurgence and revival has taken place actively in Malaysia since 1970 and there has been increasing Islamic nationalism implemented by the government. The process of Islamization has been integrated nationwide into politics, government administration systems, the judiciary, state law, banking, insurance, the economy, education, social media, and society as a whole.[42] There has been an erosion of religious freedom and there are growing tensions due to the increasing restrictions by laws and policies.[43] In 1987, more than a hundred "radicals," including NGO activists, politicians, media reporters, and artists, were detained for two years without trial under the Internal Security Act (ISA) to defuse racial and political tensions. Although the ISA was repealed, the

---

40. Collective interview data. See also Salbiah Ahmad, *Critical Thoughts on Islam, Rights, and Freedom in Malaysia* (Petaling Jaya: Strategic Information and Research Development Centre, 2007); Chandra Muzaffar, *Islamic Resurgence in Malaysia* (Petaling Jaya: Fajar Bakti, 1987); and Robert Day McAmis, *Malay Muslims: The History and Challenge of Resurgent Islam in Southeast Asia* (Grand Rapids: Eerdmans, 2002), 50–51, 79–90, and 115–17.

41. Muzaffar, *Islamic Resurgence*, 2.

42. Sadayandy Batumalai, *Islamic Resurgence and Islamization in Malaysia: A Malaysian Christian Response* (Ipoh: St. John's Church, 1996), 11–12, 39, 42–44, 57–58, 66, 81, 93, 135–39, 240–48, 259–72.

43. Batumalai, *Islamic Resurgence*, 42–44, 125, 137–39, 238, 259–72.

implications of the *Operasi Lalang* (weeding operation) have shaped Malaysia over the following decades.[44]

The Islamization agenda is also reflected in many other laws and the implementation of Islamic law in several Malay states.[45] The respective agendas of political and religious parties have led the Islamization in pursuit of an "Islamic state," although the constitution defines Malaysia as a secular state.[46] The whole nation is constantly being impacted by political struggles and conflict.[47] While there are increasing restrictions and prohibitions imposed by federal and state laws and regulations, the impingement of religious freedom and rights for the minority intensifies with religious extremism and politicization of religion.[48] Social issues and religious frictions have affected the whole Christian population and the multifaith community in the country.[49] This has impacted and shaped the mission approaches of churches over the decades.

Towards Public Witness and Nation-Building in the Twenty-First Century

Missions approaches have evolved greatly over the decades, impacted by both major internal and external factors in the local contexts. The Malaysian social influences noted above are also crucial in shaping the Malaysian church and

---

44. Anne Dorall, "What Happened with Ops Lalang 33 Years Ago?," *The Rakyat Post*, 27 October 2020, https://www.therakyatpost.com/living/2020/10/27/what-happened-with-ops-lalang-33-years-ago/.

45. Andrew Khoo, "Freedom of Religion and Extremism," in *Christians and Nation-Building in a Pluralistic Society*, eds. Hwa Yung and Helen Ting (Petaling Jaya: Strategic Information and Research Development Centre [SIRD], 2021), 117–22; Batumalai, *Islamic Resurgence*, 62–67.

46. Batumalai, 64, 88–89.

47. Muzaffar, *Islamic Resurgence*, 67–97.

48. Batumalai, *Islamic Resurgence*, 137; Lee Min Choon, "The State of Religious Liberty, 2002–2004," in *The Realities of Christian Living in Malaysia*, eds. Steven Wong, Siew Foong Lim, and Kim Kong Wong (Petaling Jaya: NECF Malaysia Research Commission, 2004), 105; Stephen Ng, "Mais and AG [Attorney General], Stop Pussyfooting Around," MalaysiaKini, 24 April 2014, https://www.malaysiakini.com/letters/260897; BBC News Online, "Malaysia's High Court Rules Christians Can Use 'Allah,'" 11 March 2021, https://www.bbc.com/news/world-asia-56356212; Umair Jamal, "Allah Row in Malaysia Is Settled for Now but Far from Over," *ASEAN Today*, 25 March 2021; Amnesty International, "Malaysia Must End Ban on Christians Saying 'Allah,'" 24 June 2014, https://www.amnesty.org/en/latest/news/2014/06/malaysia-must-end-ban-christians-saying-allah/.

49. Malay Mail, "Silence over Missing Activists 'Disconcerting,' Says Malaysian Bar," 11 April 2017, https://www.malaymail.com/news/malaysia/2017/04/11/silence-over-missing-activists-disconcerting-says-malaysian-bar/1353911; see Khoo, "Freedom of Religion," 119.

its integral missional engagement through public witness and nation-building towards greater unity in the twenty-first century.

Christian Response Towards Harmony and Unity

Living within these constraints and the government policy on Malaysianization and Islamization, Malaysian Christians have been responding and adapting with innovative missional developments: the establishment of seminaries to raise up local church leaders and workers, the Bible Society of Malaysia to print Bibles, and the formation of an ecumenical Christian federation among churches in 1985 which fostered unity among the many denominations and independent churches.[50] Churches and Christian organizations are engaging more in doing good works, charitable endeavours, and social concern ministries in the community. At the same time, there has been an increase in united interdenominational prayer networks among the evangelicals, mainline church traditions, Pentecostals, and charismatic churches under the National Evangelical Christian Fellowship, Council Churches of Malaysia, and Christian Federation of Malaysia. There has been a growth in prayer movements, mainly among Pentecostal and charismatic churches, to pray for the many issues of the nation as never before.

In this multiethnic and multireligious environment, there have been efforts to forge greater unity, peace, and harmony ever since the race riots of 13 May 1969. Over the years, various religious organizations and universities have organized interfaith dialogues, seminars, and forums to bridge the differences in the plural society. In 1983, the Malaysian Consultative Council of Buddhism, Christianity, Hinduism, Sikhism and Taoism (MCCBCHST) was established to promote harmony and cooperation to address matters pertaining to religion.[51] These are efforts to build networks and understanding among different faiths.

---

50. Batumalai, *Islamic Resurgence*, 125.

51. Kiok Nam Ng, "Islam in Malaysia," in *Islam in Asia: Perspectives for Christian-Muslim Encounter; Report of a Consultation Sponsored by the Lutheran World Federation and the World Alliance of Reformed Churches*, eds. J. Paul Rajashekar and Henry S. Wilson (Geneva: Lutheran World Federation, 1992), 97–104; Batumalai, *Islamic Resurgence*, 137, 145–47; Jin Huat Tan, "Towards a Spirited Apologetics," in *The Realities of Christian Living in Malaysia*, eds. Steven Wong, Siew Foong Lim, and Kim Kong Wong, 118–27 (Petaling Jaya: NECF Malaysia Research Commission, 2004), 118 and 124–27; see also "Malaysian Consultative Council of Buddhism, Christianity, Hinduism, Sikhism and Taoism (MCCBCHST)," HATI (n.d.), https://www.hati.my/malaysian-consultative-council-of-buddhism-christianity-hinduism-sikhism-and-taoism-mccbchst/.

Over the decades, these social influences and challenges have created political, religious, and racial sensitivity in the pluralistic society. The religious diversity in Malaysia restricts and shapes the Malaysian church and AGM's missional engagement. These factors impact AGM as a minority within a minority and shape contextual Malaysian Pentecostalism. Anderson remarks, "Contextualization not only takes into account cultural values, but also tries to make the gospel relevant to the current situation of social change and new economic and political contexts."[52] Looking forward, the Catholic Research Centre, Graduates Christian Fellowship, and Kairos Dialogue Network collectively urge all Christians to engage in nation-building and sociopolitical responsibilities to build "a better Malaysia for all."[53] These sociocultural and sociopolitical influences shape contextual Malaysian Pentecostalism to be different from Pentecostalism in other global contexts.

Holistic and Integral Missions

In its formative and pioneering period, AGM was very strong in missions, particularly church planting, door-to-door evangelism, healing rallies, evangelistic rallies, revival meetings, and so on. In the movement's growth period, there has been much diversification, involving new frontiers in missions, moving into more social concern ministries for sociopolitical reasons, and new ideas around missions. Holistic and integral missions are the way forward.

Chan Nam Chen, Executive Director of Asia Collaborative Mission Services (AsiaCMS), emphasizes, "Christian mission is always about faithfulness to the context." Serving the changing contexts requires the addressing of needs, relevance, adaptation, and retooling.[54] He affirms:

> Christian mission should always be holistic and integrated. We cannot separate the spiritual from the physical and psycho-social dimensions of life. The preaching of the gospel cannot be divorced from the totality of what individuals and communities go through. When communities and families are suddenly in forced situations of hunger, we need to provide food and basic needs. When pro-

---

52. Anderson, *Introduction to Pentecostalism*, 195.

53. Hwa Yung and Helen Ting, "Preface," in *Christians and Nation-Building*, xii.

54. Chan Nam Chen, "What Did Not Change and Should Not Change in a Changed Covid-19 World," *AsiaCMS REACH* (2021): 2. Rev. Dr. Chan Nam Chen, Executive Director of Asia Collaborative Mission Services (AsiaCMS) and AGM pioneer, specializes in intercultural missions. AsiaCMS is associated with Church Mission Society, UK, and Global CMS.

longed lockdowns, joblessness and forced changes lead to emotional breakdowns and domestic conflicts, we need to provide resources to help people cope with depression and build psychosocial health.[55]

There has been a shift in missionary motivation and emphases: from the classical emphasis based on eschatological fervour and missionary endeavours, to the contemporary emphases of diversification. Chan explains:

> Contemporary Pentecostalism in Malaysia means that we shift from a narrower perspective to a broader perspective of God's mission. We shift from the old perspective of American roots and evangelicalism on the separation between the spiritual and "the non-spiritual" or secular, and the whole emphasis on merely church planting and evangelism, to now engaging with the socio-economic. "Contemporary" also means having a more accurate understanding of what mission is all about, based on a more holistic and biblical perspective of mission. The core of contemporary Pentecostalism is the empowering of the Holy Spirit for the cause of mission. While maintaining our earlier strength in evangelism and church planting, we also need to understand missions from a more holistic perspective in the sense of integral mission.[56]

This is in line with the global trends of missions. Wonsuk Ma, in his study on "The Theological Motivations for Pentecostal Mission," concludes:

> Classical Pentecostals have the most theological and institutional resources. In non-western lands, they look radically different from their North American or European "mothers," who are not necessarily growing. This is a serious challenge to their century-old theology and constantly institutionalizing ethos. Yet they may also empower the rest of the Pentecostal-charismatic churches. Together they should continue their engagement in new frontiers of mission because to remain faithful to the scriptures, to Pentecostal spiritual heritage, and yet be relevant to the immediate context will pose a significant challenge to emerging Pentecostal mission communities throughout the world.[57]

---

55. Chan, "What Did Not Change," 2–3.
56. Interview with Chan.
57. Wonsuk Ma, "Theological Motivations," 39.

In contemporary times, AGM is still passionate about missions and moving to new frontiers and arenas, and new approaches to preaching the gospel. In a personal interview, Chan provided invaluable missional insights into moving into holistic and integral missions in this twenty-first century.

First, churches ought to be contemporary, using digital platforms for missions (certainly crucial during the COVID-19 pandemic and post-pandemic).[58] In *AsiaCMS REACH*, stressing that "Christians can live out the global unity that we have in Christ," he testifies,

> The wonders of the internet, and the apps that go with it, have allowed us to find out about each other, connect, build relationships, collaborate on projects, and share resources. We are positioned to bridge the gaps; not merely to help each other, but to better serve our world together. This was powerfully lived out . . . at the peak of the Covid-19 crisis.[59]

Second, churches should actively impact the larger community in relating to the government and business sectors and being a responsible part of the nation and even global citizens.[60] Third, the church should be involved in the alleviation of poverty of underprivileged communities by mobilizing business and social entrepreneurs:

> Integral mission today is the understanding that missions, evangelism, and church planting are very much connected with all of life and we are living in a pluralistic society. The mission goes beyond proclamation, with much sensitivity in understanding the people of other faiths, work, beliefs, and practices. We are living in a world where there is an increasing gap between the rich and the poor, and we do recognise that the eradication of poverty or helping or assisting people in the journey of human flourishing requires an understanding of mission that is more than just evangelism and church planting. This brings in an entirely new paradigm, requiring fresh skill sets, different types of vocation and expertise in different fields, yet we are Pentecostal, we stress the infusion and the work of the Holy Spirit which in the past has been regarded as secular. . . . We are also seeing the mobilisation of business and social entrepreneurs who help the underprivileged communities.

---

58. Interview with Chan.
59. Chan, "What Did Not Change," 3.
60. Interview with Chan.

These are examples of integral missions and Pentecostal empowerment in these areas.[61]

Fourth, moving from micro engagement to the broader picture of macro involvement needs to be thought through. Fifth, the church needs to get the gospel to the unreached people groups where there are pockets of unbelievers, beyond the socio-ethnic boundaries. For example, Malaysia has become a vast harvest field due to the influx of six million immigrants/migrant workers from other nations. Sixth, ultimately the emphasis should be on the Pentecostal heritage of missions and the purpose of BHS as empowerment for missions (Acts 1:8; 2). Chan stresses, "Missions is the call of the Pentecostal heritage, and the baptism of the Holy Spirit is the engine behind it."[62]

Some churches have been reaching out to society as "salt and light." Some recent examples are the following: Agape Community Church has organized missional efforts in impacting the community, engaging in community services, and building relationships with the society in the city and vicinity, such as the "Love Seremban Charity Carnival" in 2017, the "Community Care Initiative," providing a mobile clinic to small towns, the "Community Food Tree," providing food for the poor, and the "Tuition Centre" for children in need in 2018. In 2020, the church initiated the "Agape Care Package" in response to and relief of families during the COVID-19 lockdown, and a crisis response to flood victims in residential areas. Metro Tabernacle A/G and Glad Tidings Sunway, along with many other churches, set up food banks and supplied food packages and groceries to the needy during the extended COVID-19 lockdown in July 2021. The *Orang Asli* (native) ministry is one which some AGM churches have been involved in for a few decades, for example in helping them with settlement, agriculture, and resources. More AGM churches have been moving in this missional direction to impact society.[63]

Believers need the power of the Holy Spirit to preach the gospel and advance towards integral or holistic missions, embracing both evangelism and social responsibility. Every church needs to be a missional church to reach out to the society in practical ways. Wong Young Soon encourages Malaysian Christians to join in building compassionate communities and organize com-

---

61. Interview with Chan.
62. Interview with Chan.
63. E.g. Agape Community Church (https://www.facebook.com/agapegospelassembly); Rev. Paulus Wong shared about the "Love Seremban" initiatives in a BCM chapel service on 29 August 2019; Metro Tabernacle Assembly of God (https://en-gb.facebook.com/metrotab); Glad Tidings Sunway (https://www.facebook.com/gtsunway1).

passionate services in charity, development, and advocacy for the voiceless. Churches need to invest funds in equipping God's people in "social work, community development, rural or urban development, counselling, healthcare, education and early childhood education, and special needs education."[64] Mercy ministry means doing practical missions where the need is: to help the poor, feed the hungry, reach out to the marginalized and the suffering, and care for and protect the weak and vulnerable.

Marketplace Ministries and Nation-Building

The new areas of missions are marketplace ministries and nation-building. Chan also states, "In the last two elections in Malaysia, some Pentecostal Christians were getting involved as lobby groups, pressure groups, and even directly in politics as part of their calling. In the past, Pentecostals would just pray."[65] Hwa Yung encourages more Christian involvement in nation-building and calls Christians to be the "salt of the earth" and "light of the world" (Matt 5:13–14) in this pluralistic society and to be a blessing to the nation. He urges, "If the Christian community is to truly live with holiness and with integrity, take a clear stand for compassion, justice and social righteousness, and strive to be agents of reconciliation amid all the ethnic, religious and sociopolitical divisions, we can indeed become God's instrument of transformation for this nation."[66]

Call for Collaboration

The modern development of missions has encouraged diversification of the mission field towards more holistic mission and social concern ministry for sociopolitical reasons and because of new ideas regarding missions. There are shifts in and diversification of missional methods and approaches from the previous homogeneity of church planting, healing crusades, and door-to-door evangelism, to more social concern ministries and partnerships with mission organizations, overseas missions, and parachurch organizations in contem-

---

64. Wong Young Soon, "The Role of Christians in Building Compassionate Communities," in Yung and Ting, *Christians and Nation-Building*, 93–95.

65. Interview with Chan.

66. Hwa Yung, "The Church as a Blessing to the Nations," in Yung and Ting, *Christians and Nation-Building*, 1, 7, and 8.

porary times. Social influences alongside the missiological factors have been reshaping Christian missions in the country.

The core elements of contemporary Pentecostal missions are the relevance of the gospel to the community and younger generations without compromising the full gospel. It is only with the right Pentecostal spirituality that believers are filled with zeal and passion for missions, in the same way as the Spirit led many AGM pioneers in missions and church growth. Land highlights that "Pentecostal spirituality as missionary fellowship" in having "a passion for the kingdom" is ignited through BHS and glossolalia, relationship with God, and praying in the Spirit, but the heart of it is love.[67] Although AGM has been actively involved in both local and overseas missions, I suggest that an even wider vision of ecumenism in faith and mission collaborations in the international arena is instrumental in order for AGM in this twenty-first century to be impactful in the nations. AGM should have a larger vision and concertedly work towards fulfilling the common call of world Christianity, particularly "The Edinburgh 2010 Common Call" that emerged from the centenary of the World Missionary Conference.[68] Ultimately, I urge that churches unite in sharing a common missionary vision and resources (workers, finances, strategies, networks, etc.) to advance the gospel and holistic missions in the nation, and to fulfil the Great Commission. There will be powerful synergy in the interdenominational unity of the church in sharing resources for the gospel and missions.

Bible colleges play a significant role in preparing lives for ministry and "missions." Contemporary theological education should refocus on preparing lives not just for ministries, but for holistic missions with new approaches. Missions were the original and primary focus during the AGM's formative and pioneering period, with many missionaries, evangelists, church planters, and ministers being trained. Amos Yong suggests, "A theological education that serves the church ought to facilitate participation in this divine mission . . . the missiological and the pentecostal go together." Referring to Acts 1:8 and Joel 2 / Acts 2 on the outpouring of the Spirit "upon all flesh," he states that Pentecost and the "Pentecost vision for theological education" is for the "church catholic (universal and ecumenical)."[69] Indeed, AGM, as Pentecostals, and its

---

67. Land, *Pentecostal Spirituality*, 163–75.

68. "Common Call," in Lee and Ma, *Pentecostal Mission*, xiii–xiv.

69. Amos Yong, "Theological Education between the West and the 'Rest': A Reverse 'Reverse Missionary' and Pentecost Perspective," *Asian Journal of Pentecostal Studies* 24, no. 1 (2021): 27–29.

Bible colleges should always prioritize Spirit-empowered missions, especially for current and future generations, and even expand the "Pentecost vision" to the larger body of Christ through theological education and have an interdenominational united vision for missions. There is synergy in an ecumenical collaboration in holistic and integral missions in building the nation together.

Bibliography

Abeysekera, Fred G. *The History of the Assemblies of God in Singapore, 1928–1992*. Singapore: Abundant Press, 1992.

Ahmad, Salbiah. *Critical Thoughts on Islam, Rights, and Freedom in Malaysia*. Petaling Jaya: Strategic Information and Research Development Centre, 2007.

Amnesty International. "Malaysia Must End Ban on Christians Saying 'Allah.'" 24 June 2014. https://www.amnesty.org/en/latest/news/2014/06/malaysia-must-end-ban-christians-saying-allah/.

Anderson, Allan Heaton. "The Emergence of a Multidimensional Global Missionary Movement: A Historical Review." In *Pentecostal Mission and Global Christianity*, edited by Wonsuk Ma, Veli-Matti Kärkkäinen, and J. Kwabena Asamoah-Gyadu, 10–25. Regnum Edinburgh Centenary Series 20. Oxford: Regnum, 2014.

———. *An Introduction to Pentecostalism: Global Charismatic Christianity*. 2nd ed. Cambridge: Cambridge University Press, 2014.

Anderson, Allan, and Edmond Tang, eds. *Asian and Pentecostal: The Charismatic Face of Christianity in Asia*. 2nd ed. Regnum Studies in Mission. Oxford: Regnum, 2011.

Austin, Denise A., Jacqueline Grey, and Paul W. Lewis, eds. *Asia Pacific Pentecostalism*. Global Pentecostal and Charismatic Studies 31. Leiden: Brill, 2019.

Batumalai, Sadayandy. *Islamic Resurgence and Islamization in Malaysia: A Malaysian Christian Response*. Ipoh: St. John's Church, 1996.

BBC News Online. "Malaysia's High Court Rules Christians Can Use 'Allah.'" 11 March 2021. https://www.bbc.com/news/world-asia-56356212.

Bible College of Malaysia. Student information report, 2015–23.

Bible Institute of Malaya Report. "Malaysia, Missionary Force Depleting Due to the Strict Regulations Imposed by the Malaysian Government upon Missionary Visas, and Local Leadership is Much Needed in This Country." May 1981. Archive material.

Bulan, Solomon, and Lillian Bulan-Dorai. *The Bario Revival*. Kuala Lumpur: Home-Matters Network, 2012.

Calvary Church (Assembly of God Kuala Lumpur). "Calvary Church 40th Anniversary." Souvenir book. 2008. Archive material.

Chan, Kok Eng. "A Brief Note on Church Growth in Malaysia, 1960–1985." In *Christianity in Malaysia: A Denominational History*, edited by Robert A. Hunt, Lee Kam Hing, and John Roxborough, 354–78. Petaling Jaya: Pelanduk, 1992.

Chan Nam Chen. "What Did Not Change and Should Change in a Changed Covid-19 World." *AsiaCMS REACH* (2021): 1–3. https://www.asiacms.net/wp-content/uploads/2021/09/AsiaCMS-REACH-2021-HighRes.pdf.

Chong, Joeann, and Zac Gou Hao Zheng. "Together Encounter God, Empower the Church, Enforce the Kingdom, Encourage One Another." AG Biennial Report 2014–2016. 30 May – 2 June 2016. Archive material.

Choo, Christopher. *The Ba Kelalan Revival of East Malaysia*. Petaling Jaya: El Shaddai, 1994.

"Common Call." In *Pentecostal Mission and Global Christianity: An Edinburgh Centenary Reader*, edited by Younghoon Lee and Wonsuk Ma, with Kuewon Lee, xiii–xiv. Regnum Studies in Mission. Oxford: Regnum, 2018.

Dorall, Anne. "What Happened with Ops Lalang 33 Years Ago?" *The Rakyat Post*. 27 October 2020. https://www.therakyatpost.com/living/2020/10/27/what-happened-with-ops-lalang-33-years-ago/.

Engcoy, Dynnice Rosanny D. *Pentecostal Pioneer: The Life and Legacy of Rudy Esperanza in the Early Years of the Assemblies of God in the Philippines*. Pentecostalism around the World 4. Baguio: APTS, 2014.

Faupel, David W. *The Everlasting Gospel: The Significance of Eschatology in the Development of Pentecostal Thought*. Journal of Pentecostal Theology Supplement Series 10. Sheffield: Sheffield Academic, 1996.

Glad Tidings Assembly of God. *Celebrating 50 Years of God's Empowering 1963–2013: A Jubilee and Dedication Celebration*. Souvenir magazine, 2013. Archive material.

Hunter, Harold, and Cecil M. Robeck Jr. "Introduction." In *The Azusa Street Revival and Its Legacy*, edited by Harold Hunter and Cecil M. Robeck, 13–26. Cleveland: Pathway, 2006. Reprint: Eugene: Wipf & Stock, 2009.

Jamal, Umair. "Allah Row in Malaysia Is Settled for Now but Far from Over." *ASEAN Today*, 25 March 2021.

Johnson, Dave. *Theology in Context: A Case Study in the Philippines*. Baguio: APTS, 2012.

Kärkkäinen, Veli-Matti. "The Pentecostal Understanding of Mission." In *Pentecostal Mission and Global Christianity*, edited by Wonsuk Ma, Veli-Matti Kärkkäinen, and J. Kwabena Asamoah-Gyadu, 26–44. Regnum Edinburgh Centenary Series 20. Oxford: Regnum, 2014.

Khai, Chin Kua. *The Cross among Pagodas: A History of the Assemblies of God in Myanmar*. Baguio: APTS, 2003.

Khoo, Andrew. "Freedom of Religion and Extremism." In *Christians and Nation-Building in a Pluralistic Society*, edited by Hwa Yung and Helen Ting, 109–25. Petaling Jaya: Strategic Information and Research Development Centre (SIRD), 2021.

Land, Steven Jack. *Pentecostal Spirituality: A Passion for the Kingdom*. Journal of Pentecostal Theology Supplement Series 1. Sheffield: Sheffield Academic, 1993. Reprint: Cleveland: CPT, 2010.

Law, Jason. "The Bario Revival: Its Background Context and Beginnings." Christianity Malaysia. 17 July 2015. http://christianitymalaysia.com/wp/the-bario-revival-its-background-context-and-beginnings/.

Lee Min Choon. "The State of Religious Liberty, 2002–2004." In *The Realities of Christian Living in Malaysia*, edited by Steven Wong, Siew Foong Lim, and Kim Kong Wong, 100–107. Petaling Jaya: NECF Malaysia Research Commission, 2004.

Lovelace, Joshua J. *From Seedtime to Harvest: The History of the Assemblies of God in Cambodia*. Pentecost around the World 5. Baguio: APTS, 2019.

Ma, Julie C. "Pentecostal Evangelism, Church Planting, and Church Growth." In *Pentecostal Mission and Global Christianity*, edited by Wonsuk Ma, Veli-Matti Kärkkäinen, and J. Kwabena Asamoah-Gyadu, 87–106. Regnum Edinburgh Centenary Series 20. Oxford: Regnum, 2014.

———. "A Pentecostal Perspective: Challenges, Contributions and Commitment of Pentecostals in Missionary Work among Other Faiths." In *Witnessing to Christ in a Pluralistic World: Christian Mission among Other Faiths*, edited by Lalsangkima Pachuau and Knud Jørgensen, 79–89. Regnum Edinburgh 2010 Series. Oxford: Regnum, 2011.

Ma, Wonsuk. "Asian (Classical) Pentecostal Theology in Context." In *Asian and Pentecostal: The Charismatic Face of Christianity in Asia*, edited by Allan Anderson and Edmond Tang, 59–91. Regnum Studies in Mission / Asian Journal of Pentecostal Studies Series 3. Baguio: APTS, 2005.

———. "The Holy Spirit in Pentecostal Mission: The Shaping of Mission Awareness and Practice." *International Bulletin of Mission Research* 41, no. 3 (2017): 227–38. https://doi.org/10.1177/2396939317704757.

———. "Pentecostal Eschatology: What Happened When the Wave Hit the West End of the Ocean." In *The Azusa Street Revival and Its Legacy*, edited by Harold Hunter and Cecil M. Robeck, 227–42. Cleveland: Pathway, 2006. Reprint: Eugene: Wipf & Stock, 2009.

———. "The Theological Motivations for Pentecostal Mission." In *Pentecostal Mission and Global Christianity: An Edinburgh Centenary Reader*, edited by Younghoon Lee and Wonsuk Ma, with Kuewon Lee, 25–39. Regnum Studies in Mission. Oxford: Regnum, 2018.

Macchia, Frank D. "The Struggle for Global Witness: Shifting Paradigms in Pentecostal Theology." In *The Globalization of Pentecostalism: A Religion Made to Travel*, edited by Murray W. Dempster, Byron D. Klaus, and Douglas Petersen, 8–29. Oxford: Regnum, 1999.

MalayMail. "Silence over Missing Activists 'Disconcerting,' Says Malaysian Bar." 11 April 2017. https://www.malaymail.com/news/malaysia/2017/04/11/silence-over-missing-activists-disconcerting-says-malaysian-bar/1353911.

"Malaysian Consultative Council of Buddhism, Christianity, Hinduism, Sikhism and Taoism (MCCBCHST)." HATI. N.d. https://www.hati.my/malaysian-consultative-council-of-buddhism-christianity-hinduism-sikhism-and-taoism-mccbchst/.

Matacio, Doug. "Centripetal and 'Centrifugal' Mission: Solomon and Jesus." *Journal of Adventist Mission Studies* 4, no. 1 (2008): 31–42. https://dx.doi.org/10.32597/jams/vol4/iss1/4/.
McAmis, Robert Day. *Malay Muslims: The History and Challenge of Resurgent Islam in Southeast Asia*. Grand Rapids: Eerdmans, 2002.
McKinney, L. O. "A Glimpse of Malaya." 1943. Archive material.
Menzies, Robert P. *Pentecost: This Story Is Our Story*. Springfield: ACTP, 2013.
Metro Tabernacle. "30th Anniversary 1982–2012: Rejoice and Celebrate God's Favour in These Remarkable 30 Years." *Connect*, Special Edition. August 2012. Archive material.
Muzaffar, Chandra. *Islamic Resurgence in Malaysia*. Petaling Jaya: Fajar Bakti, 1987.
Ng, Kiok Nam, "Islam in Malaysia." In *Islam in Asia: Perspectives for Christian-Muslim Encounter; Report of a Consultation Sponsored by the Lutheran World Federation and the World Alliance of Reformed Churches*, edited by J. Paul Rajashekar and Henry S. Wilson, 97–104. Geneva: Lutheran World Federation, 1992.
Ng, Stephen. "Mais and AG [Attorney General], Stop Pussyfooting Around." MalaysiaKini. 24 April 2014. https://www.malaysiakini.com/letters/260897.
Ong, Stephen. "Pentecostal Movement." Bible College of Malaysia chapel service sermon on the Chinese Pentecostal movement in Malaysia and marketplace missions, 14 February 2019. Archive material.
Pagaialii, Tavita. *Pentecost to the Uttermost: A History of the Assemblies of God in Samoa*. Baguio: APTS, 2006.
Rea, John. "Book of Joel." In *Dictionary of Pentecostal and Charismatic Movements*, edited by Stanley M. Burgess, Gary B. McGee, and Patrick H. Alexander, 493–96. Grand Rapids: Regency Reference Library, 1988.
"Singapore, Malaya." *Global Conquest*. March 1961. *Global Conquest* is published bimonthly by the Assemblies of God Foreign Missions Department, Springfield, MO. Archive material.
Social Concern Works. Assemblies of God Malaysia Directory 2018–2020, 151–59. Archive material.
Soh Hui Leng Davina. "Fostering Vocation in the Here and Now: A Case Study." *Pentecostal Education: A Journal of the World Alliance for Pentecostal Theological Education* 5, nos. 1–2 (2020): 33–43. https://wapte.org/wp-content/uploads/2020/10/pentecostal-edu-vol-5.pdf.
Tan, Jin Huat. *Planting an Indigenous Church: The Case of the Borneo Evangelical Mission*. Regnum Studies in Mission. Oxford: Regnum, 2011.
———. "Towards a Spirited Apologetics." In *The Realities of Christian Living in Malaysia*, edited by Steven Wong, Siew Foong Lim, and Kim Kong Wong, 118–27. Petaling Jaya: NECF Malaysia Research Commission, 2004.
Warren, Rick. *The Purpose Driven Church*. Grand Rapids: Zondervan, 1995.
———. *The Purpose Driven Life*. Grand Rapids: Zondervan, 2002.

Winter, Ralph D. "The Two Structures of God's Redemptive Mission." Chapter 35 in *Perspectives on the World Christian Movement: A Reader*, edited by Ralph D. Winter and Steven C. Hawthorne, 220–30. 3rd ed. Pasadena: William Carey Library, 1999. First published in *Missiology* 2, no. 1 (Jan. 1974): 121–39. https://doi.org/10.1177/009182967400200109.

Wong, Paulus Too Tiang. "Anointed Marketplace Leadership." Chinese Language Division Supervisor Report, 2nd Chinese Language Division. Young Adult Starlife Camp. 16–19 July 2015. Archive material.

Wong Young Soon. "The Role of Christians in Building Compassionate Communities." In *Christians and Nation-Building in a Pluralistic Society*, edited by Hwa Yung and Helen Ting, 85–98. Petaling Jaya: Strategic Information and Research Development (SIRD), 2021.

"Worldwide." *The Pentecostal Evangel* 2786 (1 Oct. 1967): 7.

Yong, Amos. "Theological Education between the West and the 'Rest': A Reverse 'Reverse Missionary' and Pentecost Perspective." *Asian Journal of Pentecostal Studies* 24, no. 1 (2021): 21–37.

Yong, Amos, Sreedhar Subramaniam, and Sophia Tan. "Pentecostal in the Market Place." BCM Public Seminar, 15–17 July 2013. Archive material.

Yung, Hwa. "The Church as a Blessing to the Nations." In *Christians and Nation-Building in a Pluralistic Society*, edited by Hwa Yung and Helen Ting, 1–8. Petaling Jaya: Strategic Information and Research Development (SIRD), 2021.

Yung, Hwa, and Helen Ting. "Preface." In *Christians and Nation-Building in a Pluralistic Society*, edited by Hwa Yung and Helen Ting, xii. Petaling Jaya: Strategic Information and Research Development (SIRD), 2021.

9

Live in Christ, Exist for Others

The Courage and Witness of Dietrich Bonhoeffer in Situations of Rampant Injustice

Eberhardt Ngugi

Lecturer, University of Iringa, Tanzania

Introduction

Today there is a need to urgently address matters of social justice. Dietrich Bonhoeffer's legacy can challenge us as we reflect on situations of rampant injustice. His notion of "existing for others" is found early in his work and is based on his relational theological anthropology: that a human person is a being-in-relation because he or she is made in the image of the triune God. Because the church is Christ existing as community, it must strive for costly grace: it must engage in action and exist for others as Jesus did. Bonhoeffer was moved to take action in the face of injustice, even though he initially experienced no injustice himself. His witness remains a source of inspiration to guide the church as it faces new challenges today. Being a disciple of Christ entails resisting the powers of darkness, whether in the state or the church. The Bible makes social justice a mandate of faith and a fundamental expression of Christian discipleship. Social justice has its biblical roots in a triune God who time and time again shows his love and compassion for the weak, the vulnerable, the marginalized, the disenfranchised, and the disinherited. In Bonhoeffer's day, and still today, the church has been silent when it should have cried out against injustice. It has failed to speak the right word in the right way and at the right time. The Spirit of the living God speaks to us, reminding us of our calling as the church to live prophetically and speak boldly to a world that desperately needs the hope, love, and justice found in the gospel. Bonhoeffer's courage and boldness against the Nazi regime challenges each of us in our own faith to take action in the face of the many injustices in our world today.

Bonhoeffer (1906–45) was born in Germany "into a world of privilege." His parents' home "was frequented" by influential thinkers such as "Ernst Troeltsch, Max Weber, and Alfred Weber." At the age of sixteen, he began to study theology, first at Tübingen and, from 1924, at the University of Berlin. In spite of being surrounded by the liberal theologians of the day, including Adolf von Harnack, Bonhoeffer's own writings were "far from liberal." As a doctoral student, Bonhoeffer worked under Reinhold Seeberg, who "placed a great emphasis on the social nature of the church." This emphasis influenced Bonhoeffer's own ecclesiology, which is "especially evident in his 1927 dissertation 'Sanctorum Communio: A Theological Study of the Sociology of the Church.'"[1]

Andrew Walls has recognized that "theology does not arise from the study or the library even if it can be prosecuted there. It arises from Christian life and activity, from the need to make Christian choices, to think in a Christian way."[2] This observation is certainly applicable to Bonhoeffer, as throughout his life, "his theology was not formulated and displayed solely in academia or from the comfort of a pulpit, but it led him to action and ultimately death."[3] In 1930, Bonhoeffer taught at Union Theological Seminary in New York, where he engaged with African American churches in Harlem and became sensitized to issues of social justice and the many "social injustices experienced by minorities."[4] This was a foundational experience for him, and led him to later remain in Germany to actively oppose Hitler's form of National Socialism. By then a Lutheran pastor, he became one of the founding members of the Confessing Church, which opposed the effective Nazi takeover of Protestant churches in Germany. Bonhoeffer remained steadfast in his public witness

---

1. Jason G. Workman, "Existing for Others: Dietrich Bonhoeffer's Ecclesiology" (BA diss., East Carolina University, 2015), 5.

2. Andrew F. Walls, *Crossing Cultural Frontiers: Studies in the History of World Christianity* (Maryknoll: Orbis, 2017), 74.

3. Workman, "Existing for Others," 7.

4. Bernard Kabenga, "Dietrich Bonhoeffer: Biographical Approach and Theological Legacy," in *Dietrich Bonhoeffer: Life and Legacy*, eds. Traugott Jähnichen, Pascal Batarangaya, Olivier Munyansanga, and Clemens Wustmans, Theology in the Public Square / Theologie in der Öffentlichkeit 11 (Zürich: LIT, 2019), 78.

of faithful discipleship and his consequent opposition to Nazi ideology. This opposition ultimately led to his arrest and imprisonment in 1943. After time spent in two concentration camps, he was executed by hanging on 9 April 1945. Bonhoeffer left behind a legacy of decisive action, discipleship, obedience, independence, and the centrality of Christ.

This chapter describes the causes of and remedies for social injustice from Bonhoeffer's perspective, recognizing him as a real model of integration of faith and public life. His legacy should be resurrected.[5] It is hoped that Bonhoeffer's reaction to social injustice will offer a systematic approach to addressing this threat to social harmony and inclusion in contemporary societies.[6] Examining his attitude towards injustice could contribute to other scholarly efforts to awaken Christian consciousness to the menace of rampant injustice in contemporary Westernized societies.[7] As Wayne Martin Mellinger, who was himself homeless and a victim of social injustice, observes, "to bear witness to injustice is to tell a story about our world based upon firsthand observation of real-life circumstance, fueled by moral outrage, concerned for the common good, and promoting social change."[8]

Societal Justice: *Act Justly, Love Mercy, Walk Humbly with God*

Social injustice can be defined as the state in which people are treated without dignity and respect and are not provided with means to meet their basic human needs. Social justice thus incorporates both a "redistributive claim," which seeks a more equitable distribution of resources and goods, and a claim in the "politics of recognition," in which so-called minority groups are accorded equal respect.[9] Manifestations of social injustice include severe poverty, world

---

5. One of my anonymous peer reviewers points out that while Bonhoeffer is typically celebrated in English-speaking circles, historically reception of his thought has varied. During the Second World War, for example, even within the Confessing Church he "was not always accepted." In the 1960s in Germany, he remained "a controversial figure," and many Lutheran bishops and theologians did not treat his legacy with the respect accorded him in the UK and North America. In Poland in the 1980s, Bonhoeffer "was a big influence on the Solidarity movement" but "today he is almost forgotten." The situation is similar today "in Germany, outside of rather narrow ecclesiastical circles."

6. Cf. Daniel Dei and Dennis E. Akawobsa, "Dietrich Bonhoeffer's Perspective on Racism," *HTS Theological Studies* 78, no. 1 (2022): 2.

7. Dei and Akawobsa, "Bonhoeffer's Perspective," 2.

8. Wayne Martin Mellinger, "Bearing Witness to Social Injustice as a Spiritual Practice: Moving from Pain to Taking Compassionate Action" (unpublished paper, March 2021), abstract, https://www.researchgate.net/publication/349725213.

9. Mellinger, "Bearing Witness," 5.

hunger, homelessness, lack of access to healthcare, oppression[10] and exploitation based on ethnicity, gender, or social class, and violation of human rights.[11]

On 23 October 2021, Pope Francis, speaking on the social teaching of the Roman Catholic Church "particularly in regard to workers and the economy, and the relationship of the state to society," made the following indisputable statements about injustice:

> Our response to injustice and exploitation must be more than mere condemnation. First and foremost, it must be the active promotion of the good: denouncing evil and promoting the good. . . . In every area today, we are more than ever obliged to bear witness to attention for others, to go out of ourselves, to commit ourselves with gratuitousness to the development of a more just and equitable society, where selfishness and partisan interests do not prevail. . . . And at the same time we are called to watch over respect for the human person, his freedom, the protection of his inviolable dignity. Here is the mission to implement the social doctrine of the Church. . . .
>
> As Christians we are called to a love without borders and without limits. We are called to be a sign and witness that it is possible to pass beyond the walls of selfishness and personal and national interest, beyond the power of money which often decides the destiny of peoples, beyond ideological divisions that foster hatred; beyond all historical and cultural barriers and, above all, beyond indifference.[12]

It is through this kind of relationship that Christians are able to meet their fellow Christians in the midst of their misery and suffering. Because many "forms of suffering are the result of social injustices inherent in the workings of our social system," "structural transformations in the nature of that system are required to alleviate these horrendous problems."[13]

---

10. In social justice contexts, oppression is what happens when individuals or groups of people are discriminated against or otherwise treated unjustly, whether by the government, private organizations, individuals, or other groups; Tom Head, "12 Types of Social Oppression," ThoughtCo, 10 January 2021, https://www.thoughtco.com/types-of-oppression-721173.

11. Mellinger, "Bearing Witness," 5.

12. Courtney Mares, "Pope Francis: Our Response to Injustice Must Be More Than Condemnation," Catholic News Agency, 23 October 2021, https://www.catholicnewsagency.com/news/249382/pope-francis-our-response-to-injustice-must-be-more-than-condemnation.

13. Mellinger, "Bearing Witness," 4.

Christians must support one another, and, according to Bonhoeffer, they do so by listening to one another, praying for one another, bearing one another's burdens, and ultimately by continually pointing one another to the word of God and to Christ. Members of the church must belong to one another in Christ, and the way they start is by listening to and sharing in the experiences of their fellow Christians. Bonhoeffer explains:

> The first service that one owes to others in the fellowship consists in listening to them. Just as love to God begins with listening to His Word, so the beginning of love for the brethren is learning to listen to them. It is God's love for us that He not only gives us His Word but also lends us His ear. So it is His work that we do for our brother when we learn to listen to him.[14]

Yet for Bonhoeffer the church should never be merely turned inward, caring only for its own members, as we will see below.

Praying for each other is also a vital function of the church. Intercession means to "bring our brother into the presence of God."[15] Praying for a fellow believer makes it impossible to hate him or her; praying for another person brings both that person and the one offering the prayer more into the fellowship of the church. A church can only thrive and serve its members when they are praying for each other, and their neglecting to do so will cause the church to collapse. Christians owe it to the church and to their fellow Christians to pray for them daily.[16] Intercession is not general and vague, but must be real and concrete, a matter of "definite persons and definite difficulties and therefore of definite petitions."[17]

Furthermore, Bonhoeffer believes that we encounter *God* in the middle of life when we are *there for our neighbours*: "The transcendental is not infinite and unattainable tasks, but the neighbor who is within reach in any given situation."[18] Additionally, Bonhoeffer states that "the church is only the church when it exists for others"[19] – including those who are yet outside the church.

---

14. Dietrich Bonhoeffer, *Life Together* (New York: Harper, 1954), 97.

15. Bonhoeffer, *Life Together*, 86.

16. Bonhoeffer, 86.

17. Bonhoeffer, 87.

18. Dietrich Bonhoeffer, "Outline for a Book," in *Letters and Papers from Prison*, Enlarged Edition, ed. Eberhard Bethge (New York: Touchstone, 1997), 381; quoted by Richard Beck, "Letters from Cell 92: Part 6, 'The Man for Others,'" *Experimental Theology* (blog), 19 December 2010, https://www.experimentaltheology.blogspot.com/2010/12/letters-from-cell-92-part-6-man-for.html.

19. Bonhoeffer, quoted in Beck, "Letters from Cell 92."

This is consistent with earlier writing where he asserts that Christ was always there (meaning in his purpose on earth) for others. Bonhoeffer's belief that the church is Christ's presence on earth demands that as Christ existed for others, so must the true church.[20] To do this, the church must "share in the secular problems of ordinary human life, not dominating, but helping and serving. It must tell men of every calling, what it means to live in Christ, to exist for others."[21] Bonhoeffer concludes that "without Christ, to live the selfless life is impossible, but through faith that is 'held captive by the sight of Jesus Christ' one is freed from the imprisonment of the sinful nature to live as Christ. Through faith, Jesus sets the church free to live for others."[22]

Live in Christ, Exist for Others: Building Public Witness through Deeds and Actions

As noted above, for Bonhoeffer "the church is the church only when it exists for others," "not dominating but helping and serving." It must tell, and demonstrate to, persons of every calling what it means "to live in Christ, to exist for others."[23] Bonhoeffer's notion of existence for others occurs early in his work and is based on his relational theological anthropology. According to Bonhoeffer, a human person is a being-in-relation, because he or she is made in the image of the triune God who exists in a dynamic and outward moving relationship. In *Act and Being*, he points to the freedom of God for others in binding and committing himself to the church community. And in *Creation and Fall*, Bonhoeffer interprets the creation of humanity in the *imago Dei* ("image of God") in relational terms, as being free for God and others.[24]

In *The Cost of Discipleship*, Bonhoeffer further develops his notion of being-for-others, by incorporating his maturing theology of the cross. He insists upon the Christian's obligation to participate in the sufferings of Christ in and for the world. Bonhoeffer is adamant that genuine discipleship is not existence in a state of detached spiritual bliss; it means following Christ in the way of the cross. Just as Christ bears our burdens, so we are called to bear the

---

20. Beck.
21. Quoted in Beck.
22. Dietrich Bonhoeffer, *Ethics* (New York: Touchstone, 1995), 121.
23. Quoted in Beck, "Letters from Cell 92."
24. Workman, "Existing for Others," 8. Bonhoeffer's second dissertation was published as *Akt und Sein* (*Act and Being*) in 1931. *Act and Being* has been published in the English translation in various editions.

burdens of others. "When Christ calls a man," Bonhoeffer asserts, "he bids him come and die."[25]

Bonhoeffer was convinced that the saving power of Jesus must address injustices in society. For him, the correct gospel must put Christ in the community, through the public witness in word and action of Christians, and respond to the social questions of the day.[26] This approach implied that Christians should show interest in and offer substantive assistance to people in social crises.[27] Norris considers the correct form of Christianity to be one that promotes justice and love and uses these virtues as a combined paradigm for accepting people from different ethnic backgrounds to share their pain and sufferings.[28] Borrowing from Bonhoeffer, that is what it means for the church to live and exist for others. He emphasizes that the "individual becomes self-conscious by recognizing the dignity of others in the community."[29]

Living in Christ and Existing for Others in Ethiopia

Deriving from the poor, the church *should* rededicate itself to living for others, serving the whole human person, and meeting spiritual and physical needs.[30] Yonas Deressa believes that "the church is the people of God that is called out of the world together to worship God and to glorify him."[31] One powerful way for the church to glorify God is through the service the church renders to the community. The presence of the church in the world is determined by its clear voice against unjust practices in societies. For instance, in a pastoral letter in response to the Ethiopian Revolution of 1974, the evangelical church

---

25. Dietrich Bonhoeffer, *The Cost of Discipleship* (London: SCM, 1959), 87–89.

26. Dei and Akawobsa, "Bonhoeffer's Perspective," 4.

27. Dei and Akawobsa, 4.

28. Kristopher Norris, *Witnessing Whiteness: Confronting White Supremacy in the American Church* (Oxford: Oxford University Press, 2020), 9.

29. Norris, *Witnessing Whiteness*, 10.

30. Gudina Tumsa Foundation, ed., *Church and Society: Lectures and Responses; Second Missiological Seminar 2003, on the Life and Ministry of Gudina Tumsa, General Secretary of the Ethiopian Evangelical Church Mekane Yesus (EECMY)* (Hamburg: WDL, 2010), 256. While this expresses Bonhoeffer's view, we should remember, of course, that Bonhoeffer himself came from a wealthy and privileged family, and even though he was eventually martyred, even when imprisoned he was treated with relative privilege and dignity. I stress that the church *should* behave in this way with the full recognition that both historically and today this has not always been the case.

31. Yonas Deressa, "Gudina Tumsa's Understanding of the Church," in Gudina Tumsa Foundation, *Church and Society*, 262.

Mekane Yesus was clear with regard to the political witness of the church and advocacy for human rights, stating:

> We aspire for justice, respect of human rights and the rule of law. Ideologies cannot be considered as absolute. Complete allegiance is due to God alone. We recognize the urgent need of making the people aware of unjust practices. Structures for the exploitation of others must be discarded, and the crucial task of building a new society based on equality and a fair share for all undertaken with determination.[32]

The lives of Dietrich Bonhoeffer and Gudina Tumsa, the General Secretary of the Ethiopian Evangelical Church Mekane Yesus (1966–79), have been increasingly linked together[33] due to their similar stories of standing up for justice and sacrificing their lives for others (existing for others). They have both provided articulate leadership for the church under conditions of hostility and oppression.[34] Finding freedom in the confidence of God's ultimate victory, they were willing to sacrifice their own lives for others to see that injustice was not tolerated in the community.[35]

Living in Christ and Existing for Others in Tanzania

Similarly, the Diaconical Policy of the Evangelical Lutheran Church in Tanzania has the same emphasis for the church to "exist for others" through services offered to people as the church imitates the charitable work of Jesus. The policy explains that the church exists for others by engaging in action to imitate

> the six Christian Charitable works by Jesus in Mathew 25:31–42 [which] are to feed the hungry, to give water to the thirsty, to accept strangers, to give clothing to those without, to visit the sick, to visit those in prison, and to bury the dead (the last one was added in by the early church in the first century). These acts do not depend on wealth, ability, or intelligence. They are simple acts freely given and freely received. We have no excuse to neglect those who have deep needs. Jesus demands our personal involvement in caring for others' needs. It is to be noted that, depending

---

32. Gudina Tumsa Foundation, *Church and Society*, 256.
33. Gudina Tumsa Foundation, 16.
34. Gudina Tumsa Foundation, 15.
35. Gudina Tumsa Foundation, 15.

on how the church fulfills those charitable works, it will either be blessed or cursed. God blessed his people when they extended help to the hungry and afflicted (Isaiah 58:10). He will do the same today. Those works have remained a fundamental teaching of Diaconia today. God wants to receive our services through serving the needy here on earth.[36]

An important task for the church (in the eyes of the public as well) is to take up the cause of the powerless and those in need, to offer them protection, and to stand up for their rights, so that they might be enabled to live in dignity.[37] Social action is a central expression of the life of the church. This is why the church is involved in social concern and engages in public debate, even with regard to political issues.[38] For persons in need of help and care and their families, social service must continue to be clearly recognizable as a service offered by the church. Under no circumstances may the church neglect its social service tasks, even though church social service agencies may find themselves in competitive "market" situations. Manfred Sorg stresses that "the church should offer, through its 'culture of helping,' a warm-hearted, compassionate and emphatic way of accompanying disadvantaged persons. But this does not relieve the church of the duty to expose and criticize the process that leads to disadvantages for people, and to help in working to overcome them."[39] The church must use its voice to call out injustice (prophetic ministry) as well as to offer practical service (compassionate ministry):

> The church, as the body of Christ, acts by the power of the Holy Spirit to continue his life-giving mission in prophetic and compassionate ministry, and so participates in God's work of healing a broken world and bringing it into a state of reconciliation with God, the founder of mission. Communion, whose source is the very life of the Holy Trinity, is both the gift by which the church lives and, at the same time, the gift that God calls the church to

---

36. Evangelical Lutheran Church in Tanzania, "Diaconical Policy" (Arusha, 2016), 1.

37. Manfred Sorg, *A Proposal for Reform of the Evangelical Church of Westphalia: The Nature, Mission and Tasks of the Church* (Bielefeld: Evangelical Press Association for Westphalia and Lippe, 2017), 15.

38. Sorg, *Proposal for Reform*, 15.

39. Sorg, 15.

offer to a wounded and divided humanity in hope of reconciliation and healing.[40]

Live in Christ, Exist for Others: Mission as Reconciliation

We can understand mission as reconciliation, for mission reflects the work of God in reconciling humankind to God.[41] It is God who has worked throughout history and God is the one who calls believers to share and participate in God's mission. Mission is the overflow of the infinite love of the triune God. God's mission begins with the act of creation. Creation's life and God's life are entwined. The WCC's mission statement highlights this: "The mission of God's Spirit encompasses us all in an ever-giving act of grace."[42] Ecumenicity is based on the importance of reconciliation. Thus the Uniting Church in Australia was formed from Presbyterian, Methodist, and Congregational bodies joining together "in an explicit commitment to 'the mission and unity of the whole church' and the word 'mission' (and its link to unity) rings like a bell across the paragraphs of its Basis of Union.... Holy Communion strengthens the people of God for their 'participation in the mission of Christ in the world.'"[43] Verstraelen believes that "mission is ... the dynamic relationship between God and the world: God sends Himself, His Son, and His church."[44] Those who become actively involved in the vision of his redemptive will understand themselves as sent individuals or groups.

The church is on mission, as sent by and in line with the missional activity and nature of God. Therefore, the theology of *missio Dei* is developed out of the doctrine of the triune God, rather than any other doctrine. As David

---

40. World Council of Churches, *The Church: Towards a Common Vision*, Faith and Order Paper no. 214 (Geneva: World Council of Churches, 2013), 5.

41. Ronald Wayne Johnson, "Paradigm Shift in Evangelism: A Study of the Need for Contextualization in the Mission of Southern Baptists" (DTh diss., University of South Africa, 1999), xv.

42. *Together Toward Life*, the WCC's second mission statement (2012), quoted in John Gibaut, "From Unity and Mission to *Koinonia* and *Missio Dei*: Convergences in WCC Ecclesiology and Missiology towards Edinburgh 2010," in *Called to Unity: For the Sake of Mission*, eds. John Gibaut and Knud Jørgensen, Regnum Edinburgh Centenary Series 25 (Oxford: Regnum, 2014), 85.

43. Thomas F. Best, "United and Uniting Churches as Models of Mission and Unity," in Gibaut and Jørgensen, *Called to Unity*, 148–49.

44. F. J. Verstraelen et al., "Introduction: What Do We Mean by 'Missiology'?," ch. 1 in *Missiology: An Ecumenical Introduction; Texts and Contexts of Global Christianity*, eds. Frans J. Verstraelen et al. (Grand Rapids: Eerdmans, 1995), 4.

Bosch puts it, "It is not the church that has a mission of salvation to fulfill in the world; it is the mission of the Son and the Spirit through the Father that includes the church. Mission is thereby seen as a movement from God to the world; the church is viewed as an instrument for that mission."[45] The Father, the Son, and the Spirit are missional; therefore, the church ought to be missional. Speaking of the motives of mission, Berkouwer says, "These motives can never be separated from the directedness, the scope, and the goal of mission."[46] Driven by compassion for the lost and the needy and in obedience to the command of Christ, the church is called to the task of making disciples of all nations and demonstrating the love of Christ through words and works (Matt 28:19–20; 22:37–39).

Shaping the Mission of the Church through Social Justice

In speaking about the church and social justice, Calvin Van Reken has made a significant distinction between the church as an institution and the church as an organism.[47] From this also follows a distinction between church work, which is the work that a Christian does as an agent of the institutional church, and kingdom work, which is the work that an individual Christian or a group of Christians does in service of the Lord but not as agents of the institutional church. It is important therefore that we make a clear line of demarcation between the two approaches – between Christians' involvement (by persons) in social justice and church involvement (by ecclesial institutions) in social justice.

Christians' Involvement in Social Justice

Desmond Tutu used his platform as an individual Christian and a leader to call for justice beyond South Africa's borders, calling out human rights violations and actively advocating for rights for all – and for non-violent means by which to achieve them. In his 1984 Nobel Peace Prize acceptance speech,

---

45. David J. Bosch, *Transforming Mission: Paradigm Shifts in Theology of Mission* (Maryknoll: Orbis, 2005), 390.

46. Gerrit Cornelis Berkouwer, *The Church*, Studies in Dogmatics 13 (Grand Rapids: Eerdmans, 1976), 408.

47. Calvin P. Van Reken, "The Church's Role in Social Justice," *Calvin Theological Journal* 34, no. 1 (1999): 198.

Tutu reiterated, "When there is injustice, invariably peace becomes a casualty."[48] Twenty years later, he expounded further:

> For our nation to heal and become a more humane place, we had to embrace our enemies as well as our friends. The same is true the world over. True enduring peace between countries, within a country, within a community, within a family – requires real reconciliation between former enemies and even between loved ones who have struggled with one another.[49]

Tutu believed that real reconciliation goes with love and compassion. As Dearborn states, "The people of God are to be characterised by the pursuit of justice for the exploited, marginalised and abused."[50]

A basic Christian responsibility is exercising "our compassion and love for others"[51] – even those whom we think are our "enemies." This means that "Christians should feed the hungry, comfort the sorrowing, and visit the sick"[52] without any discrimination based on religious affiliation, ethnicity, colour, or sex. While in some spaces the concept of "social justice" is lamentably controversial, the broad narrative of Scripture demonstrates that "social justice [is] a mandate of faith and a fundamental expression of Christian discipleship" and that it "has its biblical roots in a triune God who time and time again shows his love and compassion for the weak, the vulnerable, the marginalized, the disenfranchised, the disinherited."[53] For those who give their allegiance to Jesus, then, existing for Christ and living for others means that a "pursuit of social justice . . . is the decisive mark of being people who submit to the will and way of God."[54]

Additionally, individual Christians can make an immense contribution to justice in the community. We can do this, individually or in cooperation with others, by appropriately addressing "the government for solutions to problems

---

48. Palwasha L. Kakar, Melissa Nozell, and Knox Thames, "Four Lessons from Desmond Tutu's Life and Legacy," *The Olive Branch* (blog), United States Institute of Peace, 29 December 2021, https://www.usip.org/blog/2021/12/four-lessons-desmond-tutus-life-and-legacy.

49. Kakar, Nozell, and Thames, "Four Lessons."

50. Tim Dearborn, *Reflections on Advocacy and Justice*, Integrating Christian Witness Series 4 (Monrovia: World Vision, 2009), 21, https://tdearborndotcom2.files.wordpress.com/2012/10/reflections-on-advocacy-and-justice-english.pdf.

51. Van Reken, "Church's Role," 199.

52. Van Reken, 199.

53. Adam Taylor, "What Does Social Justice Really Mean?," World Vision, 20 February 2012, https://www.worldvision.org/blog/social-justice-really-mean.

54. Dearborn, *Reflections on Advocacy*, 21.

that are within the government's proper sphere," by voting and lobbying for change of government policies, and by behaving as "responsible, *compassionate*, law-abiding citizens."[55] But our compassion must motivate us to take action. God requires us "to act justly and to love mercy" (Mic 6:8, NIV). Church leaders have a special responsibility to prophetically engage in witness in their public lives, to speak loudly and challenge unjust laws, and to take action to promote justice. Even secular organizations such as the United Nations allow for this. An explanation of the implications of the UN Universal Declaration of Human Rights says that

> church leaders can speak out with considerable authority about many situations. They can challenge unjust laws and promote and defend the rights of poor people. Through their example and leadership they can inspire, direct and encourage their churches to take action to promote justice. This may be through prayers, through giving, through practical caring, through speaking out and through different approaches to advocacy work on behalf of those who are suffering.[56]

Yet many church leaders fail to make use of their power to promote justice.

The Church's Involvement in Social Justice

The business of the church as an institution in society and in the world is to be in mission in terms of evangelism and social action.[57] Social action is that set of activities whose primary goal is to improve the physical, socio-economic, and political well-being of people through relief, development, and structural change.[58] The church needs to penetrate deeply into the world as salt, yeast, and light to transform society. Some claim that being concerned with issues of social justice is a distraction from the church's mission to evangelize the lost, but it is irrefutable that "social action . . . fosters evangelism, whilst the church's silence on injustice undermines evangelism."[59]

---

55. Van Reken, "Church's Role," 199; emphasis added.

56. Isabel Carter, Ruth Alvarado, and Alfonso Wieland, *Seeking Justice for All*, A PILLARS Guide (Teddington: Tearfund, 2006), 58.

57. See J. N. K. Mugambi, *The Biblical Basis for Evangelization: Theological Reflections Based on an African Experience* (Nairobi: Oxford University Press, 1989), 101.

58. Lou Gordon Levine, "How Does Evangelism Relate to Social Action in the Theologies of Michael Cassidy and Albert Nolan?" (MTh diss., University of Natal, 1996), 149.

59. Gordon Levine, "Theologies of Michael Cassidy and Albert Nolan," 149.

Some evangelicals think that it is a matter of choosing *either* "biblical righteousness" *or* "social justice." John Stott, a noted evangelical theologian, was chairman of the International Consultation on the Relationship between Evangelism and Social Responsibility which explained how this is a false choice and discussed how the church should take responsibility in bringing about social change. The following comments from their report are worth quoting at length:

> [Social action] looks beyond persons to structures, beyond the rehabilitation of prison inmates to the reform of the prison system, beyond improving factory conditions to securing a more participatory role for the workers, beyond caring for the poor to improving – and when necessary transforming – the economic system (whatever it may be) and the political system (again, whatever it may be), until it facilitates their liberation from poverty and oppression. Such social changes often necessitate political action (for politics is about power), and some evangelicals fear it because they imagine it will entail civil strife and even revolution. But this is not what we mean by "socio-political involvement." We are thinking rather of political processes which are consistent with biblical principles – such as the rights of the individual and of minorities, respect for civil authority, the welfare of the whole community, and justice for the oppressed.[60]

The church must stand for justice, take action, and defend the marginalized and oppressed, regardless of the cost. This is what Bonhoeffer calls *costly grace*. Bonhoeffer illustrates:

> Such grace is costly because it calls us to follow, and it is grace because it calls us to follow Jesus Christ. It is costly because it costs a man his life, and it is grace because it gives a man the only true life. . . . Above all, it is grace because God did not reckon his Son too dear a price to pay for our life, but delivered him up for us. Costly grace is the Incarnation of God.[61]

Unfortunately, the church has deliberately turned a deaf ear to cries for justice, not recognizing that "to turn a deaf ear to the cries of all who are

---

60. John Stott et al., *Evangelism and Social Responsibility: An Evangelical Commitment; The Grand Rapids Report*, Lausanne Occasional Paper 21 (Lausanne: Lausanne Committee for World Evangelism; Deerfield: World Evangelical Fellowship, 1982), 7.

61. Quoted in Gudina Tumsa Foundation, *Church and Society*, 10.

oppressed today is to turn a deaf ear to Christ."[62] Mellinger accuses his fellow citizens of giving up the struggle for justice. He explains:

> These are the crimes of which I accuse my fellow citizens: that apathy, indifference and cynicism have befallen you, and have led you to become numb to the suffering all around you; that you have given up the struggle for social justice and the hope that we can change the system so that all people can lead healthy lives. . . .
>
> When our observation of another person's suffering is not treated as a spiritual practice, we often turn away to not face the ugly and upsetting realities of our world, thinking that we should not watch other people's struggles. We try to avoid and dispel the flood of emotions that come over us. We don't want to think about other people's ordeals.[63]

Bonhoeffer calls any tendency to neglect justice *cheap grace*. "Cheap grace is grace without discipleship, grace without the cross, grace without Jesus Christ, living and incarnate."[64] In *Ethics*, Bonhoeffer laments the times when the church has stood apart and stayed silent in situations of rampant injustice:

> The church was silent when she should have cried out because the blood of the innocent was crying aloud to heaven. She has failed to speak the right word in the right way and at the right time. She has not resisted to the uttermost the apostasy of faith, and she has brought upon herself the guilt of the godlessness of the masses. . . . She has stood by while violence and wrong were being committed under cover of this name. The church confesses that she has witnessed the lawless application of brutal force, the physical and spiritual suffering of countless innocent people, oppression, hatred and murder, and that she has not raised her voice on behalf of the victims and has not found ways to hasten to their aid. She is guilty of the deaths of the weakest and most defenseless brothers and sisters of Jesus Christ.[65]

---

62. Emmitt Drumgoole, "Tower of Babel or Pentecost? The Church Must Not Turn a Deaf Ear to Cries for Justice," Baptist News Global, 5 June 2020, https://baptistnews.com/article/tower-of-babel-or-pentecost-the-church-must-not-turn-a-deaf-ear-to-cries-for-justice/.

63. Mellinger, "Bearing Witness," 2, 7.

64. Quoted in Robert Coles, ed., *Dietrich Bonhoeffer: Writings Selected with an Introduction by Robert Coles* (Maryknoll: Orbis, 2004), 54.

65. Quoted in Coles, *Dietrich Bonhoeffer*, 105.

In addition, the church should confess that it has witnessed in silence the spoliation and exploitation of the poor and the enrichment and corruption of the strong. The church has not proclaimed the justice of God in such a manner that all true justice must see in it the origin of its own essential nature.[66] As Bonhoeffer explains above, whenever the church fails to use her voice and her actions on behalf of victims, the church likewise is guilty of the deaths of the vulnerable brothers and sisters of Jesus Christ.[67] Either the church must willingly undergo this transformation, or else it must cease to be the church of Christ.

Conclusion

Dietrich Bonhoeffer's ecclesiology "Live in Christ, exist for others" speaks to us today. His belief that the church is Christ's presence on earth demands that just as Christ existed for others, so must the true church. To do this, the church must share in the secular problems of ordinary human life, not dominating but helping and serving. It must tell people of every calling what it means to live in Christ to exist for others. The church should exist to serve people through the humility and sacrifice of its members. Christians must support one another, and according to Bonhoeffer they do so by listening, praying for one another, bearing burdens, and ultimately continually pointing one another to the word of God and to Christ. Members of the church must belong to one another in Christ, and the way they start is by listening to and sharing in the experiences of their fellow Christians, as well as in the experiences of those outside the church.

Bonhoeffer believed that Christ is the example to be followed by the church because the church is Christ on earth. For Bonhoeffer, this call to follow Christ was a call for reformation and renewal in the context of a secular world and what had become a secular form of Christianity. Because the church is – or should be – Christ existing as community, it must strive for costly grace: it must engage in action and exist for others as Jesus did. The injustice and severity of the Nazi regime forced many Christians, including Bonhoeffer, to decide what their duties to God and fellow human beings were. If discrimination and disunity are tolerated in the church, how can we denounce them in the nation? Conversely, it is churches that visibly demonstrate the righteousness

---

66. Coles, 106.

67. On this point, see the discussion of Olivier Munyansanga, "Dietrich Bonhoeffer and the Ambiguity of Breaking Silence in Africa," in Jähnichen et al., *Dietrich Bonhoeffer*, 16.

and peace of the kingdom which will make the greatest evangelistic and social impact in the world. The salt must retain its saltiness, Jesus said; otherwise, it is good for nothing (Matt 5:13). Above all, as Drumgoole reminds us, the Spirit of the living God speaks to us, reminding us of our calling as the church to live prophetically and speak boldly to a world that desperately needs the hope, love, and justice found in the gospel.[68]

Bibliography

Beck, Richard. "Letters from Cell 92: Part 6, 'The Man for Others.'" *Experimental Theology* (blog), 19 December 2010. https://experimentaltheology.blogspot.com/search?q=Letters+from+Cell+92%3A+Part+6&submit=Search.

Berkouwer, Gerrit Cornelis. *The Church*. Studies in Dogmatics 13. Grand Rapids: Eerdmans, 1976.

Best, Thomas F. "United and Uniting Churches as Models of Mission and Unity." In *Called to Unity: For the Sake of Mission*, edited by John Gibaut and Knud Jørgensen, 141–53. Regnum Edinburgh Centenary Series 25. Oxford: Regnum, 2014.

Bonhoeffer, Dietrich. *The Cost of Discipleship*. London: SCM, 1959.

———. *Ethics*. New York: Touchstone, 1995.

———. *Letters and Papers from Prison*. Enlarged Edition. Edited by Eberhard Bethge. New York: Touchstone, 1997.

———. *Life Together*. New York: Harper, 1954.

Bosch, David J. *Transforming Mission: Paradigm Shifts in Theology of Mission*. Maryknoll: Orbis, 2005.

Carter, Isabel, Ruth Alvarado, and Alfonso Wieland. *Seeking Justice for All*. A PILLARS Guide. Teddington: Tearfund, 2006.

Coles, Robert, ed. *Dietrich Bonhoeffer: Writings Selected with an Introduction by Robert Coles*. Maryknoll: Orbis, 2004.

Dearborn, Tim. *Reflections on Advocacy and Justice*. Integrating Christian Witness Series 4. Monrovia: World Vision, 2009. https://tdearborndotcom2.files.wordpress.com/2012/10/reflections-on-advocacy-and-justice-english.pdf.

Dei, Daniel, and Dennis E. Akawobsa. "Dietrich Bonhoeffer's Perspective on Racism." *HTS Theological Studies* 78, no. 1 (2022): a7450.

Drumgoole, Emmitt. "Tower of Babel or Pentecost? The Church Must Not Turn a Deaf Ear to Cries for Justice." *Baptist News Global*. 5 June 2020. https://baptistnews.com/article/tower-of-babel-or-pentecost-the-church-must-not-turn-a-deaf-ear-to-cries-for-justice/.

Evangelical Lutheran Church in Tanzania. "Diaconical Policy." Arusha, 2016.

---

68. Drumgoole, "Tower of Babel."

Gibaut, John. "From Unity and Mission to Koinonia and *Missio Dei*: Convergences in WCC Ecclesiology and Missiology towards Edinburgh 2010." In *Called to Unity: For the Sake of Mission*, edited by John Gibaut and Knud Jørgensen, 73–88. Regnum Edinburgh Centenary Series 25. Oxford: Regnum, 2014.

Gordon Levine, Lou. "How Does Evangelism Relate to Social Action in the Theologies of Michael Cassidy and Albert Nolan?" MTh diss., University of Natal, 1996.

Guder, Darrell L. "The Church as Missional Community." Chapter 6 in *The Community of the Word: Toward an Evangelical Ecclesiology*, edited by Mark Husbands and Daniel J. Treier, 114–28. Downers Grove: IVP Academic, 2005.

Gudina Tumsa Foundation, ed. *Church and Society: Lectures and Responses; Second Missiological Seminar 2003, on the Life and Ministry of Gudina Tumsa, General Secretary of the Ethiopian Evangelical Church Mekane Yesus (EECMY)*. Hamburg: WDL, 2010.

Head, Tom. "12 Types of Social Oppression." ThoughtCo. 10 January 2021. https://www.thoughtco.com/types-of-oppression-721173.

Johnson, Ronald Wayne. "Paradigm Shift in Evangelism: A Study of the Need for Contextualization in the Mission of Southern Baptists." DTh diss., University of South Africa, 1999.

Kabenga, Bernard. "Dietrich Bonhoeffer: Biographical Approach and Theological Legacy." In *Dietrich Bonhoeffer: Life and Legacy*, edited by Traugott Jähnichen, Pascal Bataringaya, Olivier Munyansanga, and Clemens Wustmans, 75–86. Theology in the Public Square / Theologie in der Öffentlichkeit 11. Zürich: LIT, 2019.

Kakar, Palwasha L., Melisa Nozell, and Knox Thames. "Four Lessons from Desmond Tutu's Life and Legacy." *The Olive Branch* (blog). United States Institute of Peace. 29 December 2021. https://www.usip.org/blog/2021/12/four-lessons-desmond-tutus-life-and-legacy.

Mares, Courtney. "Pope Francis: Our Response to Injustice Must Be More Than Condemnation." Catholic News Agency. 23 October 2021. https://www.catholicnewsagency.com/news/249382/pope-francis-our-response-to-injustice-must-be-more-than-condemnation.

Mellinger, Wayne Martin. "Bearing Witness to Social Injustice as a Spiritual Practice: Moving from Pain to Taking Compassionate Action." Unpublished paper. March 2021. https:/www.researchgate.net/publication/349725213.

Mugambi, J. N. K. *The Biblical Basis for Evangelization: Theological Reflections Based on an African Experience*. Nairobi: Oxford University Press, 1989.

Munyansanga, Olivier. "Dietrich Bonhoeffer and the Ambiguity of Breaking Silence in Africa." In *Dietrich Bonhoeffer: Life and Legacy*, edited by Traugott Jähnichen, Pascal Bataringaya, Olivier Munyansanga, and Clemens Wustmans, 15–16. Theology in the Public Square / Theologie in der Öffentlichkeit 11. Zürich: LIT, 2019.

Norris, Kristopher. *Witnessing Whiteness: Confronting White Supremacy in the American Church*. Oxford: Oxford University Press, 2020.

Sorg, Manfred. *A Proposal for Reform of the Evangelical Church of Westphalia: The Nature, Mission and Tasks of the Church*. Bielefeld: Evangelical Press Association for Westphalia and Lippe, 2017.

Stott, John, et al. *Evangelism and Social Responsibility: An Evangelical Commitment; The Grand Rapids Report*. Lausanne Occasional Paper 21. Lausanne: Lausanne Committee for World Evangelism; Deerfield: World Evangelical Fellowship, 1982.

Taylor, Adam. "What Does Social Justice Really Mean?" World Vision. 20 February 2012. https://www.worldvision.org/blog/social-justice-really-mean.

Thomas, Norman, ed. *Reading in World Mission*. SPCK Essential Readings. London: SPCK, 1995.

Van Reken, Calvin P. "The Church's Role in Social Justice." *Calvin Theological Journal* 34, no. 1 (1999): 198–202.

Verstraelen, F. J., A. Camps, L. A. Hoedemaker, and M. E. Spindler. "Introduction: What Do We Mean by 'Missiology'?" Chapter 1 in *Missiology: An Ecumenical Introduction; Texts and Contexts of Global Christianity*, edited by Frans J. Verstraelen et al., 1–7. Grand Rapids: Eerdmans, 1995.

Walls, Andrew F. *Crossing Cultural Frontiers: Studies in the History of World Christianity*. Maryknoll: Orbis, 2017.

Walter, Daniel. "A Church for Others: A Vision of the Church Inspired by Dietrich Bonhoeffer." Unpublished paper, n.d. https://www.academia.edu/5886571.

Wayne, Ronald. "Paradigm Shift in Evangelism: A Study of the Need for Contextualization in the Mission of Southern Baptists." Doctor of Theology in Missiology diss., University of South Africa, 1999.

Workman, Jason G. "Existing for Others: Dietrich Bonhoeffer's Ecclesiology." BA diss., East Carolina University, 2015.

World Council of Churches. *The Church: Towards a Common Vision*. Faith and Order Paper no. 214. Geneva: World Council of Churches, 2013.

10

Contours of Corruption

A Challenge to and for the Church's Public Witness in the Twenty-First Century

Alfred Sebahene

Department of Theology and Religious Studies, St. John's University of Tanzania, Dodoma, Tanzania

Responding to Corruption

> I am sending you out like sheep among wolves. Therefore, be as shrewd as snakes and as innocent as doves. (Matt 10:16, NIV)

For the church to exercise faithfulness in its public life in Africa this century, it must be located, equipped, and sent within its contemporary contexts. Those contexts include endemic corruption. How can the church in Africa respond to corruption in a manner that faithfully follows Jesus Christ and bears public witness to the truth of the gospel today? As Africa responds to its post-colonial context and its place in a postmodern, pluralist, global world, and as the African continent becomes increasingly complex in terms of its contextual realities generally, how can the church faithfully exercise its prophetic voice in contexts of rapid innovation and development? Within this framework, this chapter reflects upon the current environment of the continent with reference to the public impact of the Christian faith tradition today. Christ-followers must discern biblical-theological guides for the thinking and practice of their faith as they faithfully and actively engage in both public service and private enterprise. The aim is to seek to refine the gospel's public meaning and justify its significance and impact today. Within the current state of affairs, what are the fundamental principles underlying an appropriate approach to faith and public life? Currently the global community seems to be acknowledging that the need to address the long-standing social ills facing humanity is at a crossroads. In this context, how can the church shape societal values and influence public debate? How is the public witness of the church related to a Christian response to social ills?

Although there is a wide spectrum of crimes affecting twenty-first-century African societies, this chapter focuses on corruption as a foundational area for witnessing to Christ in Africa today. How can the church effectively show that its mission relates not only to human beings but also to the whole creation, which "itself also shall be delivered from the bondage of corruption into the glorious liberty of the glory of the children of God" (Rom 8:21, KJV)? I hope that this study will help the church become a more faithful, engaged, and successful institution as it proclaims the good news that God cares about African people and hears their groaning – especially through the church's response to the social ill of corruption.

Framing the Twenty-First Century in the Reader's Mind

> The seasons change and you change, but the Lord abides evermore the same,
> and the streams of His love are as deep, as broad and as full as ever.[1]

The twenty-first century demands our attention. Though each century has had its distinctive characteristics and events, the first quarter of this century has already demonstrated that we live in an era of the world's history which needs what I call a twenty-first-century wisdom and understanding. Thoughtfulness and introspection are important here. This is reflected in the way people from all walks of life, cultures, geographical locations, and passions have understood this century as they have sought to interpret it for their own contextual applications.

As an African public theologian interested in how the church in Africa can address crucial issues of faith and public life for ordinary people, my passion for over a decade has been for a redeeming Christian presence on the African

---

1. Charles H. Spurgeon, *Morning and Evening: A New Edition of the Classic Devotional Based on The Holy Bible, English Standard Version*, revised and updated by Alistair Begg (Wheaton: Crossway, 2003), 1 July.

continent. In my roles as both an academic and a church leader, I have been seeking to contribute to the mandate of the African Union (AU), a continental body consisting of the fifty-five member states. *Agenda 2063*[2] is a continent-wide shared framework of "wisdom of the African leaders" to be honoured in how we serve for inclusive growth and sustainable development for Africa. From within that context, I wish to begin with an interpretation based on African scenarios arising from outside the church, reflecting both on what Africans do not want and on their dreams of what they do want.

Contours of Corruption
What Is Corruption? Why Does It Matter? A Secular and Biblical-Theological Definition

Before we look at the question "Why corruption?," it is important to understand it.[3] Corruption remains a complex phenomenon that has always been difficult to define, especially as it takes many forms and affects all sectors of society. In this chapter the term "corruption" will be used in two senses, first with reference to the secular world, and then from within a biblical-theological framework. In secular contexts, "corruption" refers to a misapplication of public goods to private ends. This involves acts of fraud (theft through misrepresentation), embezzlement (misappropriation of corporate or public funds), and bribery. This definition justifies the common understanding that different types of corruption tend to be closely linked. Second, from a biblical-theological viewpoint, corruption represents sin manifested in forms of abuse of civic power and/or corporate power. Such abuse of power takes place in the contexts of governance, business and commerce, NGOs, educational institutions, and within ecclesial (or church) structures. Among other forms of abuse, this includes extortion (Lev 6:2–4; Isa 30:12–13) and bribery (Ezek 22:12; Amos 5:12), both of which signify the fallen state of humankind, inseparable from the denial of God. Such corruption is an attack on the value of human dignity

---

2. In this chapter, the African Union *Agenda 2063* is adopted and used as an important mandate presenting opportunities for intensifying the discourse around corruption on the continent. For further reading see *Agenda 2063: The Africa We Want* (Addis Ababa: African Union, 2015), https://au.int/en/Agenda2063/popular_version.

3. An expanded definition of corruption from traditional discourse to anthropological, philosophical, legal, and judicial perspectives can be found in my book: Alfred Sebahene, *Corruption Mocking at Justice: A Theological and Ethical Perspective on Public Life in Tanzania and Its Implications for the Anglican Church of Tanzania* (Carlisle: Langham Monographs, 2017).

and a hindrance to human flourishing. N. T. Wright's cosmic interpretation of Romans 8 is important:

> The whole creation is waiting in eager longing – not just for its own redemption, its liberation from corruption and decay, but *for God's children to be revealed*: in other words, for the unveiling of those redeemed humans through whose stewardship creation will at last be brought back into that wise order for which it was made.[4]

Corruption: A Global Problem

> God looked on the earth, and behold, it was corrupt; for all flesh had corrupted their way upon the earth. (Gen 6:12, NASB 1995)

The crime of corruption continues to be prevalent around the world. This chapter focuses on its magnitude, its consequences, and its presence in the body of Christ, the church. For the last decade and a half, I have been immersed, as a pastor and an academic, in studying, researching, teaching, and consulting on the role of faith-based organizations (FBOs), Christian churches, their institutions, and faith as a new avenue of inquiry in addressing the harsh realities of corruption and injustice in my country, Tanzania, and beyond. Unfortunately, throughout the time of my engagement, the crime has been widespread and unabated among several political and public office holders in Africa as well as in other parts of the world. In some cases, although crime-regulating bodies are in place, the crime keeps soaring higher.

Amid all the challenges, this section is dedicated to calling the church to acknowledge and address "corruption" as we consider the overall global twenty-first-century picture. We shall argue that addressing this crime of corruption is not an addendum in the narrative of God's restorative mission, but an indispensable strand in the story of Yahweh and his people. Responding to corruption is not separate from mission but an essential part of mission. In seeking to argue this case, we have used the term "contours" to guide the church and equip twenty-first-century Christians to address corruption as part of their agenda of seeking the redemption of the world. This task needs some guidance. In the first place, the church needs to be reminded of the importance of understanding its call as people seek direction for Christian mission in the twenty-first century.

---

4. N. T. Wright, *Surprised by Hope: Rethinking Heaven, the Resurrection, and the Mission of the Church* (London: SPCK, 2007), 213; emphasis original.

The Far-Reaching Consequences of Corruption

> They covet fields and then seize them,
> and houses, and take them away.
> They rob a man and his house,
> a man and his inheritance. (Mic 2:2, NASB 1995)

The consequences of corruption are immense and endless. "Corruption is condemned in the Bible. It undermines economic development, distorts fair decision-making and destroys social cohesion. No nation is free of corruption. We invite Christians in the workplace, especially young entrepreneurs, to think creatively about how they can best stand against this scourge."[5]

Although the crime differs widely in its forms, pervasiveness, and consequences, in Africa it has been known to lower economic growth, impede economic development, and undermine political legitimacy. These consequences in turn exacerbate poverty and political instability. It is widely recognized that corruption steals from and exploits the poor. As Christians we also recognize that it steals from God. Corruption is therefore a sin against God and humanity. In a tangible way, the menace of corruption has continued to undermine the rule of law by destroying public trust in government, while perpetuating poverty and inequality.

A "Wounded Church in a Bleeding Community"[6]

> You are to be holy to me because I, the LORD, am holy, and I have
> set you apart from the nations to be my own. (Lev 20:26, NIV)

Elsewhere, in my book[7] and through engagement with churches, governments, and other secular institutions, I identify the prospects for addressing the crimes of corruption and fraud from a *faith perspective and a religious and theological vision.*[8] I have found that fingers tend to be pointed at churches. While I strongly commend some churches which are evidently flourishing and suc-

---

5. Lausanne Movement, *The Cape Town Commitment: A Confession of Faith and a Call to Action; The Third Lausanne Congress* (Peabody: Hendrickson, 2011), 64.

6. Picture language used to remind believers of the devil's schemes on the church in the community in which it is placed to serve.

7. Sebahene, *Corruption Mocking at Justice*.

8. In this concept I have been particularly influenced by John G. Stackhouse Jr., *Making the Best of It: Following Christ in the Real World* (Oxford: Oxford University Press, 2008).

cessfully ministering within their communities[9] and addressing corruption, sadly, what has always surfaced is the persistent argument that the body of Christ in my country (Tanzania) is itself not only corrupt but is an institution with serious structural deficiencies which in turn serve as a seedbed for the crime of corruption to grow. In other churches, conflicts, selfishness, and moral scandals are visible, as highlighted by Louise Kretzschmar's article.[10]

This argument, that the church itself is corrupt, is not new. Accusations range from failures in leadership and bankruptcy-causing financial corruption, to moral corruption. Such areas of corruption are often related to abuses of power within churches, especially within ecclesial hierarchies. In some cases, any power within the church is condemned as lethal in terms of access to resources, and in a grimmer picture, corruption is also embedded in the way support for and control of missions is done. In my continent, across a wide range of denominations, the abuse of power is evident in both scattered and recurring stories. Financial corruption is often accompanied by other abuses of power, including sexual abuse and social and gender discrimination. This indicates that spiritual maturity and commitment to integrity[11] are lacking, especially among Christian leaders. This is not as it should be. "Spiritually mature and morally excellent leaders can address more effectively [corruption and other] moral challenges facing the church and [the continent of Africa]."[12] This calls for the church to revisit its plan for moral formation, defined by Banzikiza as "helping people to grow in goodness by avoiding what dehumanizes oneself and others."[13] The church's deliberate engagement in moral formation is important because, as Wright affirms, "it promotes the development of Chris-

---

9. See Moss Ntlha, "Ethics and the Church in Africa," in *What Is a Good Life? An Introduction to Christian Ethics in 21st Century Africa*, eds. Louise Kretzschmar, Wessel Bentley, and André van Niekerk (Kempton Park: AcadSA, 2009), 287–97.

10. See Louise Kretzschmar, "African and Western Approaches to the Moral Formation of Christian Leaders: The Role of Spiritual Disciplines in Counteracting Moral Deficiencies," *HTS Teologiese Studies/Theological Studies* 76, no. 2 (2020): Article #5913, 10 pages.

11. Tinyiko Sam Maluleke, "A Post-Colonial South African Church: Problems and Promises," in *African Theology on the Way: Current Conversations*, ed. Diane B. Stinton, International Study Guides 46 (London: SPCK, 2010), 150–60. See also J. N. K. Mugambi and Anne Nasimiyu-Wasike, eds., *Moral and Ethical Issues in African Christianity: Exploratory Essays in Moral Theology* (Nairobi: Acton, 1999).

12. Kretzschmar, "African and Western Approaches," 1.

13. Constance R. Banzikiza, *Restoring Moral Formation in Africa* (Eldoret: AMECEA Gaba, 2001), xii.

tian moral thinking, character, relationships and behavior."[14] As the church cultivates moral formation, a central and urgent focus must be on corruption.

Repositioning and Equipping the Church for the Twenty-First-Century Mission Field Frontline

There is an unprecedented number of competing conceptions of witness today. In this context, as we rethink the contours of our involvement in public life in response to the problem of corruption, we must reflect upon some important considerations. I will reflect on three aspects that are essential to a proper concept of public witness. First, the foundation of mission is God's mission (often referred to by scholars as *missio Dei*): our participation in mission, model of mission, and parameters of engagement can be properly understood and interpreted only within the larger story of God's plan of salvation for humanity. Second, the missional goal of the church's public witness is not limited to increasing its number of members. Christ-followers must have a clear missiological understanding of the role of the church today, clearly discerning and moving beyond the commonly and generally understood mission agenda as merely the church's attempt to multiply itself and extend its sphere of influence. Third, we must consider the qualifications of believers and of churches to execute the task.

These three proposals need further exploration. We will begin by considering the scope and core of our calling to show how addressing corruption can be understood and interpreted within the larger story of God's good creation and in the light of the great story of God's redemption.

Corruption in Relation to the Scope of Our Call

For over three decades since my ordination to priesthood, having served in my church in Tanzania in different positions and capacities, I have come to realize that one of the challenges facing many servants of God in ministry is not necessarily to do with whether as a servant of God one has been called to serve or not – here I am talking about proving the validity of one's call – but rather knowing what the call is all about and its meaning. Equally significant is that the challenge becomes real when grasping the style, magnitude, and sometimes amount of work one is called to do. I bring this to the fore due to the

---

14. N. T. Wright, *After You Believe: Why Christian Character Matters* (New York: HarperOne, 2010), cited in Kretzschmar, "African and Western Approaches.," 2.

changing nature of ministry, needs, and styles. The heart of calling is what we are being called to be and do in the world. It all begins with what Christ commanded and commissioned his disciples to do. There are three key elements in the command and commission: to love God and our neighbours, to bear witness to him, and to teach others the things Jesus taught (Matt 28:19–20). Disciples, then and now, respond well to the command when we recognize its threefold christological foundation: that Christ is the way, the truth, and the life. This message reminds us Christians that we are witnesses to Jesus Christ as the way, the truth, and the life (John 14:6).

The concepts "call," "called," and "calling" are not only difficult to elucidate simply but also can be worrying to those asked to do God's work. This is especially true when we are reminded of biblical teachings such as the following:

1. If we confess that we believe in Jesus Christ, then we are called to imitate him in advancing not only our own interests but also the interests of others (Phil 2:1–4);

2. When people are called to serve, they must exercise their responsibility with wisdom and restraint (as in Gen 1:27–28 and 2:15, and Ps 8); and

3. Christians are called to be salt and light in every human society of which they are part (Matt 5:13–14).

In the context of twenty-first-century Africa, one of the key contours for locating, equipping, and sending the church for practical public witness is for the "called" to understand the scope of their call, and indeed the dimensions of Africa's and the world's need. This proposition needs expounding.

Corruption in Relation to the Core of Our Call

The foundation of God's calling can be traced back to Deuteronomy where we are told that the Israelites were called to one key task: to show the world what it means to be the people of God. They were expected to do so by loving God and by caring for their neighbours and for foreigners. It is also clear that God called Abraham and his descendants to be a blessing to the world. Important pictorial language demonstrating how this blessing activity is done is sowing the seed of the kingdom of God. These two calling "styles" are connected because of their common foundation and focus, that is, the presence of God, the Caller, and the relationship between the Caller and the called, in that the called become extremely aware of, and are inspired by, God's holiness and power. As God called Israel into *missio Dei*, so God is calling the church. Daniel L. Migliore reflects on God calling the church: "The church is a servant community that is called to minister in God's name on behalf of the fullness of life for all of God's creatures."[15] The concept "fullness of life for all of God's creatures" brings in a multidimensional interpretation of and approach to calling. Public theologians such as Sunday Agang suggest that we are called "to apply our minds to the problems that face Africa. We are called to look closely at the problems, going beyond the surface issues to the underlying causes rooted in social structures and prevailing worldviews."[16] Towards this end, I propose the following for repositioning and equipping the church for the frontline mission field in twenty-first-century Africa.

God's Plan for Humankind and Our Participation in the Plan

At the core of God's plan for humanity is his liberating, reconciling, and motivating agenda, among other dimensions of salvation design. Paul explains this fundamental teaching in his letter to the Colossians: ". . . and through him to reconcile to himself all things, whether things on earth or things in heaven, by making peace through his blood, shed on the cross" (Col 1:20, NIV). But how is this agenda linked to preparing the church and equipping it so believers can fruitfully engage the world? For the church, liberation and reconciliation generally are important because of their theological and missiological impetus which encourages believers that our participation in God's mission is possible because God's great power is already at work in us (Eph 1:19). This means that we too can bring reconciliation to a broken world by faithfully responding to corruption by word, deed, and signs, thereby making God's shalom evident. Yet how should we begin witnessing? This is possible only if we understand and accept God's liberating and reconciling logic, witness the real evidence of God's love, trust in his help to see his will done, and ensure that in our participation we are partaking in mission in God's way and for God's glory. These fundamental principles apply not only to clergy, who are often considered to be the ones responsible for God's work, but also to the laity, because both are God's stewards and bearers of his image. As Paul reminds us,

---

15. Daniel L. Migliore, *Faith Seeking Understanding: An Introduction to Christian Theology*, 2nd ed. (Grand Rapids: Eerdmans, 2004), 259.

16. Sunday Bobai Agang, "The Need for Public Theology in Africa," in *African Public Theology*, eds. Sunday Bobai Agang, Dion A. Forster, and H. Jurgens Hendriks (Bukuru/Carlisle: HippoBooks, 2020), 12.

> Therefore, if anyone is in Christ, the new creation has come: the old has gone, the new is here! All this is from God, who reconciled us to himself through Christ and gave us the ministry of reconciliation: that God was reconciling the world to himself in Christ, not counting people's sins against them. And he has committed to us the message of reconciliation. We are therefore Christ's ambassadors, as though God were making his appeal through us. We implore you on Christ's behalf: be reconciled to God. (2 Cor 5:17–20, NIV)

This is how "we participate in the reality of the kingdom of God": it is by "learning to regard the concrete world of human physical and social reality in, with, and through Christ"[17] as a witnessing community, in and through all we do. Orlando Costas summarizes what we are expected to be doing: "proclaiming, discipling, mobilizing, growing, liberating, and celebrating." For Costas, these "make up the church's mission-in-life."[18] In my opinion, the believer's motivation should be to become the visible presence of Christ in the world. We who participate in God's divine plan should avoid following our own logic instead of God's logic for our lives.

The Role of the Church

There are many different understandings of the role of the church. Some have been designed to suit a particular context as well as biblical witness and thus effectively remind the church of its role in the world. But various misinterpretations of the role of the church have led to limited or weak participation in the public square, especially at the level of the local church. First is a view of mission as a specialized vocation for specific individuals or mission agencies.[19] This approach encourages the assumption that missions and churches are two separate entities,[20] thereby persistently weakening the relationship between mission and the local church. This disturbing dichotomy results in a disconnect between believers' Christian lives and the rest of their daily lives,

---

17. Don E. Saliers, *Worship as Theology: Foretaste of Divine Glory* (Nashville: Abingdon, 1994), 132.

18. Orlando E. Costas, *The Integrity of Mission: The Inner Life and Outreach of the Church* (San Francisco: Harper & Row, 1979), xiii.

19. Esther Mombo, "From Fourfold Mission to Holistic Mission: Towards Edinburgh 2010," in *Holistic Mission: God's Plan for God's People*, eds. Brian Woolnough and Wonsuk Ma, Regnum Edinburgh 2010 Series (Oxford: Regnum Books, 2010), 42.

20. Mombo, "Fourfold Mission," 42.

between the "sacred" and the "secular" world. But it is wrong to think of the church as "self-contained and institutional. . . . Only that which is on the files in the central office is recognized as part of the Church; only those activities which are initiated and supported from that office are regarded as the Church's work."[21] This is not as it should be. It is both wrong and inconsistent with the biblical functions of the church as "witness and journey within the world."[22] It is incompatible with the cardinal call for the church to serve within the "the liberating and empowering dimension of the gospel."[23] These "threatening contours"[24] need to be revisited if the church is to be well positioned to face the challenges and opportunities of witness in the twenty-first century.

Criterion for Joining the Twenty-First-Century Mission Field Frontline: A Proposal

So every good tree bears good fruit, but the bad tree bears bad fruit. (Matt 7:17, NASB 1995)

How do we follow and bear witness to God on challenging frontlines? Words such as "frontline," "battlefield," "war," and "fighting" represent the intensity of twenty-first-century challenges. Descriptions such as "the world's deteriorating standards," "going down the drain," "violence," "dishonesty," "immorality," "disregard for human life," "materialistic greed," "human selfishness is unchecked," "darkness," and "rottenness" abound.[25] But these challenges are opportunities for the church's public witness. Twenty-first-century contexts do not prevent Christians from drawing on their spiritual resources to be effective in fighting corruption. Furthermore, fighting corruption is an obligation which stems directly from Scripture. As change occurs ever more rapidly and comprehensively (e.g. in the area of advanced communication and information technology), the church has an opportunity to expand the participation

---

21. John Taylor, *Christianity and Politics in Africa* (Westport: Greenwood, 1979), 12.

22. Vinay Samuel, "Mission as Transformation," in *Mission as Transformation: A Theology of the Whole Gospel*, eds. Samuel Vinay and Chris Sugden, Regnum Studies in Mission (Oxford: Regnum, 1999), 229.

23. Samuel, "Mission as Transformation," 230.

24. I use this phrase to indicate why it is important for the church to be aware of the constraints in witnessing for Christ in the context of the church addressing corruption in the public square.

25. These phrases have been picked to help remind the reader what challenges characterize the century. For a detailed analysis see John Stott, *Issues Facing Christians Today: New Perspectives on Social and Moral Dilemmas* (London: Marshall Pickering, 1990), 63.

of believers as they enter the public square, engaging with faith and values, in education, small groups, speaking, and service programmes, and the use of all other God-given gifts. But first the church needs to face and address problems within itself and indicate what is needed to qualify it for witness against corruption.

Witness is of paramount concern to Christians. It is the primary way to communicate faith articulately and effectively. Our witness gives testimony to who and what God is, as well as to the truth that God, who created us as human beings, wishes to restore within us the fullness of our humanity. Our witness to God's love must be unified in order to be credible and sound: our words and our deeds must match, so that both words and deeds embody God's love and make it tangible. A disunified witness belies its own testimony and thus drives people away from faith, while a unified witness verifies its testimony and draws people towards faith. Witnesses should bear in mind that their task is to communicate Christ's invitation to faith. Therefore our witness which delivers this invitation should not be separated from radical dependence on our sender, the Lord Jesus, who himself is the central content of faith and witness. If dependence on Christ is made a priority, those on the frontline will acquire bold confidence in the gospel message and know the importance of engaging respectfully, witnessing with humility, building friendship, seeking reconciliation, practising hospitality, and dialoguing authentically. This is how we should witness to our public hope. The church should consider how to give credible witness and, as John Stott aptly reminds us, how "to catch a fresh vision of Christ."[26] Such a witness is clearly centred on the unique biblical and universal witness of Jesus Christ.

Challenges along the Contours of Witness in Twenty-First-Century Africa

Agenda 2063 of the African Union (AU) recognizes that Africa is currently facing many urgent challenges: conflict, instability, and insecurity, social and economic inequalities, organized crime, the drugs trade, illicit financial flows, poor management of diversity and ethnicity, religious extremism, corruption, failure to harness the demographic dividend, escalation of Africa's disease burden, climate risks and natural disasters, and external shocks, for exam-

---

26. Quoted by Friedemann Walldorf, "Searching for the Soul(s) of Europe: Missiological Models in the Ecumenical Debate on Mission in Postmodern Europe," in *Mission and Modernities*, eds. Rolv Olsen et al., Regnum Edinburgh 2010 Series (Oxford: Regnum, 2011), 62.

ple caused by global market forces, to mention just a few. From a theological front, the voices from the church seeking to read the century are many. As Ruth Padilla DeBorst observes, "In this second decade of the twenty-first century, [we live on] a planet of rising waters and raging fires, in a world of resurgent nationalisms, blatant racisms, exclusionary ethnocentrisms, in communities racked with conflict and war."[27] Others have suggested that today we are in a century of impatience so we tend to "want knowledge, but only if it comes quickly and easily. Even more dangerous than a faulty system of learning, this virtually universal something-for-nothing mentality fundamentally undermines the growth of quality thinking skills and processes."[28] It is Smit who puts in context "shifting political, cultural and economic realities of the time . . . following different images, pursuing different metaphors, making different proposals, holding conflicting viewpoints, and raising new questions."[29] Adding to what has been put forward, I see ethics in public life as disturbing especially in relation to service provision for our communities. In my day-to-day engagement, I see clearly that faith and religion have become areas of less interest and attention.

Holistic Hope along the Contours of Witness in Twenty-First-Century Africa

It is not all bad news in this century. There is also good news. Even secular circles affirm this hope, as when the World Bank expressed in its report *Can Africa Claim the 21st Century?* that although the African continent "entered the 20th century a poor, mostly colonialized region, [as] it enters the 21st [century], a lot has changed. Education has spread, and life expectancy has increased. Many countries have seen gains in civil liberties and political participation."[30] From a theological point of view, the gospel is still intact; it has not changed. While Michael Frost affirms that "the gospel is the good news that God himself has come to rescue and renew all of creation through the work of Jesus Christ on

---

27. Ruth Padilla DeBorst, "Against All Odds – and Ends," in *Relentless Love: Living Out Integral Mission to Combat Poverty, Injustice and Conflict*, ed. Graham Joseph Hill (Carlisle: Langham Global Library, 2020), 231.

28. Philip E. Dow, *Virtuous Minds: Intellectual Character Development* (Downers Grove: IVP Academic, 2013), 86.

29. Dirk J. Smit, "Does It Matter? On Whether There Is Method in the Madness," ch. 3 in *A Companion to Public Theology*, eds. Sebastian Kim and Katie Day, Brill's Companions to Modern Theology 1 (Leiden: Brill, 2017), 67.

30. Alan H. Gelb, ed., *Can Africa Claim the 21st Century?* (Washington, DC: The World Bank, 2000), 7.

our behalf,"[31] Scot McKnight states: "The gospel is the work of God to restore humans to union with God and communion with others, in the context of a community, for the good of others and the world."[32] Whenever I am in the mission field, I see with my own eyes multitudes of people coming to faith who are not only called to live in the world and bear witness to the goodness and holiness of God, but who are faithfully participating in the kingdom-building agenda, even in an increasingly chaotic landscape across the continent of Africa. The church is unique in that it remains the longest-enduring, largest, and strongest institution in God's salvation history. Church communities live within contexts in which injustice is rampant and they understand it at an intimate level. In some countries like mine, Tanzania, the church is still very much respected as an agent of transformation and has tended to enjoy government hospitality and invitations to help in communities. And the church has done well because among its members there are believers who have responsibilities as parents, educators, extended family and religious members, and workers in public and private institutions, who all play a significant role in promoting kingdom values.

Towards a More Effective Anti-Corruption Missional Strategy for the African Church

It is not sufficient for the church in Africa to seek to understand and interpret the complex realities of our twenty-first-century era. The church must be an agent of transformation. This requires, among other things, the need to answer the central question: If the church is already located, equipped, and ready to be sent, because it is already called by God to fight corruption and to work towards creating flourishing and resilient communities on the continent, what then remains that would help it enter the public space courageously and be part of transformational interactions for practical public witness against corruption in Africa in this century? Does the church keep silent? Does Christian faith or a religious spirit recoil? Is the church conscious of the century's conflict between corruption and the church's own ideals? How can the church ensure that its message keeps gaining credibility, not only for the remaining seven decades of this century, but continuing until Christ returns?

---

31. Michael Frost in a Facebook conversation on 7 November 2019, accessed 9 December 2022, https://www.facebook.com/michaelfrost6.

32. Scot McKnight, *Embracing Grace: A Gospel for All of Us* (Brewster: Paraclete, 2005), xii.

As indicated earlier, among many categories of reasons which led to my choice to focus on corruption, three of them – namely, the far-reaching consequences of corruption, the state of the church today, and the criterion for entering this century's frontline mission field – have motivated me to engage my readers as I challenge the church to grasp the seriousness of corruption, take stock, and ask where the voice of the church is, both in the context of widespread corruption in twenty-first-century Africa and in the world as a whole.

Sacrifice and Surrender: Called to Embody the Principles of the Kingdom

This chapter does not pretend to address all the issues facing Africa which it highlights or to offer definitive solutions to all the challenges discussed as they surface on the continent in the twenty-first century. Its aim is to challenge the institution we know as "the church" to move beyond common but limited concepts of God's mission into holistic engagement within the twenty-first-century public space, examining the fruit, the impact, and the outcome of the gospel of Jesus Christ in the context of corruption. The chapter seeks to help the church consider corruption as part of its primary task of preaching the Word and equipping God's people for the work of ministry out in the world. Our central message is: Yes, the church can fruitfully engage the public and bear witness to the problem of corruption. But this is a qualified yes, conditional on the need for a thorough reflection on the gospel and its radical implications for twenty-first-century realities. In a broader context, the chapter focuses on equipping the church to boldly enter or re-enter the twenty-first-century "public space" and be able to contest for a "Christian space." The use of the term "contour" stands for the need and possibility of the church to discern what shape or form of witness it should use that suits the current situation as the church commends what the gospel teaches about the common good, part of which is the call to stand up and address corruption, for there is no aspect of life from which God's mission should be excluded. God's mission has no limits in place, entity, or structure. And the New Testament is clear when it calls the church of Christ a royal priesthood (1 Pet 2:9–10), which should include a political aspect of mission where the church is a prophetic voice speaking to the world's powers, calling the world to justice and truth, and pointing out corruption.[33]

---

33. This political aspect of mission is developed in Johannes Reimer, *Missio Politica: The Mission of Church and Politics* (Carlisle: Langham Global Library, 2017).

Conclusion

> Arise and go,
> For this is no place of rest
> Because of the uncleanness that brings on destruction,
> A painful destruction. (Mic 2:10, NASB 1995)

This chapter has explored and suggested some contours, shapes, and forms for locating, equipping, and sending the church for faithful public life and practical public witness in twenty-first-century Africa. I began by reviewing the current state of and the fast-changing nature of the twenty-first century in relation to ways of witnessing to Christ. For the purpose of missional focus, and in order to help my readers process and reflect on the challenges and opportunities for mission in the century, I identified the problem of corruption as being key in a Christian conversation about the shape of the church and its mission in the twenty-first century. I have argued that, in context, among many other challenges facing humanity, we should acknowledge that corruption, which undermines public welfare across the globe, stands as a critical missional concern which needs a Christian faith response both in private and in the public square. I emphatically maintain that the church has strong reasons to be involved in anti-corruption-related initiatives. I highlighted that this is possible because the Christian church of the twenty-first century has not lost its unique identity and, despite the challenges marking the era, is still called, and expected to faithfully respond, to the God-given task in the world of witnessing to Christ. Using the word "contours," I provided a picture of the present opportunities available and the challenges facing the church. While I acknowledged encouraging signs that in some parts of the world churches and believers are taking the issue of corruption and its realities seriously by developing and shaping relevant and appropriate contours of witness both globally and with specific reference to the continent of Africa, I also cautioned that, in order for the church to respond appropriately to this social problem, twenty-first-century church leaders, and indeed all Christ followers, need a wisdom anchored in gospel truth and rooted in a biblical narrative of the origin of and solution to human suffering, which remains of paramount importance. Our witness in this century requires that, before we enter the public square, we should first learn to hear and obey the voice of the Lord in order to be the new people God desires. These are his followers who, with transformed thinking, will be able to act with competence, vigorously contributing as a church in the twenty-first century, called to groan alongside the people they serve, as we seek to understand and remedy the causes of their suffering. Similarly, for the church in Africa to continue its mission purpose more effectively this century, the needed wisdom and discernment will help to re-engage, encourage, equip, mobilize, and shape a new generation of believers to be salt and light with authenticity for mission in the diverse world of this century. I pray that my church in Africa might grasp God's vision for the world and successfully respond to the millions on the continent and beyond who are yearning for a more human life in a new and corruption-free society.

Bibliography

African Union. *Agenda 2063: The Africa We Want*. Addis Ababa: African Union, 2015. https://au.int/en/Agenda2063/popular_version.

Agang, Sunday Bobai. "The Need for Public Theology in Africa." In *African Public Theology*, edited by Sunday Bobai Agang, Dion A. Forster, and H. Jurgens Hendriks, 3–14. Bukuru/Carlisle: HippoBooks, 2020.

Banzikiza, Constance R. *Restoring Moral Formation in Africa*. Eldoret: AMECEA Gaba, 2001.

Costas, Orlando E. *The Integrity of Mission: The Inner Life and Outreach of the Church*. San Francisco: Harper & Row, 1979.

DeBorst, Ruth Padilla. "Against All Odds – and Ends." In *Relentless Love: Living Out Integral Mission to Combat Poverty, Injustice and Conflict*, edited by Graham Joseph Hill, 231–43. Foreword by Melba Padilla Maggay. Carlisle: Langham Global Library, 2020.

Dow, Philip E. *Virtuous Minds: Intellectual Character Development*. Downers Grove: IVP Academic, 2013.

Gelb, Alan H., ed. *Can Africa Claim the 21st Century?* Washington, DC: The World Bank, 2000. https://openknowledge.worldbank.org/server/api/core/bitstreams/da4a29ac-408b-59f9-9e95-f7dcabad5a60/content.

Kretzschmar, Louise. "African and Western Approaches to the Moral Formation of Christian Leaders: The Role of Spiritual Disciplines in Counteracting Moral Deficiencies." *HTS Teologiese Studies/Theological Studies* 76, no. 2 (2020): Article #5913, 10 pages.

Lausanne Movement. *The Cape Town Commitment: A Confession of Faith and a Call to Action; The Third Lausanne Congress*. Peabody: Hendrickson, 2011. https://www.lausanne.org/content/ctcommitment.

Maluleke, Tinyiko Sam. "A Post-colonial South African Church: Problems and Promises." In *African Theology on the Way: Current Conversations*, edited by Diane B. Stinton, 150–60. International Study Guides 46. London: SPCK, 2010.

McKnight, Scot. *Embracing Grace: A Gospel for All of Us*. Brewster: Paraclete, 2005.

Migliore, Daniel L. *Faith Seeking Understanding: An Introduction to Christian Theology*. 2nd ed. Grand Rapids: Eerdmans, 2004.

Mombo, Esther. "From Fourfold Mission to Holistic Mission: Towards Edinburgh 2010." In *Holistic Mission: God's Plan for God's People*, edited by Brian Woolnough and Wonsuk Ma, 37–46. Regnum Edinburgh 2010 Series. Oxford: Regnum, 2010.

Mugambi, J. N. K., and Anne Nasimiyu-Wasike, eds. *Moral and Ethical Issues in African Christianity: Exploratory Essays in Moral Theology*. Nairobi: Acton, 1999.

Ntlha, Moss. "Ethics and the Church in Africa." In *What Is a Good Life? An Introduction to Christian Ethics in 21st Century Africa*, edited by Louise Kretzschmar, Wessel Bentley, and André van Niekerk, 287–97. Kempton Park: AcadSA, 2009.

Reimer, Johannes. *Missio Politica: The Mission of Church and Politics*. Carlisle: Langham Global Library, 2017.

Saliers, Don E. *Worship as Theology: Foretaste of Divine Glory*. Nashville: Abingdon, 1994.

Samuel, Vinay. "Mission as Transformation." In *Mission as Transformation: A Theology of the Whole Gospel*, edited by Samuel Vinay and Chris Sugden, 227–35. Regnum Studies in Mission. Oxford: Regnum, 1999.

Sebahene, Alfred. *Corruption Mocking at Justice: A Theological and Ethical Perspective on Public Life in Tanzania and Its Implications for the Anglican Church of Tanzania*. Carlisle: Langham Monographs, 2017.

Smit, Dirk J. "Does It Matter? On Whether There Is Method in the Madness." Chapter 3 in *A Companion to Public Theology*, edited by Sebastian Kim and Katie Day, 67–92. Brill's Companions to Modern Theology 1. Leiden: Brill, 2017.

Spurgeon, Charles H. *Morning and Evening: A New Edition of the Classic Devotional Based on The Holy Bible, English Standard Version*. Revised and updated by Alistair Begg. Wheaton: Crossway, 2003.

Stackhouse, John G., Jr. *Making the Best of It: Following Christ in the Real World*. Oxford: Oxford University Press, 2008.

Stott, John. *Issues Facing Christians Today: New Perspectives on Social and Moral Dilemmas*. London: Marshall Pickering, 1990.

Taylor, John. *Christianity and Politics in Africa*. Harmondsworth: Penguin, 1957. Reprint: Westport: Greenwood, 1979.

Walldorf, Friedemann. "Searching for the Soul(s) of Europe: Missiological Models in the Ecumenical Debate on Mission in Postmodern Europe." In *Mission and Modernities*, edited by Rolv Olsen et al., 57–82. Regnum Edinburgh 2010 Series. Oxford: Regnum, 2011.

Wright, N. T. *Surprised by Hope: Rethinking Heaven, the Resurrection, and the Mission of the Church*. London: SPCK, 2007.

11

Political Ideology and Biblical Interpretation

Milton Acosta Benítez

Professor of Old Testament, Fundación Universitaria Seminario Bíblico de Colombia, Medellín, Colombia

Introduction

In books on biblical interpretation, two key topics frequently fail to be included: the emotional impact of the text on readers, and the political ideology inherent within the text and within its interpreter. These statements are not meant to turn the Bible into a soap opera or to encourage political bias, as there is already enough of both. Rather, they simply point out the lack of attention given to these important hermeneutical issues. In this chapter, we will discuss the role of political ideology in biblical interpretation, while leaving the topic of emotions for another day. We will explore the intersection of political ideology, biblical interpretation, and public theology within the context of evangelical Christianity and highlight the importance of recognizing the influence of political ideologies on the interpretation of the Bible and how it shapes the perspectives and actions of believers.

The thesis we propose in this chapter is straightforward: every Bible interpreter holds a political ideology that influences his or her interpretation of the sacred text to varying degrees. This ideology may not always be explicitly formulated or expressed in writing. The thesis assumes that political ideology, whether conscious or unconscious, precedes the act of interpretation. However, the problem arises when interpreters assume that they have no political ideology or believe that the Bible itself is devoid of political ideology, or that believers can be apolitical. In reality, as political beings, we inherently hold political perspectives by the mere fact of our existence. It's a separate matter whether we align with any specific political party or its representatives, as even that indicates a political inclination. Because Christians hold diverse political commitments, they need to engage in civil and purposeful conversations, understanding, and self-reflection among themselves in order to refine their public theology and address issues of social justice effectively.

For some Christians, discussing political ideology and biblical interpretation in the same context may be seen as politicizing the Bible or distorting its nature. However, it will become clearer later on that the term "politics," as used in this chapter, does not refer to a political party but rather to a way of understanding public affairs, governance, economy, social order, and the impact of the public sphere on the private. It cannot be denied that each political party adheres to its own political ideology, and Christians are also influenced by these different ways of thinking and understanding public life.

To persuade readers of the validity of these claims, the easiest and most efficient approach is to start with biblical interpreters who openly express their political ideology. Accordingly, we will first examine three cases: liberation theology, feminist theology, and integral mission theology. Then we will provide three brief examples where interpreters unconsciously reveal that their interpretation is shaped by political ideology, even if they may not recognize or explicitly articulate it. While these interpreters may believe that their biblical interpretations remain untainted by any political ideology, the existence of divergent views among Christians on various issues demonstrates the complexity of the matter.[1]

The purpose of this chapter is not to transform the Bible into a political manifesto or turn the church into another political party. Nor do we suggest that all Christians should adopt identical political views. Christians hold diverse political views yielding the potential for polarization and division within the church. Instead, our intention is to prompt readers to acknowledge and reflect on the role of political ideologies in biblical interpretation. As human beings, we are inherently political and consistently make political choices, ranging

---

1. The history of Judaism provides a clear example of the aforementioned assertions. Despite sharing the same biblical texts and traditions, different Jewish groups interpreted their sacred texts differently, especially regarding the role of these texts in society. This disparity is evident in their diverse conceptions of the arrival of the Messiah, which ranged from a political deliverer and nationalistic saviour to a prophet, teacher, and spiritual redeemer. Given the complexity of their history, this diversity was inevitable. The Jewish people experienced different historical events, influences, interpretation methods, and sociopolitical contexts. Therefore, expecting a monolithic community would be a mistake.

from simple actions such as using a plastic bag to complex decisions such as exercising our right to vote. These choices encompass economic models and how we understand the preservation of our environment. However, it's important to note that political ideology is not the sole determinant of an interpreter's understanding of the Bible. Factors such as ecclesiastical tradition, education, personal experience, personality, and country of residence also contribute to their interpretation, but we won't address those factors in this chapter.

Liberation Theology

Liberation theology is the first authentically Latin American theology.[2] The fundamental book of liberation theology was written by the Catholic priest Gustavo Gutiérrez.[3] In this theology, the relationship between politics and theology is explicitly recognized. The argument about the determining role of political ideology in the interpretation of the Bible, as a critique of North Atlantic theology, has been built from different ideological platforms, but its ubiquity leaves no doubt about its importance.

Liberation theologians predominantly published their works during the 1970s and 1980s, although publications on liberation theology have never stopped. Even well into the twenty-first century, the impact of this theology remains significant. While there was a decline in publications and interest following the fall of the Berlin Wall in 1989, it did not signify the disappearance of liberation theology. On the contrary, it led to an explosion of various theologies across different regions of the world which embraced, to varying degrees, the central proposition of applying liberation theology to specific concerns. This section does not aim to provide an exhaustive historical account or a comprehensive summary of liberation theology, nor does it present its core ideas. Rather, its purpose is to highlight the evident influence of political ideology within liberation theology. This influence is not a matter of speculation or

---

2. However, Padilla affirms that "antes de la teología de la liberación, en el campo protestante germinó una teología emparentada con aquella, de la cual sería posible afirmar que fue el primer intento de teologizar a partir de la situación latinoamericana [before liberation theology, a theology related to it germinated in the Protestant field, which could be said to be the first attempt to theologize from the Latin American situation]." C. René Padilla, *Misión integral: ensayos sobre el Reino y la iglesia* (Buenos Aires: Nueva Creación, 1986), 201, n. 20. Padilla's thought is accessible in English in his *What Is Integral Mission? Global Voices in Latin America* (Oxford: Regnum, 2021).

3. Gustavo Gutiérrez, *Teología de la liberación: perspectivas* (Salamanca: Ediciones Sígueme, 1972). An English translation is available: *A Theology of Liberation: History, Politics, and Salvation* (Maryknoll: Orbis, 1973). Orbis published a revised edition in 1988.

deduction; it is explicitly expressed in the writings of liberation theologians. In fact, numerous works, articles, and dissertations have been dedicated to exploring the political philosophy of liberation theology.[4]

Liberation theology encompasses a range of viewpoints and topics, hence the term "liberation theologies" is used. Nonetheless, there are some fundamental concepts and concerns that are widely shared among liberation theologians. First, in liberation theology, the initial step for theological development is the theologian's involvement in a political mission for the emancipation of the impoverished and the marginalized. Therefore, the first action of theology is political. Next, the theologian interprets his or her experience in the light of the Scriptures, and vice versa. This cyclical process, called "hermeneutic circulation," is repeated continuously.

Liberation theology employs Marxist theory as a framework for understanding both contemporary reality and biblical texts. This approach is utilized due to its efficacy in explaining poverty in Latin America and seeking its eradication. It is important to note that not all liberation theologians endorsed the use of violence as a means to end poverty and oppression. Many, such as Jon Sobrino,[5] opposed violence based on the belief that it begets further violence and because it is incompatible not only with the principles of the gospel but also with liberation theology itself. However, there is a consensus among liberation theologians regarding the assertion that Christian theology and pastoral ministry are closely intertwined with the issue of poverty and oppression in Latin America. This recognition stems from the fundamental question posed by liberation theology: How do we speak about God within the context of poverty and oppression?

The exodus narrative holds significant importance in liberation theology, given its portrayal of the liberation of the enslaved Israelites from Egypt. The central theme of this theology is the image of God as the liberator of the oppressed. Applying Marxist ideology to the exodus and the conquest of Canaan led to the conceptualization of a social revolution by the Canaanite peasants to free themselves from the oppression of the Canaanite elites. This was reinterpreted during the exile as an exodus from Egypt.

---

4. E.g. William B. Duncan, "The Political Philosophy of Gustavo Gutiérrez" (PhD diss., Texas Tech University, 1995).

5. Jon Sobrino, *Jesucristo liberador: lectura histórico-teológica de Jesús de Nazaret* (Mexico City: Universidad Iberoamericana, 1994); translated as *Jesus the Liberator: A Historical-Theological Reading of Jesus of Nazareth* (Maryknoll: Orbis, 1993).

Liberation theologians, drawing from the exodus narrative and various other biblical texts, perceive God as aligning with the marginalized and disadvantaged, often referred to in the Bible as the stranger, the orphan, and the widow. Consequently, this theological perspective posits that God adopts a preferential option for the poor and the oppressed.[6] In light of this understanding, theology and the church are thus called upon to address the very issues that are of concern to God, namely, the struggles and challenges faced by the impoverished and the marginalized.

José Míguez Bonino, one of the few Protestant liberation theologians, emphasizes the necessity of a political theology in Latin America for the liberation of the poor. However, he highlights that this liberation stems from the faith of the poor themselves, rather than solely relying on Marxist ideology. Míguez acknowledges that there may be areas of convergence between the Marxist and Christian causes for the liberation of the oppressed from societal oppression, aiming to establish a more just and equitable society. Nonetheless, he contends that Marxist categories were developed in northern Europe and may not entirely align with the realities of Latin America. Thus, these categories are applied as a method rather than as rigid dogma.[7] But Latin America's liberation theology owes more to biblical texts than to modern political theory. While many social categories used by liberation theology are borrowed from Marxist analysis, the key terms – "oppression," "justice," "liberation," "poor," "rich," "oppressed," and so forth – are taken directly from the Old Testament and are key biblical themes.[8]

Critics of liberation theology have primarily focused on its methodology and outcomes; however, in Latin America, there remains a prevalence of theologies that seem to have originated in places where poverty doesn't exist. This observation suggests that the influence of political ideology in biblical interpretation is reflected not only in the topics it addresses but also in those it neglects. The absence of issues such as social justice, poverty reduction, and the struggle against oppression is indicative of a colonial political ideology

---

6. The phrase "God adopts a preferential option for the poor and the oppressed" was prominently articulated during the Latin American Episcopal Conference (CELAM) held in Medellín, Colombia, in 1968. The document produced at the conference, known as the "Final Document of Medellín," highlighted the church's commitment to solidarity with the poor and marginalized. It emphasized the need for structural changes to address the root causes of poverty and social injustice.

7. José Míguez Bonino, *Doing Theology in a Revolutionary Situation* (Philadelphia: Fortress, 1975), 35.

8. In Spanish-language liberation theology, these terms are *opresión, justicia, liberación, pobre, rico*, and *oprimido*.

that serves the interests of economic powers rather than the people. Clearly, political ideology not only influences biblical interpretation but also gives rise to a specific form of public theology – and thus of public witness – along with its associated commitments.

Political Ideology in Feminist Theology

Feminist theologians identify their theological endeavour as critical feminist liberation theology. Given the diverse experiences of women, there are various expressions of feminist theology, and a wealth of literature exists on the subject. Due to both limitations in space and my own expertise, it is not possible to provide comprehensive coverage of this vast topic here. However, it is noteworthy that feminist theologians explicitly acknowledge the political dimensions of their theology and their approach to theological inquiry. Just as the concept of liberation hermeneutics is discussed, there is also discourse on feminist biblical interpretation and feminist hermeneutics. In this theology, the political theme is clearly articulated, occupying a central and prominent position. This is evident from the titles of various works, particularly those by Elisabeth Schüssler Fiorenza, a pre-eminent feminist biblical scholar who has made significant contributions to the field of feminist biblical interpretation. She defines her work as the "critical feminist practice of biblical interpretation for liberation."[9]

Feminist theologians define their theological enterprise as a democratic political movement that aims to liberate women from systemic oppression, enabling them to fully exercise their rights and experience dignity as human beings. The objective is to achieve "radical equality" in both societal and ecclesiastical realms. To accomplish this, it is necessary to address and transform all structures and situations that perpetuate the oppression of women. In terms of biblical interpretation, Elisabeth Schüssler Fiorenza characterizes feminist theologians as "'wo/men workers' of divine Wisdom who fashion biblical studies as public-political interpretation."[10] Feminist theologians do not consider their liberation project to be any less significant than non-religious feminism; both are regarded as vital aspects of the feminist movement.

---

9. Elisabeth Schüssler Fiorenza, *But She Said: Feminist Practices of Biblical Interpretation* (Boston: Beacon, 1992), 11.

10. Elisabeth Schüssler Fiorenza, *Sharing Her Word: Feminist Biblical Interpretation in Context* (Edinburgh: T&T Clark, 1998), 21.

Feminist theology emphasizes the importance of considering both the contemporary context of interpreters and the historical context of biblical writers. According to Schüssler Fiorenza, it is essential to recognize that the biblical text is not only patriarchal but also "kyriarchical."

"Kyriocentric" and "kyriarchical" are technical terms used to critique and analyse power structures within religious and social contexts. "Kyriocentric" describes a worldview or perspective that centres and prioritizes the power, authority, and interests of those in dominant positions. The terms are derived from the Greek word *kyrios* (or *kurios*) meaning "lord" or "master." In the context of Schüssler Fiorenza's work, "kyriocentric" refers to a theology or religious framework that upholds and reinforces hierarchical systems and privileges the perspectives and experiences of those in positions of power, typically men. "Kyriarchical" is used to describe hierarchical structures of power and authority that perpetuate domination and subordination. It combines the Greek words *kyrios* and *archē* (meaning "rule" or "leadership"). "Kyriarchical" points to the ways in which systems, such as patriarchy, reinforce and sustain unequal power relations by exerting control over others based on gender, class, race, or other social categories.

While the followers of Jesus did challenge some cultural norms of their time, Schüssler Fiorenza argues that they did not go far enough in addressing issues such as the *Haustafeln* (household codes), slavery, and power dynamics between men and women. This perspective highlights the need for a critical examination of the biblical text and its historical context, taking into account the limitations and potential biases present within it.

As far as public theology is concerned, critical feminist study of the Bible acknowledges that certain texts, rather than challenging and transforming oppressive systems, can reinforce patterns of abuse, submission, and silencing of victims. Examples of such dynamics can be observed in the theology of suffering (where suffering is attributed to Christ or seen as divine discipline), in prayer (where persistence is depicted as annoying to God until he grants attention), and in the portrayal of women (as deceived by the serpent).

Feminist scholars argue that this kyriocentric language does not accurately reflect the reality experienced by women, but rather reflects the cultural context in which the biblical writers lived. By critically examining these texts, feminist theologians seek to unveil and challenge the patriarchal biases present within them, while also reclaiming the voices and experiences of women who have been marginalized or silenced. The goal is to engage in a transformative interpretation that promotes gender equality and justice in society.[11]

Feminist theologians argue that the andro/kyriocentric language of the Bible is deeply embedded in the political and social structures of the ancient world in which it was written, and that this language reinforces patriarchal and hierarchical power structures. While there are a few instances in the Bible where women play prominent roles or where the equality of men and women is affirmed, these instances are the exception rather than the rule. Feminist theologians argue that the Bible, as a whole, perpetuates the cultural norms of its time and reinforces the oppression of women. As such, feminist theology seeks to critique and challenge these patriarchal structures in both the biblical text and contemporary society.

Indeed, feminist theologians such as Teresia M. Hinga and Rosa Cursach Salas recognize that certain biblical voices, such as those found in the books of Isaiah, Amos, Micah, and Jeremiah, can be seen as authentically liberating and valuable for developing a Christian feminist theology. They acknowledge that the Bible was written within a patriarchal context by men and historically interpreted through patriarchal exegesis by men as well. As a result, women as agents of social transformation are not commonly depicted in biblical narratives.[12]

However, the biblical text is not homogeneous on this matter. While some texts denounce structures of oppression, such as the example of Judges 19, there are many others that uphold and defend patriarchal structures and relationships. Hinga, drawing from the model of Paulo Freire, proposes raising awareness among Christian women to facilitate their liberation as well as the liberation of their oppressors.[13] The aim, following Jesus's example, is to establish a "discipleship of equals" emphasizing the equality of all disciples within the Christian community.[14]

Similar to Latin American liberation theology, feminist theology also begins with a political project; in their case, it's focused on the struggle for women's liberation and against the assumption that women are not a part of

---

11. Here one notices a resemblance to Seibert's thesis regarding violence in the Bible: one thing is the "actual God" and another the "textual God." Eric A. Seibert, *The Violence of Scripture: Overcoming the Old Testament's Troubling Legacy* (Minneapolis: Fortress, 2012).

12. Teresia M. Hinga, *African, Christian, Feminist: The Enduring Search for What Matters* (Maryknoll: Orbis, 2017), 45.

13. Hinga, *African, Christian, Feminist*, 49.

14. Hinga, 44, 46.

biblical history.[15] However, it is important to note that feminist theology, while labelled as feminist liberation theology, is not ideologically dependent on Latin American liberation theology. Unlike liberation theology, feminist theology does not adopt Marxist ideology as its interpretive framework for the Bible. Instead, it employs feminist analysis as its political ideology.

One crucial concern for Schüssler Fiorenza and feminist theologians is that within the hermeneutics of liberation, the presumed interpreter remains male.[16] This issue reflects a central hermeneutical suspicion within feminist theology, as it questions both the text and the reader, particularly whether the reader produces a theology that aligns with their own affinity, such as advocating for the poor and oppressed. Feminist theology seeks to challenge the underlying power dynamics and assumptions that have shaped traditional interpretations, offering alternative perspectives that centre women's experiences and promote gender equality.

When engaging in biblical interpretation through a feminist political ideology, the interpreter is prompted to question the extent to which each text promotes democratic ideals of equality, dignity, and well-being for women and all individuals who, like them, suffer and experience humiliation due to kyriarchal structures. It is important to critically examine passages that may have oppressive implications, particularly within an androcentric culture. For instance, the statement "love endures all things" can have an oppressive impact in an androcentric culture. Feminist biblical interpretation aims to challenge such interpretations and highlight the need for inclusive and liberating readings of the text that affirm the rights and agency of all individuals.

In this concise presentation, we have observed that feminist theology emerges from a feminist political ideology and addresses biblical and societal issues that resonate with a broad audience. It carries implications for both biblical interpretation and public and ecclesiastical matters. The public theology of feminist theology is explicit and focused, stemming from its unique understanding of the Bible. However, it is important to note that the political dimensions of biblical interpretation extend beyond liberation theology or feminist theology. Building upon Schüssler Fiorenza's insights, Rosa Cursach Salas asserts that theology and biblical interpretation are inherently political

---

15. Rosa Cursach Salas, "A Christian Feminist Hermeneutics of the Bible," in *Feminist Biblical Studies in the Twentieth Century: Scholarship and Movement*, ed. Elisabeth Schüssler Fiorenza, Bible and Women 9.1 (Atlanta: Society of Biblical Literature, 2014), 173–74.

16. Schüssler Fiorenza, *Sharing Her Word*, 202, n. 21.

endeavours.[17] While this statement holds true, not all Christians, whether theologians or laypeople, men or women, are fully aware of this reality.

Similar to liberation theologians, feminist theologians employ "ethico-political imperatives as critical interpretive lenses and criteria" in their study of the Bible. They use these imperatives to evaluate the use of the Bible in theology and within the church, as well as to engage in cultural exegesis.[18]

Elisabeth Schüssler Fiorenza is interested in noting the political context of the academic discourse on biblical interpretation in the United States:

> I have done so in the full awareness that such an expressed political location may mark my reflections as unscholarly and ideological in the eyes of some colleagues. Yet liberation theologians and critical theorists have made us aware that all discourses represent political interests. Meaning is always politically constructed insofar as interpretation is located in social networks of power/knowledge relations that shape society.[19]

Schüssler Fiorenza refers here to academics, yet the statement implies that the non-academic sphere is where the situation is most prevalent. It is possible that Schüssler Fiorenza speaks from a time when there was greater trust in the objectivity of academic discourse, and individuals making political references were regarded with scepticism. Another crucial point to note is the mention of liberation theology and its role in emphasizing the political element within academic discourse, irrespective of its origins.

In feminist theology, there are two distinct alternatives for the interpretation of the Bible. One maintains the traditional patriarchal interpretation, while the other engages in critical analysis, questioning and subverting it. The choice between these alternatives reflects a political perspective that ascribes meaning to the Bible, shapes the lives of believers, and influences their understanding of the role of Christians in society. This perspective extends beyond the patriarchal issue to encompass any form of oppression or the dominance of certain members of society over others.

---

17. Cursach Salas, "Christian Feminist Hermeneutics," 164.

18. Elisabeth Schüssler Fiorenza, "Entre la investigación y el movimiento social: estudios feministas de la Biblia en el siglo xx [Between research and social movement: Feminist biblical studies in the 20th century]," in *La exégesis feminista del siglo XX: investigación y movimiento* [Feminist exegesis of the 20th century: Research and movement], ed. Elisabeth Schüssler Fiorenza, Biblia y las mujeres [Bible and Women] (Navarra: Editorial Verbo Divino, 2015), 13.

19. Schüssler Fiorenza, *But She Said*, 3.

Thus, Schüssler Fiorenza advocates what she terms "emancipatory movements." These movements aim to challenge the traditional gender hierarchy by promoting the inclusion of women in both biblical academia and other leadership positions. In this vision, women would interpret the Bible through a feminist lens, rejecting the patriarchal discourse of subservience and obedience.[20] A feminist interpretation of the Bible serves to challenge and dismantle the all-encompassing rhetoric of right-wing neo-fundamentalist Christians and androcentric liberal theology. Simultaneously, it empowers women and other marginalized individuals in their personal lives, striving for freedom, justice, and overall well-being.[21]

According to Schüssler Fiorenza, in order to bring about these necessary changes, a "reconceptualization and transformation" of biblical studies is crucial. This is because the interpretation of the Bible is determined by underlying ideological frameworks, which in turn either legitimize or challenge oppressive social and ecclesiastical structures.[22] Often, interpreters are unaware of their own political ideologies, which precede and shape their interpretations of the Bible. These interpretations are then employed to either defend or question existing political, social, and ecclesiastical systems:

> I seek to work out a process and method for a feminist political reading that can empower women who, for whatever reasons, are still affected by the Bible to read "against the grain" of its patriarchal rhetoric. Moreover, such a critical feminist interpretation is not limited to canonical texts but can be equally applied to extracanonical sources and traditions.[23]

Given that the author conceives the political as an essential component of the (androcentric) biblical text and also inherent to all biblical reading, political reading should not be understood here as a novelty but only in the feminist aspect. The term "feminist" is preferred to others because it is a political concept and a movement, unlike other adjectives for theology, such as "womanist," "Asian," "Latin American," "African," or "*mujerista*."[24] The political nature of

---

20. Schüssler Fiorenza, 4.
21. Schüssler Fiorenza, 5.
22. Schüssler Fiorenza, 5.
23. Schüssler Fiorenza, 7.
24. "Womanist" and "*mujerista*" are frameworks within feminist theology focused on the experiences and liberation of women of colour. "Womanism" addresses the unique struggles of African American women, emphasizing intersectionality and advocating for empowerment. "*Mujerista*" theology integrates feminism and liberation theology, addressing sexism, racism,

biblical texts and the inherent political dimension in all biblical reading are not seen as novelties, but rather integral aspects.[25]

Feminist theology is a type of liberation theology: "In reclaiming women's authority to shape and determine biblical religions, feminist theology attempts to reconceptualize the act of biblical interpretation as a moment in the global praxis for liberation." In order to achieve this, it is necessary to understand "the transformation of patriarchal structures both in the Bible and in our time" as a fundamental task. Furthermore, feminist theology "must seek to empower women to become theological subjects, who participate in the critical construction of biblical-theological meaning, and to establish their authority to do so."[26]

Throughout history, women have consistently engaged in the interpretation of the Bible. In the feminist hermeneutic approach, it is not a question of women interpreting the Bible for the first time, but that they do not do so "within the spiritual or theological frameworks articulated by elite men," as they have done historically.[27]

Theology of Integral Mission

In this section, our primary reference will be the book *Misión integral* (Integral mission) authored by C. René Padilla,[28] a renowned Latin American theologian. Padilla's theological reflection begins with the premise that social action and evangelization are inseparable aspects of the gospel of Christ, Christian faith, and theology. He likens them to the two wings of an aeroplane, emphasizing their interdependence. The theology of integral mission arises in parallel with liberation theology, albeit with distinct methodological assumptions and outcomes.

Padilla is critical of Western theology, liberation theology, and the Latin American church. He expresses dissatisfaction with the Latin American church's belief that it can be the church of Christ without a conscious and articulate theology. He also finds Western theology, particularly during the time he writes, to be lacking in contextual engagement. It tends to be a generic theology that pays little attention to issues of violence, poverty, and oppres-

---

and classism within Latina culture, highlighting community and solidarity. Both frameworks seek to challenge oppression and promote justice.

25. Schüssler Fiorenza, *But She Said*, 8.
26. Schüssler Fiorenza, 8.
27. Schüssler Fiorenza, 20.
28. Padilla, *Misión integral*.

sion. Moreover, it fails to offer a critical analysis of the political and economic systems that contribute to these conditions.

In the case of liberation theology, Padilla argues that while it advocates for the "construction of a new man," it risks limiting itself to an emphasis on "economic, social, and political salvation."[29] This limitation arises from liberation theology's adoption of Marxist ideology as the lens through which it interprets reality and fosters hope. Padilla asserts that theology often reflects the historical situation,[30] and this critique applies not only to liberation theology but extends beyond it.

Within this context, Padilla puts forward the theology of integral mission as an alternative. This theological framework encompasses not only a theological perspective but also ecclesiology and a methodological approach. In integral mission theology, the church is seen as a catalyst for social transformation rather than passive accommodation. It emphasizes that the church should not conform to prevailing social structures and political ideologies unless they align with the recognition of Christ's lordship over all aspects, including social and economic issues.

Padilla highlights the danger of the church accommodating itself to these structures without a critical examination of their alignment with Christ's lordship. Such accommodation can result in the propagation of a consumerist gospel that perpetuates oppressive ideologies. In essence, there is a risk of the church becoming complicit in the very systems it should challenge.

Padilla asserts that social structures are intricately linked to political and economic ideologies. He argues that if economic powers perpetuate widespread poverty, they can be regarded as evil forces. It is the flawed and unjust system itself that enslaves individuals and gives rise to the proliferation of idols. One of the most prominent and concerning idols in contemporary economies is consumerism, which manifests itself through materialistic extravagance and fashion. Consumerism has become the prevailing ideology forcefully imposed upon the modern world, even in regions marked by poverty. As a result, societies have adopted a consumerist mindset, wherein the pursuit of material possessions and immediate gratification prevails. This ideology has become deeply entrenched, even in the midst of impoverished communities.[31]

Padilla's argument revolves around the belief that if Christ is acknowledged as Lord and if we are living in the era of God's kingdom, then the gospel inher-

---

29. Padilla, 21.
30. Padilla, 86.
31. Padilla, 49.

ently opposes and rejects all forms of idolatry and oppression. Consequently, it inevitably clashes with dominant economic and political systems, regardless of our acceptance or resistance. The core message of the gospel is that God has triumphed over all these powers. However, this victory should not be misconstrued as the triumph of a particular political party or ideology.

The transformative essence of the gospel initiates with repentance and the forgiveness of sins, which necessitate a complete reorientation of life. As the gospel encompasses the entirety of human existence, it becomes inextricably linked with political and economic matters. Political and economic issues cannot be avoided since the gospel addresses and impacts all aspects of life.

Padilla holds that the gospel cannot be confused with ideologies or reduced to any one in particular since Christ surpasses our social, political, and economic categories. "As Christians we are called to testify about a transcendent, otherworldly Christ, through whose sacrifice we have received the forgiveness of sins and reconciliation with God."[32] Thus, unlike liberation theology and feminist theology, Padilla critically refers to the existence of left and right ideologies, and the influence they have on the interpretation of the Bible, ecclesiology, and pastoral care, but he does not state what his ideology is. We assume that he is neither left nor right. Biblical?[33] The truth is that integral mission is interested in noting the ethical consequences of the gospel, both in private and in public, above the numerical growth of the church and the celebrity culture of ministers.

Padilla also critiques the tendency to spiritualize the gospel, and he challenges those who fail to recognize the spiritual powers at work in public affairs, including the oppressive economic models that perpetuate poverty. A paragraph that succinctly encapsulates Padilla's perspective on public theology is as follows:

> If evangelization and social action are considered essential in the mission, we do not need a manual that tells us which comes first and which comes next. On the other hand, if they are not considered essential, the effort to understand the relationship between them is a futile academic exercise; as useless as trying to understand the relationship between the left wing and the right wing

---

32. Padilla, 41.
33. Padilla, 165.

of an airplane, when one believes that the airplane can fly with only one wing.[34]

One of Padilla's concerns is a simplistic vision of the gospel where the church is constituted as a mass without orientation or theological reflection, where ideologies come and go without anyone noticing their presence (such as consumerism, the myth of progress, and hope in economic growth or revolution, for example). Part of the problem in a good part of the evangelical church in Latin America has been to equate theology with "the letter that kills" and opposes the Spirit that gives life (referencing 2 Cor 3:6) – as if theology could be done without the Spirit, or the Spirit was opposed to theology. Padilla maintains that theology for the church cannot be done without the help of the Spirit and without the practice of Christian discipleship; the Spirit mobilizes the church to social action.

Finally, for Padilla, the antichrist is the social order based on lies. It does not always materialize in the form of persecution against Christians, but rather occurs in a much more subtle way, through seduction. The church with a mercantilist and consumer mentality is a church that has fallen prey to the antichrist.

Kirkpatrick identifies Padilla as belonging to the group of "progressive Latin American evangelicals" who "defined themselves primarily against two perceived ideological excesses: Marxist-inflected theologies of liberation and the conservative political loyalties of the Religious Right."[35] Their interpretation of the Bible became clearly post-colonial and promoted a "social Christianity." But at the same time, these progressive evangelicals were critical of what they saw as "Marxist humanism" in liberation theologies.[36]

In brief, *Misión integral* highlights that theology and Christian faith naturally intersect with public affairs. Padilla begins by defining the gospel and the kingdom of God. He then delves into an examination of the theology and practices of the church, seeking to assess whether the church primarily serves as evidence of the arrival of the kingdom of God or if it has become assimilated into the prevailing worldview and oppressive systems of the world. In essence, Padilla argues that Christian theology is inherently public, and the mission of the church is fundamentally oriented towards engagement with

---

34. Padilla, 192; my translation, for an English translation of the book see also Padilla, *What is Integral Mission?*, 93; and compare 86.

35. David C. Kirkpatrick, *A Gospel for the Poor: Global Social Christianity and the Latin American Evangelical Left* (Philadelphia: University of Pennsylvania Press, 2019), 13.

36. Kirkpatrick, *Gospel for the Poor*, 132.

the wider society. Due to his interpretation of the Bible and the implications he has articulated for Christian public life, Padilla has been regarded as too liberal by conservatives and too conservative by liberals.

"Popular" Evangelical Theology

By "popular" we mean the theology that is widely believed among evangelicals but is not easy to find in a representative book. Therefore, in this section, we depart from the direct analysis of academic texts or explicit statements by theologians regarding the political ideologies influencing their interpretations. Instead, we will explore concrete examples that demonstrate the presence of a political ideology within the interpretation of the Bible and the subsequent emergence of public theology.

The connection between context and hermeneutics is generally acknowledged, yet there are instances when this relationship is disrupted. In some cases, neither the method of interpretation nor the questions posed align with the social context of the interpreter. This is evident in countries such as Colombia, where the evangelical church, in general, has traditionally embraced conservative evangelical thought, often influenced by the perspectives of the U.S. Republican party. Those who adhere to this imported theology, with its specific methods, approaches, and pastoral concerns, often perceive their faith framework as solely biblical. They tend to view the introduction of political ideologies into matters of faith as something external to the Christian faith.

Through these examples, I seek to illustrate that, in the perception of outsiders, evangelicals do engage in politics based on their interpretation of the Bible. Merely appealing to the presence or absence of the Holy Spirit in these discussions holds limited value, as all sides of the interpretation and Christian involvement in politics make similar appeals. Few individuals would openly declare themselves to be agents of demons in these debates.

The first example has to do with the participation of evangelical Christians in politics as observed by journalists, politicians, and political scientists in Colombia. On 30 August 2022, during the inaugural speech of the former president of Colombia Juan Manuel Santos, as a professor at the National University of Colombia, he unexpectedly referred to evangelicals, or *cristianos* as we are called here. This is significant since evangelicals have historically been a minority in Colombia. The reason for Santos's mention of evangelicals was their public campaign against his flagship government programme: the signing of the peace agreement with the FARC guerrillas. While Santos acknowledged the opposition from Christians as legitimate in a democratic event, he was more concerned with understanding the underlying reasons behind their opposition.

Former President Santos commented that evangelicals voted against the plebiscite for peace without fully understanding the contents of the agreement between the government and FARC. He attributed this opposition to the influence of conspiracy theories.[37] During a panel discussion following the event, one political scientist noted that evangelicals perceived a significant presence of "gender ideology" within the agreement, even though it was not explicitly mentioned. When questioned about the specific location of this ideology, they claimed it was hidden or "encrypted" within the text.

The second example happened in October of the same year. During an interview on YouTube, Colombian writer Mario Mendoza discussed the theme of books as a refuge during the pandemic. Without any specific prompting from the journalist, Mendoza made a statement regarding evangelicals. He said that instead of dedicating themselves to their vocation of instilling hope, evangelical pastors persisted in their mission of soliciting money to further their worldly ambitions.[38] While Mendoza's statement is a generalization, it could be inferred that he believed books provided a better refuge than churches if Christian ministers behaved in such a manner.

Towards the end of 2022, I encountered a newspaper article discussing the preaching of some evangelicals in Colombia who strongly oppose the recognition of constitutional rights for individuals who identify as LGBTI. The article also mentions programmes designed by these evangelicals with the aim of attempting to change LGBTI individuals into heterosexuals. While this matter is considered theological for many evangelicals, it becomes a political issue in the context of the country's pluralist constitution, relating to individual liberties, personal development, and the rights of minority groups. It is worth noting that more extreme views within this discourse even advocate for the physical persecution of LGBTI individuals.[39]

A recurring theme in these three stories is the notion that "instead of doing this, evangelicals should be doing that" within society. It suggests that rather

---

37. Universidad Nacional de Columbia, "La paz: camino y destino [Peace: path and destiny]: Prof. Juan Manuel Santos," YouTube, 2022, https://www.youtube.com/watch?v=MR0sNAMUKjU.

38. CAMBIO, "'Mi trinchera es la de los libros [My foxhole is the foxhole of books]': Mario Mendoza," YouTube, 2022, https://www.youtube.com/watch?v=Yec4nRFy1wc.

39. Lucía Franco, "'Te liberamos: Eres libre de todo demonio y homosexualismo [We set you free: You are free from all demons and homosexuality],'" El País, 11 May 2022, https://elpais.com/america-colombia/2022-05-11/las-heridas-que-dejan-las-terapias-de-conversion-en-colombia.html.

than actively promoting peace in a historically violent country, providing solace to their congregations during the pandemic, and embracing inclusivity in a democratic society, some evangelicals vote against peace initiatives based on false assumptions, their leaders prioritize self-interest, and as a community they harbour animosity towards individuals who do not conform to their Christian ideals. This critique is quite strong and widely expressed. It is important to note that the question at hand is not whether this representation applies to all evangelicals in Colombia, but rather whether a significant number of Christians may indeed be aligned with these viewpoints. If that is the case, this raises concerns worth addressing.

Based on my personal experience, limited as it is, it appears that there are indeed evangelical Christians who have voted against the peace agreement, leaders who have focused on furthering their economic ambitions during the pandemic, and communities that support the persecution or exclusion of LGBTI individuals. While not representative of all evangelicals, these examples do exist. It is possible to disagree with the criticisms and generalizations made, but it is difficult to deny the existence of a widespread negative perception of evangelical churches regarding their public witness and involvement in public matters. Furthermore, it is undeniable that evangelicals use the Bible to express their opinions and engage with public issues.

It is evident that evangelicals hold diverse perspectives on social issues and there is no agreement on their importance or the appropriate course of action. Similarly, the public life of the church in relation to society varies among different evangelical communities. It is crucial to acknowledge this diversity and refrain from naïve assumptions. Recognizing the reality and complexity of these differences is an essential first step in engaging in meaningful conversations about these issues.

The first example has to do with our understanding of justice, the second with compassion, and the third with democracy. They all touch upon fundamental aspects of public theology. These examples highlight the significance of public theology and its impact on various societal issues.

It is evident that Christians hold diverse political preferences, and these differences have unfortunately led to polarizations and divisions within the Christian community. A subsidiary objective of this chapter is to foster a foundational understanding among Christians, enabling them to engage in respectful and meaningful discussions about social justice. The ultimate goal is to encourage a re-evaluation of the church's public life, leading to a more purposeful and impactful engagement with the pressing issues of our time.

A final example of the intersection of biblical interpretation with public witness within Latin American evangelical communities is the promotion of "prayer chains" for the peace of Israel. This is often based on the biblical verse that urges believers to "pray for the peace of Jerusalem" (Ps 122:6–9, NIV). These prayer chains are frequently mobilized in response to specific events, such as attacks on Israeli police officers or rocket attacks from neighbouring regions. This practice reflects the close spiritual connection many Latin American evangelicals feel towards Israel and their desire to express solidarity through intercessory prayer.

The problem is not prayer for the peace of Jerusalem. The issue is why the peace of one city is more important than one's own. When there is a disproportionate emphasis on praying for specific regions or issues while neglecting pressing local or global concerns, it can give the impression that some lives or situations are considered more important than others in the eyes of God. This can lead to a distorted understanding of God's love and compassion, which the Bible teaches extends to the entire world. It is important for Christians to reflect on their prayer practices and ensure that their intercessions are inclusive, encompassing a wide range of needs and acknowledging the value of all human life.

The theology from which this spirituality stems also derives from a political ideology that is disconnected from the teachings of the Bible. Arguing in favour of an exclusive focus on Israel after the coming of Christ requires accepting the validity of the entire theology of the Old Testament. However, it is important to recognize that with the coming of Christ, Israel and its institutions were assumed by Christ to make way for the establishment of the church. The church transcends national boundaries and no country or its inhabitants hold greater importance than others. In fact, they never have done. God chose Israel to demonstrate love to the nations and bless them, as part of God's promise to Abraham. This promise serves as the interpretive framework for all subsequent promises. Any notion of Israel's exclusivity is temporary and must not contradict God's ultimate promise to Abraham or God's claim of love for all of humanity in Genesis 1–2.[40] Prayer for peace is indeed commendable, as long as it is free from any undisclosed political agenda.

---

40. It would be hard to belittle the geostrategic importance of various countries, including Israel, Iraq, Turkey, Saudi Arabia, Taiwan, South Korea, Colombia, and Venezuela. These countries hold significance due to factors such as their oil reserves and their strategic value in the global balance of power.

Conclusion: A Way Forward

The purpose of this chapter is not to argue for the superiority or inferiority of any specific political ideology, nor to suggest that we can choose to be without a political ideology when engaging in public affairs. Rather, it seeks to raise awareness that as interpreters of the Bible, we bring pre-existing political ideologies (or acquire them within our church communities) that shape the way we read and understand the Scriptures, as well as how we approach public issues. Recognizing this reality is crucial in fostering mutual understanding among Christians and in refining our perspectives on public theology.

Several decades ago, theologians embraced the idea that theology is always situated within a specific context. In other words, theology seeks to respond to the theological and pastoral needs of the particular context in which it arises. This context greatly influences the exegetical methods and the way in which the Bible is read and understood by believers. One significant factor shaping the academic and popular interpretation of the Bible is the political ideology of the interpreter. In this chapter, our aim has been to explore the relationship between these three interconnected themes: political ideology (which is inherent in all of us), biblical interpretation (which is undertaken by all Christians), and Christian public witness (which seeks social justice).

The underlying premise of this chapter is that the polarization surrounding issues such as social justice, often accompanied by a denial of its biblical relevance, can be attributed, at least in part, to the political ideology through which we interpret the Bible. This premise holds true only if we acknowledge two things: first, that we all possess an ideology, and second, that this ideology significantly shapes our interpretation of the Bible. While we cannot delve into every aspect of this topic, I write with the hope that the arguments presented have at least prompted a sense of suspicion regarding this relationship.

Christianity and theology are indeed inseparable. A Christian's understanding of their faith is inherently theological, even if they may not have articulated it or developed a formal method of interpretation. Every believer holds certain truths that they have arrived at and organized in their own way. These truths shape their interpretation of the Bible, which constitutes their personal theology and method of interpretation. It is important to recognize that these theological perspectives and interpretive methods are influenced by one's way of thinking about political issues. It is worth noting that not all Christians are professional theologians who write scholarly works, as we saw in liberation theology, feminist theology, and the theology of integral mission. However, regardless of their level of formal theological training, every believer engages in theology and interprets the Bible through their own lens, which is informed by their worldview, including their political beliefs.

Political ideology is a significant factor that can polarize society, including Christians and churches. The spiritualization of the Bible and the Christian message often reflects a particular political ideology, either by downplaying its political aspects or by reducing it solely to politics. However, it is difficult to deny the political dimensions present in biblical themes such as the kingdom of God, the Messiah, and salvation; it is also difficult to deny that biblical texts speak to pressing social issues such as social injustice, patriarchalism, and the rights of minorities. It is not a mere coincidence that political candidates often present themselves as saviours, highlighting the political nature of these ideas.

Any reliable book on the history of Bible interpretation recognizes the significant influence of the political and social context on the methods of interpretation and theologies that have developed throughout time. This impact extends beyond specific movements like liberation theology and feminist theologies. The political and social environment of interpreters has consistently shaped their approaches to understanding and interpreting the Bible.

Engaging in political Bible reading is not contingent upon having read a specific book on the subject. In fact, we all engage in it to some extent, consciously or unconsciously, in various contexts of our lives, not just during election seasons. The examples of evangelicals in Colombia have one thing in common: the criticism directed towards them for their perceived negative impact on society. While the primary purpose of the church is not to seek societal approval, it can be valuable and even beneficial to listen to such criticism and engage in self-reflection, rather than hastily responding with a martyr or warrior mindset.

One common error in biblical interpretation is the tendency to disregard or downplay the political and social dimensions present in certain biblical passages. In other words, a particular political ideology can lead someone to depoliticize the Bible and instead impose their own political agenda onto the text. When a believer is excluded from a Christian community due to their political beliefs, it is not because the excluding individuals lack political ideas themselves, but rather because their own ideas differ from those of the individual being excluded.

In conclusion, this chapter has been an attempt to shed light on the relationship between political ideology, biblical interpretation, and public theology within the context of Christianity. It has underscored the impact of political ideologies on how Christians interpret the Bible and engage with public affairs using various ideologies as their starting point. It has also highlighted the need for self-awareness, dialogue, and a nuanced understanding of differing perspectives within the Christian community. By recognizing these dynamics, Christians can engage in productive conversations, refine their public theology, and witness to Christ by striving for a more inclusive and just society.

Bibliography

CAMBIO. "'Mi trinchera es la de los libros [My foxhole is the foxhole of books]': Mario Mendoza." YouTube, 2022. https://www.youtube.com/watch?v=Yec4nRFy1wc.

Cursach Salas, Rosa. "A Christian Feminist Hermeneutics of the Bible." In *Feminist Biblical Studies in the Twentieth Century: Scholarship and Movement*, edited by Elisabeth Schüssler Fiorenza, 161–77. Bible and Women 9.1. Atlanta: Society of Biblical Literature, 2014.

Duncan, William B. "The Political Philosophy of Gustavo Gutiérrez." PhD diss., Texas Tech University, 1995. http://hdl.handle.net/2346/20773.

Franco, Lucía. "'Te liberamos: Eres libre de todo demonio y homosexualismo [We set you free: You are free from all demons and homosexuality].'" *El País*, 11 May 2022. https://elpais.com/america-colombia/2022-05-11/las-heridas-que-dejan-las-terapias-de-conversion-en-colombia.html.

Gutiérrez, Gustavo. *Teología de la liberación: perspectivas* [Liberation theology: Perspectives]. Salamanca: Ediciones Sígueme, 1972.

———. *A Theology of Liberation: History, Politics, and Salvation*. Maryknoll: Orbis, 1973.

Hinga, Teresia M. *African, Christian, Feminist: The Enduring Search for What Matters*. Maryknoll: Orbis, 2017.

Kirkpatrick, David C. *A Gospel for the Poor: Global Social Christianity and the Latin American Evangelical Left*. Philadelphia: University of Pennsylvania Press, 2019.

Míguez Bonino, José. *Doing Theology in a Revolutionary Situation*. Philadelphia: Fortress, 1975.

Padilla, C. René. *Misión integral: ensayos sobre el Reino y la iglesia* [Integral mission: Essays on the kingdom and the church]. Buenos Aires: Nueva Creación, 1986.

———. *What Is Integral Mission? Global Voices in Latin America*. Oxford: Regnum, 2021.

Schüssler Fiorenza, Elisabeth. *But She Said: Feminist Practices of Biblical Interpretation*. Boston: Beacon, 1992.

———. "Entre la investigación y el movimiento social: estudios feministas de la Biblia en el siglo xx [Between research and social movement: Feminist biblical studies in the 20th century]." In *La exégesis feminista del siglo XX: investigación y movimiento* [Feminist exegesis of the 20th century: Research and movement], edited by Elisabeth Schüssler Fiorenza, 10–29. Biblia y las mujeres [Bible and Women]. Navarra: Editorial Verbo Divino, 2015.

———. *Sharing Her Word: Feminist Biblical Interpretation in Context.* Edinburgh: T&T Clark, 1998.

Seibert, Eric A. *The Violence of Scripture: Overcoming the Old Testament's Troubling Legacy.* Minneapolis: Fortress, 2012.

Sobrino, Jon. *Jesucristo liberador: lectura histórico-teológica de Jesús de Nazaret.* Mexico City: Universidad Iberoamericana, 1994.

———. *Jesus the Liberator: A Historical-Theological Reading of Jesus of Nazareth.* Maryknoll: Orbis, 1993.

Universidad Nacional de Colombia. "La paz: camino y destino [Peace: path and destiny]: Prof. Juan Manuel Santos." YouTube, 2022. https://www.youtube.com/watch?v=MR0sNAMUKjU.

12

Dialogical Model for Engagement in IFES Latin America

Public Witness in the University

Alejandra Ortiz and Josué Olmedo

IFES Latin America Logos & Cosmos Initiative

Public Life at the Beginning of IFES Latin America

The International Fellowship of Evangelical Students (IFES), which is a movement of students sharing and living out the good news of Jesus Christ locally, organized through national movements, and all coming under the umbrella of IFES in fellowship, has proposed a vision for students as they engage with the university[1] as their context for mission.[2] This vision, "Engaging the University,"[3] is for every national chapter of IFES to have an incarnational, holistic, and intellectually credible Christian witness, and the basis of this engagement implies listening well to the university context and promoting dialogue that responds to the needs and challenges of the university from a faith perspective. In this chapter, we will focus on the ways IFES, particularly in Latin America, has proposed to engage with the university since its foundation in the 1960s and

---

1. The concept of "university" includes all tertiary education institutions.
2. This vision was presented at the IFES World Assembly in 2011 in Poland.
3. IFES, "Engaging the University," n.d., https://ifesworld.org/en/university/?switch_language=en.

look briefly into the present. We will then explore some biblical and theological considerations regarding human knowledge, offering Christian meaning through conversations, and some theological considerations regarding scientific work. Finally, we will provide illustrations of present engagement in the science-faith dialogue that respond to pressing contemporary issues within the university and wider society. We consider these to be examples and expressions of public witness in university settings.

Since the inception of IFES-affiliated student movements in Latin America there has been an emphasis on the context of their mission, which is the university.[4] As different student movements in Latin America were founded in the 1960s and 1970s, leadership formation and theological and missiological reflection responded to the social context of mission, revolutions, and social unrest, and paid particular attention to the influence of Marxism in the universities across the region. IFES Latin America proposed ways of engagement with the university that followed an incarnational and intellectually credible witness under a theological framework based on two primary concepts: *misión integral* (in English, "integral mission," the term which we will use in this chapter) and the kingdom of God.

Integral mission was birthed by Latin American theologians serving in university ministry and developed in response to the social context and the desire to help university students have a deep consciousness of their place of mission, as well as of the social, political, and economic realities in which they engaged missionally and theologically.[5] In 1966, the first IFES Latin American continental event was led by Samuel Escobar and C. René Padilla (1932–2021) in Lima, Peru. The event dedicated time for Bible study, discipleship, and evangelism training, while also allowing students to delve into societal issues, as they partnered with churches in marginalized communities.[6] This event was a marker for all other training events and for the ways in which mission, theology, context, and practice came together in IFES, which would be later coined "integral mission." Alongside training events, the writings published in the Latin American IFES magazine *Certeza*, as well as publications from Escobar, Padilla, and other IFES theologians, show the commitment to Scripture and

---

4. Timothée Louis Joset, "The Priesthood of All Students? Historical, Theological and Missiological Foundations of a University Ministry: The International Fellowship of Evangelical Students (IFES)" (PhD diss., Durham University, 2021), 17–18.

5. David C. Kirkpatrick, *A Gospel for the Poor: Global Social Christianity and the Latin American Evangelical Left*, Illustrated ed. (Philadelphia: University of Pennsylvania Press, 2019), 48.

6. Kirkpatrick, *Gospel for the Poor*, 47.

being relevant to the different national realities around Latin America, trying to respond to the challenges of university students.[7]

Samuel Escobar, one of the IFES pioneers in Latin America, models dialogue for missional engagement and public witness. Escobar encourages Christian students to listen and to dialogue, to understand the other person's concern or philosophy, and to connect the gospel. He does this magnificently in his writings, which are a response to what he sees around him. Among other influences, Escobar explains that this way of understanding faith and connecting it to what was happening in the university was inspired by John A. Mackay (1889–1983), as he called for a faith that was contextual and connected to the whole of life.[8] He is also influenced by Cecilio Arrastía in how he connected faith and culture and how, through conferences given in the universities and through his writings, Escobar creatively bridged philosophy and the arts in dialogue with the biblical narrative.[9] In his *Diálogo entre Cristo y Marx* (Dialogue between Christ and Marx), Escobar engages Marxism from a Christian perspective that goes beyond the surface and caricature that bolstered the polarization of Christians and Marxists in the 1960s and 1970s around Latin America.[10] Escobar dialogues with ideas and ideologies which are contrary to the Christian faith, but does so graciously, with the conviction that real encounters and dialogue was Jesus's way.[11] As IFES national student movements in Latin America were established, they had a deep commitment to evangelization and the contextualization of the gospel, which also implied listening well and entering into dialogue with others.

The other element that laid the foundation for IFES's missional engagement and public witness was a particular understanding of the "kingdom of God," and there were at least two key historical moments in the development of this theological understanding of the kingdom of God in IFES Latin American circles. One was in 1966, after René Padilla returned from his doctoral studies and taught in the continental training for Latin American leaders of IFES

---

7. Samuel Escobar, *Chispa y la llama* [Spark and flame], vol. 2 (Lima: Ediciones PUMA, 2022), 207.

8. Samuel Escobar, *En busca de Cristo en América Latina* [In search of Christ in Latin America] (Buenos Aires: Kairós, 2012), 148.

9. Escobar, *En busca de Cristo*, 166. See also Samuel Escobar, "Cecilio Arrastía: Teólogo y predicador [Theologian and preacher]," *Textos para la Acción* [Texts for Action] 7 (Dec. 1996): 27–31.

10. Samuel Escobar, *Diálogo entre Cristo y Marx* [Dialogue between Christ and Marx], 2nd ed. (Lima: AGEUP, 1969), 15–16.

11. Escobar, *Diálogo entre Cristo y Marx*, 15.

national movements about the gospel of the kingdom of God and the social and political implications of the kingdom's eschatology. The second moment was in 1972, at the Second Consultation of the Fraternidad Teológica Latinoamerica (Latin American Theological Fellowship), in which the theme of the kingdom of God was discussed.[12] These discussions led to a greater projection of Latin American evangelical theology presented at the Lausanne Congress for World Evangelization in 1974 and the Lausanne Covenant.[13] This understanding of the kingdom of God provided the theological basis for what we have already mentioned about training and writings. As Padilla wrote: "To talk of the kingdom of God is to talk about God's redemptive purpose for the whole of creation and of the historic vocation that the church has regarding that purpose here and now, in the 'in-between times.'"[14] The theological framework of the kingdom of God was an antidote to a shallow understanding of the gospel and provided a vocation for IFES movements as they desired to encourage disciples who would be able to think and reflect on their own studies, disciplines, and social contexts from a kingdom perspective. This invited people to lives of service in the university and the wider society.

An Enriched Practice of Public Life in the University

IFES Latin America has a rich history of public life in the ways it has engaged in the university. As we have highlighted some key elements of its initial history, we now want to bridge to the present in IFES Latin America, to then explore some biblical and theological considerations regarding the sciences, as well as some theological considerations on scientific work. As we do this, we will highlight recent efforts at "engaging the university" within IFES, focus on the work of Terry Halliday and Vinoth Ramachandra and, finally, provide some examples of present engagements that lead to faithful public life in the universities in Latin America.

As IFES globally focused on "engaging the university" to live out in evangelism, service, and dialogue within the university, there were also efforts in IFES Latin America to understand how national movements and student

---

12. Escobar, *En busca de Cristo*, 271–72.

13. Escobar, 298.

14. C. René Padilla, *Misión integral* [Integral mission] (Buenos Aires: Kairós, 2012), 283; translation by authors of this chapter.

leaders were integrating faith and public life. In a report of a consultation[15] from 2018 made on the big issues of the university[16] in Latin America, there are indicators of how students and movements from across Latin America were engaging in public witness in the university, in topics ranging from creation care and climate change to violence, peace, religion, and faith dialogue. The engagement was expressed in invitations to dialogue, forums, creating awareness of societal problems, and partnering with organizations inside the campus that were involved with issues concerning campus life. In the second half of 2018 the IFES "Engaging the University" online course was launched in three languages (English, French, and Spanish). This course was developed to help students and staff understand the university and learn to listen well, to relate academic disciplines to the Christian faith, and to provide a robust theology that would allow dialogue with others. The course takes on many of Vinoth Ramachandra's teachings that connect to Escobar and Padilla's concerns and has been important in Latin America for recovering our commitment to listening to the university context. In 2019, David Bahena, who was regional secretary for Latin America, formed a small "Engaging the University" team of leaders from national movements in the region[17] in order to promote contextual approaches to new university realities in the region. This same team worked on the publication of a book on engaging the university,[18] which features articles from Ramachandra and Halliday, as well as from members of the Latin American team.

As we mentioned, Vinoth Ramachandra is an excellent example of promoting dialogue as mission and has written about civility as a basis for living as Christians in our societies. Ramachandra understands civility as the basis for dialogue and invites Christians to live in the public sphere seeking peace (shalom) and justice for the cities we inhabit.[19] Civility and dialogue are based

---

15. Consultation funded by the John Templeton Foundation, led by Professor Ross McKenzie, and implemented in several IFES regions.

16. IFES, "Informe de la consulta-investigación los retos importantes de la universidad [Consultation-research report on the major challenges facing the university]" (Panamá: IFES América Latina, 2018).

17. The team was formed by Sarah Nigri, Gustavo Sobarzo, and Alejandra Ortiz, led by Josué Olmedo.

18. Terence C. Halliday et al., *Conectar con la universidad: La fe y el servicio en el ámbito académico* [Connecting with the university: Faith and service in academia] (Lima: Certeza Unida, 2022).

19. Vinoth Ramachandra, *Compromisos subversivos: Cristo y la iglesia en la esfera pública* [Subversive engagements: Christ and the church in the public sphere] (Lima: Certeza Unida, 2019), 190.

on listening, opening oneself up for the other to be right, and dedicating the time needed for dialogue. For Ramachandra, who is dialoguing with other authors[20] and furthering their ideas, civility is sacrificial as it seeks the well-being of others and recognizes the innate dignity of all human beings.[21] Mission as dialogue has also been proposed by missions scholar Andrew Kirk, as he develops his ideas as to how Christians can engage with secular culture. For him, dialogue is about developing relationships of trust in order to comprehend others better and to allow mutual witness,[22] but he also acknowledges that the issue of dialogue has been present in missiological thinking, albeit mostly in reference to people of other faiths.[23] John Stott and Chris Wright have also written about dialogue in the context of Christian mission, bringing forth some biblical reflections and proposing four qualities for true dialogue, which are authenticity, humility, integrity, and sensitivity.[24] From a non-Western, post-colonial perspective, Silber proposes dialogue as a means to salvation, as he states that God has always been in dialogue with humanity. He goes so far as to propose that dialogue is the *missio Dei* itself, as it is not an imposition but an offer that comes from God's initiative.[25]

Theological Considerations for Public Witness in the University

As stated in the previous sections, the witness of faithful public life of IFES Latin America in the universities of the region is carried out within the tradition of contemporary theological reflection on public theology in the evangelical context,[26] and more specifically is inscribed in the theological frameworks of integral mission and engaging the university. Thus, the public testimony of IFES Latin America is framed within the search for the human flourishing of the university community. This practice of public witness is informed by

---

20. Stephen Carter and Jonathan Sacks.

21. Ramachandra, *Compromisos subversivos*, 190–91.

22. J. Andrew Kirk, *Mission under Scrutiny: Confronting Current Challenges*, 1st ed. (London: Darton, Longman & Todd, 2006), 28–29.

23. Kirk, *Mission under Scrutiny*, 29–30.

24. John Stott and Christopher J. H. Wright, *Christian Mission in the Modern World*, updated and expanded ed. (Downers Grove: InterVarsity Press, 2015), 128.

25. Stefan Silber, "Sinodalidad y poder: Aportes poscoloniales a la misionología actual [Synodality and power: Post-colonial contributions to today's missiology]," *Spiritus: Edición hispanoamericana* 61/3, no. 240 (Sept. 2020): 127–28.

26. Rudolf von Sinner and Nicolás Panotto, eds., *Teología pública: Un debate a partir de América Latina* [Public theology: A debate from Latin America] (São Leopoldo: Gemrip, EST, 2016), 12–14, 89–90.

certain theological considerations regarding the sciences and the university, which are developed below.

Biblical-Theological Considerations Regarding Human Knowledge

What do the Scriptures tell us about the considerations of God's people regarding human knowledge? This is an important question, the response to which helps to lay a biblical-theological foundation to public witness in the university. Throughout time, IFES and its associated national movements have produced several resources to guide students to understand biblically and theologically their role as witnesses of the gospel in the universities. For the purposes of this reflection, two biblical accounts will be briefly explored, one from the Old Testament, with a focus on the character of Daniel, and another from the New Testament, with a focus on the experience of Paul's missionary sojourn in the city of Ephesus.

Daniel in Babylon: First and Ultimate Loyalty to God

Daniel is a kind of patron saint for university students. He models excellence in studying and integrity of character in public service, both nurtured in a committed loyalty to God. Chapter 1 of the book of Daniel narrates the experience of the young Jew Daniel, who along with others sees his country invaded by the Babylonian Empire and as a result is uprooted from his nation and geographically relocated to Babylon, where a forced process of cultural assimilation awaits him. This cultural assimilation was intended to prepare Daniel and others for public service in the Babylonian imperial court (Dan 1:4), and the device primarily used for this purpose was what could be called "higher education." The account describes how, for admission to the educational process, young people had to have a certain profile: physical aptitudes (handsome and without physical defect), intellectual aptitudes (ability to learn, good sense), and performance skills (wisdom and service). Under the tutelage of Ashpenaz, chief of the officers, this group of young Jewish nobles would experience a three-year curriculum that would encompass Babylonian language, literature, and science (1:4, 5, 17). The programme would be implemented in the same court as that of King Nebuchadnezzar, who would also provide for their food; in addition, the change of their original Jewish names to those of Babylonian gods was compulsory (1:5, 7, 10, 13).

What were Daniel's actions and attitude towards this cultural assimilation via Babylonian imperial education? Christopher Wright points out that Daniel and three other young men – Hananiah, Mishael, and Azariah – responded positively to three of the required changes but rejected one. This group of exiles said "yes" to Babylonian education, public service at the Babylonian court, and the change of their names; but they said "no" to the king's food and wine, preferring to be fed with only vegetables and water (1:8, 12–16).[27] Daniel and his colleagues said "yes" to the acquisition of knowledge produced by none other than the invading and dominant nation. It is even highlighted in the story that God himself enabled them to distinguish themselves among others in their intellectual performance: "To these four young men God gave knowledge and understanding of all kinds of literature and learning" (1:17).[28] And this was well known by its chief qualifying judge, King Nebuchadnezzar: "He found none equal to [them]. . . . He found them ten times better than all the magicians and enchanters in his whole kingdom" (1:19–20). Here is a group of young Jewish exiles who have achieved academic excellence in an educational programme quite alien and hostile to their faith and practice. At the same time they show that their first and ultimate loyalty is to God and his law, which is the reason they resolved not to defile themselves by expressing loyalty to the king in sharing the table with him (1:8).

From this section of Daniel's experience in Babylonian higher education, what are some of the important biblical-theological considerations regarding human knowledge for public witness in the university? On the one hand, there is a positive assessment of Babylonian knowledge: it is a knowledge that must be willingly learned even to the point of excelling in it. On the other hand, there is a critical assessment of the fundamental assumption of the Babylonian educational system: the demand for ultimate loyalty to the king and his imperial project. Christian public witness in the university supposes, first, a willingness and aptitude to engage proficiently with human knowledge in a higher educational system, and, second, a resistance to and critique of some of its fundamental assumptions, such as loyalty to or complacency regarding a political imperial project.

Paul in Ephesus: The Centrality of Dialogue
The apostle Paul visited the city of Ephesus during his second missionary trip (Acts 15:36 – 18:22). He was on his way back to Antioch, his missionary home base, and arrived at the city in the company of Priscilla and Aquila. He visited

---

27. Christopher Wright, *Probados por el fuego* [Tested by Fire] (Barcelona: Andamio, 1998), 19–23. See also Juan José Barreda, "Daniel," in *Comentario bíblico contemporáneo* [Contemporary biblical commentary], ed. C. René Padilla et al. (Buenos Aires: Certeza Unida, 2019), 1056.

28. All Scripture quotations in this chapter are from the NIV.

the local synagogue and talked to the Jews there, who asked him to stay longer, so Paul promised to return.

During his third missionary trip, after travelling through the regions of Galatia and Phrygia, Paul returned to the city of Ephesus. Upon his arrival in the city, the apostle carried out two activities. The first was to get in contact with some followers of Jesus, whom he instructed on baptism and on the Holy Spirit. The second was to attend the local synagogue to talk about God's kingdom, boldly trying to persuade his listeners about it. But the initial enthusiasm these Jews had previously shown for Paul's teaching (18:20) dissolved and "some of them became obstinate; they refused to believe and publicly maligned the Way" (19:9).

Faced with this resistance, unbelief, and offence, Paul decided to turn away from these Jews and to establish a separate group, which gathered daily at the lecture hall of Tyrannus with the purpose of "discussing" the gospel with Jews and Greeks (19:9–10). In several ways this had a significant impact on the entire region and the city which is evident as the story develops. These two elements from Paul's missionary journey in Ephesus should be noted: the non-religious venue in which this newly established community chose to gather, and the dialogical approach they took to sharing the gospel. The group of disciples in Ephesus led by Paul chose to use a non-religious place, "the lecture hall of Tyrannus," as their base for public witness. One can see a dialogical approach to mission especially in chapters 17, 18, 19, and 20 of the book of Acts. The Greek verb used to describe Paul's approach to sharing the gospel is *dialego*, from which we get the words "dialogue" and "dialogical"; it can be translated as to reason, to lecture, to argue, or to discuss, which in context implies a commitment to careful argumentation. The apostle used careful argumentation as his strategy in his interactions with the Jews in the synagogues, people in the marketplace, the Athenian philosophers, and people in Ephesus who attended the lecture hall of Tyrannus.[29]

From this section of Paul's experience in Ephesus, what are some of the important biblical-theological considerations for public witness in the university? Or why the interest in all these details regarding venue and approach? It is because there are similarities in the kind of venue and approach Paul and

---

29. The French philosopher and theologian Jean-Luc Marion states that from the beginning of Christianity the believers used argumentation as one of the ways to make the proclamation (*kerygma*) of Christ known to the pagans. He gives several examples: Paul in Athens, Peter in his letter (1 Pet 3:15), Justin Martyr, Tertullian, and Augustine. See his lecture "Philosophy and Martyrdom: Tertullian and Justin Martyr," Lumen Christi Institute, 21 February 2013, YouTube, https://www.youtube.com/watch?v=PFBDHzM3_P0&t=3219s, starting at 32:19.

his group decided to use for the preaching of the gospel and the venues and approaches IFES Latin American students use with the similar aims of sharing the gospel. IFES students use the classrooms, green spaces, and lecture halls of their universities, and privilege a dialogical approach for sharing and articulating the good news. Christian public life in the university supposes a wise and creative use of university venues as legitimate spaces in which the message of Christ should be argumentatively dialogued among other ideas.

Offering a Christian Meaning through Conversation

From the exploration of these two biblical accounts around the characters of Daniel and Paul, the focus now turns to some biblical-theological considerations as developed by two IFES thought leaders: Terence Halliday and Vinoth Ramachandra, both global pioneers for IFES Engaging the University, among others. Halliday and Ramachandra built and offered a theological and practical framework for the concept and practice of Engaging the University, which easily took hold in the IFES Latin American context, given the previous reflections and practices described above regarding integral mission and awareness of context.

Terence Halliday[30] points out three premises underlying Christian witness in the university.[31] The first is that God is everywhere in the university. The Christian does not take Christ into the university, because he is already present throughout the life of the institution: in research, in teaching, in laboratories, in formal and informal conversations. Much of the believer's task is to discern God's work and point others to it. The second is that God has given believers the call to know him and serve him in the university. This demands of believers at least two intellectual virtues: open-mindedness and humility. Since God is already present in the university and in the different academic disciplines, it means believers are invited to expand their knowledge of God, the world, and themselves in ways they had not previously considered there in the university. The third premise is that Christians in the university are called to articulate a Christian meaning of the vocation and activities of the university, amid other meanings that are also offered.

---

30. There are more resources produced by this author and others on the following sites: Global Faculty Initiative, https://www.facultyinitiative.net/; and Resources for Engaging the University, https://engage.Universityresources.org/. Dr. Halliday remains involved in IFES's Engaging the University.

31. Terence Halliday, "Engaging Our Disciplines in Conversations," YouTube, 2022, https://youtu.be/gZ3Vo-LiHy0.

Regarding the third premise, Halliday points out that the modality that must be privileged for the articulation of a Christian meaning is the "conversation" or dialogue. Every conversation is an exchange that must, in the case of the believer, be a genuine expression of inquiring, of wonder, of building a relationship, of mutual discovery. The significant advantage of the conversation or dialogue modality, Halliday states, is that it allows new meanings to the previous understandings and practices that have developed in the lives of believers, as individuals or as a community: (1) The university can deepen the believer's understandings of the different aspects of human life and of God's character and working, as noted above; (2) the Christian community in the university can enrich the university for kingdom purposes, through affirming values and practices such as compassion, truth, beauty, and goodness; (3) the Christian community can strengthen the very purposes of the university as the search for truth, from its ethical and theological convictions.

Regarding conversation as a modality for engaging, Halliday points out that it is necessary to pay attention to the following: the types of conversation, the partners in the conversation, and the development of the conversation as a Christian virtue. The university has several types of conversations: those of academic disciplines, interdisciplinary issues (e.g. globalization, environmental crisis, human mobility, politics, religion), university management, student and teacher welfare, and the social issues of the locality in which the university is inserted (e.g. identity, gender, indigenous peoples). The partners of these conversations are diverse: students and teachers (Christians and non-Christians), other groups or associations of the university, the administrative staff of the entity, to name just a few. Regarding the cultivation of conversation as a Christian virtue, Halliday suggests these attitudes or practices: *humility*, as the ability to say "I don't know"; *affirming*, as the ability to say "I learn from you, I value what you know"; *patience*, as the ability to admit "I don't like what I hear, but I'm going to keep paying attention"; *mutuality*, as the attitude of showing genuine interest in the other and their academic project; and, finally, *respect*, as recognition of the dignity of the interlocutor as a bearer of the image of God.

Conversation is the primal modality for Christians to engage the academic world and thus to contribute with their Christian interpretation of reality, to which Halliday adds two nuances: refining the art of asking and refining the art of listening.[32] These are added with the aim of effectively connecting with the conversation partner. Thus, Halliday suggests the following elements. Start

---

32. Terence Halliday, "Getting Practical in Dialogic Engagement of the University," YouTube, 2022, https://youtu.be/4lGVgx8K7I4.

by asking about the trajectory or life history of the person, or the history of their interest in a certain academic area. Knowing someone's life trajectory arouses interest, compassion, and joy, as well as helping the group locate their colleague in their own story. In addition to trajectory, Halliday suggests that to refine the art of asking one must identify the interests which arise in one by listening to the other. After identifying the interest, one should try to find a connection: personal and close, or from third parties and distant. The next element is to request a simplification, that is, an explanation in simple language of the topic or academic problem with which the interlocutor in the conversation is dealing. It can be requested, in addition to a simplification, by analogies or metaphors that help one understand what the colleague in the academy is dealing with. Regarding refining the art of listening, Halliday suggests paying attention to the following: the words used to describe the academic problem that colleagues are dealing with, the emotions that such a research problem is generating, and the location of this person's academic interest in the great debate of their scientific discipline.

Some Theological Considerations Regarding Scientific Work

As seen in previous sections, the integration of Christian faith and public life in the university entails an attitude and practice of careful listening and dialogue, but also a resistance to and critique of some aspects of knowledge production that hinder human flourishing or threaten faithfulness to God. In this section, following Vinoth Ramachandra's reflection, two elements of scientific work will be pointed out. One is the faith assumptions science has, which are not always clearly recognized. The other is the moral responsibility that scientific work entails and is accountable for in society. Neither of these elements should be ignored in the development of Christian public witness in the university.

Let us start with the first element. Ramachandra points out two aspects of scientific work that account for this activity as an act of faith.[33] The first aspect is that scientific work requires the basic assumption that there is a real world outside the mind of the scientist that is structured in an orderly and intelligible manner. This coincides with the biblical understanding of the universe as creation: orderly, intelligible, and contingent. The second aspect is that scientific work requires an additional basic assumption, which is the confidence that the human mind is capable of discovering and exploring the world truthfully.

---

33. Vinoth Ramachandra, *Gods That Fail: Modern Idolatry and Christian Mission*, rev. ed. (Eugene: Wipf & Stock, 2016), 133–45.

This coincides with the biblical understanding that the human being has been given the vocation to care for and cultivate the world, which presupposes the need to know it, and therefore God's enabling human beings to obtain such knowledge for their task.[34] From the fact that human beings, as bearers of the image of God, are called to a responsible administration of creation, it follows that they will seek to understand the created world. It is then expected that there will be a sort of correspondence between the minds of human beings and the physical world that these minds explore. Therefore, Ramachandra affirms that the contingent rationality of the universe and the rationality of the human being find their foundation in the rationality and ultimate fidelity of the Creator. This author points out that these two assumptions are an act of faith on the part of science: a world that is possible to explore by being orderly and intelligible, and a mind capable of exploring such a world.

To these two assumptions of the "faith" of science, which coincide with biblical convictions about the world and the human being, Ramachandra adds a further theological consideration, namely, that scientists have moral responsibility for the work they do. The scientist is a "map maker." There is a real world with events and entities in a network of relationships which the researcher wants to make sense of or understand through concepts, models, and theories. That is their scientific map. Such a map is not only descriptive, but prescriptive and predictive. The laws established by the scientist are not prescriptive in the sense of specifying what cannot happen, but guide the expectations that should be had regarding a situation. That is what makes a reliable theory, but every theory is fallible and limited, hence the need for the combination of trust and humility in the research initiative. With "map-making" comes a moral responsibility. In the biblical notion of knowledge, knowing and being responsible go hand in hand. The one who knows must act according to what they claim to know, otherwise they do not really know. The scientist is a generator of knowledge, but compared to other professionals, they have greater responsibilities regarding this knowledge. The divorce between knowledge and responsibility is a manifestation of the fall, in theological terms. The separation between theory and practice is assumed, and in some circles it is even celebrated. It will always be easier to enjoy the technical aspects of a discovery than face the hard ethical questions the discovery might raise.

In light of the theological considerations about science and scientific endeavour – that the world is intelligible, the human mind is capable of truth-

---

34. See also e.g. John G. Stackhouse Jr., *Need to Know: Vocation as the Heart of Christian Epistemology* (Oxford: Oxford University Press, 2014).

fully exploring the world, and such generation of knowledge carries with it a moral responsibility – Ramachandra proposes that the challenge Christian faith poses to science is that of a responsible practice of scientific work. That is, it should be directed by love: love for God and love for neighbour. This is a challenge that must be embodied and modelled first and foremost by believing scientists or scholars. In the absence of love, science enslaves and does not liberate. Love for God will generate respect for truth and integrity at work. Thus, fame, prestige, or wealth are not the main motivators. Love for one's neighbour will prioritize human needs over self-realization, and compassion rather than mere curiosity. This will manifest itself in certain areas of research having clear legal restrictions because they can easily be abused – for instance, research on human embryos. Knowledge is not to be pursued for the sake of knowledge – such an affirmation is empty – for knowledge is such insofar as it relates to and integrates with ideas from other disciplines and coexists with other ends such as justice and human flourishing. Thus, scientific initiative will have to be accountable to society. A science responsible to society is that which, according to the Christian point of view, is done as an obedient response to the intelligibility of the world, which believers recognize as the work of the Creator.

Some Examples and Final Reflections

In line with IFES Latin America's commitment to the public witness of the gospel with a dialogical approach and relevance to the context at its core, the following projects are offered as samples. These projects were formulated and implemented as a key element of the IFES Logos and Cosmos Initiative, led by Professor Ross McKenzie, whose aim is to strengthen the capacity of IFES Latin America and Francophone African Christian scholars to dialogue their faith in Christ with their academic disciplines. These and other projects are funded by the John Templeton Foundation with the counterpart of the IFES National Movements involved.[35]

"Breaking new ground for justice and peace in Mexico" is the project carried out by social psychologist Dr. Sandra Márquez. It aims to better understand perceptions and practices of social violence in order to design and implement educational spaces for reflection and training in justice and peacebuilding. With theoretical frameworks and tools from the social sciences and theology, empirical research was implemented to identify Christian university students'

---

35. For more details, see IFES, "The Logos and Cosmos Initiative," https://lci.ifesworld.org/en/.

perceptions on war, justice, and peace. From this, two seminars were held to train a group of students in basic issues of reconciliation and peacebuilding, and, finally, an academic forum was organized on the same topic with the participation of experts in these areas. The project will continue now in its next phase, being implemented with university students from two countries: Mexico and El Salvador. This time, narratives on violence will be identified as students struggle with structural and gender violence.[36]

Another project focuses on the relationship between Christian theology and the arts. A mentoring programme on the arts was planned and implemented by architect and PhD student Marcio Lima, whose aim was to train art students in their theological skills to understand art.[37] The basic theological framework used was the grand biblical narrative of creation, fall, and restoration. As a result, those students involved in the programme created artistic products and theological reflections. One outcome was the research paper written by one of the participants, Beatriz Nishikawa from Brazil, in which she explored some of the feeling-based responses of a group of university students to the presence of certain objects around them – objects which were part of their everyday lives, such as cell phones (screen devices), mirrors, clothing, a table, a chair, and a glass.[38] Her main research question focused on the potential of objects to elicit feelings of optimism, hope, and well-being, and thus the responsibility of designers to create things that nurture a sense of transcendence in people through material means.

A final example is the project implemented by social communicator and PhD student Lorena Brondani on "Christian women scholars in Argentina at the interface of sciences and theology." The project explored how a few women from an academic and Christian background perceived in their lives the relationship between spirituality, womanhood, and academic life. Six women were

---

36. Details of the three projects described here are from IFES Logos and Cosmos, "Projects in Latin America," 17 January 2023, https://lci.ifesworld.org/en/projects-in-latin-america/. For more details on Dr. Sandra Márquez's project, visit Abriendo Caminos de Justicia y Paz, https://ilccatalizador11.blogspot.com/.

37. For more details on Marcio Lima's project, visit Arte, Arquitetura e Teologia, https://ilccatalizador7.blogspot.com/.

38. Beatriz Nishikawa Venturim, "Design & esperanca: Un vislumbre do trascendente através do material [Design & hope: A glimpse of the transcendent through the material]" (unpublished paper presented at the XIV Congreso de Enseñanza del Diseño [14th Congress on Design Teaching in Argentina], 17 July – 4 August 2023).

interviewed on how they have woven together the opportunities and challenges of their faith in Christ, academic life, and family life.[39]

These projects reflect the concepts and practices of public witness in the university that IFES Latin America has been trying to flesh out for decades under theological paradigms such as "integral mission" and "kingdom of God," with an acute awareness of the context. They also reflect the most recent emphasis on the dialogical approach to academic life and scientific work under the model of Engaging the University. In light of the above-described projects, some big social issues such as gender or structural violence are being dealt with in their different expressions with academic and theological rigour, looking for the transformation of people and circumstances.

The realities of universities around the world differ greatly; however, the challenge to Christian public life in tertiary education institutions may be enriched by the story of IFES Latin America, its current development, as well as the theological concepts we have explained and articulated. From what we have shared, to respond to the challenges of different contexts is a missiological imperative that requires a commitment to listen to and to enter into dialogue with others. The hope in which the followers of Christ rest is that the same God who provided the concepts, tools, and courage for a faithful public witness in the experiences of Daniel, Paul, IFES, and others, will continue to do so for the advancement of his kingdom.

Bibliography

Barreda, Juan José. "Daniel." In *Comentario bíblico contemporáneo* [Contemporary biblical commentary], edited by C. René Padilla, Milton Acosta Benítez, and C. Rosalee Velloso da Silva, 1051–75. Buenos Aires: Certeza Unida, 2019.

Escobar, Samuel. "Cecilio Arrastía: Teólogo y predicador [Theologian and preacher]." *Textos para la acción* [Texts for action] 7 (Dec. 1996): 27–31.

———. *Chispa y la llama* [Spark and flame]. Vol. 2. Lima: Ediciones PUMA, 2022.

———. *Diálogo entre Cristo y Marx* [Dialogue between Christ and Marx]. 2nd ed. Lima: AGEUP, 1969.

———. *En busca de Cristo en América Latina* [In search of Christ in Latin America]. Buenos Aires: Kairós, 2012.

González, Justo. *Hechos de los Apóstoles* [Acts of the Apostles]. Comentario bíblico iberoamericano [Ibero-American biblical commentary]. Buenos Aires: Kairós, 2000.

---

39. For more details on Lorena Brondani's project, visit Blog del Proyecto de la Catalizadora Lorena Brondani (Abua) en la Iniciativa Logos y Cosmos IFES AL, https://ilccatalizador6.blogspot.com/.

Halliday, Terence. "Engaging Our Disciplines in Conversations." YouTube. 2022. https://youtu.be/gZ3Vo-LiHy0.

———. "Getting Practical in Dialogic Engagement of the University." YouTube. 2022. https://youtu.be/4lGVgx8K7I4.

Halliday, Terence C., Vinoth Ramachandra, Alejandra Ortiz, Gustavo Sobarzo Aguayo, Sarah Nigri de Angelis, and Morgana Boostel. *Conectar con la universidad: La fe y el servicio en el ámbito académico* [Connecting with the university: Faith and service in academia]. Lima: Certeza Unida, 2022.

IFES. "Engaging the University." n.d. https://ifesworld.org/en/university/?switch_language=en.

———. "Informe de la consulta-investigación los retos importantes de la universidad [Consultation-research report on the major challenges facing the university]." Panama: IFES América Latina, 2018.

Joset, Timothée Louis. "The Priesthood of All Students? Historical, Theological and Missiological Foundations of a University Ministry: The International Fellowship of Evangelical Students (IFES)." PhD diss., Durham University, 2021.

Kirk, J. Andrew. *Mission under Scrutiny: Confronting Current Challenges*. London: Darton, Longman & Todd, 2006.

Kirkpatrick, David C. *A Gospel for the Poor: Global Social Christianity and the Latin American Evangelical Left*. Illustrated ed. Philadelphia: University of Pennsylvania Press, 2019.

Lumen Christi Institute. "'Philosophy and Martyrdom: Tertullian and Justin Martyr'; Jean-Luc Marion." 21 February 2013. YouTube. https://www.youtube.com/watch?v=PFBDHzM3_P0.

Padilla, C. René. *Misión integral* [Integral mission]. Buenos Aires: Kairós, 2012.

Ramachandra, Vinoth. *Compromisos Subversivos: Cristo y la iglesia en la esfera pública* [Subversive engagements: Christ and the church in the public sphere]. Lima: Certeza Unida, 2019.

———. *Gods That Fail: Modern Idolatry and Christian Mission*. Rev. ed. Eugene: Wipf & Stock, 2016.

Silber, Stefan. "Sinodalidad y poder: Aportes poscoloniales a la misionología actual [Synodality and power: Post-colonial contributions to today's missiology]." *Spiritus: Edición hispanoamericana* 61/3, no. 240 (Sept. 2020): 122–33. https://www.academia.edu/44515918/.

Sinner, Rudolf von, and Nicolás Panotto, eds. *Teología pública: Un debate a partir de América Latina* [Public theology: A debate from Latin America]. São Leopoldo: Gemrip, EST, 2016. https://www.otroscruces.org/wp-content/uploads/2016/08/Teologia_Publica_RvS-NP-FINAL.pdf.

Stackhouse, John G., Jr. *Need to Know: Vocation as the Heart of Christian Epistemology*. Oxford: Oxford University Press, 2014.

Stott, John, and Christopher J. H. Wright. *Christian Mission in the Modern World*. Updated and expanded ed. Downers Grove: InterVarsity Press, 2015.

Venturim, Beatriz Nishikawa. "Design & esperanca: Un vislumbre do trascendente através do material [Design & hope: A glimpse of the transcendent through the material]." Unpublished paper presented at the XIV Congreso de Enseñanza del Diseño [14th Congress on Design Teaching in Argentina], 17 July – 4 August 2023.

Wright, Christopher. *Probados por el fuego* [Tested by Fire]. Barcelona: Andamio, 1998.

13

Theological Education as Formation of Prophets for the Church and Society

The African Context

David Tarus

Executive Director, Association for Christian Theological Education in Africa (ACTEA)

Theological Education and the Transformation of Society

Cameroonian theologian Jean-Marc Éla insisted in *My Faith as an African* (1988) that the church must be awake to the cries of villagers and poor urban dwellers sleeping hungry because of empty granaries.[1] Éla's assertion is significant for what we think about God and theological education. God is concerned with the cries of people sleeping hungry, not just their spiritual well-being. In the same vein, theological education should help the church to be conscious of the cries of people wherever they live. A church that is not attuned to the cries of villagers and poor urban dwellers is a dead church. This calls for a carefully crafted theological education able to inspire such a conscious mindset. Such theological education is inspired by courageous innovation, questioning, being questioned, open exchange, and experimenting through the guidance of the Spirit. What hope does theological education have for and give to the majority impoverished by disasters, hunger, and exploitation around the world? What

---

1. Jean Marc Éla, *My Faith as an African*, trans. John Pairman Brown and Susan Perry (Maryknoll: Orbis, 1988), 92–97.

kind of theological education enables a robust engagement with the realities of a complex world? Healthy theological education focuses on the formation of men and women in Christlikeness to enact a different reality in a warped world. Theological education appropriately done should produce men and women who are able to engage society in transformation.

Theological education has played a significant role in the transformation of the church and society in Africa. While some missionaries were indeed complicit in the colonial project, theological education itself proved subversive to imperialistic designs.[2] Theological education has promoted, and continues to promote, literacy not only in the lingua francas such as English, Swahili, and French, but also in vernacular languages.[3] Today, literature in indigenous languages exists because of the efforts of theological educators. Today, many Africans who did not receive formal education are able to read their Bibles in the vernacular because of the efforts of theological educators. Christian theological education helped to lay the foundations for the revival of indigenous African cultures and languages and has contributed to patriotic nationalism through its commitment to holistic approaches to life. So many of Africa's beloved heroes – whether Christian or opposed to Christianity – were prepared for their roles in gaining national independence and building national unity by theological educators.[4]

The church also has been a partner in development. Religious institutions work alongside governments and other development partners to contribute to the flourishing of societies. For example, the church provides spiritual, social, psychological, and often material support for families and individuals facing various challenges. The church has built hospitals, schools, colleges, and universities and has dug wells to help communities get water. Research shows that

---

2. Kwame Bediako, "De-sacralization and Democratization: Some Theological Reflections on the Role of Christianity in Nation-Building in Modern Africa," *Transformation* 12, no. 1 (1995): 5. Lamin Sanneh notes that during the colonial period in Africa, Christianity contained an inherent though "implicit conflict with colonial priorities"; *Whose Religion Is Christianity? The Gospel beyond the West* (Grand Rapids: Eerdmans, 2003), 18. See also the discussion of Andrew F. Walls in "Overseas Ministries and the Subversion of Theological Education," *International Bulletin of Mission Research* 45, no. 1 (2021): 7–14.

3. See especially Lamin Sanneh, *Translating the Message: The Missionary Impact on Culture*, 2nd rev. and expanded ed., American Society of Missiology 42 (Maryknoll: Orbis, 2009); Lamin Sanneh, "Gospel and Culture: Ramifying Effects of Scriptural Translation," in *Bible Translation and the Spread of the Church: The Last 200 Years*, ed. Philip C. Stine, Studies in Christian Mission 2 (Leiden: Brill, 1990), 1–23; and Andrew F. Walls, "The Translation Principle in Christian History," in Stine, *Bible Translation*, 24–39.

4. I thank my colleague Joshua Robert Barron, a member of the ACTEA staff, for helping me draft the second and third paragraphs of this chapter.

development projects which work with religious leaders perform better.[5] We see this historically within the Roman Empire, as community welfare development projects launched by Christian leaders far surpassed what the Roman state was able to accomplish.[6] Today, secular development projects tend to be materialistic in focus and lack the holistic approaches that development can have when done in partnership with religious leaders.[7] Because holistic approaches resonate with holistic African worldviews, they are more likely to generate redemptive uplift and less likely to result in dependency.[8] Moreover, because of the respect accorded to religious leaders in their communities, they are positioned to raise awareness and influence the behaviours and attitudes of community members.[9] The resulting buy-in by the community increases the likelihood of success of a given developmental project.

In "De-sacralization and Democratization," Kwame Bediako is concerned that, whereas Christianity subverted imperialistic designs and participated in transforming the post-colonial African society, "African Christianity, now with greater consciousness of its African identity and characters, may face an even greater challenge to be of service to Africa in the political realm."[10] This is particularly true because African states seem to have made little progress since independence. In 1986, Ali Mazrui vividly described the crisis facing the African continent: "Things are not working in Africa. From Dakar to Dar es Salaam, from Marrakesh to Maputo, institutions are decaying, structures are rusting away. It is as if the ancestors had pronounced the curse of cultural sabotage."[11] Almost forty years later, little has changed. Corruption is still rav-

---

5. See, for example, Emma Tomalin, *Religions and Development* (London: Routledge, 2013), which explores the relationship between religion and development and examines the positive impact of faith-based organizations in both Christian and Islamic contexts.

6. Frederick W. Norris, *Christianity: A Short Global History* (London: Oneworld, 2002), 70, 99.

7. Gerrie ter Haar and Stephen Ellis, "The Role of Religion in Development: Towards a New Relationship between the European Union and Africa," *The European Journal of Development Research* 18, no. 3 (2006): 355.

8. Stephen Maxwell, "'Delivered from the Spirit of Poverty?' Pentecostalism, Prosperity and Modernity in Zimbabwe," *Journal of Religion in Africa* 28, no. 3 (1998): 350–73; Joshua Robert Barron, "Is the Prosperity Gospel, Gospel? An Examination of the Prosperity and Productivity Gospels in African Christianity," *Conspectus: The Journal of the South African Theological Seminary* 33, no. 1 (2022): 88–103.

9. Health Communication Capacity Collaborative, "The Role of Religious Leaders and Faith Communities," n.d., https://healthcommcapacity.org/i-kits/role-religious-leaders-faith-communities/.

10. Bediako, "De-sacralization and Democratization," 5.

11. Ali A. Mazrui, *The Africans: A Triple Heritage* (London: BBC), 11.

aging the continent.[12] Political instability is destroying African nations. There were thirty-seven attempted unconstitutional regime changes (coups d'état) in Africa from 2010 to 2021.[13] Consequently, despite vast deposits of minerals and precious metals, huge hydraulic potential, incomparable biodiversity, exceptional human capital, and impressive geographical wonders, Africa lags behind other continents of the world.

In *The Challenge for Africa* (2009), Nobel Peace Prize-winner Wangari Maathai notes that, despite Africa's wealth, beauty, and prosperity, the image of sub-Saharan Africa is one of devastation, pain, primitive tribal customs, civil disorder, armed militias, child soldiers, mud huts, open sewers, corruption, dictatorship, genocide, and other dysfunctions.[14] Emmanuel Katongole laments in *The Sacrifice of Africa* that "churches and coffins are perhaps the two most prevalent images associated with Africa today."[15] That churches and coffins comfortably coexist in Africa is a sad reality and one that betrays the God whom Christians worship, as Jean-Marc Éla observes: "We glimpse the dangers of blasphemy and of betrayal to which churches open themselves when human distress and situations of death provide more evidence each day for the trial of the God whom they announce."[16] Sadly, many of the churches spread throughout the continent are those that view faith as "a performance-enhancing drug or a soothing balm rather than as a resource to orient their life in the world."[17] Such a warped faith, Volf, adds, "is merely a crutch to use at will, not a way of life."[18] Christians attuned to prosperity theology are preoccupied with prosperity and health and rarely see themselves as witnesses of a different reality.

The church needs robust theological education able to meet complex contextual issues and to help form people for faithful public life. Seminaries must be facilitated and equipped to carry out their mission. This facilitation includes developing relevant accredited programmes, institutional facilities to support

---

12. See Alfred Sebahene, "Contours of Corruption: A Challenge to and for the Church's Public Witness in the Twenty-First Century," chapter 10 in this volume.

13. Charles Onyango-Obbo, "What Africa's Coups Reveal about Us," *Daily Nation* (Nairobi), 9 September 2021, https://nation.africa/kenya/blogs-opinion/opinion/what-africa-s-coups-reveal-about-us-3543530.

14. Wangari Maathai, *The Challenge for Africa* (London: Arrow, 2009), 78–79.

15. Emmanuel Katongole, *The Sacrifice of Africa: A Political Theology for Africa* (Grand Rapids: Eerdmans, 2011), 29.

16. Éla, *My Faith as an African*, 179.

17. Miroslav Volf, *A Public Faith: How Followers of Christ Should Serve the Common Good* (Grand Rapids: Brazos, 2013), 23–24.

18. Volf, *Public Faith*, 16.

the programmes, well-equipped libraries, well-trained and resourced faculty, robust executives, and engaged boards.

Informed by the need to serve a broader constituency, some seminaries have become liberal arts universities. These institutions are informed by the belief that faith speaks to all spheres of life – education, arts, science, politics, communications, and so on. Some reputable Christian universities in Kenya, for example, started as Bible schools. These include Africa International University (formerly Nairobi Evangelical Graduate School of Theology), St. Paul's University (formerly St. Paul's United Theological College), Scott Christian University (formerly Scott Theological College), Kenya Highlands University (formerly Kenya Highlands Bible College), and others. Similarly, some theological institutions have been integrated into state-funded universities as departments of religious studies, for example at the University of South Africa (UNISA).

These Christian universities and religious studies departments struggle to avoid mission drift, a seductive liberal ethos, and secularistic bents (e.g. the temptation to move education away from the influence of faith),[19] as happens to many faith-based organizations.[20] Nevertheless, many Christian universities are salt and light, helping to bring the Christian faith to the public arena by providing a Christ-centred education and worldview to thousands of students who, in turn, go out to infuse society with the gospel of Christ. The church needs to support such institutions as Christopher Wright notes: "Wherever Christians enter professions that do give them public space – in politics, journalism, broadcasting and other media – they need to be supported and encouraged by the church to understand the front-line nature of their calling."[21] These institutions prepare frontline workers for the marketplace. They must not take their responsibility arbitrarily but with the commitment and dedication it deserves.

---

19. Harriet Akugizibwe Caroline Kintu, "Effects of the Transition of Theological Seminaries in Kenya to Universities on Their Evangelical Christian Identity: An Inquiry into Africa International University," ch. 9 in *Governance and Christian Higher Education in the African Context*, eds. David K. Ngaruiya and Rodney L. Reed, ASET Series (Carlisle: Langham Global Library, 2019), 160; Semeon Mulatu, *Transitioning from a Theological College to a Christian University: A Multi-Case Study in the East African Context*, ICETE Series (Carlisle: Langham Global Library, 2017), 190–201.

20. Peter Greer et al. observe in *Mission Drift: The Unspoken Crisis Facing Leaders, Charities, and Churches* (Minneapolis: Bethany House, 2014) that mission drift is a pervasive problem that faces all faith-based organizations of all varieties. Theological institutions must therefore be alive to this reality.

21. Christopher J. H. Wright, *The Mission of God's People: A Biblical Theology of the Church's Mission* (Grand Rapids: Zondervan, 2010), 271.

Six Critical Areas of Formation

There are at least five critical areas that theological education needs to pay attention to in forming students for witness in the public realm. These include (1) Theological anthropology: who are we, and why do we need to be formed? (2) Transformation: what exactly are we attempting to do? (3) Telos: what is the end of theological education? (4) Time: how much time does it take to form? Is formation instant or gradual? (5) Technology: how do we facilitate spiritual formation, and guard against misuse of technology, in this digital age? and (6) Technique: how do we form students for God's mission? Where do we form them?

Theological Anthropology

Spiritual formation is necessary because of who we are; we are human beings created in the image and likeness of God but greatly marred by sin (Gen 1:26–27; 5:1; 9:6; 1 Cor 11:7; Jas 3:9). Our creation in the image of God means everyone bears a God-given intrinsic worth that cannot be compromised. The fallenness of all human beings means that we cannot extricate ourselves from the powers and forces of darkness without divine assistance. Because of sin, we are not naturally drawn to God but away from God and will need God's intervention for us to align with God's purpose for our lives. This divine aid comes through Jesus Christ by the Spirit. The redemptive activity of God in Christ frees us from the enslaving power of sin.

Theological anthropology is essential for how we conduct theological education. We must see students as people created in the image of God. This perception is vital in many ways, including respecting students and valuing them as worthy contributors of knowledge and people being prepared to go and serve other image bearers. Acknowledging the fallenness of students helps the theological educator to be charitable and patient and to invest time and energy in spiritual formation. A proper pedagogy also flows from a proper view of humanity. As James K. A. Smith convincingly argues, we need to view students as affective beings shaped and reshaped by things around them "to be a certain kind of person."[22] Smith regrets that Christian education still operates as if students were mere "containers for ideas," or "thinking things," rather than "loving, desiring, affective, liturgical animals who, for the most part,

---

22. James K. A. Smith, *Desiring the Kingdom: Worship, Worldview, and Cultural Formation*, Cultural Liturgies 1 (Grand Rapids: Baker Academic, 2009), 25.

don't inhabit the world as thinkers or cognitive machines."[23] Smith urges us to see Christian education as the formation of "a peculiar people" rather than as mere dissemination of information.[24] These "peculiar people" are those who shall make a difference in society as they faithfully and courageously witness to a different way of public life.

Transformation

Theological education forms believers in Christlikeness to serve the church and transform society. It is a holistic formation of a peculiar people – men and women transformed in Christlikeness. It begins from the premise that people have already been *de-*formed by sin and Christian education *re-*forms them afresh in Christlikeness. It is a formation that counters worldliness – the values that are contrary to God's values. Structural, institutional, and interpersonal spheres are all affected by a God-infused presence as believers manifest a different way of life. The implication for theological education is that our task is to provide an education that is formative, an education that goes beyond the mind to other areas of life.

As students become connected to God, the source of life, God draws them to himself and away from "the patterns of sin and death which mark our past and present, and into his own future of which resurrection is both the sign and the pledge."[25] Students formed in Christlikeness are peculiar people commissioned to serve their churches and societies. They have been appropriately formed as agents of Christ's redemption (2 Cor 5:18, 20). As they embody the fruit of the Spirit (Gal 5:22–23), they model to the world a different reality. They become the face and flesh of Christ, "concrete embodiment [and] enfleshment . . . a people who are called to present to the world a visible alternative to the world's arrangements."[26] They live by kingdom values wherever they are. Miroslav Volf agrees:

> When we embrace faith – when *God* embraces *us* – we become new creatures constituted and called to be part of the people of God. That is the beginning of a journey: our insertion into the

---

23. Smith, *Desiring the Kingdom*, 32, 34.
24. Smith, 31.
25. Richard Bauckham and Trevor Hart, *Hope against Hope: Christian Eschatology in Contemporary Context*, Trinity and Truth (London: Darton, Longman & Todd, 1999), 72.
26. William H. Willimon, *Calling and Character: Virtues of the Ordained Life* (Nashville: Abingdon, 2010), 52.

story of God's engagement with humanity. As we embark upon it, faith guides us by offering itself as a way of life that indicates paths to be taken and dark alleys or dead-end streets to be avoided, and that tells us what our specific tasks are in the great story of which we are a part. Finally, the story itself gives meaning to all we do, from the smallest act to the weightiest.[27]

Telos

The end of theological education is to contribute to a God-glorifying world through formation of God-glorifying disciples. These are men and women shaped and sent for God's mission. They have been shaped to contribute "to God's cosmic vision of restoration and new creation in the world and the divine intent to morally rehabilitate all peoples and nations in Christ."[28] Such people will not spectate but will actively engage in God's kingdom work through different vocations and spheres of life. They will go out as active image bearers "cultivating God's good creation, working to renew a fallen world, bearing witness to how the world can be otherwise, bearing fresh olives to a world battered by the floodwaters of injustice."[29] This formation begins with connecting learners to God in Christ by the Holy Spirit. Their connection to Christ will shape their lives and ministry and show them what they are intended to be and do because it is Jesus the Christ who exemplified what we are called to be and destined to be. He showed, lived, and offered life in its fullness.

Time

The renewal of the image of God occurs through Jesus Christ by the Spirit. It is not instantaneous. It takes time. It is a progressive journey. Writing about the sixteenth-century theologian John Calvin, Matthew Boulton envisioned formative education as "a sanctifying, disciplinary, recuperative path, and in that sense a humble and humbling return, little by little, to full humanity

---

27. Volf, *Public Faith*, 16.

28. Celucien L. Joseph, *Theological Education and Christian Scholarship for Human Flourishing: Hermeneutics, Knowledge, and Multiculturalism* (Eugene: Pickwick, 2022), 68.

29. James K. A. Smith, *Imagining the Kingdom: How Worship Works*, Cultural Liturgies 2 (Grand Rapids: Baker Academic, 2013), 5.

in Christ's image."[30] Ruth Haley Barton observes, "Spiritual transformation takes place *incrementally over time with others in the context of disciplines and practices that open us to God.* In general, while we are still on this earth, our transformation will happen by degrees (2 Corinthians 3:18), and we need each other in order to grow (1 Corinthians 12)."[31]

Technology

The concern for formation increases significantly with the use of technology. Students often have unrestricted and unmonitored access to the Internet and often stray to areas that end up de-forming them in profound ways. Pornography, intrusion of other people's privacy, and even radicalization are just a few examples of misuse of technology. Our students are constantly being shaped and reshaped by digital culture. If we genuinely believe that our role as a seminary is to form students for the church and society, then we cannot abandon this role. We must think of ways of actualizing formation, even online. Joanne J. Jung's *Character Formation in Online Education* is a helpful resource for seminaries and professors as they find ways of facilitating spiritual formation of online students.[32] We can partner with local churches, alumni, and different communities to facilitate formation of students.

Technique

Theological education forms people for God's mission through a holistic education that embraces a broader vision of humanity in its comprehensive nature. God's people need to be "equipped with new intellectual reservoirs and skills for thinking" as well as "new habits and desires and virtues."[33] Such an education should be holistic. It should train the mind (knowing), transform the heart (being), and provide vocational competencies (doing).

Where does this holistic formation happen? It happens in the classroom, the playground, discussion forums, chapels, the explicit and implicit curriculum, the written and unwritten curriculum, curricular and extra-curricular

---

30. Matthew Boulton, *Life in God: John Calvin, Practical Formation, and the Future of Protestant Theology* (Grand Rapids: Eerdmans, 2011), 4.

31. Ruth Haley Barton, *Life Together in Christ: Experiencing Transformation in Community* (Downers Grove: InterVarsity Press, 2014), 13; emphasis original.

32. Joanne J. Jung, *Character Formation in Online Education: A Guide for Instructors, Administrators, and Accrediting Agencies* (Grand Rapids: Zondervan Academic, 2015).

33. Smith, *Imagining the Kingdom*, 5.

activities, and online discussions. Thus, it is important to view formation happening in various ecological systems that include the institution, the church, the wider community, and even the digital space.[34]

Seeing theological education from the perspective of ecology is significant because schools will not limit the work of formation to the campus environment. They will fulfil their role in imparting knowledge and shaping students' character in collaboration with different partners such as local churches, practitioners (pastors, counsellors, mentors), and local communities where students live and serve. Therefore, students need not be physically together to experience community and to be formed because they always live in formative communities (e.g. church and community). Students are part of different communities. The seminary is a community, the community outside the campus walls is another community, and the church is another community. All these different communities shape the lives of seminary students.

For residential seminaries, a greater task is placed on professors and college mentors to ensure personal, pastoral, and vocational formation. However, for online theological education, the church is the primary centre of formation. Kevin Smith, President of South African Theological Seminary (SATS), a fully online theological school, writes, "The paradigm of how the Lord, the seminary, and the church work together to equip the saints for ministry is different in distance education from in contact training. The seminary provides content and learning activities; God nurtures character and calling; the church recognizes and validates it."[35] I will now suggest three critical things for theological institutions to do as they train men and women to serve as prophetic voices for the society today.

What Theological Institutions Should Do
Clarified Mission

The Association for Christian Theological Education in Africa (ACTEA), the organization I serve as executive director, partners with ScholarLeaders International in helping theological institutions clarify their mission in their path to sustainability. Through the Vital Sustainability Initiative, theological institutions look again at their mission because mission drives everything a

---

34. E.g. see Stephen D. Lowe and Mary E. Lowe, *Ecologies of Faith in a Digital Age: Spiritual Growth through Online Education* (Downers Grove: IVP Academic, 2018).

35. Kevin Smith, "Reflections on ACTEA's Draft Standards for OdeL," communication by email, 14 September 2020.

school does and is. It shapes student recruitment, formation, prophetic voice, faculty development, learning, pedagogy, resources, sustainability, executive leadership, and board governance.[36] The school's mission should be attuned to God's comprehensive mission for the world because a theological seminary exists to serve God's mission.

The comprehensiveness of the *missio Dei* means we go beyond mere affirmation of evangelical tenets, as important as they are – conversion through Christ; active sharing of the word of God in word and deed; the centrality of the Word of God; and the significance of the cross of Christ for the salvation of humanity[37] – to "other priorities such as cultural discipleship, a theological vision of work, a re-appreciation of beauty alongside truth and goodness, a commitment to social improvement and a vision of impacting the world of ideas as well as the personal lives of individuals."[38]

Theological institutions should therefore clarify their mission in the local context. What is God calling us to do in our local context? Be sure that the answer is comprehensive. It should not be limited to doctrinal affirmations and teaching but should also include other areas of life. Once the members of the institution have understood what it is here for, they should go ahead and fulfil that calling with faithfulness. They should work with the church in supporting the institution to serve God's mission on earth. The Lausanne *Cape Town Commitment* clearly articulates the missional nature of theological education:

> The mission of the Church on earth is to serve the mission of God, and the mission of theological education is to strengthen and accompany the mission of the Church. Theological education serves *first* to train those who lead the Church as pastor-teachers, equipping them to teach the truth of God's Word with faithfulness, relevance and clarity; and *second*, to equip all God's people for the missional task of understanding and relevantly communicating God's truth in every cultural context.[39]

---

36. ScholarLeaders, "Critical Lessons from VSI Engagement" (unpublished document, 2022).

37. David W. Bebbington, *Evangelicalism in Modern Britain: A History from the 1730s to the 1980s* (London: Routledge, 1989), 7.

38. Marvin Oxenham, *Character and Virtue in Theological Education: An Academic Epistolary Novel*, ICETE (Carlisle: Langham Global Library, 2019), 58.

39. Lausanne Movement, *The Cape Town Commitment: A Confession of Faith and a Call to Action; The Third Lausanne Congress*, foreword by Doug Birdsall and Lindsay Brown (Lausanne Movement, 2011). https://www.lausanne.org/content/ctc/ctcommitment#capetown.

Theological education accompanies and strengthens the church in fulfilling God's comprehensive and holistic mission. Christopher Wright avers, "Mission was not made for the church; the church was made for mission – God's mission."[40] John Stott asserts, "Mission arises from the heart of God himself, and is communicated from his heart to ours."[41] Howard Snyder and Joel Scandrett agree: "The church is on mission because God is on mission."[42]

Prophetic theological education helps the church to "speak on behalf of the independent Divine Auditor . . . [offering] the voice of evaluation, of critique or approval, according to the standards we learn in God's own revelation."[43]

A theological institution animated by a faithfulness to God's mission will serve local communities even if that service means putting everything on hold. This has happened several times in some of the institutions that are part of the ACTEA network. Université Shalom de Bunia (USB), in the eastern part of the Democratic Republic of Congo (DRC), and Faculté de Théologie Evangélique de Bangui (FATEB), also known as Bangui Evangelical School of Theology (BEST), located in the Central African Republic (CAR), are beacons of light in war-torn countries. DRC and CAR have been subjected to war for decades.

Université Shalom de Bunia, then called Theological School of Northern Congo (ETCN), became a university in 2007 to serve the wider public through relevant education. The university chose Shalom as its preferred name because the seminary had then been seen as a place of shalom; it was a place "where reconciliation will start" and a place to enhance "wholeness of life and fullness of life."[44] USB has lived up to its name. Apart from its varied programmes such as environmental studies, medicine, administration and management, agriculture, development studies, and theology, USB is known for being a haven of peace and reconciliation. George Atido, who serves as vice-chancellor, notes that USB has slowly been exerting its prophetic voice in a country devastated by war, corruption, and poverty.

> The Development Faculty worked the last seven years to help Pygmies make a transition from essentially indentured servitude to

---

40. Christopher J. H. Wright, *The Mission of God: Unlocking the Bible's Grand Narrative* (Nottingham: Inter-Varsity Press, 2006), 62.

41. John R. W. Stott, *The Contemporary Christian: Applying God's Word to Today's World* (Downers Grove: InterVarsity Press, 1992), 335.

42. Howard A. Snyder and Joel Scandrett, *Salvation Means Creation Healed: The Ecology of Sin and Grace; Overcoming the Divorce between Earth and Heaven* (Eugene: Cascade, 2011), 117.

43. Wright, *Mission of God's People*, 271.

44. Mike Saum, "Moving towards Shalom," AIMStories, n. d., https://www.aimstories.com/blog/moving-towards-shalom.

timber barons to become sustainable farmers who also take care of the environment. The Faculty has initiated informal reforestation programs that encourage Pygmies to take care of nature as they draw their daily bread from it. As a result, 90 hectares (222 acres) of forest has been legally secured for a Pygmy band as their own and 17 Pygmy households have successfully embarked on farming and reforestation using tropical species. This experience is now being replicated from 2 to 9 other villages and the total secured forest area has increased from 90 hectares to 1,110 hectares (approximately 2,741.7 acres).[45]

FATEB, led by Nupanga Weanzana, has been a hub for refugees since 2010 when the war broke out in the region.[46] At one time they hosted more than four thousand refugees from different ethnic communities and religions. The university has also hosted several peace meetings and consultations. It is because of this that Pope Francis visited the institution in 2015. In addition, FATEB's preschool, primary, and secondary schools are dependable schools in the community providing education to thousands of children. Every day they receive more than three thousand school children. This doesn't mean that FATEB has a lot of resources. On the contrary, it is barely surviving. Despite this, the institution soldiers on. They now have a campus in Yaoundé, Cameroon, and a primary school in Kinshasa, the Democratic Republic of Congo. Through education, the college shapes the morals and future destiny of children.

Jesus's prayer in John 17:18 (NIV), "As you sent me into the world, I have sent them into the world," is a reminder that a seminary must understand its mission (prophetic voice). Missional questions include the following: What does it mean for our seminary to be sent like Jesus into the world? What is God calling our seminary to do in the local context? Is what we do advancing God's mission? Is it the best way to advance God's mission? How should we align all our programmes and resources with our mission? These are relevant questions that an institution must answer as it seeks to clarify its mission so that it can better serve the church and society.

---

45. George Atido in an email to the author on 2 May 2023.

46. Kate Tracy, "Surge in Christian-Muslim Strife Stirs Genocide Fears in Central African Republic," Christianity Today, 12 December 2013, https://www.christianitytoday.com/news/2013/december/christian-muslim-genocide-central-african-republic-bangui.html; Inna Lazareva, "'Now We're Back It's Even Worse': The Bangui Residents Who Preferred a Refugee Camp to Their Home City," The Guardian, 5 July 2017, https://www.theguardian.com/cities/2017/jul/05/mpoko-airport-bangui-residents-return-city-worse-refugee-camp-internally-displaced-central-african-republic.

Contextually Relevant Curriculum

Africa's seminaries, Bible colleges, and university departments of theology and biblical studies have a long way to go in providing a contextually relevant curriculum. After many years, the theological curriculum still needs to be decolonized because it still bears the stamp of colonialism. It was hand-delivered to institutions by well-meaning Western missionaries. The church and its seminaries received it as if it was cast in stone. They never questioned the assumptions the curriculum bore. They never asked what needed to be done to make sure the curriculum was actually addressing the questions asked by local communities. It was assumed to be normative for the whole church everywhere. It was fully dressed in Western thoughts. It looked Western. It was taught using Western language, idioms, and even illustrations. In my own studies at Scott Theological College, I studied Wayne Grudem, Millard Erickson, and other Western systematic theologians. I did not study the works of African systematic theologians because it was assumed that Grudem and Erickson were standard textbooks for "proper" systematic theology. The others were deemed "contextual" theologies, which are typically considered to be "second-rate endeavours."[47] This ignores the fact that "all theology is contextual [and] is culturally contingent."[48]

Sadly, to date, many seminaries do not care to understand their contexts and to use context-relevant materials. That is why many seminaries still depend on Western-generated resources, teaching patterns, and ideas, ignoring home-grown resources, pedagogies, and epistemologies. A theological education able to transform society must be home-grown. It must speak to the local context by understanding it fully and then walking backwards to the kind of education that will achieve that purpose.[49] It must be thoroughly flexible, relevant, yet faithful to Scripture. It must be dynamic, always adjusting and learning from the culture and context and positioning itself to serve that context. Theological education that is not alive to the context is irrelevant. Thus, it is unacceptable for seminaries to import curricula without connection to local contexts. Excellent theological education is alive to the context. It is in constant conversation

---

47. Kenneth R. Ross, "Decolonizing the Theological Mind: Work in Progress," ch. 2 in *Decolonizing the Theological Curriculum in an Online Age*, eds. Felix Chimera Nyika et al. (Zomba: TSM, 2022), 31.

48. Joshua Robert Barron, "The Camel Has Four Legs: A Contextual African Practical Ecclesiology," in *Ecclesiology in Africa*, ASET (Carlisle: Langham Global Library, 2024), 367.

49. See Rupen Das, *Connecting Curriculum with Context: A Handbook for Context Relevant Curriculum Development in Theological Education*, ICETE (Carlisle: Langham Global Library, 2015).

with the local context, always providing context-relevant curricula and looking for ways to be of more significant influence in local communities.

Theological education is not merely an academic discipline. It is a transformational discipline working to strengthen and accompany the church in its mission for the transformation of God's good but fallen world. It is a theological education of salt and light, a prophetic theological education able to facilitate a different way of life. It is a theological education that produces hopeful possibilities and the necessary commitments to realize those possibilities. It is a theological education of hope in a world of hopelessness; a voice for justice and reconciliation in a world of injustice and conflict; a theological education that witnesses to the Lord's presence on earth. It is a theological education with the courage to speak. But it cannot speak unless it understands the message and those to whom it speaks. It understands God's message clearly spelled out in Scripture (it has the resources and the personnel to exegete the Word) and context (it also has the resources and personnel to exegete the world). This exegesis of the world must be done in partnership with other disciplines – political science, sociology, anthropology, and others. The saltness of theological education calls for "a critical distance"[50] from the world, being careful not to be immersed in it so that we become blind to its distorting nature (Rom 12:1–3). Thus, theological education must look beyond itself and even beyond theology itself to utilize the resources available in social science, and must go beyond library-focused research to actual immersion in communities and churches. Gregg Okesson observes, "The task of unfolding the many rich nuances of Christian witness requires tools with greater animation than words printed on a page."[51] Such theological education must be courageous to innovate in order to be relevant in a complex world.

Courage to Innovate

Theological education that facilitates prophetic public life needs the courage to innovate in order to speak to complex issues affecting the church and society today. Seminaries are barely surviving. They have fewer and fewer students. Facilities are barely maintained and need to be more utilized. Teachers are underpaid. Churches are not supporting seminaries as they used to. In *Leading Financial Sustainability in Theological Institutions: The African Perspective*,

---

50. Wright, *Mission of God's People*, 271.

51. Gregg A. Okesson, *A Public Missiology: How Local Churches Witness to a Complex World* (Grand Rapids: Baker Academic, 2020), 149.

Emmanuel Bellon provides a graphic picture of many theological institutions in Africa today: "The carcasses of struggling institutions littering every corner of the continent bear witness to [endemic financial challenges]."[52] Is there a way out? Bellon writes, "These ailing institutions are still hopeful that somehow a contextually relevant remedy will emerge to set them on a path to financial sustainability."[53]

It is a reality that the typical seminary student is likely going to be an adult interested in bi-vocational ministry. Seminaries are no longer attracting younger students who favour full-time residential training. Students prefer to study in the comfort of their homes and closer to their workplaces and families. The rapid acceleration of Internet access and widespread use of smartphones have contributed to newer ways of theological education. With this kind of reality, "the future is campus-free," as Matt Ayars avers.[54] Steve Hardy observes, "Training programs of the future are likely to function as theological resource centers serving a number of off-site programs, rather than as a single location where all teachers, classes, books and students can be found."[55]

Survival is not the only reason for innovation in theological education. Mission is of primary importance. Mission is driving new ways of training. Innovative seminaries are conscious of their mission to make theological education "accessible, more affordable, and cheaper to deliver."[56] This is of particular importance because seminaries need to meet the growing demands of the more than 95 percent of untrained pastors worldwide. According to the Center for the Study of Global Christianity at Gordon-Conwell Theological Seminary, which conducted a comprehensive global survey on theological education, there are "5 million pastors/priests in all Christian traditions worldwide (Catholics, Orthodox, Protestants, and Independents, including bi-vocational)." Of these only "5% (250,000) are likely to have formal theological training (undergraduate Bible degrees or Master's degrees)."[57]

---

52. Emmanuel O. Bellon, *Leading Financial Sustainability in Theological Institutions: The African Perspective* (Eugene: Pickwick, 2017), 3.

53. Bellon, *Leading Financial Sustainability*, 3.

54. Matt Ayars, "The Future Is Campus-Free," *Christianity Today* 66, no. 7 (Oct. 2022): 32–33.

55. Steven A. Hardy, *Excellence in Theological Education: Effective Training for Church Leaders*, ICETE (Carlisle: Langham Global Library, 2016), 121.

56. Ayars, "Future Is Campus-Free," 32.

57. Center for the Study of Global Christianity, "What Percentage of Pastors Worldwide Have Theological Training?," Frequently Asked Questions, n.d., https://www.gordonconwell.edu/center-for-global-christianity/research/quick-facts/.

What needs to be done to scale up ministerial training for the 95 percent who need training? Is this going to be achieved by traditional seminaries alone? Are seminaries bold enough to make drastic decisions about how and who they educate? Are they willing to adapt to new methods and strategies? Are they willing to utilize innovative technologies in the formation of ministers for the church and society? Are they willing to brutally assess the curriculum, even retiring courses that are no longer relevant and instead offering relevant courses? Are they willing to hold their professors to a high threshold in who they are and what they do? Are they willing to collaborate with others (e.g. other disciplines) in the formation of students? Or are they going to be protective of their spaces to avoid being "tainted" by other disciplines? Are they willing to descend from their ivory towers of academic scholarship to the levels below?

Marvin Oxenham poses some critical questions in his *Character and Virtue in Theological Education* which show that we need to be thinking beyond traditional theological education:

> As we consider the failure of theological education in your region, could it not be that the very definition of traditional theological education is problematic? If, for example, faith communities are tired of polished academic graduates and are looking for lay leaders, why should theological education be restricted to "tertiary level"? Is it really even necessary to produce "degrees"? Furthermore, if students are mobile and are looking to be trained in a quick-paced society, why do we continue to operate in traditional "institutional" contexts? Might we not break down this church-academy dichotomy and explore shared educational spaces? And again, if the "Berlin" model is too limited in its "academic and vocational purposes," should we not investigate other purposes?[58]

The reality is that theological institutions are very slow to investigate other viable models. They are afraid to experiment with new ways of training. In *Living above the Level of Mediocrity*, Charles R. Swindoll challenges Christians to rise above traditionalism. He defines that as "an attitude that resists change, adaptation, or alteration" and "being suspicious of the new, the up-to-date, the different."[59] He advocates "openness, allowing room for the untried, the unpre-

---

58. Oxenham, *Character and Virtue*, 22.

59. Charles R. Swindoll, *Living Above the Level of Mediocrity: A Commitment to Excellence* (Dallas: Word, 1987), 163.

dictable, the unexpected – all the while holding fast to the truth."[60] Tokunboh Adeyemo, former general secretary of the Association of Evangelicals in Africa and Madagascar (AEAM), urged theological institutions in Africa to be innovative, creative, yet sensitive to the leading of the Spirit.

> In our theological education process renewal may demand flexibility as opposed to rigidity, freedom of the Spirit as opposed to legalism, and originality of symbolism and thought forms as opposed to traditionalism. Of necessity, our pedagogy will shift emphasis from formal to informal, from "communication to" to "communication with," from clandestine individualism to community, from obligation to commitment, and from mere display of talents to discovering, developing, and deploying the charismata.[61]

Martin Accad, currently president of Arab Baptist Theological Seminary, observes that the traditional theological education that limited training to vocational service of ordination is no longer relevant, especially for regions where Christianity is the minority religion. In such contexts, theological education is about preparing people for prophetic ministry. "In seminaries that are conscious of their 'prophetic' role, whether in the [Middle East and North Africa] or outside of it, theological education consists in a process of 'deconstruction,' 'paradigm shifting,' and the 'reconstruction' of an alternative consciousness."[62]

Jean-Marc Éla urged African churches to innovate and explore new directions in theological education for the whole church. "We need to *imagine* new solutions that do not simply copy former models, which are too marked by the historical characteristics of a particular period of Christian life."[63] He argues that the future of the church in Africa depends on "declericalized" ministries – "making full use of the diaconal and priestly potential of the Christian laity."[64] This calls for courageous innovation, questioning, being questioned, and experimenting with the guidance of the Spirit in order to make full use

---

60. Swindoll, *Living Above the Level*, 163.

61. Tokunboh Adeyemo, "The Renewal of Evangelical Theological Education," in *Evangelical Theological Education: An International Agenda*, ed. Paul Bowers (Springwood: ICAA, 1994), 12; ICAA is now ICETE. AEAM was founded in 1966; in 1993 the organization simplified its name to Association of Evangelicals in Africa (AEA), though evangelical groups in Madagascar are still included.

62. Martin Accad, "Theological Education as Formation for Prophetic Ministry," Arab Baptist Theological Seminary, 1 August 2019, https://abtslebanon.org/2019/08/01/theological-education-as-formation-for-prophetic-ministry-2/.

63. Éla, *My Faith as an African*, 63; emphasis original.

64. Éla, 63.

of God-given resources available to the church. This courageous movement involves a "return to our people, becoming their companions in life and their travelling partners."[65] Therefore, a theological education that is alive to the context will need to deconstruct, shift, and reconstruct so that it can provide a robust theological education able to serve the needs of society and the church. This consciousness helps the seminary to be in tune with the church and society.

Conclusion

Theological education plays a critical role in the transformation of communities. It does this by walking alongside the churches and supporting them through the formation of men and women to serve the church and transform society. The church transforms society through its teaching, character development, and actual practical acts of charity and compassion. The church is also a moral compass for society. Through its prophetic voice, the church speaks to society and draws it back to God's purpose. It speaks to societal realities such as political conflict, poverty, health, religious violence, tribalism, and corruption, which adversely influence society. But the church cannot speak well if the voices of the leaders are muted or distorted. Leaders must receive proper biblical and theological training so that they can courageously and faithfully speak to and address societal issues. Proper training comes in different forms – formal or non-formal – and is offered in a variety of ways. Theological education, whether residential or not, whether designed for lay leaders or those preparing for full-time Christian ministry, has the high calling of forming men and women to be witnesses in the society for the glory of God. This will happen through a clarified mission, contextually relevant curriculum, and the courage to innovate.

Bibliography

Accad, Martin. "Theological Education as Formation for Prophetic Ministry." Arab Baptist Theological Seminary. 1 August 2019. https://abtslebanon.org/2019/08/01/theological-education-as-formation-for-prophetic-ministry-2/.

Adeyemo, Tokunboh. "The Renewal of Evangelical Theological Education." In *Evangelical Theological Education: An International Agenda*, edited by Paul Bowers, 5–12. Springwood: ICAA [ICETE], 1994.

---

65. Éla, 182.

Ayars, Matt. "The Future Is Campus-Free." *Christianity Today* 66, no. 7 (Oct. 2022): 32–33.

Barron, Joshua Robert. "The Camel Has Four Legs: A Contextual African Practical Ecclesiology." In *Ecclesiology in Africa*, edited by David K. Ngaruiya and Rodney L. Reed, 365–399. ASET Series. Carlisle: Langham Global Library, 2024.

———. "Is the Prosperity Gospel, Gospel? An Examination of the Prosperity and Productivity Gospels in African Christianity." *Conspectus: The Journal of the South African Theological Seminary* 33, no. 1 (2022): 88–103.

Barton, Ruth Haley. *Life Together in Christ: Experiencing Transformation in Community*. Downers Grove: InterVarsity Press, 2014.

Bauckham, Richard, and Trevor Hart. *Hope against Hope: Christian Eschatology in Contemporary Context*. Trinity and Truth. London: Darton, Longman & Todd, 1999.

Bebbington, David W. *Evangelicalism in Modern Britain: A History from the 1730s to the 1980s*. London: Routledge, 1989.

Bediako, Kwame. "De-sacralization and Democratization: Some Theological Reflections on the Role of Christianity in Nation-Building in Modern Africa." *Transformation* 12, no. 1 (1995): 5–11.

Bellon, Emmanuel O. *Leading Financial Sustainability in Theological Institutions: The African Perspective*. Eugene: Pickwick, 2017.

Boulton, Matthew. *Life in God: John Calvin, Practical Formation, and the Future of Protestant Theology*. Grand Rapids: Eerdmans, 2011.

Center for the Study of Global Christianity. "What Percentage of Pastors Worldwide Have Theological Training?" Frequently Asked Questions. https://www.gordonconwell.edu/center-for-global-christianity/research/quick-facts/.

Das, Rupen. *Connecting Curriculum with Context: A Handbook for Context Relevant Curriculum Development in Theological Education*. ICETE Series. Carlisle: Langham Global Library, 2015.

Éla, Jean-Marc. *My Faith as an African*. Translated by John Pairman Brown and Susan Perry. Maryknoll: Orbis, 1988.

Greer, Peter, and Chris Horst, with Anna Haggard. *Mission Drift: The Unspoken Crisis Facing Leaders, Charities, and Churches*. Minneapolis: Bethany House, 2014.

ter Haar, Gerrie, and Stephen Ellis. "The Role of Religion in Development: Towards a New Relationship between the European Union and Africa." *The European Journal of Development Research* 18, no. 3 (2006): 351–67.

Hardy, Steven A. *Excellence in Theological Education: Effective Training for Church Leaders*. ICETE Series. Carlisle: Langham Global Library, 2016.

Health Communication Capacity Collaborative. "The Role of Religious Leaders and Faith Communities." N.d. https://healthcommcapacity.org/i-kits/role-religious-leaders-faith-communities/.

Joseph, Celucien L. *Theological Education and Christian Scholarship for Human Flourishing: Hermeneutics, Knowledge, and Multiculturalism*. Eugene: Pickwick, 2022.

Jung, Joanne J. *Character Formation in Online Education: A Guide for Instructors, Administrators, and Accrediting Agencies*. Grand Rapids: Zondervan Academic, 2015.

Katongole, Emmanuel. *The Sacrifice of Africa: A Political Theology for Africa*. Grand Rapids: Eerdmans, 2011.

Kintu, Harriet Akugizibwe Caroline. "Effects of the Transition of Theological Seminaries in Kenya to Universities on Their Evangelical Christian Identity: An Inquiry into Africa International University." Chapter 9 in *Governance and Christian Higher Education in the African Context*, edited by David K. Ngaruiya and Rodney L. Reed, 159–86. ASET Series. Carlisle: Langham Global Library, 2019.

Lausanne Movement. *The Cape Town Commitment: A Confession of Faith and a Call to Action; The Third Lausanne Congress*. Foreword by Doug Birdsall and Lindsay Brown. Lausanne Movement, 2011. https://www.lausanne.org/content/ctc/ctcommitment.

Lazareva, Inna. "'Now We're Back It's Even Worse': The Bangui Residents Who Preferred a Refugee Camp to Their Home City." *The Guardian*. 5 July 2017. https://www.theguardian.com/cities/2017/jul/05/mpoko-airport-bangui-residents-return-city-worse-refugee-camp-internally-displaced-central-african-republic.

Lowe, Stephen D., and Mary E. Lowe. *Ecologies of Faith in a Digital Age: Spiritual Growth through Online Education*. Downers Grove: IVP Academic, 2018.

Maathai, Wangari. *The Challenge for Africa*. London: Arrow, 2009.

Maxwell, Stephen. "'Delivered from the Spirit of Poverty?' Pentecostalism, Prosperity and Modernity in Zimbabwe." *Journal of Religion in Africa* 28, no. 3 (1998): 350–73.

Mazrui, Ali A. *The Africans: A Triple Heritage*. London: BBC, 1986.

Mulatu, Semeon. *Transitioning from a Theological College to a Christian University: A Multi-Case Study in the East African Context*. ICETE Series. Carlisle: Langham Global Library, 2017.

Norris, Fredrick W. *Christianity: A Short Global History*. London: Oneworld, 2002.

Okesson, Gregg A. *A Public Missiology: How Local Churches Witness to a Complex World*. Grand Rapids: Baker Academic, 2020.

Onyango-Obbo, Charles. "What Africa's Coups Reveal about Us." *Daily Nation*. 9 September 2021. https://nation.africa/kenya/blogs-opinion/opinion/what-africas-coups-reveal-about-us-3543530.

Oxenham, Marvin. *Character and Virtue in Theological Education: An Academic Epistolary Novel*. ICETE Series. Carlisle: Langham Global Library, 2019.

Ross, Kenneth R. "Decolonizing the Theological Mind: Work in Progress." Chapter 2 in *Decolonizing the Theological Curriculum in an Online Age*, edited by Felix Chimera Nyika, Mzee Hermann Y. Mvula, and Kenneth R. Ross, 23–45. Zomba: TSM, 2022.

Sanneh, Lamin. "Gospel and Culture: Ramifying Effects of Scriptural Translation." In *Bible Translation and the Spread of the Church: The Last 200 Years*, edited by Philip C. Stine, 1–23. Studies in Christian Mission 2. Leiden: Brill, 1990.

———. *Translating the Message: The Missionary Impact on Culture*. 2nd revised and expanded ed. American Society of Missiology 42. Maryknoll: Orbis, 2009.

———. *Whose Religion Is Christianity? The Gospel beyond the West*. Grand Rapids: Eerdmans, 2003.

Saum, Mike. "Moving towards Shalom." AIMStories. N.d. https://www.aimstories.com/blog/moving-towards-shalom.

ScholarLeaders. "Critical Lessons from VSI Engagement." Unpublished document, 2022.

Smith, James K. A. *Desiring the Kingdom: Worship, Worldview, and Cultural Formation*. Cultural Liturgies 1. Grand Rapids: Baker Academic, 2009.

———. *Imagining the Kingdom: How Worship Works*. Cultural Liturgies 2. Grand Rapids: Baker Academic, 2013.

Snyder, Howard A., and Joel Scandrett. *Salvation Means Creation Healed: The Ecology of Sin and Grace; Overcoming the Divorce between Earth and Heaven*. Eugene: Cascade, 2011.

Stott, John R. W. *The Contemporary Christian: Applying God's Word to Today's World*. Downers Grove: InterVarsity Press, 1992.

Swindoll, Charles R. *Living Above the Level of Mediocrity: A Commitment to Excellence*. Dallas: Word, 1987.

Tomalin, Emma. *Religions and Development*. Routledge Perspectives on Development. London: Routledge, 2013.

Tracy, Kate. "Surge in Christian-Muslim Strife Stirs Genocide Fears in Central African Republic." Christianity Today, 12 December 2013. https://www.christianitytoday.com/news/2013/december/christian-muslim-genocide-central-african-republic-bangui.html.

Volf, Miroslav. *A Public Faith: How Followers of Christ Should Serve the Common Good*. Grand Rapids: Brazos, 2011.

Walls, Andrew F. "Overseas Ministries and the Subversion of Theological Education." *International Bulletin of Mission Research* 45, no. 1 (2021): 7–14.

———. "The Translation Principle in Christian History." In *Bible Translation and the Spread of the Church: The Last 200 Years*, edited by Philip C. Stine, 24–39. Studies in Christian Mission 2. Leiden: Brill, 1990. Reprinted as chapter 3 in *The Missionary Movement in Christian History: Studies in the Transmission of Faith*, 26–42. Maryknoll: Orbis, 1996.

Willimon, William H. *Calling and Character: Virtues of the Ordained Life*. Nashville: Abingdon, 2010.

Wright, Christopher J. H. *The Mission of God: Unlocking the Bible's Grand Narrative*. Nottingham: Inter-Varsity Press, 2006.

———. *The Mission of God's People: A Biblical Theology of the Church's Mission*. Grand Rapids: Zondervan, 2010.

Contributors

Milton Acosta Benítez is Professor of Old Testament and Biblical Interpretation at the Seminario Bíblico de Colombia in Medellín. He has worked at the seminary since 1995, where he has also served as Academic Vice-Rector and Dean. His areas of research include rhetorical patterns in the Hebrew Bible and forced migration and violence in the Bible. He is the author, co-author, and editor of numerous articles and books, including *El humor en el Antiguo Testamento, Comentario Bíblico Contemporáneo*, and *Fe y Desplazamiento: La investigación-acción misional ante la crisis colombiana del desplazamiento forzoso*. He publishes regularly on his blog, *Pido la Palabra*.

Sunday Bobai Agang was born to unchurched parents in 1958 in Nigeria. He came to faith and began his walk with the Lord in April 1977. He later led both his parents to saving faith in Christ before they went to be with the Lord. He and Sarah have been married since 1987 and are blessed with four children. He has served as Provost of ECWA Theological Seminary, Kagoro (2012–17), and since 2020 has been Provost and Professor of Christian Ethics, Theology, and Public Policy at ECWA Theological Seminary in Jos, Nigeria (JETS). He is a research fellow in the Department of Systematic Theology and Ecclesiology, Faculty of Theology, Stellenbosch University, South Africa, and a prolific author, his books include *Endangered Moral Values: Nigeria's Search for Love, Truth, Unity and Empathy* (HippoBooks, 2021) and *When Evil Strikes: Faith and the Politics of Human Hostility* (Pickwick, 2016). He was also the general editor of *African Public Theology* (HippoBooks, 2020).

Ruth Barron is a #metoo and #churchtoo activist who has worked in full-time ministry since 2000 and as a missionary in Kenya since 2007. With degrees in English and psychology (BA from Milligan University) and Christian doctrine (MAR from Emmanuel Christian Seminary), her focus is on the intersection of trauma, theology, literature, and church polity. She has developed curricula for Maasai and Turkana churches and writes academic articles, essays, poems, and stories.

Brenda Darke is a missionary with Latin Link. She was born in the UK and graduated from Southampton University in 1973 with a BEd. She has taught children with severe cognitive disabilities in schools in England. She also has completed studies in transcultural mission (All Nations Christian College, 1984–5) and theology of disability (Oxford Centre for Mission Studies, 2001). In 1985, Brenda moved with her husband and two young children to Peru. Since 1995 they have lived in Costa Rica. Brenda works towards the inclusion of people with disabilities in churches through teaching in a Bible college in San José and through networks across Latin America as well as being a published author on the subject. She is also involved with pastoral ministry for Personas con Discapacidad (PcD, [People with Disabilities]) and their families.

Eunice Kamaara is from Kenya. She is a Professor of African Christian Ethics at Moi University, Eldoret. She loves teaching and learning for life. She is Presbyterian by birth, Roman Catholic by marriage, and Christian by choice. She teaches like a mother and mothers like a teacher.

James A. Lemons is a neonatalist physician at Indiana University Health and a Professor of Pediatrics Practice at the Indiana University School of Medicine in Indianapolis. He served as co-director of the Clinical Pastoral Education (CPE) project at Moi University and the Riley Mother and Baby Hospital (RMBH), both in Eldoret, Kenya, and was responsible for the building of RMBH.

Víctor Manuel Morales is from Monterrey, Mexico. A lay preacher of the Lutheran Church, he is trained as a teacher of philosophy and Spanish. He has studied in South Africa, holds a PhD in New Testament from the University of Liverpool, and is the author of *Contours of a Biblical Reception Theory* (2011), which examines the reception history of Romans 13:1–7. He is currently in Germany as a postdoc researcher in systematic theology on the topic of sustainable development. He loves the outdoors and is a hobby gardener, taking care of a variety of flowers including twenty roses and six orchids. He is also a founding member of A Rocha Germany, an evangelical ministry devoted to environmental care.

Eberhardt Ngugi is the Head of Department of Theology and Lecturer of Practical Theology at the University of Iringa. He received a bachelor of divinity degree from Tumaini University in Arusha, Tanzania (1999), a master's in pastoral care and counselling from the University of Kwazulu Natal, Pietermaritzburg, South Africa (2005), and a doctor of philosophy degree in practical theology from the University of Stellenbosch, Cape Town, South Africa (2013). After graduating from Stellenbosch University, he took a job working at Sebastian Kolowa Memorial University in Lushhoto, Tanzania, as a Director for Postgraduate Studies and afterwards the Deputy Vice-Chancellor for Planning, Finance and Administration, from the same university. He later became the assistant to the bishop, Evangelical Lutheran Church in Tanzania, North Eastern Diocese. He lives in Tanzania with his wife and their three children: a daughter and two boys.

Josué Olmedo is an International Fellowship of Evangelical Students IFES staff-worker and co-leader of the IFES Latin America Logos & Cosmos Initiative. He is from Ecuador with studies in education (Universidad de Guayaquil), Bible (Regent College), and theology (Pontificia Universidad Católica del Ecuador). He lives with his wife and their two daughters in Quito, Ecuador.

Alejandra Ortiz is an International Fellowship of Evangelical Students (IFES) staff-worker and co-leader of the IFES Latin America Logos & Cosmos Initiative. She is from Mexico and studied history (Universidad Autónoma de Baja California) and later specialized in church history (Regent College). She lives with her husband and their two daughters in Tijuana, Mexico.

Lucy Schouten conducted her doctoral research in world Christianity at the University of Edinburgh, studying the response of Arabic-speaking Jordanian churches to the refugee crisis since 2012. Her research focuses on synthesizing interviews and observations from her multiple fieldwork trips to Amman, Jordan, with insights from scholarship in migration studies, political theology, and Christian-Muslim relations. She also served as the project coordinator for the Christian-Muslim Studies Network for the University of Edinburgh from 2017 to 2020, in addition to teaching courses on religion, violence and peacebuilding, and Islam and Christian-Muslim relations. She currently lives in Arizona with her husband, James, and their two children.

Alfred Sebahene is a senior priest in the Anglican Church of Tanzania and a public theologian. A graduate of Stellenbosch University in South Africa (PhD, systematic theology and ecclesiology) and Oak Hill Theological College at Middlesex University in the UK (BA and MA, both in pastoral and theological studies), he is currently serving at St. John's University in Dodoma, Tanzania, as senior lecturer in systematic theology and ethics, Head of Department of Theology and Religious Studies, and founding coordinator for the Unit for the Study of Corruption. He consults for churches, NGOs, the government of Tanzania, and other public and private organizations on matters of ethics, anti-corruption, capacity development, and higher education practice. Alfred is married to Ruth Niyonzima Sebahene; they have two teenagers, Joanna Niyonkuru and Samuel Niyitegeka.

David Tarus serves as Executive Director, Association for Christian Theological Education in Africa (ACTEA), a project of the Theological Commission of the Association of Evangelicals in Africa (AEA). ACTEA's mission is to strengthen theological education through accreditation, scholarship, and support services in order to serve the church and transform society. David is a graduate of McMaster Divinity College (PhD, Christian theology), Wheaton College (MA in historical and systematic theology), both in North America, and Scott Christian University (BTh) in Kenya. David is an ordained minister in the Africa Inland Church (AIC). He serves as Associate Pastor at AIC Milimani, Nairobi.

Myrto Theocharous was born in Cyprus and now lives with her husband in Athens, Greece. She specializes in the Old Testament (PhD University of Cambridge) and teaches Hebrew and Old Testament at the Greek Bible College. She is also the president of Nea Zoi Anti-Trafficking Association in Athens, Greece.

Eva Wong Suk Kyun is the Director of Malaysia Pentecostal Research Centre and full-time lecturer at Bible College of Malaysia. She holds a PhD in theology (Pentecostal studies) from the Oxford Centre for Mission Studies in partnership with Middlesex University, UK. She is an ordained minister of the Assemblies of God Malaysia. She currently serves on the Executive Committee of the Asia Pentecostal Society and Lausanne Global Analysis Editorial Advisory Board, and co-leads the ScholarLeaders Women's Peer Leader Forum.

Langham Literature and its imprints are a ministry of Langham Partnership.

Langham Partnership is a global fellowship working in pursuit of the vision God entrusted to its founder John Stott –

to facilitate the growth of the church in maturity and Christ-likeness through raising the standards of biblical preaching and teaching.

Our vision is to see churches in the Majority World equipped for mission and growing to maturity in Christ through the ministry of pastors and leaders who believe, teach and live by the word of God.

Our mission is to strengthen the ministry of the word of God through:
- nurturing national movements for biblical preaching
- fostering the creation and distribution of evangelical literature
- enhancing evangelical theological education

especially in countries where churches are under-resourced.

Our ministry

Langham Preaching partners with national leaders to nurture indigenous biblical preaching movements for pastors and lay preachers all around the world. With the support of a team of trainers from many countries, a multi-level programme of seminars provides practical training, and is followed by a programme for training local facilitators. Local preachers' groups and national and regional networks ensure continuity and ongoing development, seeking to build vigorous movements committed to Bible exposition.

Langham Literature provides Majority World preachers, scholars and seminary libraries with evangelical books and electronic resources through publishing and distribution, grants and discounts. The programme also fosters the creation of indigenous evangelical books in many languages, through writer's grants, strengthening local evangelical publishing houses, and investment in major regional literature projects, such as one volume Bible commentaries like *The Africa Bible Commentary* and *The South Asia Bible Commentary*.

Langham Scholars provides financial support for evangelical doctoral students from the Majority World so that, when they return home, they may train pastors and other Christian leaders with sound, biblical and theological teaching. This programme equips those who equip others. Langham Scholars also works in partnership with Majority World seminaries in strengthening evangelical theological education. A growing number of Langham Scholars study in high quality doctoral programmes in the Majority World itself. As well as teaching the next generation of pastors, graduated Langham Scholars exercise significant influence through their writing and leadership.

To learn more about Langham Partnership and the work we do visit **langham.org**

www.ingramcontent.com/pod-product-compliance
Lightning Source LLC
Chambersburg PA
CBHW060945230426
43665CB00015B/2063